RIGHTSIZING

INFORMATION

SYSTEMS

SECOND
EDITION

PROFESSIONAL REFERENCE SERIES

RIGHTSIZING INFORMATION SYSTEMS

SECOND EDITION

Steven L. Guengerich and
George Schussel

201 West 103rd Street, Indianapolis, Indiana 46290

SAMS
PUBLISHING

Thanks to our families for supporting and encouraging us throughout the project.—*Steven L. Guengerich and George Schussel*

Copyright © 1994 by Sams Publishing

Trademarks

Overview

Contents

Appendixes

Foreword

Rightsizing Information Systems: Moving to a Client/Server World

by George Schussel

The First Three Generations of Rightsizing

The rightsizing of information systems began with the minicomputer in the 1970s. At that time, innovative companies were able to devise ways of building more responsive and inexpensive solutions to data processing problems at the departmental level. Through the 1980s, networks of 32-bit minicomputers became very popular and fueled the explosive growth of vendor companies such as Prime Computer, Digital Equipment Corporation, Data General, and Wang Computer.

The second generation of rightsizing started with the advent of the IBM PC in the early 1980s. By the 1987 time frame, it had become abundantly clear that networks of these smaller PCs (from IBM, Apple, Compaq, and many clone vendors) and scientific workstations (from Sun, Hewlett Packard, Digital Equipment Corporation, and so on) were going to take over much of traditional business data processing. This second generation of rightsizing had important new vendors providing the necessary products. Companies like Novell, 3Com, Microsoft, Apple, Borland, and Compaq were the leaders of this new wave of rightsizing.

Potential cost saving from the earlier mainframe to minicomputer rightsizing efforts were significant, but major minicomputer-based networks were still large in terms of budget and support requirements. The potential savings of all types—hardware costs, software, electricity, air conditioning, space, and so on—from the second generation of rightsizing were astounding by comparison, however. The mid-1980s PC/AT-class computers costing $2,000–$3,000 were capable of running programs at the same speed as many minicomputers that were priced more in the $40,000 to $60,000 range. The idea of replacing a computer that was the size of your desk with a PC that was positioned on your desk was also revolutionary.

Innovative companies began porting their business applications to desktop PCs using new types of languages and databases. Products such as dBASE, Paradox, PC Focus, and Clipper were born and sold to millions of developers who realized that they could solve data processing problems on home-style computers. By 1990, manufacturing, insurance, banking, retail, and many other types of companies had proven that the process of porting business applications to PC-style networks would work.

This second generation of rightsizing was characterized by that word *porting*. In general, the PCs were doing the same style of computing that had previously run on minicomputer and mainframes, but they were doing it on a lower cost platform.

We are now into the third generation of rightsizing (3GEN). This generation is much different from the last. 3GEN is typified by graphical, event-based computing on client/server networks. This is in contrast with the character-styled, program-controlled, time-shared networks of the past.

As in the past, new vendors are emerging to lead us on the path and to profit from selling the products necessary to support third-generation rightsizing. The following table gives key differences in older and in new/future 3GEN approaches to computing:

CURRENT	*3GEN FUTURE*
The primary users are clerical and production workers.	The current users are still supported, but business users and MBAs doing decision-support are more typical of users and of the uses of the new systems.
The key information is in the data, which is shared and controlled by a production-style DBMS. The language used to access this data is SQL (if we're modern) or an older, proprietary hierarchical style DBMS DML, if the application was built before 1990.	Data is still fundamental, but it is more diverse than what can be stored with SQL. Text, pictures, graphics, voice annotation, and video clips are typical new data types. The key to this new data is providing a communication backbone that allows all necessary users to tie in and access as necessary.

The primary purpose of our computing is to support the basic business processes, for example, production inventory control, reservations, billing. Transaction-processing applications prevail.

Custom application systems are built with an engineering approach based on structured methodologies.

The application system is designed to support internal staff and to improve efficiency or lower costs.

Users of applications are connected to the network by a PC/terminal positioned on the desk. The only way to interact with the application is through this PC/terminal. The system's users are all employees of our company.

Decision-support applications that affect the management and customer service application to improve our service are more important in their capability to make the company competitive.

Visual software construction techniques are used. Assembly of custom software from existing software modules is standard. Object-based software allows software assembly. Prototyping and user involvement at all stages of application construction are essential.

The better service that the system provides to our customers means that we are selected as the preferred vendor.

Many users are only connected to the network on an occasional basis. They travel and need the most current information possible. Replication techniques are used to keep such users up to date. Many users of the system are our customers or suppliers—the outside world.

The computer architecture is primarily minicomputer- and mainframe-based with terminals or PCs mimicking terminals and time-shared or transaction-processing types of operating PCs systems.	The computer architecture is client/server with high-speed networks replacing the internal computer bus as the primary communication technique among processes. with GUIs are the primary clients. Many diverse types of servers and networks are part of the overall architecture.

In rebuilding and designing their applications for 3GEN, customers (rightly) want their applications to have more flexibility and longevity. Current approaches to computer-based systems are very much tied to the underlying technology, and the resulting applications become undesirable when new technological approaches surface. Customers want technologies that are modular, expandable, reusable, and friendly.

A very important component of applications designed for 3GEN is that they should be "open." The exact definition of "open" can be and is debated. For the user, it should mean that a product architecture is widely recognized as a standard and that there are many choices for add-on products and services. Open shouldn't be confused with "proprietary," which is the opposite of public domain. I would argue that it's very possible for an open standard to be proprietary. The key issue here, then, is whether interfaces to that product are openly published and whether the vendor encourages alternative sources of supply. In this context, I would consider NetWare and the various Windows APIs to be open.

The Components of the New Client/Server Architecture

Important new markets are being opened by the worldwide migration to 3GEN. Initially, the three most important and largest technology markets will be these:

1. Client and desktop operating systems
2. Server operating systems
3. Object-based frameworks for creating and connecting applications across the network

These product classes are "enablers." Once they are in place, their availability will allow the true value (which always lies in the applications for end users) to be delivered. These enablers are software-based, of course, because that's where the toughest decisions with the most impact on users will be made. Hardware issues, such as whether the server is based on Pentium or SPARC processors, are less interesting and less important to the typical user.

The leading contenders for dominance on the client are shown in Figure FW.1. Microsoft, IBM, Apple, and various UNIX vendors are the fighters for your desktop-standard dollar. In the 1970s, the analogy that was used was "Snow White and the Seven Dwarfs." At that time, the computer industry consisted of IBM and various pretenders to IBM's market dominance, such as RCA, Honeywell, GE, Control Data, and Univac. Today in client operating systems, there is a comparable dominance by one vendor, but that vendor is Microsoft, not IBM. The DOS/Windows combination will have shipped more than 50 million copies by year-end 1994. The closest competitors are Apple's System 7 and IBM's OS/2, both of which are shipping at a rate that is 10 percent of Microsoft's sales rate for DOS/Windows.

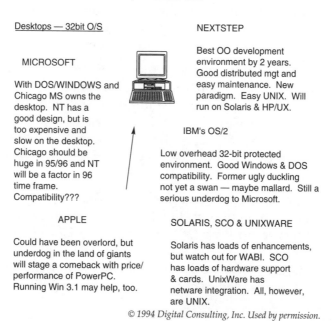

Desktops — 32bit O/S

NEXTSTEP

MICROSOFT

Best OO development environment by 2 years. Good distributed mgt and easy maintenance. New paradigm. Easy UNIX. Will run on Solaris & HP/UX.

With DOS/WINDOWS and Chicago MS owns the desktop. NT has a good design, but is too expensive and slow on the desktop. Chicago should be huge in 95/96 and NT will be a factor in 96 time frame. Compatibility???

IBM's OS/2

Low overhead 32-bit protected environment. Good Windows & DOS compatibility. Former ugly duckling not yet a swan — maybe mallard. Still a serious underdog to Microsoft.

APPLE

SOLARIS, SCO & UNIXWARE

Could have been overlord, but underdog in the land of giants will stage a comeback with price/performance of PowerPC. Running Win 3.1 may help, too.

Solaris has loads of enhancements, but watch out for WABI. SCO has loads of hardware support & cards. UnixWare has netware integration. All, however, are UNIX.

Figure FW.1. *O/S competitors for the desktop.*

It should be pointed out that Apple preceded Microsoft with a simple GUI for the desktop user. Apple, however, is notoriously closed about its hardware environment, while the IBM PC standard that supports Windows is cloned by more than 100 alternative vendors on a worldwide basis. Apple won the battle to convert users to a graphical form of computing but lost the marketing war to Microsoft because the Microsoft products run on open systems while Apple's system is closed.

Most analysts today are predicting that the market shares of the major desktop contenders will stay approximately where they are today, while the overall dollar value of this market increases significantly. Various UNIX players like NeXT, Sun, and Santa Cruz Operation will all continue to have significant annual desktop sales. But their sales are measured in the hundreds of thousands rather than in the tens of millions as Microsoft's market has grown to be. Windows 4.0 (Chicago) will likely replace the majority of client sites in client/server networks during the 1995–1997 time frame. Windows NT will carve out a niche in high-end applications, where it will compete for marketshare with OS/2 and UNIX. But the huge market for client operating systems in the latter part of the 1990s is Microsoft's to lose; and in order to lose it, Microsoft would have to commit some major marketing and technical blunders. Blundering hasn't been part of the Microsoft tradition, and I'm glad that I don't have to compete against them in this arena!

A second major emerging market is for server operating systems. Servers, in effect, are the next generation of minicomputer. They represent the shared, multiuser database and multiuser-services provider. Where a client machine is designed to service a single user with an easy and flexible user interface, the server has to be more like traditional computer architectures. It is multiuser and therefore has to be secure and very quick and responsive.

The server operating system market is not dominated by a single supplier like Microsoft on the desktop. Novell's NetWare is the dominant supplier in workgroup-sized LAN-based servers. However, UNIX from various suppliers and in various forms is the dominant environment in mid-size to larger servers. OS/2 has a small piece of this market, and Windows NT is expected to become a serious competitor for some of this market in the mid 1990s.

A critical component of server services is data base management. Now, the DBMS function is typically performed by a relational DBMS programmed with the SQL language. The dominant providers of relational

DBMSs are, in order of their marketshare, Oracle, Sybase, Informix, and ASK/INGRES. Of course, IBM's DB2 family, Digital Equipment's Rdb, and Hewlett Packard's Allbase also have significant marketshare, but usually the relational DBMSs sold by IBM, Digital Equipment and Hewlett Packard are sold almost exclusively into the customer base that has the hardware vendor's hardware also.

Server relational DBMS engines are more functionally robust than the same types of products offered on older mainframes and minicomputers. The server versions have picked up added programmability on the server side, with features like stored procedures and triggers.

Another important new relational server capability is replication. Replication allows for system-managed copies of data in asynchronous fashion. Relational DBMSs with replication capability allow the user to update data locally with the system worrying about how to distribute that update to other locations that need it.

Replication is not the only new relational DBMS technology that is creating excitement among users. During 1994 and 1995, RDBMS vendors are delivering an array of new products that are enabled to parallel processing hardware servers. Informix, for example, offers its Dynamic Scalable Architecture to take advantage of symmetric multiprocessing computers with 4 to 16 processors. Scalability in some applications is almost linear.

As another example, IBM is offering parallel processors in symmetric (shared memory), shared disk, and/or shared nothing configurations. The new IBM mainframes are built from parallel CMOS implementations of System 390 architecture chips. IBM's new AIX (UNIX)-based server series (SP2) is a parallel architecture based on the Power PC chip.

Relational DBMSs can be improved in more ways than just copy management and performance. The world of object technology has brought some good ideas to the technology table. These ideas include the need for a DBMS to explicitly support complex data types with structure and the need to have a programming environment that supports the object notion of inheritance. We can be sure that the RDBMS vendors will be busy adding support for these features over the next few years. While it will continue to expand in both functionality and performance, the Relational DBMS that we know today with its SQL language is likely to remain dominant as the repository for most corporate information systems in the remainder of this decade.

While the contestants in client software, servers, and databases are well known, an important emerging marketplace for object frameworks is where the main battle of the mid '90s will be fought. Object frameworks are the standards by which software developers will create and distribute the software objects and components that will redefine software markets in the 1990s. Up until now, the operating system provided the supporting standards that application developers required. In the future, the underlying operating system will be largely hidden from view while the developer works with object frameworks.

The contestants in this new battle for supremacy in object frameworks are the old gladiators, but repackaged into new alliances. No one should be surprised to find that Microsoft is once again a leader in defining object standards (see Figure FW.2). The Microsoft technology is OLE (object linking and embedding). Whereas OLE is designed for the desktop environment, Microsoft is cooperating with Digital Equipment to develop versions of OLE that will work across networks.

OBJECT MARKETS

- MICROSOFT'S OLE 2.0 & DEC COM

- APPLE's OPENDOC + IBM's SOM & DSOM

- SUN/NEXT/HP OPENSTEP, OBJECT ORIENTED APPLICATION ENVIRONMENT

- APPLE/IBM/HP TALIGENT

© 1994 Digital Consulting, Inc. Used by permission.

Figure FW.2. *Leading candidates for object standards.*

Almost every other vendor is working with Component Integration Labs (CIL) to create an alternative to OLE. The critical pieces of this other (United Nations) object framework are Apple's OpenDoc, IBM's System Object Model and Distributed System Object Model, and the Object Management Group's CORBA (Common Object Request Broker Architecture).

A ten-second synopsis on the major competitive lineups for object framework standards is then this:

■ Microsoft with OLE and its partner Digital Equipment are in the lead in 1994 with

    1) a technology that is already deliverable

    2) ownership of most of the current and future desktop operating systems

    3) the allegiance of developers that this market position buys

    4) an important application product suite—for example, Word, Excel—that will show off OLE technology, and

    5) a resulting market of billions of dollars that will punish developers who can't or won't move to this technology.

■ IBM, Apple, Novell, and everyone else are working together to deny Microsoft the home run that was achieved with Windows. Other vendors want a competitive market, and they'll work together to deliver a superior (especially when distributed) object environment. It'll be later than Microsoft's, however.

■ NeXT with its NeXTStep is the prototype of the object-framework environments of 1996. You can buy it from NeXT today. Sun realized that and has joined forces with NeXT to create OpenStep, which runs on NeXT and Sun hardware and software. This combination ensures more support for a truly superior development environment that NeXT was too small to pursue by itself. The ultimate importance of this combination, however, will depend on how far ahead technically it can stay of its two much larger competitors previously mentioned.

■ Taligent, a joint venture of Apple and IBM, is attempting to create a next generation object framework that offers superior technology to the other three contenders mentioned previously. As an interim capability, Taligent's object frameworks will run on existing operating systems such as OS/2 and System 7. Taligent's stuff is supposed to be in the market in the 95/96 time frame. On this one, I'm afraid that if it's too late a set of market standards will have already coalesced around one or two of the previously named products, and the market won't readily accept a new competitor.

The Software Environment of the '90s

If you think the layered look in clothing software was good, you haven't seen "nothin" yet compared to the layered look in computer software for the '90s. Figure FW.3 illustrates the typical user environment of the '90s with many independent but interdependent software layers, each taking advantage of service provided by others.

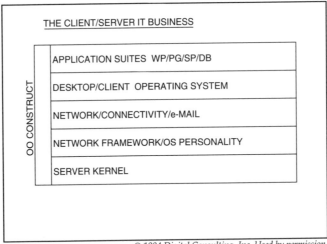

© 1994 Digital Consulting, Inc. Used by permission.

Figure FW.3. Many software layers.

At the top are applications that provide services to the end user. These can be word processors, spreadsheets, order entry, or any other application. The horizontal categories like word processing, of course, are likely to be sold by the major software vendors. Specific business applications can be developed on a custom basis or purchased also.

These applications take direct advantage of the desktop operating systems like Windows. Such GUIs control the display and scheduling of the work accomplished at the client.

In the networked enterprise, the client GUI will take advantage of services that are available across the network. E-mail and database services come to mind, but more advanced communications services to others in the company or across the world (through the Internet, for example) can be provided by the network layer. Those services are delivered to the application through the desktop operating system.

Connectivity to mainframe databases, shared object stores (for example, Lotus Notes) or e-mail servers are just applications that run over the network. As network applications, these functions use the lower-level services that the network operating systems provide.

Most current server operating systems are complete tightly integrated products. In the future, however, many operating systems will become layered themselves. The most invisible part is the kernel, which provides access to the basic machine. The higher level parts of the operating system, features like priority, rollback, scheduling, directory, security, and user addressing will be incorporated in object software modules or components that exist in the operating system personality. There will be only a very few players building server kernels (probably the best known example is Carnegie Mellon's MACH, which is the chosen kernel for Digital Equipment's OSF/1 and for IBM's OS/2 and AIX operating systems).

The unifying element for all of these layers will be services provided by the object model or construct that provides the standard for messaging, security, and the other defining elements of an object environment. In other words, an OLE or OpenDoc architecture will unify the diverse elements. It's even possible, even probable, that multiple object architectures can be present in components across a corporate client/server network. In other words, heterogeneity will likely be the norm.

Looking at the six boxes presented in Figure FW.3 can give you an idea as to how strong a player Microsoft is likely to be in providing components of your future client/server architecture. Microsoft competes in all six boxes illustrated. At the top layer, it sells Microsoft Office, the dominant current player in application suites. Its combination of DOS and Windows has 70+ percent of the market for desktop operating systems. It is too early to make any prediction based on Microsoft's next generation, Chicago/Windows 4.0, but few dispute the probability that Microsoft will continue or even extend its mastery over the desktop.

In the middle layer of network or network connectivity, Microsoft's market penetration is far below Novell's (with NetWare or UNIX) or Lotus' (with Notes). However, Microsoft is not abandoning any market here yet. It has mounted a multiyear attack on this market, first with LAN Manager and more recently with Windows NT. NT is very capable of providing connectivity network services and will be contesting this market for the foreseeable future. Windows 4.0 will have expanded embedded connectivity function also.

Furthermore, with its two future operating systems—Chicago, the replacement for DOS/Windows, and Cairo, the follow-on enhancement of NT—Microsoft is building its own micro kernels and the Windows personalities that sit on top of the kernels. With OLE, Microsoft is establishing its own standards for software objects.

IBM, by contrast, is not an original developer of application suites and isn't a significant seller of any kind of application software. IBM's two desktop operating systems, OS/2 and AIX, are good products with significant (except by Microsoft standards of marketing) market volumes. Both of these products can also work as server operating systems. If you add LAN Server then, IBM competes in the middle three layers of software. The company has announced that both AIX and OS/2 will become personalities that sit on top of the MACH kernel. IBM is also a major player in the emerging world of object standards with its SOM/DSOM initiatives. So IBM is competing in four of the six software blocks.

Novell is probably the only other major player that is attempting to compete with Microsoft in all the software segments. Outside of the networking and UNIX areas, however, Novell is a minor or insignificant participant.

The Future of the Software Business

When one puts all of this together and looks at it from a macroeconomic viewpoint, it becomes clear that the software business is quickly maturing into an industry that is organized like other mature industries, automobiles, for example. In the early days of the auto business, there were dozens of vendors of cars. Eventually, they all disappeared or merged to form three behemoths (in the United States). These three dominant players sold finished product through established brand names and an unassailable distribution system. Even in the years when Detroit's product was perceived as inferior and more expensive than cars produced in Japan, the dominance of the Big Three's dealers in numbers and geography made purchase of an American car a reasonable alternative. It's very tough to attack a superior distribution system.

The software business, in like fashion, is bound to shake out in the near future to a smaller number of major brands (Microsoft, Lotus, IBM, and Novell?). The smaller companies, then, will become parts and component suppliers. These parts and components will be built to the object standards of the small number of emerging standards. That is what happened to the auto industry, and it's about to happen to the software industry.

With this scenario, most application software systems will be built or assembled from object-based components that are the parts built by a vast industry of parts builders. Some companies will choose to do their own assembling, but others will rely on systems integrators with expertise in defined markets.

The end result of all this is going to be better software made more inexpensively. It took the auto industry 70 years to reach maturity. The software industry is accomplishing the same in about 35 years. Client/server will be the backbone architecture. Database concepts, especially relational, will remain vital. Object standards will become the glue that ties together the entire computing environment and allows the final maturation of this industry.

George Schussel

Chairman and CEO of DCI

June 1994

Preface

"This is a book about Downsizing Information Systems..."

That's what we wrote three years ago, in this same space, in the first edition of this book. Since then, much of what is covered in this book has been experienced by thousands of companies across the globe. PCs and networks are pervasive today. As their costs continue to drop, they continue to be adopted as the new technology driver for information systems development and operations.

However, no longer is the majority of activity occurring based on top management pressure to downsize. Instead, the biggest difference between now and when the first edition of this book was published two years ago, is that the term *rightsizing* is much more applicable for what is happening now and what will happen in the future in computing. The reliability, costs, and richness of choice of new client/server technologies have increased to the point that—whether companies are growing, expanding, and increasing their automation, or whether they are reducing, trimming down, and reengineering—they are rightsizing to new technologies.

Thus, when we developed this revised edition of the book, we decided to rechristen it *Rightsizing Information Systems* as a more appropriate name for today. While a majority of the subjects are the same, we've made many updates to the technologies, added several new developments, and fixed a few of the nits that found their way into the first edition.

Then, as now, it might be good to start by allaying some Management Information Systems (MIS)-related fears of rightsizing. First, it is not synonymous with "headcount adjustment." Instead, research shows this is one of several myths of rightsizing, with others to be covered in Chapter 1, "Understanding the Importance of Rightsizing." For example, a survey of 200 companies engaged in rightsizing showed a decline in the MIS workforce in only 16 percent of the respondents. What's more startling is that the same survey showed an increase in MIS staffing due to rightsizing in 14 percent of the cases!

Second, rightsizing has joined the ranks of its new buzzword brethren like total quality, customer responsiveness, and competitive advantage. What CEO doesn't have those three on the tip of the tongue?

Third, we can finally stop talking about rightsizing and do it!

Most technological barriers to rightsizing have been overcome—the majority of them in the last two or three years. The local area network (LAN) "server" has matured to a point where performance, reliability, and capacity are comparable to traditional mainframe and minicomputer standards. What's more, network-based development and application software rivals, and often surpasses, the functionality of much larger systems.

The elusive relational database has taken hold in the network computing realm. Companies such as Oracle, Sybase, Gupta, Informix, Ingres, IBM, Borland, and many others are, at long last, putting Structured Query Language (SQL) in the corporate technological arsenal.

But probably the most compelling quality of rightsizing is the dramatic reduction in cost, as we've mentioned. A $35,000 server can do the work of a $2 million mainframe or a $400,000 minicomputer. The server has no special environmental requirements, such as a raised floor, water cooling, or meat-locker temperatures. It runs software that costs in the thousands—not the tens or hundreds of thousands. And it is easily serviced. For critical applications, a fully redundant hardware configuration can be installed economically. Try buying a duplicate mainframe!

What we're really talking about here is the emergence of the LAN-based network computing platform as the preferred domain for data processing. It spells the "beginning of the end" of monolithic, centralized information systems, as it places the personal computer at the top of the information technology (I/T) heap in a new, "heterogeneous" information systems infrastructure.

The largest global corporate powers are putting their lifeblood—information—in the hands of devices that literally are no larger than a breadbox. MIS executives that embrace the LAN platform have graduated from being "pioneering" and "reckless," to being "visionary" and "savvy." In fact, the term "MIS executive" was viewed as somewhat of an oxymoron before corporate America saw information as a strategic asset.

In this spirit, let's define rightsizing as the migration of corporate mission-critical applications and information to the network computing platform.

Notice that "migration" has no directional component—no "up" nor "down." That is, rightsizing can be approached either from above or below. A typical scenario, however, is for MIS to identify a few key, large systems applications, modify them to work on the LAN platform, and relocate them to the network in their entirety.

Conversely, rightsizing also involves the aggregation of individual PC workstations into a common network or LAN. The benefits of this "upward rightsizing" (upsizing) include electronic connectivity—the ability to share information expeditiously—and standardization, the simplification of training and systems implementation processes across many users.

Clearly, these trends will continue for some time, with companies that possess costly, centralized systems downsizing, and with others that have growing, disparate PCs and networks upsizing.

That's really why the "rightsizing" name sticks.

Acknowledgments

A fundamental shift has occurred in the way businesses go about using information systems for their competitive advantage. New techniques, such as business process reengineering, have led to systems reengineering; and as businesses continue to decentralize and rightsize, information systems will follow suit. In the years ahead, we believe analysts will look back at this as a time when computing was reinvented.

Along with the tremendous potential, however, comes tremendous confusion and chaos in the marketplace. Open systems, object orientation, graphical user interfaces, UNIX and Windows network and systems management, mobile and wireless computing, databases, and superservers—these are terms that can impact information systems choices in various ways. But in today's rapidly changing business and computing environments, how do you decide which solution is best for your needs? And how do you go about implementing that solution?

We wrote this book to provide answers to these and similar questions. As one would expect, the information in *Rightsizing Information Systems* comes from years of experience and first-hand implementation of new technologies. As a hands-on integrator and an established technical author, Steve Guengerich, President of BSG Education, deserves credit as principal author and orchestrator of the effort put forth in creating *Rightsizing Information Systems*. In this edition, we are very pleased to add George Schussel, Chairman and CEO of Digital Consulting, Inc., as a co-author of the book.

Special thanks go to the team at BSG Corporation, who edited and produced the original manuscripts, including Andrew D. Dunlevie, Kim W. Padgett, and Susan Wilson. In addition, David Menendez was instrumental in putting together the original outline and gathering raw material for the chapters. Thanks also to Lara Weekes and Kathleen Saux who helped develop the second edition.

Thanks go to Mitch Shults, Linda Richardson, Steve Brewer, and George Jones, who were gracious enough to spend some brief—but important—interviews early on to bring focus to certain sections of the book. Michael Bang and Kathy Wollerman contributed material to the hardware and software passages in the book, as well.

Thanks also to Cheryl Currid, President of Currid and Company; and Susan Scrupski, President, SS Consulting, for their interest and words of encouragement during the early stages of manuscript development. Their thoughts and ideas are sprinkled in at several points in the book.

Thanks also go to Peter Klinkow of Strategic Systems Funding, who deserves much of the credit for ideas contributed on the subject of financing rightsized systems. Likewise, Daryl Conner, President of ODR, a leading consultancy on managing corporate change, deserves the credit for much of the material in the chapter on change management.

Most of the credit for the knowledge in this book must be attributed to the professionals at BSG, a leading integrator of corporate computing systems. We worked with experts in each of BSG's divisions—Alliance/ IT, Consulting and Education—to develop a complete picture of all the issues in the rightsizing process. Among them, special thanks go to Ben Mayberry, Richard Scruggs, Eileen Birge, Ginny Green, and Steve Douty, who helped to keep the manuscript on track by lending their many combined years' experience in the SI industry to the review process. Others involved in the technical review process included Andy Roehr, Martin B.H. Weiss, James J. Sobczak, and Dwight Williams.

We hope that you gain a better understanding of and appreciation for the marvelous possibilities of rightsizing as you read *Rightsizing Information Systems* and that you feel better prepared to ride the fundamental shifts in business and computing throughout the next several years.

Steve G. Papermaster

Chairman, BSG Corporation

May 1994

About the Authors

Steven L. Guengerich is president of BSG Education, a division of BSG Corporation, and also serves as its senior communications officer. He cofounded the *NetWare Advisor* technical journal and has written numerous articles and books on client/server technology and its role in business change. In addition to his authoring role for this book, he is also the series editor for *Client/Server Computing* and *Enterprise-Wide Networking*, both from Sams Publishing.

George Schussel is the Chairman and CEO of Digital Consulting, INC. (DCI), Andover, Massachusetts. DCI sponsors large conferences and trade shows for data processing professionals. Schussel chairs both the Client/Server and DATABASE WORLD conferences and trade shows. An expert of database, downsizing, and information management issues, his lectures are held all over the world, typically before audiences that number in the hundreds. He has authored many important published papers on client/server subjects and as Editor of *Schussel's Downsizing Journal* devotes considerable space in that publication to the subject.

Introduction

The Systems Integration Industry

This book is one in a series of three books in Sams Publishing's *Professional Systems Integration* series. The other two books are *Client/Server Computing* and *Enterprise-Wide Networking*. There are two objectives in each book:

■ To explain the particular subject matter at hand and its meaning for the systems integration community and its followers.

■ To provide a common thread of guidance for how systems integrators must be organized to meet the demands of information technology (IT) through the next decade.

This series was conceived to provide information and guidance to professionals in the systems integration field, as well as those affected by and involved in systems integration issues. The audience for this series includes

■ Corporate managers and executives who must make and execute systems integration decisions for their organizations

■ Computer-systems integrators

■ Value-added resellers (VARs)

■ Manufacturers of computer systems

■ Communications providers

■ Third-party consultants

■ Corporate information-systems professionals

The size of this audience has grown dramatically in recent years and, based on industry figures, is expected to continue growing. For example, worldwide systems integration is projected to grow from $25 billion in 1989 to $70 billion in 1994 (see Figure IN.1).

Total Worldwide Market
$70 Billion

Source: GR Research

Figure IN.1. *Estimated worldwide systems-integration expenditures for the '90s.*

This growth, both current and projected, can be traced to four major trends:

- ■ The realization that information is a strategic asset
- ■ An expanded awareness of the advantages of distributed processing
- ■ The evolution of the microprocessor, which has enabled network technology to evolve to the point where corporations around the world accept PCs as alternatives rather than just adjuncts to mainframe technology
- ■ Greatly increasing choices for systems components and solutions

These trends have had a *push me, pull you* effect on corporate IT resources. On one hand, the rapid evolution of technology at all levels pushes companies to deliver new and better systems to their users. On the other hand, business executives feel the need to pull together their increasingly dispersed information systems in order to have some reasonable sense of coherence and control.

The bottom line is that these forces have led to an overloading of in-house staff. Staff responsibilities have expanded from enhancing and maintaining existing systems to developing solutions for a constant flood of new demands, prompted by user expectations and complex new business operating requirements. At the same time, the in-house staff must remain current with numerous new developments in distributed hardware, software, and communications.

In light of these increased demands, it's becoming increasingly clear that, by coordinating the best available outside resources with in-house staff capabilities, organizations can

- Achieve the highest performance, timeliness, and integrity of information and communications systems solutions in support of mission-critical needs.
- Take advantage of leading technologies, methodologies, and tools.
- Benefit from the best skilled people available.
- Optimize the return on large investments made in these systems and avoid dead-end technical choices.

Enter the systems integrator, or SI. You can expect undivided attention, maximum efficiency, and economy from a third-party systems integrator. You also can obtain assurances through contracts or other written agreements with the SI regarding costs, schedules, and performance. A systems integrator can assume the task of coordinating and efficiently scheduling the work of all vendors and MIS staff directly or indirectly involved in a project, and the SI can be responsible for the quality of the finished system.

Having a single contract and single point-of-contact insulates the corporate executive and the user alike from the burden of incompatible platforms, interfacing difficulties, contract loopholes, hidden technical shortcomings, and other problems that multiply geometrically with the number of vendors engaged in a systems implementation project. The systems integrator offers greater assurance of the quality and timely completion of the project in conformance with your stated objectives and needs.

From a financial view, corporate executives are attracted to systems integrators because of the increasing complexity of buying computer products. These executives choose to share some of the project-management risk with outside parties. Flexible pricing, risk-sharing, and profit or equity participation arrangement enable the corporate customer to feel more comfortable undertaking these complex implementation projects.

What does this mean for the systems integrator? Clearly, whether your systems integrator is an independent consulting company or an in-house MIS group, there is an "up-side" opportunity. The current growth rate and impact of the four major trends cited earlier are likely to continue unabated. The major players in the SI market, therefore, should enjoy this market growth for the foreseeable future.

Already, strong players have emerged in at least three different areas of SI services, as illustrated in Figure IN.2. Tier 1 integrators, such as EDS and Andersen Consulting, are traditional providers of large-scale, mainframe SI contracts and outsourcing. Tier 2 integrators, such as BSG and CTP, are leaders in applying the emerging technologies—for example, client/server network computing—in an area G2 Research calls *microsystems integration*. Tier 3 integrators, such as US Connect and Lotus Consulting Services, focus on providing network computing platforms and vertical, vendor-specific applications environments.

Although the market holds a variety of opportunities for these and other

SI Type	# of Companies	Typical Size	Leaders
Tier 1 Legacy out-sourcers and systems integrators	10	$1B+	EDS ISSC IBM CSC Andersen Consulting
Tier 2 Early out-sourcers and client/server integrators	40	$200M-1B	SHL Systemhouse Technology Solutions Cambridge Tech. Ptrs. BSG Corporation
Tier 3 Vertical application and network integrators	200+	$50-$200M	USConnect Lotus Consulting Svcs. Oracle RBOCS

Source: BSG, 1994

Figure IN.2. *System integration categories and leaders.*

integrators, the risks are numerous. Perhaps the greatest of these risks is keeping up with the fundamental changes occurring in business itself. In the aftermath of the corporate mergers and acquisitions of the 1980s and early 1990s, the need to link disparate systems has become a major problem. Les Aberthal, Chairman of EDS, has commented on the inability of both his company and the SI industry as a whole to "keep the promise of the great sword of technology from rusting in its scabbard."

Another change in the industry is the shift of the authority for systems decision-making from corporate MIS to the individual operating units. This is both good and bad for systems integrators. As operating units look to maximize their return on investment in information systems, they turn to outside sources for systems integration solutions. On the other hand, these same operating units are relatively uninitiated in the systems-development process and are likely to be disappointed because of unrealistically high expectations.

Executives are attracted to systems-integration providers whose approach to product and service delivery matches their own—an open, market-driven approach that combines concepts like "smaller, cheaper, and faster" ways of doing business while maintaining "the best and the brightest" professionals.

With the growth of this market, it's ironic that few established integrators are capable of decentralizing, rightsizing, and distributing systems for companies. Too many integrators are steeped in the traditional monolithic, hierarchical structures they have installed for customers over the years and around which they have organized themselves. What's required is a new, open architecture and delivery philosophy that better matches where corporate customers and IT are headed.

This new delivery philosophy is illustrated in Figure IN.3. This illustration shows the open architecture structure that SIs must adopt, which provides entry points at several levels. Users can start at the bottom and work their way up through the SI, getting increasingly more service. Users also can enter from the side, taking just the SI services they need. Freedom of choice is the rule.

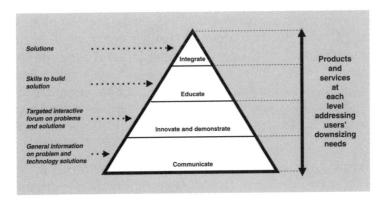

Figure IN.3. Open architecture systems integration delivery.

PART 1

Downsizing, Upsizing, or Rightsizing?

Downsizing information systems (IS) is one of the most talked about subjects in business. When asked what it is, however, professionals and lay-people alike struggle for a clear, concise definition. The press and public often associate downsizing with related trends in information technology, including client/server network computing, distributed-applications development and processing, object-oriented programming, and enterprise-wide networking. Although it's true that downsizing makes use of these technologies, they don't by themselves define downsizing.

So, what is downsizing? In a nutshell, it is a process. The best definition for downsizing is that it is the process that organizations must undertake to get from the current generation of information technology (I/T) to the next generation.

Admittedly, this is a broad definition. In fact, the breadth of interpretation of this definition already has resulted in the demise of the word *downsizing* as a useful term in many quarters. New terms have emerged to represent downsizing's trend toward distributed-processing solutions and away from the problems of traditional data processing. For example, the terms *rightsizing* and *client/server computing* have become, in many firms, synonyms for downsizing; or, they're used in place of *downsizing*. In others, the related term, *upsizing*, is being used. Upsizing represents the use of client/server network-computing technologies for more sophisticated, mission-critical applications not previously automated in an organization.

Regardless of the term, many technical challenges and cultural problems of downsizing and upsizing are the same in definition and approach. The combined forces of the push from above (downsizing) and below (upsizing) have created an interesting, new dynamic as shown in Figure I.1. The figure demonstrates how an optimal combination of decentralized and centralized systems makes for a maximum return in information systems benefits, such as productivity, efficiency, and flexibility, among others.

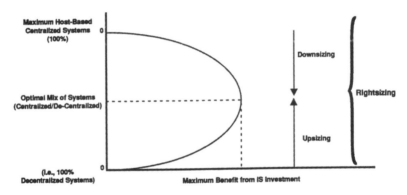

Figure I.1. Rightsizing curve.

In Figure I.1, the vertical axis represents the degree of host-based, centralized systems in a company, ranging from zero to maximum, and the horizontal axis represents the amount of benefits realized. Theoretically, every company is somewhere along the vertical axis and is trying to move up or down to reach its optimal mix of systems. In general, most large corporations are too high on the axis and, thus, through the process of downsizing their information systems, they can and will move down the axis and out on the curve to realize greater MIS benefits.

The result of this process is an increased mix of personal computers (PCs) and workstations, local- and wide-area networks, and mainframe and minicomputer hosts from multiple vendors. The resulting multivendor mix has forced companies to adapt their existing mainframes to work in concert with PC LANs. An example of the kind of information-systems infrastructure that this new mixed, or *heterogeneous*, approach to information processing can create is illustrated in Figure I.2.

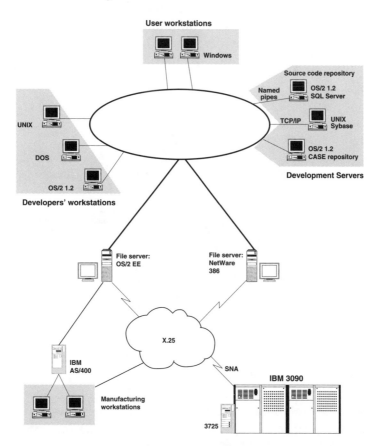

Figure I.2. *A heterogeneous, multivendor computing environment.*

In addition to the dynamics at work in Figure I.1, another reason the alternative terms *rightsizing* and *upsizing* have grown in favor over *downsizing* is the psychological discomfort caused by the word. In a general business sense, "downsizing" often is used as a euphemism for "layoffs." A management information system (MIS) corporate staff employee might have fears that downsizing computer applications could result in reductions in support staff.

According to research, however, this fear is one of the many myths of downsizing (others are discussed in Chapter 1, "Understanding the Importance of Rightsizing"). To the contrary, analysts don't foresee many MIS staff members being laid off because of the downsizing of information systems. In fact, typical of the research, one survey of 200 companies that downsized their information systems showed that central MIS staffers were cut at 16 percent of the sites that downsized, but increased at 14 percent of the sites. As shown in Figure I.3, staffing levels remained the same at more than 69 percent of the sites.

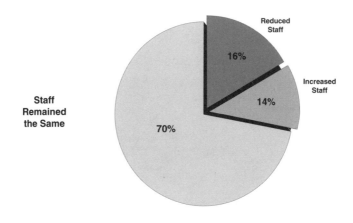

Source: PC Week, September 10, 1990, vol. 7 no. 36.

Figure I.3. Change in central MIS staff levels.

The reason for the relatively insignificant impact on staffing numbers is that business downsizing and computer downsizing are not similar processes (see Chapter 2, "Rightsizing Origins," for more information about this subject). Rather, downsizing information systems is another name for the way that organizations take advantage of improvements in information technology (it would, more correctly, be called rightsizing). Until now, computers have just automated tasks that previously had been done mechanically or manually. The process of downsizing (rightsizing) and its related technologies are evidence that correct, imaginative use of computers can fundamentally change the way we work. Downsized (rightsized) systems enable new processes to occur and provide new ways to bring together formerly unlinked resources. These processes enable companies to improve their use of information to gain a competitive advantage—a grail that all companies seek.

Pursuing the benefits of competitive advantage is one thing; *achieving* competitive advantage, however, is one of those "easy to talk about, hard to do" goals. Chapter 3, "Where We Are Today and Opportunities for Tomorrow," provides concrete information about just how important rightsizing information systems can be. Consider this tiny sampling of benefits:

- *Price/performance*—The price per millions of instructions per second (MIPS) on a mainframe, for example, is typically given as $45,000. The price per MIPS on a desktop PC is $10–50. The price advantage is thus between 900 and 4,500 to 1.

- *Productivity*—Dunkin' Donuts has reduced the average time it takes to develop computer applications from 3–6 years to 9–12 months by rightsizing to PC-based networks. The new applications support five times as many users.

- *Scalability*—Before rightsizing to a PC LAN, Consolidated Insurance Group needed a $200,000 mainframe-based, general-ledger program to keep track of its debits and credits. After rightsizing, Consolidated keeps track with a $595 off-the-shelf program. The price advantage of the application is more than 300 to 1.

Of course, examples such as these don't, by themselves, win the argument for rightsizing. They illustrate, however, that rightsizing has some tremendous advantages. Chapter 4, "Finding and Measuring Rightsizing Benefits," discusses measuring these benefits and the feasibility aspects for rightsizing. Helping you to understand how to work with executives and staff in your company (or how to work with your clients, if you are an independent integrator) to recognize and then implement rightsizing projects is the goal of the chapters in Part I.

1

Understanding
the Importance
of Rightsizing

Great businesses turn on a little pin.

—George Herbert (1640)

Objectives:

1. To illustrate the possible benefits of rightsizing.
2. To introduce you to the strategic technology and systems methodology that set rightsizing apart from traditional, mainframe systems development.
3. To preview some of the topics in this book and how they relate to one another.

Just how important is rightsizing information systems? Consider the results of a study Forrester Research conducted in late 1992 called the "Mainframe Voyage." In it, the researchers reported that a staggering 80 percent of respondents (interviewed were seventy-five Fortune 1000 firms in seventeen vertical industries) told Forrester that rightsizing interest is increasing. The average savings reaped by respondents was $1.7 million per year. As one respondent from a forest products company put it, "It's a 100:1 cost difference per MIP [millions of instructions per second] between PCs and the host. By 2001, it will be 700:1. Why not take advantage of this and more processing closer to the user."

Based on actual street selling prices, not fictional published prices, the sharp diverging trend predicted for the future is even more remarkable (see Figure 1.1). In 1990, a PC instruction cycle cost only 1/160th of a mainframe instruction cycle—that is, less than 1 percent. Yet by 1996, this fraction will be more like 1/6000th, an improvement of almost 50 fold in six years! As we approach the middle of this decade, the difference in these cost ratios will be so striking that information system designers will be well advised to consider the costs of PC MIPS as free when planning new systems.

Certainly, when compared to staff, software, and other large budget items, the cost of PC MIPS will become almost invisible. This kind of analysis is coming into vogue at aggressive rightsizing sites.

The astounding power of the numbers in Figure 1.1 recalls a comment by Steve Gibson in the July 13, 1992 issue of *InfoWorld:* "I believe that the radical advances in the PC's power/cost ratio will have another far ranging impact: all competing hardware platforms are dead. Inertia may carry them forward for a while, but their justifications for existing have completely evaporated." So, the power of PCs and the enabling technology of network computing can tackle tasks that once were the exclusive domain of "big iron." Today's microprocessor-based systems have the memory capacity and processing speed of the largest commercial mainframes. Combine those ingredients with the multiuser capabilities of the LAN, and you've got a recipe for full-scale, all-out data processing.

		$/MIPS				$/MIPS	
YEAR	PC $/MIPS	MAINFRAME $/MIPS	RATIO	YEAR	PC $/MIPS	MAINFRAME $/MIPS	RATIO
87	2,000	130,000	65:1	92	75	58,000	775:1
88	1,600	111,000	70:1	93	37	49,000	1,325:1
89	1,000	94,000	94:1	94	18	41,000	2,280:1
90	500	80,000	160:1	95	9	35,000	3,900:1
91	150	68,000	450:1	96	5	30,000	6,000:1

Figure 1.1. Cost per millions of instructions per second.

But why is rightsizing so *big?* Does it rank with engineering marvels like the internal combustion engine, fiber-optic cable or the digital signal processor? Maybe, but that isn't the whole story. The basic thesis of Chapter 2, "Rightsizing Origins," is that there's more to the rightsizing equation than technology. We can say safely that without the string of recent microprocessor advancements, this book would be but a gleam in our collective eye. But the combination of technological breakthroughs, strong economic pressures, and the rise of the "quality imperative" have made rightsizing a legitimate mechanism for excellence in business—if not for *survival.*

Putting I/T All Together

The tremendous competitive pressures of the 1970s, and especially the 1980s, placed a premium on access to accurate and timely information about customers, competitors, business measurements, and so on. We've all known for years that the mainframe is an expensive, inflexible, temperamental, and imposing being. In the early days, however, information beggars could not be platform choosers. There simply was no other way to manage the volumes of collected data in a reasonable time frame.

But processing power came at a great expense, both in terms of dollars and amenities. Not even the manufacturers would dispute that large systems had their shortcomings and disturbing trade-offs. Rightsizing, on the other hand, offers some interesting alternatives to the classic compromise among power, user friendliness, and cost. In fact, a new genre of I/T, called the client/server, combines the best of all worlds:

- The rich user interface of the PC
- The power of mainframes and large LAN-servers
- A much smaller price tag

To be sure, rightsizing is not a panacea—but it does address the problems that have plagued large systems for decades. Remember, as we said in the introduction to Part I, rightsizing is "the process that organizations must undertake to get from the current generation of information technology to the next generation."

The User Interface

No matter how hard it tried, the mainframe just could not produce the environment that would draw *technophobes* (read "executives" and "management") into its lair. There's only so much you can do with a darkened TV screen covered with 1,960 blinking characters. The fancier the program, the more precious CPU time is gobbled up. In a world where the smallest upgrade to a system could cost you $500,000, cute colors and user conveniences quickly fell by the wayside.

In the meantime, the PC was blasting through five generations of microprocessor architecture in just 12 years (from the now-archaic Intel 8086 to the latest commercially available Pentium). Initially fashioned in the image of its maker, the PC got its start with that same dreadful screen of 1,960 characters. But the Macintosh turned the world upside down with the graphical user interface (GUI) and, for the first time, "real people" were using computers.

Object-Oriented Programming

Software companies saw GUI's potential and worked the visual power of the user interface into the application development process. This solved the "United Nations effect," in which some translation is required for every user/programmer conversation. Because you can see a mock-up of the end product in the early stages of program development, and because the process is not entirely dependent on the use of English, the application design cycle is shortened dramatically. The Fortune 1000 has heard the call to arms for objects. A 1993 report called "The Object Voyage," by Forrester Research, showed that 70 percent of those interviewed were actively investigating object technology or were developing at least one application based on this new development style.

In addition, the use of *objects*, or functions—instead of nested menus—is more representative of "real world" processes and can be grasped more easily by the novice (see Chapter 10, "Joint Application Design (JAD)," and Chapter 16, "Rapid Application Development (RAD)").

The Number Cruncher

PC/mainframe debates used to end abruptly when the mainframe side would ask: "OK, OK—but can *yours* handle a multikeyed, reverse-indexed search over a 10-gigabyte hyperspace?" Long pause; stony silence. "What's a gigabyte, anyway?"

Mercifully, those days are numbered. LAN-server architectures, unlike traditional mainframe architectures, are ideally suited to the blistering speeds offered by UNIX. The incredible pace of microprocessor technology and its impact on rightsizing are covered in more detail in Chapter 3, "Where We Are Today and Opportunities for Tomorrow." For now, suffice it to say that with the network server, mainframes finally have met their match.

The Money Pit

There was a time when the MIS department was viewed much like the power company: it was far too expensive, you didn't always notice it until the first "temporary outage," and you simply couldn't survive without it. Undoubtedly, CFOs spent years grudgingly approving huge amounts of the budget for something they didn't understand or enjoy. However, the new breed of executive takes a more proactive approach to I/T; the catch phrase of the 1990s is "computers are our friends." But new breed or not, executives wince just as hard at the computer bill.

It's true: when you add up all its bite-sized pieces, the cost of a rightsized system is more than just a fraction of the cost of large systems. Consider the components: a PC for every user, multiple servers, cabling, and lots of software. If you were to start from scratch, the initial layout for a rightsized system wouldn't lag far behind a large system.

The fact is, most professionals already have a PC on their desktop, so the largest rightsizing cost component already has been spent! Beyond that, the real "killers" in the computer cost game are the recurring charges: maintenance, staffing, and environmentals. Here the network platform wins, hands down.

So, with powerful, economical servers doing the work of mainframes and a revitalized set of users champing at the megabit, the picture is complete. A network of GUI-laced PCs and one or more database servers truly has the capability of running large, mission-critical applications.

Here's the bottom line: If you're trying to refute the merits of rightsizing with a technological argument, you're barking up the wrong tree. The real issues confronting rightsizing involve not machines, but organizations and people.

Are We "There" Yet?

Rightsizing isn't without its challenges. Rightsizing a company's systems demands an organizational agility and resiliency that, in many cases, simply doesn't exist. Nowhere is this more evident than in the MIS department.

Change Management

MIS teams schooled in data processing during the 1970s and 1980s continue to cling to time-tested paradigms. Clearly, 30 years or so of IBM, DEC, and Honeywell have established a durable culture—one that hasn't seen much dramatic change until now. In addition, the years have produced a solid base of computer operations and systems management practices that are hard to dispel.

There are, for example, proven procedures for data backup, batch processing, job scheduling, disaster recovery, and network fault isolation. Problems typically have been wrestled to the ground by large vendor and end-user support staffs. With this kind of attention, the large systems environment is thoroughly broken-in and understood.

Network computing, in contrast, has at most five years under its youthful belt. Robust operational practices are either new or still under development. MIS veterans have looked askance at these rich, new whiz-kids (Bill Gates?

Michael Dell? Steven Jobs? Phillippe Kahn?) and their toys—literally waiting for them to fail. But they have not failed.

Sometimes you really can't teach an old dog new tricks. For some, it's hard to imagine a computing world without batch processing. For others, the transfer of gigabyte-sized databases to the network server is beyond comprehension. Finally, the organizational changes that accompany this technological revolution often are simply too much to handle.

But isn't this what "quality" and "reengineering" are all about? It means changing the way you do business. Rightsizing isn't about reorganization. Nor is it about automation. It involves fundamental corporate and organizational change, discussed in detail in Chapter 6, "Reengineering."

Chapter 7, "Change Management," discusses a critical, often-overlooked step in the rightsizing process. This chapter isn't talking about changes in technology but, rather, organizational changes in the way people work. These changes can be implemented, and are being implemented, by visionaries in the I/T field. The effect of change on an organization is too important to be overlooked.

The "Production" Environment

The other consideration with rightsizing systems is in the design of operational support processes. Again, the mainframe and minicomputer paradigms come replete with procedures, rules, and standards that make for a smooth-running and reliable operation. The LAN platform just recently has adopted its analog of this environment.

Remember the movie *The Andromeda Strain?* To descend from one sublevel laboratory to the next, the beleaguered scientists had to go through a dreadful series of decontamination, radiation, laser beams, air locks, and other grisly measures—some of which had to be accomplished in the nude. Once you made it down without being contaminated by that ghastly virus, getting back up was even tougher! Welcome to the mainframe "production" environment.

Large system operations often maintain two or more parallel computing environments. The distinction between them is simple: some are used for testing, whereas others are "the real thing," for example, "production" applications. The latter category includes the set of programs that are "live"— they are directly engaged in running the business. These applications have survived that technological rite of passage called "migration to production."

For all practical purposes, they are flawless—tested seven ways to Sunday to ensure error-free operation and peaceful coexistence with all the others.

For all the slings and arrows undoubtedly suffered by large system trouble-shooters, the exhaustive rigor of the production environment simply makes good sense. When a company's survival depends on the proper functioning of its systems, the production set of applications is not taken lightly. In fact, entire MIS organizations are known to have been kept up all night when a new set of applications is "cut over." The continual repetition of these bonding experiences has created, in part, today's rightsizing-resistant mainframe culture.

So What?

Consider the typical PC user. Knowing just enough to be dangerous, this independent soul likely has created a custom-built computing environment known only to his or her *id* (in the Freudian sense). Files are organized into directories and subdirectories that are nearly indecipherable except under hypnosis. Yet it works.

Reared in the safety of shrink-wrapping, the free-wheeling nature of personal computing stands in stark contrast to the grim practicalities of large systems. Until very recently, many hard-core MIS professionals saw the PC as an annoyance—the user's ill-advised declaration of independence. The realm of PC computing simply wasn't taken seriously.

Often confused with empire protection, resistance to rightsizing is a reluctance to compromise the sacred production environment. It is similar to the reaction you might get from asking someone to move the family fortune from Chase Manhattan to Louie's Savings and Loan. Saddled with the ultimate responsibility of corporate computing, and without the assurances of robust support processes, it's understandable that rightsizing isn't always an instant "no-brainer."

All glitz aside, the fact remains that user-friendly, GUI-based, object-oriented applications cannot be implemented successfully without the parallel deployment of an ongoing application and hardware support environment. This is where LAN implementers can take a few lessons from the "old timers." Operations and support issues are just as real in the LAN world as they were in the mainframe age. Rightsizing project managers cannot disregard this critical aspect of the new systems without asking for real trouble down the road.

Savvy MIS leaders will orchestrate a migration of the mainframe-skill base to the network arena by recycling time-honored procedures. Most experienced mainframe staffers realize that their future lies in the LAN realm, as discussed more in Chapter 9, "Assembling the Team for Client/Server Applications Development." With the proper transition and training, LAN-based tools can be applied to create an environment just as robust as the traditional "glass house."

Myth or Salvation

The answer is that although rightsizing isn't necessarily our salvation, it is a tremendously powerful tool in the information age. It has a potential role in almost every company—at least those that need information to stay in business. Indeed, the technological, organizational, and economic arguments for rightsizing are so strong that the responsible businessperson cannot ignore them.

So, rightsizing as salvation? For some maybe. For others, rightsizing is the next growth stage in the life of their information system. One thing is assured: rightsizing is no myth.

Centralization Versus Decentralization

For many years, companies supported computing with a centralized MIS function. In fact, there was no other practical option. Applications could be developed only with software that required programming professionals, and the cost of hardware precluded establishing multiple data centers. It's important to note that even though the general rightsizing trend is to move both the computing capability and the MIS support function closer to the end user, the two are not necessarily linked. It is conceivable that a centralized MIS function could develop applications for PCs and workstations on a company-wide basis. Similarly, applications could be developed by personnel much closer to the end user, who nonetheless could continue to operate at a central data processing center. For these reasons, the two areas should be looked at separately.

Shortcomings of Centralized MIS Functions

The trend toward rightsizing in companies is due in no small part to the shortcomings of the large, centralized MIS function. These shortcomings include

- A lack of appreciation for business requirements
- Poor responsiveness to user requests
- Internal transfer payment practices that provide economic incentive for end-user groups to perform their own system development

Business Requirement Appreciation

Even when MIS functions were in their infancy, a debate raged over whether the personnel in these groups should have technological backgrounds and be taught to appreciate business needs, or have business experience and be taught the technology. The debate continues today. A major result of the debate is a high turnover rate among MIS managers. This reflects growing senior management frustration with results produced by their MIS leaders, as the expenditures for I/T become a significant expense item without an apparent return on that investment. This frustration has provided a major impetus to the rightsizing trend.

The belief is that the closer the application development is moved to the end user, the more likely it is that the application will be successful. At the same time, the ability to exercise direct management control increases. These two forces are so strong that it is unlikely the rightsizing trend will ever be reversed, even if some unforeseen technological development removed the economic incentive to do so. This trend has been made possible by continuing improvements in software that allow applications to be developed by nonprogramming professionals.

This discussion does not mean to imply that no role exists for the centralized MIS function. As is discussed throughout this book, however, the role of central MIS is changing dramatically as the result of rightsizing activities.

Poor Responsiveness

As with the users of any centralized service function, would-be users of the MIS function must compete for resources. Few MIS functions are given budget resources to support all requests made of them. As a result, many user requests are placed in a queue.

Further, on-going maintenance requirements of applications consume a growing part of the MIS workforce. As fewer resources are available to assign to new application development, the request queue grows even larger. This situation then is exacerbated further by company-wide cost-reduction programs. The senior management frustration level with MIS makes it a prime target for budget reductions.

This never-ending spiral has caused serious problems for MIS functions faced with rigid budget constraints on one side and growing user dissatisfaction on the other. The results are predictable. Technology developments now have made it possible for users to consider developing their own applications using their own hardware…and they do!

Cost Chargeback Mechanisms

Most companies require that costs associated with MIS and data processing be allocated to individual departments through an internal transfer payment system. Centralized MIS groups often have acted as their own worst enemy by charging significantly more than actual costs. This attempt to make a profit provides incentives for organizations to form their own MIS function, using the reduction in internal transfer payments as part of the cost justification. Chapter 5, "Cost Justifying and Financing Rightsizing," deals with the subject of chargeback systems in more detail.

Are There Limitations to Rightsizing?

There are situations in which rightsizing is not the appropriate course of action. The situations are mostly limited to very specific scenarios. Some of those scenarios include

- Development of very complex systems in which experienced systems designers are critical
- Applications with high security exposure
- Existing applications for which it's not cost-justified to migrate to a smaller platform
- Applications that possess characteristics better suited for a mainframe

Complex Systems

In the early days of MIS, many systems failed even though the hardware and software worked perfectly. These systems failed because systems designers did not consider the human element associated with their design. Good designers learned very quickly to define the boundaries of the system to include not only the hardware and software changes, but the people changes required of the system. In many cases, end users either don't know or are unable to communicate what they want. Professional system designers have learned to factor this into their design approach. In short, professional systems designers possess an expertise that may not exist in a decentralized, downsized operation. Today's software has developed to the point that fairly complicated systems can be developed by inexperienced systems people, but the design issues discussed previously remain.

Managers of downsized operations should consider the issues just mentioned when staffing their operations. As the complexity of the system grows, the need for professional systems developers—most likely to be found in the centralized MIS group—becomes more important.

Security Exposure

Large data centers and MIS groups have considerable expertise in providing adequate system protection from a wide array of threats. These groups possess a general appreciation of the need for security. There are those who predict that many downsized operations are a "disaster waiting to happen" because precautionary measures are not in place to protect information assets from unauthorized disclosure, modification, or destruction. They believe internal control deficiencies in downsized operations could lead to serious risks and exposure to the corporation.

Inaccurate processing or miscalculation of balances in financial systems could expose the company to significant financial loss, customer dissatisfaction, or product liability claims. Establishing adequate control is always difficult. The importance of adequate control becomes magnified in decentralized operations where there may be less appreciation and experience in dealing with such issues. Formal testing and validation procedures also are less likely to be understood.

Operational threats fall into two main categories: people-related threats and physical threats. People-related threats include human errors and accidents, dishonest employees, disgruntled employees, and hackers. Physical threats include damage caused by water, fire, electrical outage, and natural disasters such as earthquakes, tornadoes, and floods.

The first step in avoiding a security problem is to understand any vulnerability that exists. It is critical that those responsible for managing downsized operations analyze the risks involved. A *risk analysis* is a process used to develop an estimate of loss expectation due to specific threats. It involves identification of vulnerabilities and determination of countermeasures. At a minimum, a set of baseline controls should be put into place. Databases must be securely, accurately, and completely maintained. Proper control must be exercised over access to data. Rigorous change-management procedures must be established both for the applications and the network. A disaster-recovery plan should be established. Finally, backup and recovery procedures must be in place.

Applications that a risk analysis show to have high vulnerability may require a significant cost outlay to establish protection. In most cases, applications of this type should be left at the central data center, where elaborate security measures are already in place.

Rightsizing Candidates

When considering any new application, it makes sense to first consider developing it on a rightsized platform. First, the organizational situation should be analyzed. Who will be the end users of the system? Where does the data for the system originate? Will you be dependent on a separate organization outside your control to support the system? If the success of the application requires the cooperation of several organizations not part of the rightsizing organization, a warning flag should be raised. If the developing organization cannot control the application, problems are sure to occur.

Good first candidates for rightsizing are applications that involve data entry and editing, statistical and mathematical analysis, decision support, and highly interactive applications such as computer-aided design. If possible, get the first rightsized applications "under your belt" and into production so you can understand many of the technical and organizational implications. Tackle mission-critical applications after your first pilot projects: in these projects you will be dealing with complex applications with high security requirements and high-volume database updating, many of which span organizational boundaries.

Rightsizing does not necessarily mean that an entire application should be moved off a mainframe. It may mean moving only parts of applications to a new platform. For example, this might entail moving data entry and editing functions to a PC platform while the mainframe continues to process changes to the database. A good, "real world" example of this approach is automated-teller machines (ATMs). ATM applications perform user authorization and gather all transaction input before communicating with the mainframe to process the customer database changes.

There also exists a class of applications that originally were developed on a mainframe but are more suitable for a rightsized platform. There may not be sufficient cost justification to migrate such applications off the mainframe. Many companies have chosen to be very selective in rightsizing these types of applications.

Pluses and Minuses of Rightsizing

In summary, don't look to rightsizing to cure all ills associated with centralized system development and computing. Rightsizing can, at times, provide significant savings. Perhaps more important, rightsizing can produce applications that meet your needs more closely because they're developed by people closer to you with a better appreciation of the business requirements. These two powerful motivators probably justify a development philosophy that first considers a rightsized platform and supports a mainframe-only platform when absolutely advantageous to do so.

Some rightsizing advocates believe the mainframe has outlived its usefulness and should be eliminated. Others take the opposite point of view and argue that the mainframe should remain the primary platform. Both are wrong. There are cases in which moving systems or parts of systems to smaller platforms brings significant cost savings, improves efficiency, and results in systems that more closely meet the needs of the end user. Similarly, there are applications in which a full or partial mainframe implementation offers clear advantages. The true systems professional understands the advantages and disadvantages of each approach and uses both to maximize the value a company receives from its I/T expenditures.

Rightsizing
Origins

Rightsizing Origins

2

*Those who ignore history are
doomed to repeat it.*

—Santayana

Objectives:

1. To help you understand the business origins and tenets of rightsizing.
2. To illustrate why business downsizing and information systems rightsizing aren't related.
3. To show you societal forces at work and why they are part of the rightsizing process.
4. To help you understand the technological origins of rightsizing and what makes it so different from the practices of just a few years ago.

Rightsizing, as a specific information systems strategy, developed in a climate created by the general business trends of the 1980s, rapid changes in demographics, and developments in computing technology. This chapter discusses some of the conditions and events that contributed to and made possible the phenomenon of rightsizing information systems.

Business Origins of Downsizing

Popular management rhetoric of the 1980s and 1990s has promoted a work environment well-suited to rightsized computer systems. Few of these management theories, however, have called specifically for rightsizing. Tom Peters, author of *In Search of Excellence*, exhorts business leaders to adopt a number of "beyonds" thinking beyond the management theories in vogue. For example, Peters says we must move beyond "empowered" individuals to "informated" individuals. Being "informated" implies not only having the authority to make decisions, but also having at your fingertips the information necessary to make smart, reasoned business decisions.

In a 1991 study, a task force of the Financial Executives Institute found that the lower the level at which information decisions are made, the better the results. The key to the success of ideas like this one is in creating systems that are small (in terms of size, not power), flexible, and distributable—in other words, rightsized information systems.

Whatever positive rightsizing concepts have been borrowed from management theory, however, rightsizing information systems is first related to the concept of general business downsizing: eliminating the excessive bureaucratic infrastructure. Robert Tomasko, author of *Downsizing:*

Reshaping the Corporate Future[1], stresses the reduction of staff and operating costs through careful, *selective* elimination. In particular, he stresses cutting out excessive, unjustifiable layers of management and support staff.

Some of the objectives Tomasko lists for planned downsizing are the following:

- Lowered costs
- Quicker decision making and responsiveness
- Less distorted communications
- Higher morale, facilitating synergy within the company
- Individual empowerment
- Increased productivity

Tomasko suggests achieving these objectives by strategically examining and changing organizational structure, company culture, and company policies. Downsized information systems that encourage peer-to-peer communication are especially well-suited to this environment. Lotus Development Corporation's Notes is a good example of a software tool that provides peer communications. The mail and discussion features of Notes enable users to communicate with one another and conduct ongoing discussions. Additionally, the software retains the history of the discussion, including relevant facts and knowledge that are traded.

The process of rightsizing information systems has greatly expanded its relevance beyond being a useful information systems reaction to business downsizing. Today, the differences between general business downsizing and information systems rightsizing are huge. Business downsizing, as it usually is practiced, is a desperate, defensive reaction. Examples of United States companies in the process of business downsizing span all industries, including the information technology industry, with IBM Corporation having downsized its worldwide workforce in half in recent years. On the other hand, the planned rightsizing of information systems is a strategic migration from one stage of technology and business processes to a new, more relevant stage.

Although some firms have rightsized their information systems in pursuit of the single goal of reducing costs, rightsizing is more often undertaken for proactive rather than reactive reasons. For example, information systems

---

[1]*Reprinted, with permission of the publisher, ©1990 AMACOM, a division of the American Management Association. All rights reserved.*

rightsizing is conducted for critical reasons, such as reducing the time-to-market of goods and services or responding more quickly to business, regulatory, and economic change. Other reasons include increasing worker communication, easing data access, and creating more flexibility. In general, this proactive, strategic introduction of rightsizing technologies is the subject of this book, rather than the reactive measures of business downsizing.

Business Reengineering

Before moving on, another business management principle should be discussed. The principle of business reengineering is well suited to rightsized systems and is related to the principle of general business downsizing. Business reengineering means fundamentally rethinking what a business does and how it does it. Business reengineering breaks down current work processes and introduces a new order.

Reengineering has its roots in the management philosophies preached by business gurus such as W. Edwards Deming, Peter Drucker, and Michael Porter. Their ideas, and the efforts of Michael Hammer and other thinkers in the information technology industry, have contributed to an atmosphere in which a fundamental rethinking of business basics is considered essential to remaining competitive.

Applying reengineering principles has resulted in a sharper focus on

- Flattening the hierarchical pyramid
- Improving quality, including quality of service
- Facilitating communication within the organization
- Empowering people at all levels within the organization with tools, information, and the authority necessary to make decisions
- Becoming customer-driven

Rightsizing information systems can facilitate and guide us down the path to these objectives. Chapter 5, "Cost Justifying and Financing Rightsizing," and Chapter 6, "Reengineering," discuss specific objectives of business reengineering in more detail, including methods of measuring success.

Societal Origins of Rightsizing

Psychologists, historians, anthropologists, writers, and other observers of human life have labeled our era the Information Age. Although we humans always have sought to improve our methods of gathering, analyzing, and applying information, author John Naisbitt of *Megatrends* fame pinpoints the start of the Information Age as the late 1950s. That, he says, is when white-collar workers outnumbered blue-collar workers for the first time. Since then, information has become central to our lifestyle. Now that information flow is in place, however, the need to perfect information delivery is essential.

Too Much Data

Today, more data than ever before is readily available to us. According to IBM studies, however, only about 2 percent of all corporate data currently resides on a computer. With the advent of electronic data interchange (EDI), image processing, and other new information-management technologies, not only is more data going to be entered into computers, but this data is going to be processed in more ways by more people than ever before.

Just as computers have no intrinsic productivity value in and of themselves, data by itself is useless—and more data actually can hinder, rather than facilitate, progress. Misinformation, deliberate or unintentional, adds to the confusion. Too much data can lead to analysis paralysis, which stalls decision making. Now, more than ever before, obtaining quality information and knowing how to use it is vital to achieving goals. Rightsizing information systems is a step toward better focus on information quality and the achievement of business goals.

Constant Change Is Reality

In 1970, Alvin Toffler's *Future Shock* detailed the effects of the accelerating rate of change on our lives and lifestyles. That book, other more recent works by Toffler (*The Fourth Wave* and *Powershift*), and the works of others drive home the point that constant, rapid change is a reality of modern life. To survive, humans must learn to cope with these rapid changes. These include changes in business strategies and tactics, in personal relationships, in systems planning and implementation, and in ongoing maintenance. To thrive, businesses cannot simply cope with change, but must anticipate and respond to changes with changes of their own. Rightsized systems alone cannot manage change, but proper rightsizing creates an environment that enables corporate employees to more effectively anticipate and respond to change.

Technological Origins of Rightsizing

As strategic planners began reexamining their established procedures and organizational infrastructures, they also paid close attention to how their companies were using their information systems. At about the same time, a new star made its debut on the corporate stage: the personal computer, or PC. The phenomenon of rightsizing information systems has its technical origins in the PC explosion of the early 1980s. The introduction of affordable, powerful machines that put the technology directly in the hands of the individual user changed the entire approach people took to data processing.

The advent of the PC coincided with, and contributed to, the management principles that gained popularity throughout the 1980s. The PC allowed individual workers to gain more control over their work. The individual worker became the driving force behind the increase in productivity. Studies have shown that increases in productivity take place when individuals are granted the authority, incentive, and tools to make and implement decisions. Key among these information-technology tools is the personal computer.

When managers realized they could prepare schedules or plans on a PC, including conducting and compiling the research, analyzing the data, and creating a professional-looking report *by themselves,* they were reluctant to use anything else. Thinking and making changes based on the results of that thought became an intuitive, productive work process. Simply put, the PC became the tool that got the job done more quickly and efficiently.

The PC, however, wasn't the answer to all computing needs. For many reasons—including the expense of output devices such as printers and the inconvenience and inefficiency of sharing files by floppy disk—local area networking using PC LANs became increasingly popular throughout the 1980s. Simultaneously, PC and networking technology improved, providing better, more powerful, and faster environments and innovative, versatile software. The late 1980s saw the flourishing of LANs.

Still, many companies have not reaped the hoped-for benefits of increased productivity just by installing and maintaining PC networks. Technical advancement alone can't change the world. The fax machine existed for nearly a century before the market for it exploded in the 1980s. More than technological improvement is needed to get the most out of information technology.

Indeed, in some situations, PCs can have detrimental effects. Tomasko points out that although microcomputers can be great time-savers and grasp-extenders, they also can become tools that promote inappropriate micromanagement and excess analysis. They can chain managers to desks when they should be walking around. The availability of PCs tempts some managers into doing tasks themselves that would be better delegated to another staff member.

Completely replacing centralized mainframe systems with distributed PC networks is unlikely to solve all information processing problems. Rightsizing is not simply a matter of replacing hardware and software. Nor should rightsizing automatically be translated to mean "100 percent PCs." Partial downsizing or upsizing efforts are the most common instances of rightsizing. In many cases, rightsizing can take place without having to go through the immediate pain of making mainframes obsolete or the wholesale conversion of applications.

There is no single solution to the information-processing requirements of an organization, and there is no single path to flexible, powerful systems. That's part of the reason rightsizing is a muddled term and part of the reason it can be such a painful process.

Rightsizing Snapshot: Natural Gas Clearinghouse

The following case study provides a good example of a company that chose "mainframe avoidance" with strategic success.

Company Background

The company in question is the largest independent gas marketing company in operation today. Almost five years ago, the company employed a dozen people, working with six PCs. At that time, it hired a consulting company to develop an integrated computer system that would grow with the company. The consulting team set up the company on a PC LAN with custom applications to meet its needs. Today, the company employs 300 people in twelve district offices around the country and still uses an extended version of the initial LAN with the same applications.

Business Need

The gas marketing company needed an integrated system for tracking the buying, transporting, and selling of gas, from bid origination through final disposition and accounting. The company communicated a set of initial needs to the consulting team it hired. The solution needed to support critical business functions, such as tracking a prospect through final account balancing and providing market data. The company also wanted something that was easy to use and that it would not outgrow.

System Design

The consulting team chose a PC LAN for three reasons:

- A PC LAN would support the data the company had acquired over the primary phase of its business.
- Its potential for expansion was limitless.
- It was the most cost-effective solution.

The gas marketing company had begun operation three years before, when deregulation in the gas pipeline industry opened up commercial opportunities. Because gas marketing was a relatively new industry, no off-the-shelf software packages were available to meet the needs of the company. The consulting team chose to custom-design the required applications in the Advanced Revelation DBMS (database management system).

The entire project was completed in 18 months. By then, the gas company had a total of 85 employees in four regional offices. The consulting team installed Compaq desktops and portables as the nodes on the LANs and a Compaq SystemPro file server with a 130-megabyte disk drive. Novell's NetWare network operating system manages the LANs. The remote offices are connected to the Houston office through a wide-area network (WAN).

Results

In the gas marketing business, all companies provide the same product. The only difference among the various competitors is the quality of service that they provide. This company's integrated system enables it to consistently provide accurate, timely service. Its reputation for such service has contributed to its growth. At the time the company implemented its integrated system, it estimated its growth to be 15 percent annually. The company's actual annual growth rate since then has been almost 50 percent. The gas company's business has grown very quickly; however, its staffing requirements have not. The efficiency and speed of its computer system have allowed the company to grow without significantly increasing the number of employees.

Trends Contrary to Downsizing

It would be a mistake to leave the impression that all companies are rushing to dismantle their centralized MIS functions and large data centers. In March, 1992, *Network World* published the results of a downsizing survey it conducted. Although the survey showed that the majority of respondents either were presently downsizing or planning to downsize, 42 percent reported plans to continue development of new mainframe applications, and another 26 percent said that they would not downsize present mainframe applications even though most of their new development was LAN-based. These results are an indication that some applications do not lend themselves to downsizing and that the costs of migrating applications to downsized platforms cannot always be justified.

There actually are two trends in which central data centers are being expanded. The first is called *outsourcing*. The second involves the consolidation of large data centers into fewer, but even larger, centers. In both cases, the computing power actually is being moved farther from the end user.

Outsourcing

Outsourcing generally can be defined as contracting with third parties to perform some or all of the information technology functions of the company. One of the best known examples of this trend is the Eastman Kodak contract with Digital Equipment Corporation, IBM, and Businessland to take over major portions of their telecommunications and computer operations. Of course, long before the term *outsourcing* came into vogue, systems integrators such as Electronic Data Systems (EDS) were pursuing a business strategy that attempted to convince companies that EDS could handle the company's data-processing requirements more efficiently.

The motivation for outsourcing usually is cost-based. The belief is that economies of scale allow large companies, such as EDS, to operate at a lower unit cost. Another major motivation stems from the aforementioned frustration senior management feels with the MIS function. Management hopes that contracting with companies with specific expertise in information technology will offload the burden of overseeing the MIS function. One could argue that, in the long run, outsourcing actually will stimulate rightsizing by encouraging end user departments to develop their own applications on their own computers instead of dealing with an outside agency. For now, outsourcing remains contrary to the downsizing trend.

Data Center Consolidation

Another trend indicating that the announcement of the death of the large data center is premature is that many large companies are closing data centers and moving applications to even larger data centers. Downsizing usually is not an alternative because of the nature of the applications serviced by these centers, which tend to span organizational boundaries, have high security requirements, and involve frequent updating of centralized data bases. However, these moves, too, almost always are cost-based.

Bank of America, Westinghouse, and Johnson & Johnson are among many large companies who have pursued this strategy over the past few years. These firms traditionally operated several large data centers, each serving specific geographic or business unit constituencies. What they have found is that terminals and workstations don't know, or care, about the length of the wire connecting them to the host computer. Electronically, it makes no difference whether that wire is several hundred feet in length or spans thousands of miles. The longer wire may cost much more, but that cost is small when compared to the costs associated with operating a large data center.

The costs of operating a data center involve much more than the hardware and software. Even though in 1992 mainframes dropped more than 30 percent in price, according to *Datamation* magazine, the cost of using a mainframe remains high. The costs associated with the people employed to operate the center, floor space, security systems, and specialized environmental-control systems often are much greater than the incremental cost of consolidating applications at another existing data center.

Where We're Going

Rightsizing—in either of its most recognizable forms, upsizing or downsizing—is not simply a matter of using cheaper computers to generate the same volume of information being generated by hand or on mainframes. Technological advancements in data storage, indexing, and retrieval devices can provide us constantly with more data, more quickly. Rightsizing is the first step in preparing an organization to keep pace with the accelerating rate of change. The computer networking revolution—in particular the advent of shared processing between client and server devices and associated elements such as GUIs, pen-based computing, and geographically dispersed networks—has as great an impact on today's business world as assembly-line procedures had on manufacturing at the beginning of the 20th century.

In order to capitalize on these trends, a company must analyze where it is today. Then the company must recognize what rightsizing opportunities are available to it now and which ones will be available in the near future. This self-analysis can put a company well on its way toward using information more effectively than its competitors, and help it achieve a measure of competitive advantage right off the bat.

Where We Are Today and Opportunities for Tomorrow

Where We Are Today and Opportunities for Tommorrow

3

*Hath not the morning dawned
with added light?*

—Henry Timrod

Objectives:

1. To help you understand the major information technology platforms and their differences.
2. To introduce technology developments that are likely to shape systems in the near future.

Forty years ago, the computer industry was primitive by today's standards. The only owners of computers were large banks, insurance companies, manufacturers, airlines, and the federal government. Thomas J. Watson, Sr., the founder of IBM, once described the computer as a prohibitively expensive "giant brain"—of interest only to the scientific community and, perhaps, extremely large businesses. For the small business or individual, the benefits offered by computer processing were just wishful thinking.

But times have changed. Today's MIS staff often is faced with overwhelming choices in computer systems, even in small companies. To better understand the opportunity that rightsizing information systems holds, it's vital that you understand just how technology got to where it is today. This chapter provides a look at the choices confronting today's MIS staff person or manager.

Mainframes

The term *mainframe* was coined in the mid 1960s, when computers were large and bulky. The term referred to the cabinets in which the *central processing units* (CPUs) were housed. Today, *mainframe* refers to the largest commercial computer systems, including their associated peripherals. The marketplace for mainframes is dominated by IBM and several Japanese and European companies, as shown in Figure 3.1. Most big users of information technology have one, if not several, mainframes as the core of their information systems.

In most cases, the mission-critical business applications for companies still are run on mainframes. Without these applications, the company would not be able to operate its business. These mainframe systems may be handling several hundred, or even several thousand, online terminals. They probably contain hundreds of megabytes of main memory and hundreds of gigabytes of disk storage. In some cases, smaller computers are used in conjunction with the mainframes as front-end processors that link directly to data and telecommunications networks.

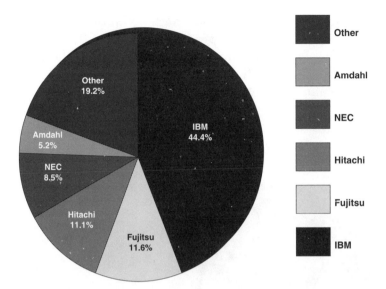

Figure 3.1. *The top five in large-scale systems.*

The most important distinguishing feature of mainframes is their cost in comparison to mini- and microcomputers. The processor alone can cost millions of dollars, with upgrades to new processors costing tens or hundreds of thousands of dollars, as shown in Figure 3.2. Also, the supporting hardware, software, and "required" vendor maintenance can add another 50 to 100 percent of the base mainframe cost, making it very expensive to keep a mainframe functioning efficiently.

Description	Machine Type	Model	Purchase Price
Processor Unit	9021	340	$ 2,125,000
Processor Unit	9021	500	4,100,000
Processor Unit	9021	580	5,715,000 (1)
Processor Unit	9021	620	8,050,000
Processor Unit	9021	720	10,545,000 (2)
Processor Unit	9021	820	16,025,000
Processor Unit	9021	900	22,280,000 (2)

1. Feature #7430 required.
2. Features #7430 and #7431 required.

Note: See A190-201 for administrative details.

Source: IBM Product Announcement Pricing System/390 Announcements, September 5, 1990

Figure 3.2. *3090 processor purchase prices, when announced in 1990.*

The systems and applications software running on one of these corporate mainframes is likely to be a mix of products, both from the mainframe vendor itself and other large software vendors. For example, the largest mainframe providers also sell software (see Figure 3.3). In an IBM "shop," for example, the systems software mix is likely to be VM/MVS or DOS/VS for the base operating system, or some upgrade combination of the three, for example: VM/ESA (for VM), MVS/XA or MVS/ESA (for MVS), or DOS/VSE or VSE/ESA (for DOS/VS).

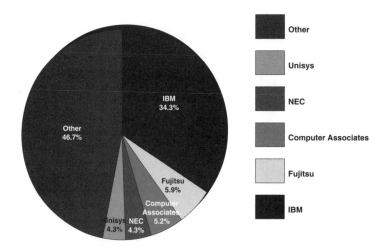

Figure 3.3. The top five providers in mainframe software.

On top of the operating system, the most likely teleprocessing monitor is VTAM. The online transaction processing software is probably some version of IBM's CICS. Database management software includes DB2, SQL/DS, and IMS (as well as IMS/ESA), depending on the type of mainframe and operating system in use. Finally, other software thrown into the fray includes Remote Batch Processing (RJE), Security (ACF2, Top Secret, and RACF), and Network Management (Netview and Systemview)—and that's just for starters.

It is likely that corporate mainframes have complex data storage, peripherals, and communications facilities. The communications products and services are most likely provided by both large data and telecommunications providers, as shown in Figure 3.4. In an IBM shop, the mainframe is likely to be employing Systems Network Architecture (SNA) as its primary communications architecture or protocol. Generally, the computers, communications equipment, and related equipment are enclosed in a special environmentally controlled computer room, commonly called the "glass house" (or, by frustrated and dissatisfied users, the "black hole"). The mainframe computer rooms usually are located in or near the company's headquarters.

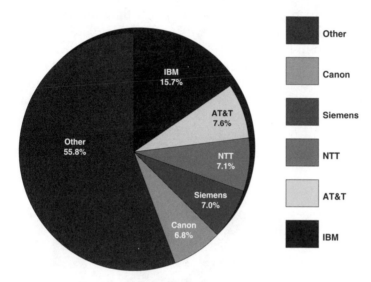

Figure 3.4. *The top five providers in communications.*

Other than PCs, the predominant desktop device is the dumb terminal, which enables users to interact with the applications and programs residing on the mainframe. Through mainframe gateways, personal computers also are likely to communicate with the mainframe, probably by virtue of 3270 or 5250 emulation. Mainframe users often are located at various locations nationwide, logged on to the mainframe and using its software virtually 24 hours a day.

Minicomputers

As powerful as mainframes are, they can't do everything. During the evolution of computers, *minicomputers* (minis) appeared around the 1970s and 1980s to handle applications requiring dozens, and sometimes several hundred, online terminals. The first minicomputer, the PDP-1, was launched by Digital in 1959. Shortly thereafter, other major vendors—such as Data

General, Hewlett-Packard, Wang, and Tandem—followed suit. IBM also has introduced many lines of minicomputers, including the System/38, Series 1, and the AS/400.

Today, most large users of information technology have multiple minicomputers, typically running specialized applications deemed more appropriate or more productive for the minicomputer than for the mainframe. The minicomputers in use probably are IBM, DEC, Hewlett-Packard, or one of the others shown in Figure 3.5. Like their big brothers the mainframes, the minis run operating systems and applications software that are proprietary to their particular designs. This means that the amount of connectivity and sharing of programs and data with other computers in the overall information system is limited. Minis typically are used for stand-alone applications, such as office productivity, manufacturing, process control, and similar jobs. Other minis play simple supporting roles such as telecommunications.

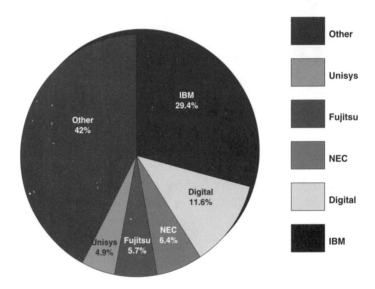

Figure 3.5. The top five providers of minicomputers.

In any case, wherever there's a minicomputer in a company, you can just about bet that it's a high-priority target for replacement by a network and microcomputers.

Microcomputers

Probably the most visible information systems component in any company today, large or small, is the *microcomputer*—also known as the PC or personal computer. Since its introduction, the microcomputer has enjoyed a rich period of growth and diversity, with several definite categories of micros emerging. Industry leaders in the PC marketplace are shown in Figure 3.6.

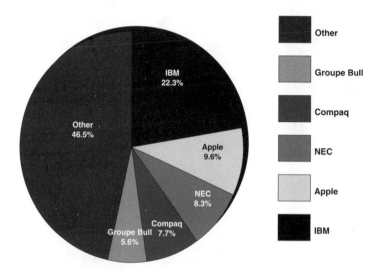

Figure 3.6. The top five makers of PCs.

First, there are floor-mounted superservers. These computers actually start at a low-end of $10,000 before additional features are loaded in. Servers are usually configured to act as LAN controllers, or supervisors, handling a network of workstations, but are not necessarily used as workstations themselves. The Compaq SystemPro is a good example of a base superserver. The SystemPro consists of multiple microprocessors and is capable of handling multiple workstations on a network.

Down the line are the workstations and desktop PCs. Although the lines between workstations and PCs are blurring, the main difference between the two is that a workstation usually has a true multitasking operating system (usually a UNIX derivative), a high-resolution display card and monitor, and a math coprocessor. A workstation is used mainly for scientific applications, in contrast to the commercial applications of the PC. Workstations in the corporation are most likely to come from Sun, DEC, HP/Apollo, or one of the other providers shown in Figure 3.7. Each workstation or desktop PC typically is used by only one person at a time.

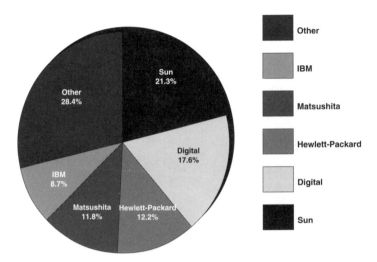

Figure 3.7. The top five providers of workstations.

Another broad category of microcomputers being integrated into corporate life includes the notebook and laptop computer. These computers are quite portable, usually including their own rechargeable battery packs; yet, in many cases, they are as powerful as desktop units. The cost of one of these smaller computers is comparable to the cost of a desktop PC. They are gaining acceptance, particularly from many business travelers and other mobile workers.

Finally, there are many other smaller categories, such as diskless workstations, palm-top micros, personal digital assistants and pen-based PCs—all discussed later in this chapter. With PCs have come a splendid array of software for tasks ranging from simple personal time management to complex statistical data analysis—with applications for everything in-between. More than likely, the applications on these PCs come from Microsoft, Borland, WordPerfect, Lotus, or one of a few other dominant developers.

Although estimates vary, there is consensus that more than 50 million PCs have been sold over the past 10 years, with high projections at 100 million units. No other computing resource is so pervasive. In many companies, PCs have become the desktop computing resource, replacing the dumb terminal tied to the mainframe. In other companies, PC LANs have taken over workgroup computing requirements as wholesale replacements for minicomputers or mainframe applications.

Into the Fifth Generation

Where this leaves the modern MIS staff, manager, and executive—not to mention their end users—is in the middle of a complex, perplexing, often incompatible, ever-changing sea of mainframes, minis, micros, communications equipment, and other related I/T resources. As if this weren't enough, the innovations occurring right now already are yielding new information-technology products and services, which big I/T users have begun to evaluate. These innovations are described in the following sections.

The Electronic Frontier

Telephone, cable television, and computers were once distinct industries. However, a wave of technology advances and competition-fired joint ventures and mergers during the early 1990s have formally marked the end of this distinction. The Baby Bells have been angling for a piece of the computer communications industry and the cable business for several years. Likewise, cable companies have been looking for ways to leverage their television hookups into interactive mediums. The all-encompassing service they all seek to build and control is the "information superhighway"—the name given to the nation-wide network to deliver digital services of all kinds.

Most computer users have become accustomed to the concept of their computer being online. However, the term "online" will soon apply to multiple mediums. The television is the prime target for heightened connectivity. Americans have become very attached to their televisions, and the advent of shopping via television has already shown how well true interactive services via television can do. Bank services, airline reservations, and theater tickets are just a few of the services being proposed for interactive television and the information highway.

While these services are not yet widely available, more and more services are becoming available online and thus are accessible to the end user on an individualized basis. This tailoring of services to the individual's needs has been dubbed WYNIWYG (pronounced "WINnie-wig"), for "What You Need Is What You Get." The principle is simple: Evaluate what an end user's requirements are; then make sure that user gets only the portion of the data that he or she wants or needs.

There are a host of information sources that will provide the data. First, there are large public and private information services, such as CompuServe, the Internet, America Online, MCI, Dow Jones News, LEXIS, NEXIS, and others. Next, there are a growing number of dial-in electronic bulletin board systems. Most bulletin boards are public but have different levels of security. Some allow anyone to access their question-and-answer programs. Others require an ID and password just to access the bulletin board. Last, but certainly not least, is information from remote, real-time gathering sources, such as grocery store scanning machines or warehouse barcode reading units.

These information services deliver information to the typical network user in various ways. As far as the PC user is concerned, large information services and bulletin boards operate much as traditional host sessions: the LAN user dials the service and a connection is established. However, the simplest way to connect a remote workstation to a LAN is by using a LAN communications server with a modem for dial-up into the network from the remote PC. When connected, the remote PC functions just like a network workstation.

Some have defined this flurry of activity providing services to the business user on a PC network (and soon, a child at home on a TV set) as the age of "social computing." Social computing is what happens when technologies create new ways for people and organizations to communicate. The thought is that, in addition to the technology forces that are shaping the electronic frontier, there are societal forces as well. Those societal forces involve the need for people to regain control (to try to get closer to a "normal life" in the era of longer work hours, two wage-earner families, and so on) and the emergence of the "techno-tuned" consumer (Americans today embrace new technologies, whereas barely a decade ago ATM cards and home PCs were cult objects).

Mobile Computing

In the hustle of a busy world where travel is a necessity, mobile computing advances have made it easier for workers to take their computers with them when out of the office. For example, notebook PCs have given computer users the ability to work on a PC virtually anywhere. On-going improvements in displays, keyboards, and memory capacity have made working with the notebook PC more and more like working with the desktop PC. The communications software available has also made mobile computing a viable method of connecting to a network, giving a much broader meaning to the term "connectivity."

The first generation of notebook computers appear to be anything but portable when compared to the latest generation. The latest generation has now been labeled "subnotebooks;" the average weight has been reduced by half. The power of a 486 has been packed into some models weighing less than four pounds. Battery packs are still heavy; even so, most users choose to carry the additional weight of extra batteries for the benefit of extended notebook use, when one battery pack goes out.

The small monochrome monitors of the first notebooks strained the eyes of users. In comparison, the 7 1/2-inch color displays that are common in subnotebooks make GUI applications a feasible option. These displays are continually being improved, and the brightness and readability will soon be comparable to a desktop monitor.

Human physical needs constrain subnotebooks in the area of keyboards also. The human finger does not adapt well to keyboards reduced to less than 90 percent of the standard keyboard size. Users complain that cursor-control keys are too small and placed in awkward positions. Similarly, pointing devices fail to meet users' expectations for an easy-to-use interface. Design improvement can only do so much to correct these problems, compelling innovators to look to new technology for a solution.

As an alternate to straight keyboard use, pen-based computing technology has made promising advances during the 90s. In fact, some industry experts see pen-based devices, personal digital assistants, and PC "mutants" (as they're sometimes called) as the next major wave in the information technology revolution, following mainframes, minicomputers, and PCs. From an interface point of view, direct pen input is the next improvement over the cursor and mouse.

From teletype, to full-screen editing under keyboard cursor control, to the GUI under mouse-cursor control, the human/machine interface has improved, enabling people to learn to use computer applications more easily. Under pen-based computing, the user interface resembles that of paper and pen; the user "writes" on the computer screen using the pen. This process will improve efficiency and ease of use for such tasks as filling in forms, editing, drawing, annotating existing documents, and building a spreadsheet. Most likely, the keyboard will not become obsolete; it still will be the best choice for fast, high-volume data entry and for word processing.

In any case, personal digital assistants (PDAs) are catching on in the business world. For example, computerized "clipboards" are used now by most national delivery services, allowing the courier to "write" information on a screen, as well as providing an electronic means of storing the customer's signature. Software that can translate handwriting is improving each month. Although Apple's Newton PDA endured much industry ridicule when its first release did not meet the high expectations created by the marketing hype, the pen-based interface is now being acknowledged as a practical and viable one.

Yet another important addition to these mobile computers is wireless modems. Storage capacity becomes far less of a concern when users can connect to their network to work on data stored virtually anywhere. These modems also allow users to send faxes and to connect to printers.

Work-Flow and Document Imaging

Work-flow systems automate a process, its related tasks, and the route information must follow through an organization. Work flow extends computing beyond office automation tools, bringing the process itself—not just the work caused by the process—into the system. Work-flow systems enable business process reengineering activities to be combined with low-cost computer tools to reinvent organizations productively. Imaging vendors invented the work-flow business. They added work flow to their imaging applications to route documents around a work group.

Document imaging uses a facsimile-based technology to replace paper documents with electronic images. These images are stored, retrieved, displayed, printed, and distributed as necessary. Document imaging on personal computer-based LANs has caught the attention of business executives and technologists in many organizations. It appeals to management because it offers opportunities to improve service while reducing costs. It appeals to technologists because it incorporates many areas of technology in an innovative and productive way.

High-speed lines, such as 56-Kbit/sec or 1.5-Mbit/sec T1 lines, enable people in remote locations to view images using the same tools as users directly attached to the LAN. Compared with typical data transmissions, the telecommunications overhead is low relative to the data sent. However, an average document-page image is 50–70,000 bytes when compressed; even with T1 lines, retrieving an image can take 30 seconds or more. LAN-based imaging has come into its own because vendors have begun to support four key technologies: network operating systems, Windows 3.x on clients, SQL-based databases to maintain image system tables, and standard hardware components.

LANs are particularly good for imaging because they are standard, fast, and able to support the transfer of images among all nodes—workstations, scanners, storage devices, and printers. LANs also allow for greater flexibility in host access because users have a variety of gateways from which to choose.

Imaging applications are still relatively expensive to design and implement, compared to a more standard database-driven accounting application. However, many organizations have found that work-flow-based applications justify imaging systems. How imaging can benefit your organization depends on your industry and the state of your automated systems. For example, if your industry or company is heavily committed to electronic data interchange, you probably don't need imaging for these transactions.

As the open systems world has grown, many organizations have already selected electronic mail systems and Windows development tools and expect to be able to add a lower cost work-flow alternative to their environment. They also want to be able to view images, but this is not the primary reason that they want work-flow systems. Their desire for work flow is based on its ability to manage processes electronically. In these organizations, work flow will be accomplished with tools that can be "bolted on" to the existing applications architecture.

Several benefits are achieved through work-flow systems, either embedded in imaging systems or "bolted on" to client/server applications.

> **Reduced Information Float**: Work-flow applications optimize time-based tasks, because there is very little time between the completion of one activity and the time the next activity is ready to begin. This can result in higher quality and better customer service.
> **Productivity:** Users are able to process more information in less time with better results, resulting in higher levels of productivity. Work-flow systems give organizations a tool for evaluating productivity. The system's and users' actions either add value to the customer and process or they are cut.

Improved Communications: Work-flow applications frequently result in more continuous and effective communications among team members because they are able to interact asynchronously.

Increased Information Integrity: Work-flow processes have built-in security and controls that make them more measurable and reliable than paper-based processes. Additionally, the processes allow a bigger opportunity to integrate the information from separate tasks due to increased automation.

Groupware

It is generally acknowledged that, after spending upwards of $800 billion on information systems, corporations have yet to realize significant productivity gains from automation. Some analysts attribute these disappointing results to the fact that today's computers and software deal only with the end results of work—spreadsheets, documents, budgets, and databases—and not with the process of producing work. To this end, *groupware* has appeared as a new class of cooperative applications that promises to democratize information and channel it quickly throughout an organization.

The term *groupware* is very ambiguous; it is sometimes defined as *collaborative software*, whereas others call it *strategic confusion* or an *adhocracy of information*. Perhaps the most appropriate (and optimistic) definitions of groupware are Microsoft's "Information at your fingertips" campaign or Lotus' "Working Together" slogan.

The best-known example of groupware is Lotus Notes, which integrates aspects of electronic mail, document management, computer imaging, full-text search and retrieval, and work-flow processing. In addition, several key component technologies have attracted the attention of standards committees and consortiums in an effort to promote the acceptance of technologies that will enable groupware to become a reality.

One of these technologies is called *mail-enabled applications*, a key for simplifying the task of information sharing among individuals and groups. Three alliances have been formed for mail-enabled groupware-related technology: Microsoft's mail-enabled applications interface (MAPI), Lotus/Apple/Novell/IBM vendor-independent messaging (VIM), and Apple Computer's open collaborative environment (OCE).

As the computing industry gropes with the corporate trend to eliminate middle-management in its drive to become more competitive, the significance of groupware and the enabling technology it represents will increase as a core component of tomorrow's information-processing strategies.

Forecasts

Forecasts in the computing world are no better than those in any other industry, even with all of the technology used to generate them. Change will be continuing and unpredictable. However, based on history and recent evidence, there are some pretty good hunches about what developments in the next computing generation will be like.

Advances in the Microcomputer

In terms of the advances in hardware architecture, there are mixed feelings as to who will be the leaders and the followers. Bill Ablondi and Portia Isaacson, principals with CAP BIS Strategic Directions, believe that the momentum of Intel Corporation's 80x86 computer chip architecture is much greater than that of any other in the history of computing. They base their beliefs on Intel's command of end-user hardware shipments; resales; software shipments; publication pages, software, hardware, and peripherals development; and knowledgeable individuals.

On the other hand, new industry partnerships and players can rise up and quickly assume a strong "challenger" dominating role in an industry that changes so rapidly. Some come, and some go. For example, an alliance between MIPS, Compaq, Microsoft, and Santa Cruz Operations that looked on paper as though it could end the monopoly of Intel, fell apart when the partners couldn't agree on technological direction.

In another alliance with a much better chance of success, IBM, Apple, and Motorola teamed to develop the PowerPC, a next generation reduced instruction set computer (RISC) design. IBM and Apple both have long, successful market niches in the microcomputer world. In the past, communication between these two systems was difficult, but possible. Through their PowerPC alliance, these two companies, with Motorola, may develop a new standard type of system, thus setting a new threshold of leadership in the microcomputer world.

In any case, if one were forced to look ahead based on what we know today, expectations of the power of computers by the year 2000 would most likely fall in the following ranges:

- The average $8,000 desktop workstation would have applications integrated with expert systems, with object-oriented multimedia databases that include video, sound, voice, images, and data.

- These workstations also will have a drawing- or writing-pad extension, with "sketching assist" and drawing- and character-recognition capabilities.

- All of these drawings will be displayed on a color WYSIWIG ("What You See Is What You Get") monitor.

- The printer of choice—and default—will be a high-speed, laser page printer.

- The PC will have multisensory input/output capabilities with "touch screen" (input by way of fingers or pen) capability.

- The midlevel superservers might possess complete scalability to mainframe-like power, with growth paths for optionally adding or subtracting processors, memory, disk subsystems, and I/O interfaces. They will have nonstop processing functionality, with auto-reconfiguration as a standard feature. They will share object-oriented, multimedia databases with full location-independence of data, meaning that applications will no longer need to be concerned about where data resides in order to access and utilize it.

In terms of communications, by 1995 half of all desktop systems will be linked to LANs, with a total installed base of about 60 million desktop computers. Between 1990 and 1995, the 9 percent cumulative annual growth rate of total desktop systems installed will pale in comparison to the 24 percent rate of desktop systems connected to LANs. Beyond the LAN, telecommunications technologies like the integrated services digital network (ISDN) and switch multimegabit data services (SMDS) are expected to provide the speed, bandwidth, flexibility, and lower cost required to make enterprise-wide networking across disparate geographical locations popular and affordable.

The Darden Convergence Theory

What about the minicomputer and mainframe hosts? What will they look like? In answer to this question, consultant and scientist David A. Darden believes there will be a convergence of mainframes, minicomputers, and microcomputers, forming a single, extremely scalable product line by the late 1990s. Darden bases his theory on the speed with which the performance of PCs has been catching up with the performance of mainframes. PCs, in general, pick up seven years of mainframe technology every three years. By this standard, PCs should converge with mainframes by 1996. At that point, PC technology can be incorporated into mainframes and minicomputers, essentially combining these three distinct products into one. No longer would there be a mainframe, a minicomputer, and a microcomputer. All that would be left would be the computer.

The Everlasting Mainframe

With all these advances in microcomputer technology expected, we're back to the same bothersome question others have asked: What happens to the dusty mainframe that exists today? Is its demise just around the corner? Such a turn of events seems possible in light of what's happened to IBM in recent years. In early 1991, there were stories of massive layoffs at IBM in conjunction with reports of its first-ever quarterly loss. A much leaner IBM now can only dream of recreating the luxurious 1980s, in which mainframes and minis yielded large profit margins and there were continuing service contracts and software leasing agreements.

As much as it seems that PC LANs are taking over the computing industry, however, they aren't likely to eliminate the entire worldwide base of installed mainframes in the near future. Instead of going away, mainframes are adapting to their new environment. As Figure 3.8 shows, they have a new role in many organizations that have downsized or are considering rightsizing. IBM's processors, with new, long-distance fiber-optic attachments and the 3172 controller/gateway, are making mainframes more powerful and easier to connect with other products. Bridges are being developed between PCs and mainframes, so companies can use mainframes for large, number-crunching, mission-critical, transaction-processing applications, and for network and data management, but can still utilize PC LANs to build more flexible and user-friendly applications.

Some companies, after switching to LANs, continue to use their mainframes as part of their network. They understand that rightsizing takes time and planning to be accomplished properly. During the transition, mainframes are used to manage the system. After the transition occurs, mainframes work their way into a niche in the system and can handle certain large applications that are more difficult on a PC.

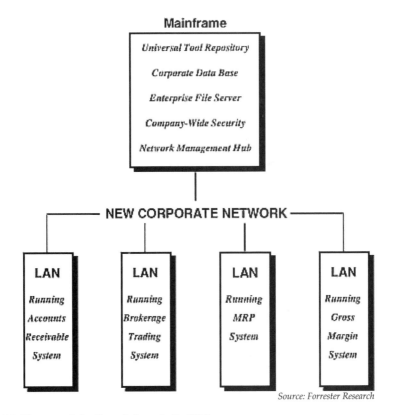

Figure 3.8. *The new role for the mainframe in the 1990s.*

So, taking a glimpse of the information technology landscape through the eyes of the modern information systems professional, this is where we've come from, where we are today, and where we're headed. The technology for rightsizing certainly is within reach. But rightsizing involves much more than taking advantage of the recent advancements in computer technology. Successful rightsizing also requires changes in the way work is performed— both the tasks of the business and the tasks that support the information technology. This fundamental rethinking of the operations of the organization is called *reengineering*, or business process redesign.

Whether by design or by happenstance, and whether the principals know it or not when they get started, rightsizing always takes place within an environment of reengineering.

Finding and Measuring Rightsizing Benefits

Finding and Measuring Rightsizing Benefits

4

Many decisions that clearly appear to have been correct from today's perspective were neither easy nor obvious at the time they were reached.

—Eric K. Clemmons
The Wharton School,
University of Pennsylvania

Objectives:

1. To understand the key benefits that are possible from rightsizing systems.
2. To understand the primary motivations for beginning a rightsizing project.
3. To understand the importance of establishing benchmarks and ways of measuring rightsizing's benefits.
4. To learn the main areas of risk to concentrate on when assessing a possible rightsizing project.

Although the benefits of rightsizing seem obvious, determining those benefits for your particular situation sometimes is more difficult than you might think. Measuring them often is even harder. In this chapter, we examine the benefits gained from rightsizing and offer ways you can measure the impact of rightsizing—both before and after the process begins.

Opportunities: Faster, Better, Cheaper

Rightsizing, done correctly, can save your company huge sums in acquisition, installation, and maintenance costs. At the same time, your company can increase computing power, flexibility, and response time, while improving user satisfaction, productivity, and knowledge. The trick is knowing what you can get, knowing what you want, and knowing how to get it.

Knowing the benefits of rightsizing is the first step in determining what it can do for you. Rightsizing offers nine principal benefits. They are

- Cost savings
- Efficiency
- Simplicity
- Flexibility
- Specialization
- Responsiveness
- Usability
- Independence
- Empowerment

Later in this chapter, each of these benefits is examined in depth. Before you dive in too deeply, however, let's examine the problem areas specific to the situation that prompts the rightsizing of systems.

What's Your Need?

To fully reap the benefits of rightsizing—and to be able to evaluate how successful your rightsizing efforts are—you should know what you want to accomplish through rightsizing. Rightsizing is a strategic answer to business challenges and should not be initiated for vague or superficial reasons.

Overall, information systems projects commonly are initiated for one of three reasons:

- To solve operational problems (including mechanizing manual systems)
- To create a new business activity
- To replace existing technology

Solving Operational Problems

Over time, operational problems can occur in even the best systems. As a company grows, as product lines expand and contract, and as economic environments shift, systems which were once sound quickly can become impediments to the company's ability to operate effectively in a new business climate. A manufacturer's order-entry and inventory systems, for example, no longer fit the way the company needs to do business.

Rightsizing can help solve order-entry and inventory problems, along with other, less tangible types of operational problems—including some that at first seem only indirectly related to information systems. For example, rightsizing can help solve inadequate customer service, excessive bureaucratic procedures, and even low employee morale by putting more powerful, decentralized systems at the source of operational problems.

Creating a New Activity

Rightsizing can be a specific strategy that enables a company to enter new business lines. Andrei Chivvis, an I/T writer, says that a more capable, rightsized information system can dramatically expand a company's internal information processing capability. This additional capability enables management to reevaluate the company's business objectives and strategies, to improve the delivery of products and services, and even to increase the company's ability to enter new marketplaces. A good example of this is the creation of a new cottage industry of desktop publishing companies. These companies have taken advantage of PCs, networks, and new printing capabilities to greatly expand the newsletter and other print publishing fields.

Replacing Existing Technology

Existing systems have to be replaced from time to time. Systems grow old and are altered so much over time that proper maintenance becomes almost impossible. For example, an accounting system installed in the early 1960s contains the technology available at that time. If it was installed on a large IBM mainframe, the computer was probably a second-generation computer; the language was likely an assembly-level programming language or an early version of COBOL. Vendor support for both hardware and software probably was withdrawn long ago. The expertise that the MIS department once had in this technology has almost certainly disappeared—even though both the machine and the programs may continue to function.

Machines that were technologically outdated more than 20 years ago may still be operational today. A system's functions may have been well thought out and advanced for its time, and the system's requirements may have been established through meaningful user involvement. It's likely, however, that the company's accounting practices and procedures have seen major changes through the years. In a situation such as this, the user may or may not be satisfied with the system as it was originally designed. In either case, establishing the benefits of rightsizing the existing system is an important step.

Goal Setting

When the existing problems are understood, it's time to set goals for rightsizing. Often, the overall goals in rightsizing are the same as the goals for business reengineering outlined in Chapter 6, "Reengineering": to improve quality, reduce costs, and stave off competition. Knowing what you hope to accomplish by rightsizing is crucial if you hope to measure how successful the rightsizing actually is. Although exact goals may be difficult

to set, you should be able to benchmark the success on a scale of high positive impact, no impact, or high negative impact. One way to do this is to use
a worksheet such as the one in Figure 4.1.

Downsizing Project:_____		IMPACT				
BENEFIT	**BENCHMARK**	High Positive	Somewhat Positive	None	Somewhat Negative	High Negative
Cost savings						
Simplicity						
Specialization						
Efficiency						
Flexibility						
Response						
Qty of interface						
Independence						
Potential						

Figure 4.1. *Rightsizing evaluation worksheet.*

The idea is to determine what impact on your business you seek, or you
believe can occur, for each benefit of rightsizing. This qualitative exercise
should validate your overall feeling about the value of a particular rightsizing
project. The next several sections describe how to assess in more detail the
impact of each benefit. Chapter 5, "Cost Justifying and Financing
Rightsizing," provides specific quantitative analysis of the benefits of
rightsizing.

Cost Savings

The reason business people overwhelmingly cite first for investigating
rightsizing systems is that they want to reduce the tremendous costs of their
information systems platforms, applications development, and hardware and
software maintenance and administration. Most believe rightsizing offers a
way to perform the same information systems functions for less money.

Dramatic rightsizing success stories based on cost savings abound. The *Wall
Street Journal* reported the story of how Consolidated Insurance Group

(Wilmington, DE) replaced a $3 million IBM 3090 with a $300,000 network with seven "no-name" servers. Additionally, an article in *PC Week* reported that Turner Construction Corporation saved $300,000 annually in mainframe hardware and software costs by replacing a mainframe with remote LANs connected to a central database. Various characteristics of rightsized systems contributed to the cost savings by these and other companies, including hardware, software, and personnel. Let's take a look at some of the specific dynamics of each characteristic.

Hardware

Without a doubt, the cost savings of rightsizing are a direct result of the PC and networking revolutions. Mainframe computers, as profiled in Chapter 3, "Where We Are Today and Opportunities for Tomorrow," are complex machines with strict physical environmental requirements. They are manufactured by only a few companies. PCs are smaller, have fewer components, are much more portable, and can be used in a larger variety of physical environments. PCs are manufactured by hundreds of companies, none of which completely dominates the marketplace.

The competitive market for PCs originated when IBM allowed other manufacturers to use IBM-developed technology in their personal computers. The Industry Standard Architecture (ISA) that led to the proliferation of "IBM-compatible" computers became a de facto industry standard. The personal computer became a commodity, driven by demand and competition, and its low cost acquainted more people than ever before with the power of computing. Throughout the 1980s and into the 1990s, more and more people have used computers for the first time.

There are many reasons why PCs currently cost less than larger computers and why they will continue to cost less. The significant forces that make PCs more affordable than larger systems include the ones listed in the following sections.

Many Suppliers

There are hundreds of PC manufacturers in the world. Along with the many brands of PCs available, there also are many ways to buy PCs. In the early days of the personal computing revolution, PCs were sold mainly through authorized dealers and, to a lesser extent, resellers. The rationale behind this distribution approach was that dealers were PC experts who could offer technical support at a local level. This approach also enabled a manufacturer to take advantage of a sales network without adding a sales force of its own. However, as user awareness of PCs proliferated, more vendors began offering their products directly to the public.

Buyers today can purchase computers from any of the following channels: the traditional dealer, direct from the manufacturer, through a mail-order house, from a retail outlet that may or may not specialize in computer equipment, from a computer superstore such as COMP USA, Computer City, or even the neighborhood electronics and stereo store.

Economies of Scale

Manufacturers produce millions of PCs a year, as opposed to hundreds of mainframes. PCs have fewer components, take less time to make, and cost less to transport and install. There also are numerous suppliers of replacement and enhancement parts, and the knowledge required to install these parts is easier to come by.

Low Barriers to Entry

Only ten years ago, few people had heard of Dell, Compaq, Apple, or Sun. Today, these companies are some of the largest and fastest-growing corporations in the world. Michael Dell got his start by selling PCs from a dorm room at the University of Texas. PC technology, compared to mainframe internal design, is remarkably simple. Numerous books are available on the general topic, "How to build your own PC." In addition, PC components are available from numerous sources.

Rapid Technological Advancement

In less than 10 years, the PC evolved from what many considered a toy or a fancy typewriter to the central information processor of many businesses. This couldn't have happened without incredible improvements in the underlying technology, especially in the main microprocessor—the integrated circuit chip that performs the PC's central functions. (For most PCs, this chip is either an Intel 80x86 series or a Motorola 680x0 series microprocessor.) Technical advancements in fields not strictly related to personal computers have contributed to the PC's success as well. These include the rapid advancements in communications such as fiber optics, satellite technology, micro-wave, infrared, radio, and cellular communications.

Not only can more people afford computing than ever before, but the PCs themselves are more powerful than ever before. The proof is in the figures: Sales of microcomputers to Fortune 1000 corporations rose 130 percent from 1987 to 1989; sales of workstations rose 85 percent; sales of mainframes de-clined 3 percent for the same time period.

Scalability

Another hardware cost advantage of PCs stems not from the economics of the market, but from the fact that distributed networks allow you to buy only as much computing power as you need. The days of excess capacity are gone. Networks, by design, consist of discrete hardware (and software) components that can be easily acquired as needed. One of the major reasons that network-ing emerged in the early days of PCs was to connect expensive output devices such as laser printers and plotters. As with PCs, the prices of periph-erals have dropped while performance has improved. Moreover, components can be redeployed when necessary, with much less effort than it takes to move the parts on a larger system.

Hardware costs, of course, depend on an organization's unique situation. You already may have a large base of suitable PCs installed that can run rightsized applications. In general, it's better to determine hardware requirements only after the functions of the network are defined. As a guideline, however, it is reasonable to estimate a cost of at least $3,000 per node and $10,000 per server. Remember, this figure is for hardware only; it does not include annual main-tenance and management or additional software.

Software

Like mainframe hardware, mainframe software is sold by just a few compa-nies. Mainframe software tends to be complex, with limitations to the user interface. Mainframe software usually must be altered to suit a company's specific needs. These alterations can be costly and time-consuming. PC soft-ware, like PC hardware, is developed by many different companies, tends to be less complex, and often interacts easily with other PC software.

Because PC software is supplied by hundreds of companies and the compe-tition is so intense, software developers must pay attention to product functionality and quality. PC applications developers, therefore, place great importance on accommodating user requirements. For all of these suppliers, having their products work with more than one software package is not an option—users demand it.

In one-on-one comparisons of packaged software between mainframes or minis and PCs, the price comparison is so vast as to be almost ludicrous. Typical PC packages cost from $50 to $500; typical mini and mainframe packages cost from $5,000 to $50,000. The 100-to-1 advantage in cost is a good rule of thumb.

But what happens when there are dozens, or even hundreds, of PC users who require the same software? Now that networks are prevalent, most software companies have responded with versions of software specifically designed for networks. Typically, software manufacturers offer packages licensed for multiple users, often at an accelerated price discount based on larger numbers of users. Thus, you buy only as many licenses as the number of users you have, and you can license additional users as you grow.

Personnel

Savings on systems-support-personnel costs is, for some firms, the largest area of cost savings. These are the administrative and maintenance personnel for the traditional MIS department. Of course, this is a sensitive area for most firms; decreased personnel costs mean fewer people.

Instead of maintaining large MIS staffs, some companies support their networks with up to 75 percent fewer people once the networks are up and running. CBS-Fox Video reduced its support staff from 50 to 8 people after replacing two mainframes with an enterprise-wide network. Although some companies can get by with as few as half the number of systems administration and maintenance staff, Turner Construction Corporation kept the same amount of staff but redeployed half of them to support branch-office networks.

Not all companies, however, report reductions in support personnel. Other companies report, at least initially, an increase in the number of support personnel when rightsizing and reengineering. Also, the development staff is likely to grow during this time, to build the new systems that the reengineering projects mandate. Even so, over the long run, personnel costs usually decrease.

Indirect Benefits, Maybe; Soft or Intangible, No Way!

The history of evaluating the benefits of information systems has been one of separating the direct benefits from the indirect benefits. This process is a little like determining the liquidity of assets: cash is the most liquid, whereas everything else has value but must be discounted somewhat because of its degree of illiquidity. After cost savings, the remaining benefits of rightsizing information systems are a little like illiquid assets. They may be of great value, but sizing up their direct liquid value may be difficult.

Efficiency

One of the more powerful advantages of any PC-based, rightsized system is that it complements and facilitates the way people work. The corporate worker receives information, analyzes it, transforms it (or chooses not to), and passes it on. As we provide users with more accurate, timely data and manipulate that data in more ways, an improvement in efficiency is likely to be the by-product.

Remember that efficiency is not a measure of how well something gets done— that is effectiveness. Rather, efficiency is a measure of input versus output. To make something more efficient, the goal is to decrease the ratio of input to output until it is 1:1, and then begin improving the output side of the equation. Rightsized systems can help make processes more efficient because they can reduce the number of information sources (input) from several systems to one—the PC.

Simplicity

Another benefit of rightsized systems is the simplicity of PCs. Because the technology is easy to grasp, PCs are the tool of choice for many people. Personal computers are just that—personal. For the most part, users understand what their machines can and can't do.

This principle of design simplicity is a powerful one. In 1985, Michael E. Porter and Victor E. Millar wrote in the *Harvard Business Review* that executives have a growing awareness that technology can no longer be the exclusive territory of EDP or MIS departments. The authors described how the "information component" of products is increasing, and products are becoming "smarter." As an example, Porter and Millar described a "smart" drill that measures geological conditions and enables engineers to make adjustments while drilling for oil wells.

It would be distressing if computers, of all tools, did not also increase their information components. The information component of computers is advancing principally in the area of ease of use. For example, GUIs are making computers simpler to use by replacing words with pictures or symbols whenever appropriate.

In addition to design simplicity, another benefit of rightsized systems is simplicity of installation and maintenance. True, professional expertise is required to install a large network. However, most PCs and their applications are what traditional mainframe shops would term *customer-installable*.

Flexibility

Flexibility is one of the greatest benefits to using rightsized systems running on distributed networks of PCs. Compared to a host platform, flexibility exists in the size, scope, and configuration of the network. Flexibility enables the network to be customized for optimum support of specific functions.

For example, many electronic designers and graphic artists prefer Macintosh computers for their design work, whereas other professionals choose the Macintosh for general business use, such as database and accounting functions. Through network flexibility, the hardware and software of many different vendors can be used in the same network with Macintoshes, as opposed to having Macs available only as stand-alone, "closed" computers.

The physical size and environmental constraints of a computer system are also considerations in regard to flexibility. Most mainframes are physically huge. Some are cooled by liquid and demand constant temperatures. PCs are more tolerant of temperature fluctuations and are, by virtue of their size, more portable.

Then, consider the variety of products available for PCs—talk about flexibility! Look at your choices for printers: laser printers, ink jets, fax/printer combinations, plotters, color printers, printers for labels, envelopes—and the list goes on. This variety, apparent in hardware and peripherals, is even more obvious in software applications. Applications can be built from scratch in a variety of languages. Some applications even are designed to write other applications. All in all, there are thousands of applications, written by multiple vendors, offering similar products at various levels of complexity and sophistication.

Specialization

Another key benefit of rightsized systems is system specialization: different networks can be designed to handle different tasks. In some ways, specialization is the "other side of the coin" of flexibility. Because rightsized systems can deliver so much information, business people can focus on specialized tasks that previously were difficult to address.

For instance, a payroll application in a company may require a large database, whereas the production department requires an imaging network. Data and communications can be shared through the enterprise-wide system's hardware and software, while specialized needs of the various departments can be addressed by their individual networks.

Responsiveness

What good is a host computer that operates 24 hours a day, seven days a week, when users sometimes must wait hours, or even days, to receive reports? Often the answer is very little good—especially when users can receive the same report instantly from their PCs. In addition, people can access and input data as they need to, then manipulate it as they choose. Gone are the days of waiting for reports that are outdated by the time you receive them. Today's networked systems truly can be called responsive.

Usability

GUIs are to computers what handles are to razor blades: you can get along without them, but it's much more painful. Using a GUI also is like knowing how to drive: once you learn, it's the same, no matter which road you're on. Applications take advantage of similar features built into the operating system software, which present choices to the user in a consistent, intuitive way. Even if you don't know the features of a program in depth, you can "feel" your way along, reducing both your anxiety level and the time it takes to get up and running. This helps to make such systems much more usable by the average PC user than alternatives.

Independence

This intangible benefit could easily be subtitled, "Escape From MIS." As mentioned earlier in this chapter, it is often beneficial to depart from the host-based, MIS-controlled systems environment. Besides factors already cited, users of "breakaway" rightsized information systems tend to adopt an increased appreciation for the value of their information systems, as well as the effort involved in keeping them current.

Empowerment

As we have discussed, rightsized systems can offer significant cost savings in hardware, software, and maintenance, and these savings are the primary justification for starting the rightsizing process. Aside from the cost savings, distributed computer networks offer advantages in the way they allow users to work. Rightsizing does not have to be merely replacing the mainframe and performing the same tasks with PCs. Certainly, rightsized systems are capable of that. You can, however, realize additional benefits from rightsizing. Rightsized systems running on PC networks can, and should, usher in innovative ways of working.

This innovation stems from the fact that PC networks fit the management style of empowerment—a key weapon in running "lean and mean." In an empowered environment, every individual has personal responsibility and accountability for advancing the causes of the business. Individuals at every level are given the power to make decisions that affect the business, without always having to get prior approval. Implemented poorly, this management model can thrust the company into an out-of-control situation. When properly implemented, however, the empowerment philosophy can dramatically help in growing the business.

LAN-based systems not only are capable of providing this kind of information system empowerment, but also enable new processes and technologies to be integrated more easily into the business. As testament, among the three major platforms—mainframe, minicomputer, and PC—PCs are where innovation is occurring most often today. Pen-based technology, portable computing, desktop publishing, desktop video, presentation, imaging, laser printing—these are all examples of innovations that have occurred since the PC gained wide acceptance.

Competitive Advantage: American Versus United

The question is, Have companies been successful in rightsizing and distributing data onto PC LANs? The answer is an emphatic yes. Why haven't we heard these stories then? Because large companies in the process of rightsizing have decided to be quiet. They don't tell the world *because their new computer systems are a competitive advantage point.*

United Airlines sells the world's dominant airline reservation system, Computerized Reservation Systems (CRS), called Apollo in the U.S. But, the largest flight reservation system in the U.S. is Sabre, which is owned by American Airlines. What both of these airlines are attempting to do with their reservation systems is to provide a new layer of service for ticket agencies. Because a ticket agency subscribes to only one reservation system, all of their customers' airline reservations, car rentals, and hotel reservations are made using that network. Both airline companies place a surcharge on reservations made on other airlines using their system. These airline companies are prospering through their reservations systems—in 1990, Sabre's profits were equal to that of American Airlines.

United and American are in combat, and their weapons are LANs. United is currently installing 9,000 corporate rings; United installs three per day using its own employees—no subcontractors. Domestically, it will have 25,000 servers running within two years. Over the next five years, American will install 15,000 token rings. We haven't heard more about these installations because neither American nor United wants to talk about its new technological advantages.

Baxter's Success Story: Buying the Customer

Another company that has successfully rightsized is Baxter International, Inc. Baxter does $5 billion each year in revenue. It is the largest hospital supplier in the United States, providing supplies such as bandages, syringes, and bed-pans. Baxter carries over 120,000 line items, and does $1 million dollars worth of word processing per hour.

Baxter used to conduct its business in the traditional manner—when a hospital needed supplies, the hospital would call the local Baxter sales representative to place an order. Then, the Baxter representative would input that information into the computer, the order would be centrally processed, and inventory would be returned in a few days. That system worked fine, but it was not going to make Baxter number one. So, Baxter decided to rightsize. To get the attention of the data processing department, it cut both the IS staff and budget by 15 percent and told the department to rightsize and improve the corporate system.

Baxter's rightsizing efforts were extremely successful. Baxter is now running an order-entry application on a client/server architecture using Windows and LAN Manager. In each hospital it services, Baxter placed a client in the nurses' stations. Now, when care-givers need an item, they walk to the station and type in the order. Think of it as a Sears catalog, put into a Windows environment and placed on a desktop. This new order-entry system eliminates the need for Baxter's sales/data-entry personnel. It eliminates order-entry and inventory errors, and it gives immediate feedback to the hospital on the availability of the items ordered. This accuracy gives Baxter the ability to guarantee two-hour delivery times in their ten largest metropolitan areas. Such quick turnaround means that the hospital can transform its supply rooms into floor space for patient care. In this case, both parties win— the hospitals win with more floor space, better inventory accounting, and quick, reliable service; and Baxter wins because now it owns the business of that hospital. That hospital will never leave Baxter!

Baxter, like American and United, is fundamentally changing the way it does business through the process of rightsizing. All three of these companies are moving to client/server technology and are installing LANs, PCs, and servers in order to secure customers.

Rightsizing Information Systems Snapshot: A Natural Gas Pipeline Company

Background

Imagine, if you will, trying to compete in a modern-day Formula One auto race with a car that has a Model-T engine. No amount of aerodynamic tinkering to the chassis or improvements to the wheels or high-performance fuel will make a difference. This is the situation that this gas transport company, a subsidiary of one of the nation's largest provider of natural gas, confronted in 1991.

The company's senior management surveyed the landscape of their industry and came away with a sense of mission and urgency from what they saw. What they saw were continuing regulatory changes, decreasing barriers to entry in the marketplace, and increasing competition. To counter these marketplace truths, the company developed a set of business requirements to guide them through the 1990s.

These requirements included improving pipeline processes, such as optimizing gas volume and monitoring throughput to prevent imbalances. Other requirements included producing more timely and accurate bills and maintaining a program of constant improvement in quality and service. In particular, customers wanted more accurate and timely information, through whatever mechanisms worked best—electronic data interchange (EDI), online access, or networking with the field locations.

Unfortunately, the company found that the information technology that it had in place fell short of helping to meet these new business requirements. Specifically, what it found were computer systems with marginally acceptable functionality, not what it needed to help it compete in the dynamic gas transportation marketplace. The company found systems that lacked flexibility at a time when it was reengineering its business processes. Its systems also lacked the capability to provide for individual operating group accountability, at a time when its parent company's commercial entities were decentralizing. Also, the company was dealing with 1986/87 technology, even though significant technological changes had occurred since 1987. It had a Model-T system in a Formula One business.

Business Need

In response to these systems shortcomings, the company developed a set of systems requirements for the '90s. Clearly, its first step was to streamline systems in support of streamlined business processes. The company set a requirement for cost-effective solutions that had short-term payback, that is, less than three years (less than one, ideally). It decided to require that all systems be flexible and portable, and be able to grow with the company and migrate to new and different technologies as they were introduced. The company also decided to establish a dedicated systems support group. In the course of taking advantage of new technologies that were sized specifically for its needs, the company wanted to make certain that it could provide its own support of mission-critical applications.

System Design

In September 1991, the company started developing a set of applications that supported its core business requirements. These included an application to process gas pipeline contracts (TCS); an application to process customer nominations for gas transportation, scheduling of the gas within the pipeline, and accounting for the actual delivery (NSA); and an application to allow pipeline customers to set up their own nomination requests (TCI). The applications were constructed for an environment with Novell NetWare v3.11, Microsoft Windows v3.0 with PowerSoft's PowerBuilder development package, and a Sybase database engine with a UNIX operating system for the database server. The system also interfaced with electronic flow measurement, scheduling, and accounting systems running on IBM 3090 and DEC VAX equipment.

Results

The strategy for developing this system encompassed several important decisions. For example, the company chose to adapt core business systems to the new technology by using the existing systems as building blocks. It also chose to prototype development on a local area network (LAN) for quick results, because it wanted no project phase to exceed six months. And, it chose applications-development tools for optimum flexibility and portability. This decision paid off when the company switched from one type of database server software used in prototyping and development to another type of database server for production use of the application. The entire process took less than two weeks—a vast difference from the months of effort such switches often mean in the traditional host environment. Finally, putting as much of the system functionality in the hands of its front-line business people—empowering them to make key business decisions nearly instantaneously at the request of customers—was extremely beneficial to the business.

Measuring Benefits

Determining how successful rightsizing efforts can be is, for many companies, an inexact proposition. One reason is that some of the benefits are so-called "soft" benefits—things such as user independence, higher morale yielding increased productivity, efficiency gains, and flexibility. These soft benefits can have significant impact on your organization. But even with "hard" benefits, such as reduced transaction or personnel costs, it can be difficult to measure exactly how much you have gained through rightsizing.

The same problem has existed throughout the information age. Assigning a hard value to a strategic information system is a slippery task, unlikely to lead to more effective decision making. So, then, is the question "How do we measure the value of our system?" a valid one, or should we ignore the costs and simply go with intuition?

Clearly, neither of the extremes is the right choice. The problems with measuring the value of systems are complex. The numbers never will be known with sufficient precision to enable you to decide what action to take without risk. Insisting on a dollars-and-cents analysis on every project can seriously damage an organization's competitiveness. On the other hand, decisions made on pure intuition always are suspect. So a middle ground position makes sense.

Let's look at the way business analysis is taught in our universities. Discounted cash flow, net present value, and value assignment to soft benefits are taught as the only means of investment-decision analysis. Because many benefits cannot be estimated within a comfortable degree of precision, analysts are taught to assign a value of zero to those benefits.

A better starting way to analyze soft benefits and, ultimately, performance against them is to go back to the evaluation worksheet in Figure 4.1. Add new columns that, at key milestones, can be assessed in terms of whether the benefit was realized. This evaluation should be done in combination with a series of feasibility tests that establish whether or not the benchmarks are achievable.

Rightsizing Feasibility

Because rightsizing is not without its pitfalls, the surest way to validate the potential benefits of rightsizing, as opposed to its risks, is to work through the feasibility of the project on a number of levels. According to Davis and Olson, in *Management Information Systems: Conceptual Foundations, Structure and Development*, there are five types of feasibility that must be assessed: technical, operational, schedule, motivational, and economic.

Technical Feasibility

Technical feasibility addresses the issue of whether the technical aspects of a proposal are practical and achievable. Usually, this type of feasibility is more of an issue if the technology involved in the project is new, or new to the organization. Technical feasibility is lacking when the problems you are solving have no known algorithms or when the algorithm is not efficient enough. Some scheduling problems and many problems currently being researched in artificial intelligence have this characteristic.

Operational Feasibility

Operational feasibility concerns whether the system concept is appropriate for the operating environment for which it is proposed. For example, while a traditional, keyboard-based system might be the most economical for an oil-field application, it might be difficult for the user to learn to use. Also, portability might be a requirement for the user that makes a desktop-based system unusable.

Schedule Feasibility

Schedule feasibility involves verifying that the schedule for developing and installing the proposed system is realistic and reasonable in light of upcoming business events and business requirements. Certain times of the year may be natural conversion dates, for example, and some seasonality factors may be insurmountable.

Motivational Feasibility

Motivational feasibility ensures that the users want the proposed system badly enough that they are willing to participate in a development project and undergo disruption of their daily routines to absorb the changes introduced by the new system.

Economic Feasibility

Economic feasibility deals with the issue of whether the resources needed to develop and operate the proposed rightsized system can be justified by the returns from installing it. Cost-and-benefit analysis is the key part of this aspect of a feasibility study. However, economic feasibility does not imply that all systems should have direct cost savings as part of their justification. The subject of cost/benefit justification and overall financing of rightsizing projects is the subject of Chapter 5, "Cost Justifying and Financing Rightsizing."

PART II

Planning

Planning

So, a company is sold on the benefits of rightsizing. It believes in the realities rather than the myths (Chapter 1); understands rightsizing's history and credentials, so to speak (Chapter 2); recognizes the available opportunities and has bought into the promise of new technology (Chapter 3); and knows how to find and measure rightsizing benefits (Chapter 4). What's the next step?

The answer to this question takes you from *considering* rightsizing to *acting* on it. The next step involves moving into a deliberate set of major activities that can best be described as a methodology.

The methodology for rightsizing information systems is an evolutionary one. Like other elements of rightsizing, its methodology has evolved from the traditional computer-systems development life cycle. The traditional approach to computer-systems development generally is regarded as a generic life cycle of major phases; each phase is related to the other only in that each one comes after another and before the next, as shown in Figure II.1.

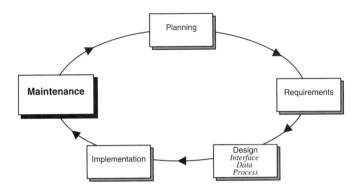

Figure II.1. *Generic systems development.*

Further, you can look at the traditional systems development life cycle as resembling a cascading waterfall of phases, as shown in Figure II.2. Each step in development is a hurdle in the development process. The result is that the development effort usually takes many months, or often years, to complete.

The development methodology for rightsizing has evolved well beyond the traditional life cycle. The methodology for rightsizing systems is compact and overlapping, and, as such, multiple phases blend into one. Parts of the completed system emerge throughout the project. Rightsizing requires new ways of thinking and an understanding that at times it employs revolutionary techniques at some very specific points in the development life cycle.

You can further compact and speed up this process by changing tradition at some key steps along the way. As Figure II.3 shows, the rightsizing methodology includes, at the highest level, four major phases: planning, design, implementation, and maintenance. The first departure of this methodology from the traditional life cycle involves collapsing the requirements-analysis phase into the design step and, to a lesser extent, the planning step.

The second departure from the traditional life cycle is the overlapping of steps in the rightsizing methodology. As Figure II.3 shows, sometimes certain steps are concurrent. For example, the next portion of a system's design is often in process while the current portion is being implemented. This approach keeps the development activity, by its nature, always forward-looking and fast.

The third departure is that the process often is planned as iterative so that parts of the new system can be in use long before the entire system (or project) is completed. This planning allows for earlier return on investment and acceptance of the new system in "bite-sized, digestible" pieces.

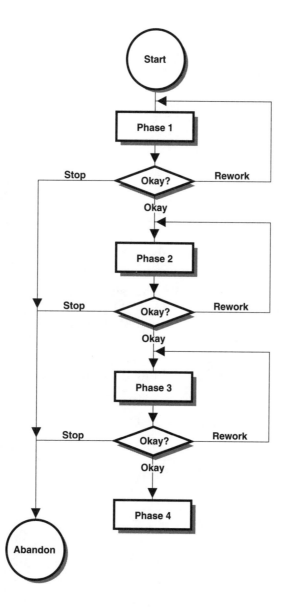

Figure II.2. Waterfall systems development life cycle.

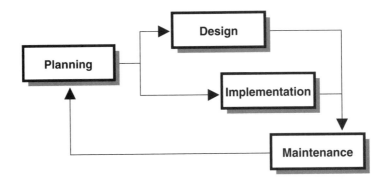

Figure II.3. Rightsizing development methodology.

Rather than march entirely through the rightsizing methodology and explain it step-by-step for a rightsized system, the remaining sections of this book focus on the key success points for rightsizing and those that differ from traditional methods. This section focuses on the steps in the first box—planning–and discusses five key subjects that are important for planning the development of rightsized information systems: cost-justifying and financing the systems; business reengineering; change management; understanding the rules for success; and assembling the rightsizing development team.

5

Cost Justifying
and Financing
Rightsizing

*The computer is the most significant addition
of capital…since the printing press.*

—Richard Cyert,
President,
Carnegie-Mellon
University (1984)

Objectives:

1. To help you understand how to perform financial analysis of rightsizing projects.
2. To help you understand the alternatives for funding a proposed rightsizing project.

The approach to justifying your rightsizing project, like so many other aspects of rightsizing, most likely will be determined by your intentions, goals, and reasons for rightsizing in the first place. For instance, a company that considers rightsizing for immediate financial relief will take a different approach from a firm that wants to rightsize to increase flexibility and position itself for the future. It's important to know the reasons for embracing rightsizing, because the initial investment costs can be significant depending on the scope of the transition and the company's needs and operations. Senior management must be willing to provide the necessary funding to achieve the desired rightsizing impact.

You read at the end of the preceding chapter that the economics of rightsizing must be investigated thoroughly before undertaking a project of any significant size or scope. Financial issues associated with rightsizing projects can be both complex and inexact. The following questions have to be asked and, to the extent possible, answered:

■ How do we determine that a rightsizing project is a good investment?

■ How much will rightsizing really cost?

■ How do we account for rightsizing in our accounting records?

The answers to these questions can make the difference between a successful transition to the next generation of computing and turning your company systems into a disorganized mess. Unfortunately, rightsizing does not always lend itself to traditional cost justification methods. There are two reasons for this:

■ As mentioned in Chapter 4, "Finding and Measuring Rightsizing Benefits," many of the benefits of rightsizing are intangible and difficult to measure. These benefits include flexibility, speedier decision-making, efficiency, productivity, improved service, and expansion of potential.

■ The costs often cannot easily be tied to any specific returns on investment, not even to a payback period, even though the payback period for rightsized systems generally is recognized to be shorter than that of traditional host-based systems.

Yet, sooner or later, every proposal to implement a major new rightsized system is measured by its hard-dollar impact, not just by its technical or indirect merit. Whoever is proposing a rightsizing project therefore should have a cost/benefit analysis ready. The accounting department will be grateful, and senior executives will feel more comfortable when they can evaluate the direct business impact.

The Cost/Benefit Analysis

The purpose of a cost/benefit analysis is to summarize the relevant costs and benefits of a proposed project in sufficient detail to permit management to decide whether to proceed with a project. Many estimates in the analysis are probable ranges of costs and benefits. Management should not expect precise estimates at this stage because there still is much that is not yet known about the costs of installing and operating the proposed system. Subsequent phases of the development process enable you to make a more accurate cost/benefit analysis as more detailed information is gathered. Estimating has been likened to "trying to guess what the core of an onion will look like as you peel off its outside layers."

The general format of a cost/benefit analysis is illustrated in Figure 5.1. The following information is needed before the analysis can be prepared:

■ An estimate of the cost of operating the current system

■ An estimate of the cost of operating the proposed system

■ An estimate of costs for subsequent phases of the development project

■ A description of intangible benefits

■ A basis for estimating how these costs and benefits will change during the next few years (for example, assumptions about volume increases and inflation)

■ An identification of the quantifiable risks associated with either doing or not doing the project

Cost/Benefit	
First-Year Costs:	
Equipment	$
Software	$
Application:	$
Word Processing Application (__users)	$
Spread sheet (__users)	$
Other	$
Accounting	$
Networking Software	$
(Minus software discounts)	$
Staffing Costs	$
Consulting Fees -- (establish)	$
MIS Organization	$
Consulting Fees	$
Training	$
Additional Corporate MIS Charges	$
For Data Conversion Assistance	$
Existing Corporate	$
Charges (6 months)	$
TOTAL FIRST YEAR COSTS:	
Subsequent Year Costs:	$
Staff	$
Salaries/fringe (6 people)	$
Training costs	$
Employment agency fees/recruiting	$
Outside Consultants	$
Hardware/Software Upgrades	
User Training Material/Courses	$
TOTAL SUBSEQUENT YEAR COSTS	$

Cash Flow Analysis - 5 years	YEAR					
	1	2	3	4	5	Total
Cash expended under distributed approach Current Systems Cost Savings						
Net present value of savings using 10% discount factor						

* Negotiated Amount

Figure 5.1. *A typical cost/benefit analysis worksheet.*

The organizational units impacted by the project should assume primary responsibility for the various components of the cost/benefit analysis, under the overall coordination of the project team. Economic analyses prepared at the completion of the design phase are much more comprehensive than this analysis, although the format essentially is the same. At any point in the process, however, the following guidelines apply:

- State the costs and benefits conservatively.
- Make and clearly state all assumptions for financial projections.
- Assess realistically the elements of project risk.

Estimating Costs

Returning to the first step, the cost of operating an existing mainframe or minicomputer application is compared to the cost of developing what typically end up being client/server, PC network replacement options. There are three main categories of computer system costs:

- Initial hardware, software, communications, and personnel costs
- Application development costs
- Maintenance and operating costs

Although new systems usually have costs in all three categories, the existing system ostensibly is "free" except in the category of maintenance and operating costs. The first hurdle to overcome is to ensure that the existing system's initial and original development costs are considered. Otherwise, you will seem to be lobbying to replace a free system with one that costs money, and you might lose.

This area is where the ideas of a system life cycle come in handy. (These ideas are described in the introduction to Part II, "Planning.") You want comparisons that show all costs associated with the life cycle of the current—rather than the proposed—system over the application's projected life. Five years used to be a good rule of thumb for figuring software life. Today, groups such as Forrester Research propose that the life cycle for systems be planned for two years or less.

The next step is to compare costs incurred over time. A number of financial mechanisms help determine costs over time, including *discounted future cash flow*, *internal rate of return*, and *net present value* (NPV), among others. The specific advantages and disadvantages of each are beyond the scope of this book. For purposes of illustration, however, let's "walk through" an example of one of the more often-used mechanisms: NPV.

NPV is a financial formula for comparing costs incurred at different times. Having identified the costs of two or more alternative systems over the multiyear life cycle, the NPV formula lets you reduce life cycle costs to a single dollar figure representing the total cost of the system if it were paid today. The lowest NPV "wins." More than likely, your spreadsheet program or favorite business calculator already has the specific NPV formula built in. The point to remember is that to get a result, you must supply not only the costs, but also an interest rate to be used in the calculation. This interest rate is how the formula converts a future cost to an equivalent present cost.

Think about it: If you have to spend $100 today, or $110 a year from now, which is better? Answer: It depends on the interest rate. Suppose that the interest rate is 10 percent. You can spend $100 today, or bank that $100 at a 10 percent interest rate for a year, and spend $110 then. The two costs are equivalent if the interest rate is 10 percent. If the interest rate is lower than 10 percent, you are better off spending the $100 today and vice versa if the interest rate is higher. Where do you find your interest rate figure? Check with the company comptroller. If he or she doesn't have a favorite figure for use in cost/benefit analyses, use 10 percent.

Table 5.1 shows the calculation of the net present value of two cost streams at different interest rates. The costs add up to the same total, but as the interest rate goes up, the NPV of the first stream—with lower first-year costs—looks better.

Table 5.1. NPV calculations assuming two interest rate options.

Total Costs		NPV @ Annual Interest Rate of:		
First Year	Second Year	0%	5%	10%
$ 900	$1000	$1900	$1764	$1645
$1000	$ 900	$1900	$1769	$1653

Let's apply the method to a real situation. A company with an application running on a mainframe wanted to get the same or better functionality and reduce costs. They knew that the annual operating cost of the current system was $200,000, including charges for CPU, memory, disk storage, maintenance, programmers, and operators.

Various solutions were analyzed in terms of one-time costs (hardware, software, development, and training) and recurring costs (hardware maintenance, license fees, and support staff.) The results are shown in Table 5.2. Option A was a client/server PC-based LAN running Oracle on a Banyan Vines network. Option B was the current mainframe system. The startup cost plus projected annual maintenance costs for Option A is better than Option B using either of the interest rates examined.

Table 5.2. An NPV evaluation of alternative systems.

			Life Cycle Costs				
Year:	0	1	2	3	4	5	Total
Option A	$114,848	$25,101	$25,101	$25,101	$25,101	$25,101	$ 240,351
Option B	0	200,000	200,000	200,000	200,000	200,000	1,000,000

	Net Present Value		
Interest Rate:	0%	5%	10%
Option A	$240,351	$218,052	$202,998
Option B	$1,000,000	$824,662	$713,697

In this case, the relative financial merit of the two options doesn't change significantly within the broad range of interest rates used for the analysis. We can, however, imagine situations in which the raw costs are close enough, and the differences in the timing of expenditures of competing systems large enough, that the rank order of the NPVs would differ for different interest rates. In any case, life cycle cost analysis and the concept of net present value form a sound basis for comparing systems alternatives and for justifying good rightsizing proposals to nontechnical decision-makers.

Estimating Intangibles

Rightsizing, like any large-scale systems project, sometimes may be difficult to justify using only numbers. For some reason, systems projects do not lend themselves to hard statistical analysis and prediction as well as do other important business decisions, such as whether to expand into a specific geographic area or for what price a new product should be sold.

Assessing the Risks

In assessing the risks of rightsizing, you should ask these questions: "What are the risks of proceeding with the program, and how can they be managed?" and "What are the risks of not proceeding with the program?"

There are many forms of risk to consider:

- Financial ("Too expensive.")
- Technical ("It can't be done.")
- Project ("We don't know how.")
- Functionality ("Once done, no good.")
- Systemic

Systemic risk is the risk that the system has so great an impact that it changes the rules of the game and causes any assumptions about costs and benefits to become obsolete.

Continuing to work backward in the list, functionality risk should be assessed in light of the view that sometimes an investment, not currently essential, should be undertaken to ensure that future courses of action remain open to the firm. Project risk can be addressed by skills inventories and proper training. Financial risk, aside from being assessed in terms of the pure financial exposure to the firm, can be dealt with in different ways. For example, if there is no resource advantage or barrier to competitors' duplication, the question should be asked: "Would it make more sense to develop a system cooperatively, if the opportunity is appropriate?" Likewise, if the firm lacks financial resources, might it make more sense to develop with strategic partners to counter these resource problems?

Of all of these risks, technical risk is perhaps the most difficult to assess. With the incredible pace of change in the I/T industry, major research and development effort is required for most companies just to understand, in general terms, what their options are.

The bottom line is that there is no absolute right or wrong way to estimate the intangible benefits of the proposed strategic system. To make a good decision about the value of intangible benefits, you must ask yourself and the company management a series of questions:

- What is the expected competitive impact?
- What proprietary resource advantage does it exploit?
- What competitive advantages are sustained and protected?

Understand that changes in the firm's future operating environment, either externally imposed or actually caused by rightsizing, are likely to alter the assumptions on which you based your decision.

Financing Alternatives

The funds for any corporate purchase must come from either or both of two sources: internally or externally generated funds. Internal funds are accessed through capital and operating budgets. Virtually all corporations use a combination of operating and capital funds to support systems integration projects.

The capital budget typically is used for computer hardware, especially large CPUs and related peripheral devices, and most components of large-scale external contracts with systems integrators.

The operating budget typically is used for internal corporate charges for "soft" services (software development and other "people" expenditures). These charges commonly are called *internal charge-backs* and cover a variety of activities and expenses. The operating budget is used also for the components of systems integration contracts associated with project feasibility.

Despite the obvious need for funding, the financing of systems integration projects—of which rightsizing projects are a leading category—typically has been a low-profile activity. Such traditional funding sources as banks and leasing companies have been slow to appreciate the intrinsic value of integrated systems. Hence, their financial offerings have followed time-honored formats: bank loans predicated on general creditworthiness, and equipment leases based on forecasted equipment resale values. The imagination evidenced by "financial engineering" in markets such as corporate mergers and acquisitions has been notably absent from external funding sources for systems projects.

The historic demand for project-specific systems integration financing also has been modest. In fact, a 1991 survey of 100 large organizations indicated that only 5 percent use external financing on an exclusive basis for systems integration projects. This percentage is in contrast to computer hardware leasing, which is used by approximately 50 percent of those surveyed. The fundamental reason for this difference is that, until recently, traditional corporate financing sources, such as bank loans or stock or bond offerings, have been plentiful for most system buyers. Treasurers have drawn on those sources with a minimum of inconvenience. When conditions are unfavorable for traditional financing, such as during recessions, the response is to slash or defer capital appropriations budgets.

This lack of alternatives to traditional funding has the potential to leave the beneficiaries of rightsizing projects, whether users or MIS departments, "in the lurch." As sponsors of projects, users and MIS departments are influential in the appropriations process; as Figure 5.2 illustrates, however, the people who hire systems integrators and have veto power over funding include executive management, executive steering committees, and others, such as the board of directors. The practical effect is to hold perfectly good projects hostage to circumstances outside the control of the project beneficiaries. To understand your options with each of these sources, let's look at them in more detail.

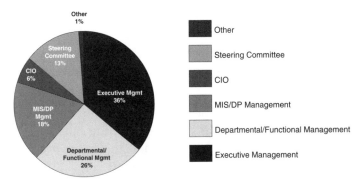

Figure 5.2. Who hires the integrator?

Leasing

Leasing companies, especially computer leasing companies, have been a significant source of funds for systems integration rightsizing projects. Computer leasing companies offer a variety of benefits to hardware buyers:

- Low rates, based on a willingness to assume risks about the value of the computer equipment at the end of the lease
- Flexibility in equipment planning; for example, in addressing CPU upgrades and increased storage capacity
- The accounting benefit of "off-balance sheet" financing and operating budget treatment

What these benefits mean to buyers of rightsized information systems is that attractive financing of the new computer equipment often is available from computer leasing companies. Note however, that buyers should avoid lease terms and conditions that limit subsequent flexibility, especially terms that limit competitive bidding for hardware upgrades.

Bank Financing

Bank financing has started to become available for systems integration projects. Often, such financing is made available through bank leasing or commercial financing subsidiaries. Unfortunately, although this might be a different form of financing—the title of the document often says "lease" rather than "loan"—the structure of most bank offerings is unchanged from that of traditional bank loans.

The Lease-Versus-Buy Decision

The guiding principle behind the lease-versus-buy analysis for computer hardware is to compare the cost of leasing to a company's after-tax cost of capital—the weighted average cost of debt and equity—taking into account the tax deductibility of interest but not of dividend payments. The logic behind using the cost of capital rather than the cost of debt is as follows: To retain their debt ratings and to comply with lender and investor expectations, companies maintain a certain level of debt in proportion to equity. Although management has considerable discretion in the timing and techniques of debt management and equity management, an increase in debt in general will be matched eventually with a proportionate amount of equity.

Systems Integrators

Another response to the funding dilemma is for buyers of rightsized information systems to obtain financial concessions from their suppliers: systems integrators. Many systems integrators have been creative in accepting what amounts to deferred payment for services rendered. Most integrators have assumed this position unwillingly, usually in response to competitive pressures or from clients pleading limited budgets. Keep in mind, too, that the systems integrator often is the representative for a number of "players" brought to bear in the implementation of your new system, as shown in Figure 5.3.

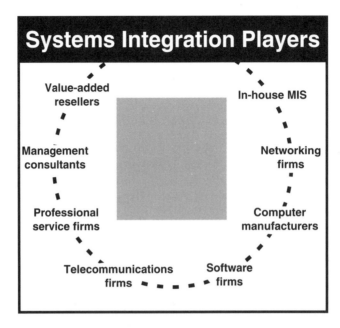

Figure 5.3. *The team members of a typical systems integration project.*

The most common form of integrator financing is to offer a "back-loaded" payment schedule in the systems integration acquisition contract. With this type of payment schedule, the integrator assumes a negative cash-flow position during the time in which the system is being built. Specific terms vary by transaction and are related directly to competitive factors.

Another means of financing rightsizing is through system buyers obtaining limited royalty rights. This method involves a royalty payable to the buyer when a similar system is sold, in whole or in part, to others. A factor limiting the prevalence of such royalty agreements is buyers who do not want to lose their "competitive advantage" as a result of selling their systems innovations to competitors.

Finally, selected systems integrators are making equity investments in their clients, thereby assuming direct financial interest in the client's success. Some refer to this arrangement as *outsourcing*. For example, EDS regularly makes investments in companies, ranging from Enron Corp. to System One. Occasionally, these investments have been made in financially ailing clients and therefore have been subject to external factors—such as bankruptcy courts and rising interest rates—outside of their immediate control.

In a variation on this theme, system buyers are starting to require systems integrators to assume an equity interest in projects. The theory is that having money at risk will financially motivate the systems integrator to assure the long-term success of the project. Although the frequency of equity investments is growing, you should note that the number of integrators with *both* the financial resources and the will to invest is limited. Therefore, this method of project financing is unlikely to become a primary technique.

Getting into the Driver's Seat

The most positive development for financing a systems integration project is that the financial community is beginning to comprehend the significance and long-term value of systems to corporations. The primary step for systems buyers, therefore, is to contemplate the financial issues surrounding the acquisition of systems. Stated another way, buyers should determine the most important financial aspects of the deal.

For example, financial motivations could include:

- Minimizing immediate operating expenses
- Cash constraints
- Balance sheet constraints
- Finding additional income

After determining their financial motivations, buyers should consider how to satisfy these requirements, and should challenge system suppliers to do the same. For example, here are some creative responses to these issues:

- Minimize immediate operating expenses by entering into an operating lease of "in-house" implementation costs.
- If you have cash constraints, consider a sale and leaseback of an existing system to pay for the acquisition of a new and different system.
- If you have balance-sheet constraints, pursue operating leases of hardware and software.
- To acquire additional income, consider a sale and leaseback of a system that was "expensed." The sale proceeds might be considered income. Consider a royalty arrangement with the system supplier.

It's important to challenge not only systems integrators but also computer-leasing companies and banks, especially those who already are dealing with the buyer, to come up with innovative financing solutions. After all, when a real demand for funds occurs, the supply will follow.

As you consider creative financing alternatives for your rightsizing project, you should seek the active, constructive participation of your company's chief financial officer and the financial analysis team. Most firms, in particular publicly owned corporations, have certain finance and accounting "rules" and techniques they must follow consistently. If a creative financing option violates one of the "rules," you will not be permitted to adopt it.

Evaluating Performance

After the system has been bought and paid for, it's important to understand just how well the cost savings and benefit goals were achieved. How do you know if your rightsizing project reached the expected levels of savings and performance? Some methods, imperfect at best, nonetheless are useful.

Begin by setting up expectations during the planning stage of the project. You should have specific expectations about how the system will work and how users will spend a typical day using the system. With rightsizing, there often are additional, unforeseen uses, but for evaluation purposes, you will probably want to ignore them. Set up performance benchmarks for the machines. The performance measurements can be divided into three categories:

- The technical aspects of the system itself. For instance, how fast can the network transfer data? What are the available communications options and relative speeds? What are the advantages and drawbacks of each one?

- The measurement of cost savings in terms of service and support. Measure the average cost per month of a service contract. Determine the cost of salaries for support personnel. How many hours per month of downtime are there? How has customer service improved?

- Performance measurements in terms of utilization, such as logon time, session duration, number of users logged in to the system, user acceptance, the number of e-mail messages handled, the amount of network storage utilized, and user requests for assistance. What are the number of applications and tasks handled on the LAN? Perform research. Ask users to list the purposes for which they use the network. Ask them whether they use the network instead of doing something another way—a way they previously had to do it.

The financial issues raised by a rightsizing project are similar to those raised in any strategic application of information technology. As such, the starting point for justification is an estimate of the value of the expected, direct cost savings and revenue increases, compared to an estimate of the direct costs involved in undertaking the project. Unfortunately, as stated at the beginning of this chapter, traditional quantitative cost/benefit analysis of this sort ignores many of the indirect benefits that comprise some of the most compelling reasons to rightsize.

Again, however, quantitative analysis should not be discounted completely. On the contrary, reasonable estimates of costs, both of the rightsizing project and of the costs of maintaining the rightsized system, usually are the most convincing evidence that rightsizing makes sense—especially for firms experiencing excessive I/T costs. Just don't count on being able to predict precisely how much money will be saved by rightsizing. In the final analysis, it matters only that the value is superior to (in other words, less negative than) the alternatives.

A Rightsizing Snapshot: A Case Study of Cost/Benefit Analysis at a Major Gas Company

Let's review a specific case study to determine in detail how a cost/benefit analysis was actually developed in a real-world environment.

Background

A major gas company conducted a preliminary analysis of the charges from its information systems department for two of its subsidiaries. Based on this analysis, it was concluded that potential material savings were possible because the annual charges were in excess of $2.4 million, and the preliminary alternatives suggested savings in excess of $1 million per year.

The company then requested that a consulting firm conduct a review of sufficient depth to determine the answers to these questions:

- Was a stand-alone approach to data processing for the two subsidiaries feasible? That is, could the systems running on the parent company's mainframe be replicated by the use of a local area network?
- What would be the probable total cost of such a system—including equipment, ongoing staffing, software development, and so on?

Conclusions

The implementation of a stand-alone, distributed system for the two subsidiaries was feasible. This conclusion was based on the functions performed, number of users, and transaction volume. The consulting firm provided both a theoretical projection and a comparison of the company's transaction volumes to those of its other consulting clients performing similar functions in a distributed network environment.

The two subsidiaries could be completely converted to new systems and be off the mainframe by the end of the year, assuming a start date on or before the second quarter of the same year.

The forecasted cost of staying with the current approach was $12 million over a five-year period. The projected costs of the distributed approach over the same period ranged from $4.4 million to $5.9 million. Thus, the potential savings over a five-year period ranged from $6.1 million to $7.4 million without an adjustment for discounting. Using a discount factor of 10 percent, the savings ranged from $4.3 million to $5.6 million, as shown in Figure 5.4.

To put this projection in perspective, the data-processing costs would be reduced by a factor of between 51 percent and 64 percent. Under any of the alternatives, the profitability effect of changing the data-processing approach is positive in each one of the five-year periods analyzed.

Each day that the gas company continued with its original data-processing approach cost an additional $9,600. This figure contrasts with the projected recurring costs of the distributed system of $2,000 to $2,500 per day.

Summary of Discounted Cash Flow: All Alternatives

Discount Factor: 10%

	Year 1	Year 2	Year 3	Year 4	Year 5	Total
Alternative 1						
Low end	$83,870	$1,611,675	$1.450.508	$1,305,457	$1,174,911	$5,626,420
High end	(117,505)	1,539,855	1,385,870	1,247,283	1,122,554	5,178,056
Alternative 2						
Low end	(262,879)	1,621,508	1,459,357	1,313,421	1,182,079	5,313,485
High end	(972,314)	!,550,970	1,395,873	1,256,286	1,130,657	4,361,471
Alternative 3						
Low end	(153,439)	1,533,870	1,380,483	1,242,435	1,118,191	5,121,539
High end	(920,824)	1,512,495	1,361,246	1,225,121	1,102,609	4,280,646

Savings Range: $4.3 million to $5.6 million

Figure 5.4. The financial analysis of a distributed processing alternative.

A Description of the Solution

Figures 5.5 and 5.6 illustrate the financial forecasts of a distributed, client/server-based solution for the gas company. Both a high- and low-end were forecasted in order to provide a comfort range from which to plan.

The key activities and plans on which the forecasts are based are these:

- The two subsidiaries converted to a distributed system consisting of one or more local area networks, with a minicomputer (or a high-end microcomputer) as a database server (computer).
- Conversion to the distributed system occurred in the summer before the project—thus, mainframe data-processing costs remained at current levels throughout the first six months of the year.
- Existing programs, which supported subsidiary operations, were written in SAS. This alternative takes as an assumption the consulting firm's capability to make a successful conversion of the mainframe SAS programs to run on the PC network (using PC-SAS).

■ An accounting package was installed and modified to serve the needs associated with the company and its subsidiaries. The alternative assumed significant enhancements in the areas of invoicing, accrual processing, and consolidations.

■ The subsidiaries hired their own personnel to administer, operate, and maintain the new data-processing systems.

■ The subsidiaries owned the equipment and software.

■ The consulting firm was hired to procure the equipment, install the network, install and modify the accounting systems, convert the operational systems from the mainframe, and manage the conversion of historical data from the mainframe to the PC network.

■ To simplify comparisons, none of the projections made any assumptions about inflation—all costs were in constant dollars.

■ No costs were imputed to the time users were to spend in training.

A Description of Intangible Costs and Benefits

We have reviewed the tangible financial costs and benefits of the migration to new rightsized information systems, as well as key assumptions made by the subsidiaries. But what about all the important intangible costs and benefits? These often are the "make or break" factors and are therefore reviewed in the following sections.

Costs

■ The subsidiaries assumed a risk of insufficient support for existing systems during the conversion period. (This risk was addressed in the consulting firm's proposal.)

■ User efficiency was reduced during the user-training and self-study period of implementation.

■ Subsidiaries experienced a greater amount of management time to recruit and supervise in-house systems department personnel.

Alternative 1 Cash Flow Analysis-- Five Years-- Low End

YEAR

	1	2	3	4	5	Total
Cash expended under dist. approach	$2,311,716	$515,000	$515,000	$515,000	$515,000	$4,371,716
Current Systems cost	2,400,000	2,400,000	2,400,000	2,400,000	2,400,000	12,000,000
Savings	88,284	1,885,000	1,885,000	1,885,000	1.885.000	7,628,284
Net present value of savings using 10% discount factor	83,870	1,611,675	1,450,508	1,305,457	1,174,911	5,626,420

Alternative 1 Cash Flow Analysis-- Five Years-- High end

YEAR

	1	2	3	4	5	Total
Cash extended under dist. approach	$2,523,689	$599,000	$599,000	$599,000	$599,000	$4,919,689
Current Systems cost	2,400,000	2,400,000	2,400,000	2,400,000	2,400,000	12,000,000
Savings	123,689	1,801,000	1,801.000	1,801.000	1.801.000	7,080,311
Net present value of savings using 10% discount factor	(117,505)	1,539,855	1,385,870	1,247,283	1.122.554	5,178,056
Savings	123,689	1,801,000	1,801.000	1,801.000	1,801,000	7,080,311
Net present value of savings using 10% discount factor	(117,505)	1,539,855	1,385,870	1,247,283	1.122.554	5,178,056

Figure 5.5. Analysis of distributed processing alternatives: a cash-flow analysis.

Alternative Description 1:

	Low End	High End
FIRST YEAR COSTS:		
EQUIPMENT:	$502,897	$560,171
SOFTWARE:		
Application		
WordPerfect (80 users)	23,800	23,800
Lotus 1-2-3, v2.2 (80 users)	39,600	39,600
SAS (assume 50 users)	6,500	12,000
Other	12,000	15,000
Accounting (assume Platinum)	7,000	8,000
Novell NetWare 386 (2copies)	15,998	15,998
Less software discounts	(15,880)	(15,880)
STAFFING COSTS:		
Salaries and fringe	150,000	150,000
(assumes 6 people hired for avg. of 5 months)		
Employment agency/recruiting fees	72,000	72,000
CONSULTING FEES-ESTABLISH		
MIS ORGANIZATION	11,000	13,000
CONSULTING FEES		
Accounting system installation/		
enhancements	54,000	90,000
Conversion of operational systems	60,000	90,000
Historical data conversion	30,000	60,000
Production monitoring	24,000	24,000
Network installation	36,000	36,000
Project management	40,800	60,000
TRAINING		
Network training (assume 80 attendees)	8,000	10,000
Word processing (assume 40 attendees)	8,000	10,000
System manager/network administration	6,000	10,000
ADDITIONAL CORPORATE MIS CHARGES		
FOR DATA CONVERSION ASSISTANCE	20,000	40,000
EXISTING CORPORATE		
CHARGES (6 MONTHS)	1,200,000	1,200,000
Total first year	$2,311,716	$2,523,689
SUBSEQUENT YEAR COSTS:		
STAFF		
Salaries/fringe (6 people)	$360,000	$360,000
Training costs	9,000	12,000
Employment agency fees/		
recruiting	36,000	72,000
(low end=1/year, high=2/year)		
OUTSIDE CONSULTANTS	35,000	60,000
HARDWARE/SOFTWARE UPGRADES	60,000	80,000
USER TRAINING MATERIAL/COURSES	15,000	15,000
TOTAL	$515,000	$599,000

*Also includes tasks associated with training,
development of user procedures and testing.

Figure 5.6. *Analysis of distributed processing alternatives: a cost analysis.*

Benefits

■ The new systems could be modified more easily and applications developed more rapidly in response to changing business environments.

■ The new systems also improved the company's capability to customize security procedures over and above the current environment.

- The new systems improved user productivity because it provided all users with access to word processing, spreadsheets, e-mail, and other productivity aids.
- The new systems improved flexibility, making information more quickly available to office locations, remote sites, and third parties.

Pricing Computer and Network Usage

Companies with rightsized installations often are faced with the challenge of properly allocating costs among users. As the preceding snapshot has just shown, many centralized MIS operations have cost structures that appear increasingly prohibitive. If these costs are at all artificially inflated, then the decision to rightsize might be partly based on some false financial assumptions. What sometimes has happened is that MIS organizations have, in effect, overcharged their users, charging high prices. IS professionals must be careful not to make this mistake. The urge to make a profit must be resisted. Appendix F, "The Importance of Cost-Reflective Pricing," discusses the design philosophy to follow in developing a charge-back system.

Reengineering

Reengineering

6

Organizations will now resemble spider webs more than pyramids.

—Robert M. Tomasko
Downsizing: Reshaping the Corporate Future (1990)

Objectives:

1. To understand the definition and underlying goals of business reengineering.
2. To understand the relationship between business reengineering and rightsizing.
3. To identify and understand the requirements of successful business reengineering efforts.
4. To learn from examples of business reengineering projects.

As mentioned earlier, successful rightsizing requires careful planning at several levels. To be sure, there is the planning of the required system functionality, the physical layout of the PC networks, the determination of the technical requirements of the network components, and the planning of training for users. First and foremost, rightsizing requires high-level strategic planning to determine the impact it will have on your organization and to clearly define the goals of specific rightsizing activities. The comprehensive nature of rightsizing demands that principles of business reengineering are included in the planning process; in a sense, rightsizing is the reengineering of the information technology and human resources of your organization.

When undertaking a program as important as overhauling how your firm uses information, planning must be approached seriously and comprehensively. Even if your reengineering analysis results in a decision *not* to change the organizational structure (which is highly unlikely), you will be rewarded with a deeper understanding of how your firm works and what helps it work better. In this chapter, we discuss how to plan rightsizing efforts using principles of business reengineering.

What Is Reengineering?

Business reengineering is the fundamental rethinking and radical redesign of business processes to achieve dramatic improvements in critical measures of performance, such as cost, quality, capital, service, speed, and so on.

The process of reengineering is one of examining existing business processes and structures in an organization, determining what are the better ways to achieve the organization's performance goals, and then implementing changes to better facilitate progress towards those goals.

Like rightsizing, reengineering is a term that has been applied to many different business activities. Some executives use reengineering as a polite term for "massive layoffs to reduce costs," but true business reengineering is something else altogether. Some people use "business process redesign" (BPR) as a synonym for reengineering and quality improvement efforts, and restructuring programs as "reengineering." Although it's true that quality improvement often is a product of reengineering efforts and that reorganizational activities often occur in tandem with reengineering, reengineering is something more.

What sets business reengineering apart from these related activities is that reengineering involves a comprehensive examination and evaluation of the very essence of the work being performed. This includes the rationale for the work itself, the logic of the way the work currently is performed, and the investigation of alternate ways to achieve the goals of the work. Colloquially, reengineering takes a "big picture" perspective.

The hallmarks of business reengineering are these:

- Ambition—It's all about *dramatic* change. Reengineering efforts seek performance improvements in the range of 80 percent reductions in costs, cycle times, and so on; or, conversely, ten-times increases in quality, customer satisfaction ratings, and so on. If you are aiming for improvements just in the 10–20 percent range, then business reengineering is not for you.
- Breaking the rules—It's all about *radical* steps. Reengineering efforts focus on identifying and recasting fundamental assumptions and associated beliefs.
- Process orientation—It's all about the *process* (or the journey), not the destination. The emphasis is on fundamental business processes, not artifacts and organization boundaries.

Reengineering Background

Reengineering arose in the late 1980s to address the question of why investments in information technology, particularly in automation, hadn't resulted in the anticipated benefits. Reengineering proponents attribute the failure of MIS to follow through on its promises to the misapplication of computing technology to business problems.

In a milestone article on reengineering, "Reengineering Work: Don't Automate, Obliterate," (*Harvard Business Review*, July-August, 1990), Dr. Michael Hammer, one of the best-known reengineering spokespersons, said companies tend to use technology to mechanize old ways of doing business. Later, in the book that he wrote with James Champy, *Reengineering the Corporation* (Harper, 1993), he asserted that reengineering is using technology to fundamentally change the way you do business, not simply to speed it up. Reengineering efforts take analysis from the "Which processes can we speed up by using computers?" level to the "What are the best processes to accomplish our business goals?" level.

As a metaphor for how reengineering differs from an investigation for alternative technical solutions to an existing work process, consider transportation. A traveler wants to go to Los Angeles from New York. In the past, the traveler has always driven. A non-reengineering perspective would limit decisions to the type of vehicle the traveler should drive (including model, color, body style, and so on) and the route the traveler should take.

A reengineering perspective first examines more fundamental issues, including asking whether driving is the best form of transportation or whether flying, traveling by train, or bicycling would be better. Another question is the rationale for the trip to Los Angeles: A vacation? To visit a friend? To make a sales call on a client? To examine property investments? Further, are there other ways to accomplish the goals of the trip to Los Angeles: A trip to London? A phone call, fax, or letter? What about sending an employee?

The important aspect of reengineering is that it involves *considering* complete abandonment of old processes. It strips existing work to its bare essence and throws out preconceived ideas of how the work is done and the goals are achieved.

The reengineering process of identifying fundamental business objectives and of forming a detailed strategy to achieve those objectives results in redesigned business policies and procedures. When successful, these new policies and procedures result in an improved flow of information through an organization. With the resulting rightsized system, the company works smarter, faster, and better. The visible results of reengineering are the often-dramatic changes in how business problems are approached as well as the methods used to achieve the corporate goals. A case in point may be a rightsized, distributed PC-based network that replaces an expensive, centralized, mainframe system that has outlived its usefulness.

Why Reengineer?

Certainly, every company wants to improve quality, remain competitive, and reduce costs, but do companies really need to reengineer to accomplish these goals? Why, especially, should reengineering efforts include a strong emphasis on information technology? Corporations have not been willing to take the steps needed to solve problems. Reengineering just seemed too drastic. Rather than periodically examining fundamental business activities, organizations take a number of actions that postpone—but do not eliminate—the need to reengineer. These methods include incremental quality improvements, indiscriminate budget and personnel cuts, and throwing more technology at the problems.

From a pure IS perspective, much of IS is uncomfortable with the "reengineering style." This style calls for improvisation and evolution; intense and unrelenting focus on achieving the process changes and ultimate objectives; team-oriented and collegial working environments; and exploratory and inductive thinking and approaches to problems. The IS style, in many ways, has not been in sync with this reengineering style. As a result, IS people worry about the devaluation of their skills, their inability to acquire new ones, negative impacts in their power and authority and, ultimately, the possibility of losing their job.

These are some of the reasons why reengineering is hard and why it takes extraordinary commitment from a company's executive and IS management. However, in general, the "try something, try something else, try anything" approach hasn't worked. Instead, the evidence shows that reengineering does work, as the following examples demonstrate.

Examples of Projects

Business reengineering projects have been launched at many corporations, including Ford Motor Company, AT&T, and Digital Equipment Corporation. They typically have reported an increase in productivity and an approximate 80 percent decrease in staff. At DEC, a reengineering team converted 20 incompatible accounts-payable systems to a DEC VAX minicomputer standard and consolidated 55 accounting groups down to 5, eliminating 450 jobs in the process. At Ford, the company similarly examined the accounts-payable function, composed of 500 people, and reduced the staff by 75 percent through process reengineering and better use of the power of its computer systems.

There's more to reengineering than just shifting or eliminating jobs. Reengineering should not be viewed as a crisis-management technique— rather, as a technique for affecting situations ripe with opportunity. Although reengineering often is a reaction to outside forces, it is not necessarily a purely defensive response. It is a catalyst for creating opportunities for improvements. The key is to be ready to reengineer and not to shy away from it. Approach the process with the idea that you prepare to reengineer before you have to, so that you can enact changes when it makes the most sense to do so.

When Is Reengineering Necessary?

It's one thing to say that only through continually asking yourself if you can do something faster, better, or cheaper does reengineering yield the benefits it promises. You can watch for some telltale signs that signal when it's time for you to examine your business from a reengineering perspective. Some of these signs include

- Widespread user dissatisfaction with information systems. Be alert to a lack of alignment between the expectations of senior line managers and MIS people.
- Decreasing competitive position; for example, a stable or declining marketshare in a growing market.
- Poor communications between divisions or departments. You can test this by asking members of each division what they think the other divisions are doing.
- Outgrown procedures. If you've just experienced (or anticipate) rapid growth in a particular market, the procedures that were adopted when the department was small may not be sufficient to handle the volume of data and the current workload. The problem may lie with the workflow, with the information-processing tools used, or with the application of resources.
- Competition. Examine other firms' approaches to similar business problems. Look both at your competitors and at firms in businesses dissimilar to your own.
- Emergence of departmental reengineering efforts. Middle management tends to see problems before upper management does and often considers beginning their own quality-improvement programs or departmental reorganizations.

- Intensive quality programs that have no I/T connection and large MIS replacement projects that are disguised reengineering opportunities.

- The inability to leverage opportunities: Were you unable to seize a business opportunity because of organizational inertia or other systemic constraints?

Reengineering and Rightsizing

Rightsizing information systems may be the expected result of business reengineering. Rightsizing, however, is not always the answer that comes out of the reengineering process. Thus, it is important to recognize that the reengineering perspective impacts the decision to rightsize.

- *Rightsized systems differ from traditional systems.* Although it may not be obvious to a casual observer or even to an experienced information systems professional, rightsizing represents an approach to information processing that is radically different from traditional, centralized systems. Radical changes without reengineering analysis are changes for the sake of change, not advancements. Specifically, rightsizing information systems without legitimate justification, without a solid understanding of how rightsized systems need to work, and without expectation of corresponding radical changes in organizational structure and work flow has little chance for success.

- *Rightsized systems are supported differently.* In rightsized environments, there is less dependence on MIS personnel as an interface between users and their applications. Rightsized applications often interact with productivity applications, such as spreadsheet and word processing software, which allow end users to manipulate and analyze information without having to rely on MIS personnel to provide reports.

  Support personnel in a rightsized environment need skills and training different from traditional MIS support. Network administrators must be able to understand the entire network. They need to be meticulous about recording network events and performing backups faithfully, and they must be able to respond quickly if problems develop.

Users have a much greater responsibility for knowing how a rightsized system works and need different kinds of training. In many instances, users are responsible for taking care of their own computer files, just as they are responsible for taking care of their desk space. In order to take advantage of all the network services, users need to be taught how to use the different applications available on the network singly and in concert. Users need to learn to reengineer their approach to the tasks they perform.

■ *Rethinking an organization's approach to information management enables you to achieve the maximum benefits from rightsizing.* The main reason to plan with a reengineering perspective stems from the fact that a rightsized, distributed system is a very different creature than a mini or mainframe system. Rightsizing isn't simply replacing large, expensive computers with smaller, less expensive computers. Many of the benefits of rightsizing are possible only when the organization changes its fundamental information-management approach. Bringing in PC networks for the sole purpose of emulating existing mainframe applications usually is frivolous and does nothing to exploit the benefits of the PC environment.

Reengineering efforts don't end with rightsizing. Even rightsized systems need to be reexamined with a reengineering perspective at some point. Fortunately, the flexibility of rightsized systems assists in further reengineering efforts. Powerful, distributed systems have the flexibility required when reengineering efforts take place. Additionally, the lower cost of replacing or obsoleting various components of a rightsized system makes subsequent reengineering less painful. You don't get tied to a particular technology or a single vendor.

The Other Side of Reengineering: Obstacles Along the Path

Mike Hammer says, "The risk is not in reengineering, it's in not reengineering." Managing change in relation to reengineering and rightsizing means striking a balance between the risk associated with taking new approaches and the risk of failing to maintain competitiveness in a chaotic environment. Along the way toward achieving this balance, there are obstacles that are easy to understand, but which often require great effort to knock down, as illustrated in Figure 6.1.

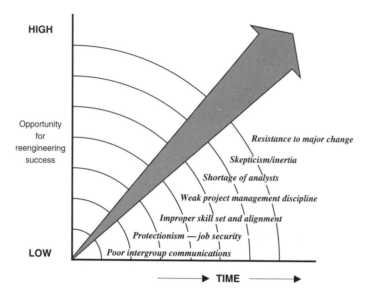

HIGH

Opportunity
for
reengineering
success

LOW

Resistance to major change

Skepticism/inertia

Shortage of analysts

Weak project management discipline

Improper skill set and alignment

Protectionism — job security

Poor intergroup communications

TIME

Figure 6.1. *Breaking the obstacles to reengineering progress.*

Skepticism

To some line and staff people, changes come and changes go—usually with the people that fostered them. It's not uncommon to have employees who would swear they've seen every kind of management program that exists tried at least once during their time with the company. Given time and employee skepticism, these programs often fail, allowing things to "get back to normal" in the employees' eyes. The only way to overcome this obstacle is to create a committed, near-fanatical management team determined to see the reengineered processes succeed.

Resistance to Change

Some critics of reengineering insist that reengineering is a ploy by suppliers of information technology services and products to create demand for their skills. Other business people resist the promise of reengineering, believing it to be simply a new name for an old package of management theories and other business ideas. To some extent, this is true. Reengineering is a long-run strategy to achieve the traditional business goals of increasing shareholder value, improving quality, reducing costs, and beating the competition. The rate of change in business today, driven partially by rapid improvements in information technology, demands that businesses remain open to the radical types of changes reengineering may suggest—now more than ever. What exists, in effect, is a kind of commercial Darwinism. Companies are faced with the following choices: evolve, adapt, or die.

Inertia

Consultant/author Tom Peters was asked to define the "Tom Peters approach" to getting employees who are solidly opposed to new business processes to accept them. Peters responded, "The Tom Peters approach? Don't bother." As cutting as it sounds, his response is in many ways the only method of dealing with people when there's no time and great resistance. The more likely case, however, is that there exists the need to involve employees in the process of changes resulting from reengineering. This process of change management is covered in detail in Chapter 7, "Change Management."

The Seven Steps to Successful Reengineering

The reengineering process varies from firm to firm, but successful reengineering efforts have the following seven steps in common.

Step 1: Start at the Top

Successful reengineering requires major commitment from senior management. Furthermore, management should convey its support for reengineering efforts to subordinates and encourage them to support the efforts as well. Because reengineering efforts typically cut across all departments and may also involve elimination or redistribution of departments, these efforts must receive enthusiastic support from management at a sufficiently high level so that departmental priorities do not drive rightsizing. Reengineering one department may make incremental improvements, but only by implementing an enterprise-wide reengineering effort can a company hope to improve its business to the fullest extent.

Reengineering has to start at the top. Without this commitment, reengineering is doomed to failure. Commitment does not necessarily require intense involvement on the part of senior management, but it does require intense vision. Upper management must be able to envision the firm in the future and must be willing to leave the past—and present—behind.

Step 2: Set Broad Goals and Keep the Purposes Clear

Make sure the purposes of reengineering are clear. Everyone must understand the expectations for what is to be accomplished. Emphasize that the three major motives that compel reengineering efforts in business today are improving quality, reducing costs, and maintaining competitiveness.

Quality

The somewhat-vague goal of improving quality has become a top priority of global business, especially in the United States. Throughout the 1980s, American businesses centered on quality improvement as a path to success. Many firms adopted an approach of continuous quality improvement. Continuous quality improvement is something everybody in the organization can do. Once begun, the organization makes incremental changes that, over time, can accumulate into significant change.

Firms seeking to improve quality have attempted to instill a sense of contribution and responsibility at every level of the organizational structure. This empowerment is most visible in the manufacturing sector, for example, where assembly-line workers now are commonly given the authority to halt the production process if they notice problems. A similar embracing-of-empowerment theory is occurring in the white-collar sector. The focus on quality and individual contribution in clerical, management, and support staff positions has resulted in the emergence of the *knowledge worker*, expected to be able to gather, analyze, and act on information with much more responsibility than ever before. Reengineering should empower the knowledge worker.

Cost Reduction

Reengineering efforts often are prompted by a desire to reduce operating costs, particularly in I/T investments. In 1992, the Fortune 500 companies' information technology investments—including hardware, software, and data and telecommunications—averaged as much as 45 percent of their total business capital spending, a trend mirrored in smaller businesses as well. Yet national productivity figures, according to some sources, have not increased since 1973. Some firms have even suffered productivity losses following massive I/T investments. If companies are spending more and more on information technology, why are they not becoming more efficient? Reengineering often is undertaken to address the productivity problem. Reengineering can reduce costs effectively as a by-product of removing outdated, unproductive steps in procedures.

Competition: The New Challenge of the 1990s

The third major force driving reengineering efforts is competitive pressure. Indications of threatening competition range from a competitor's ability to introduce a product more quickly to a declining marketshare in an expanding market. In addition, American firms are feeling more threatened than ever by foreign interests. The pressure of global competition comes not only from Japan and the European Community but also from emerging industrialized nations, such as South Korea and Brazil. With more and more nations adopting capitalistic economies, competition will be even more fierce. The threats are well-documented in a plethora of books and articles, to the point where it's a virtual cliche. It's best for a company to concentrate on doing what they do better. Look at the competition, learn from them, even imitate them if necessary. Remember, however, that reengineering is a proactive response to problems, not a reactive one.

Step 3: Generate Support

When the decision has been made to fundamentally reassess the resource application of the firm, it's time to get talented people from various divisions of the company involved. Involving a cross-section of people from your organization accomplishes a number of things: it demonstrates the high-level commitment to reengineering, emphasizes the company-wide nature of reengineering, and provides a means of communicating the progress of the ongoing reengineering efforts. The people selected for this multidivisional task force ideally share the following characteristics. They have

- Credibility among the other members of their division
- A solid understanding of the tasks performed by the people in their division and how their work contributes to the activities of other divisions
- Strong communication skills
- The ability to see the big picture

Management commitment also must take the form of committed resources: human, material, time, and financial. Successful reengineering requires total commitment—commitment to action and commitment to making the reengineering work. Once started, reengineering is a difficult process to stop. Reengineering can be an extremely emotional process that, if done wrong, can cause severe, even fatal, damage to an organization.

Step 4: Break the Rules

Successful reengineering requires vision; reengineering can work only when managers and strategic planners allow themselves to question everything. In his writings, Michael Hammer has said the essence of reengineering is "discontinuous thinking…breaking away from the outdated rules and fundamental assumptions that underlie operations. Unless we change these rules, we are merely rearranging deck chairs on the Titanic." The questions asked should encompass every aspect of the business. Often they will be prefaced with words like "Why do we…?" and "What if we…?" Reengineering efforts also involve examining the approaches other organizations use to accomplish their goals. Other organizations can be competitors, firms in other industries, nonprofit organizations, and government agencies.

Even if all the reengineering team members possess all the characteristics mentioned, reengineering efforts will fail unless they are *led by* someone with credibility, vision, and the ability to create an atmosphere in which everything can be questioned. Because it is extremely difficult for most people to take a wide-angle perspective on activities in which they are involved from day to day, the ideal leader of the reengineering task force often is a newcomer. For instance, a recently hired executive, such as a Chief Information Officer or Chief Operating Officer, can lead the reengineering charge. Another tactic is to hire business consultants to help with the reengineering process.

Step 5: Take Stock of the Current Situation

What are the firm's strengths and weaknesses? Compare current conditions to past performance, and compare the company's strengths and weaknesses in relation to its competitors. Extensive examinations of each division, including extensive audits, are recommended during this step, which can take weeks or even months. At the completion of this phase, the work performed in the organization should be precisely described, particularly with regard to the flow of information and products. You are looking for the procedures and tasks that are unjustifiable, that duplicate work, or that cause bottlenecks and errors in the processing of information. Recognize that inefficient procedures are not always obvious.

Step 6: Investigate I/T Possibilities

While most task force members are examining and analyzing existing procedures, others should investigate ways in which information technology can be applied to the business problems being identified. Information technology plays a central role in reengineering efforts by implementing and supporting the information systems that reengineering specifies.

There are several characteristics of information technology systems that make I/T a logical place to focus your reengineering/rightsizing efforts.

Expense of Investments

Information systems, which are typically one of a firm's largest capital investments, account for a significant portion of its operating costs.

Size of Systems

In most organizations, everyone performs at least a portion of their time at work each day using one or more of the company's computer systems. Fundamentally changing the computer platform has the potential to change how each of the employees in the firm performs work.

Time to Develop and Maintain Systems

I/T projects are not completed overnight. The I/T answers to many reengineered processes are in the seedling stage right now: imaging, wireless communications, pen-based systems, personal mass storage/retrieval, multimedia document integration, modeling and design applications, and others are just coming into their own.

How does one know which, if any, of these new weapons in the I/T tactical arsenal is appropriate? The first step is recognizing that these *are* tactics, not strategies. Reengineering efforts don't have to be based on computer-related processes or even include computing technology. Being aware of these technologies and considering their use, however, is an important part of reengineering.

Step 7: Don't Patch Holes, Change the Tire...or Build a Whole New Car...or Grow Wings

Once again, the analysis has been completed; it's time for action. Reiterate the goals, redouble the commitment, and hang on. Reengineering calls for broad, systemic changes, not temporary solutions. Automating a slow process provides a temporary fix but doesn't address the inefficiency inherent in the process itself.

A tale from a Chief Information Officer (CIO) describing the scene when he first joined his new company (a Fortune 500 communications-product manufacturer) is perhaps the best way of describing the reengineering challenge, especially as it relates to I/T.

"As I surveyed the scene at the MIS division I was about to take over, I couldn't help but think of a train analogy I had heard before that seemed applicable. I was the new conductor and my mission was to replace the wheels and change the engine of this speeding electric train I was on.

"But there were problems to overcome. In the locomotive at the head of the train, there were three people. One of them was an engineer rifling back and forth through the pages of a book the size of the New York City phone directory with the title on it 'Everything You Need to Know About Running an Electric Train.'

"The second person was also an engineer who was standing nearby somewhat purposefully but with a confused look on his face. Although on an electric train, he was holding a shovel full of coal. The third individual in the locomotive was the brakeman, holding a brake that had obviously broken off at the handle, but who continued to grimace while gripping it with all his might.

"As I worked my way back among the passenger cars, I found them empty. Most of the passengers had climbed to the top of the cars to get a better look for soft places along the side of the tracks to land. Those passengers that hadn't climbed out had instead made their way to the caboose, where they were working shifts to hammer out the linchpin holding the caboose to the rest of the train."

The CIO's analogy, presented at a conference on downsizing and systems integration, led him to discuss how taking the helm of the Information Systems division at his company was much like the train conductor analogy.

The people in charge of the division before he arrived were desperately seeking ways to improve the division's performance, either by looking for answers within the current way of doing things or by trying to force outdated or improper techniques on the division.

At the same time, users of the Information Systems division's services were trying to correct the problems they sensed by dealing with them in the only ways they knew how. In some cases, they were looking for alternate delivery methods and channels to supply the information they needed. They were either reprocessing information on PCs they brought in-house or getting by with manual systems. In other cases, they openly were advocating breaking from the Information Systems division and creating independent, semi-autonomous work groups of PC networks that could address the business applications needs of the end-user department.

After surveying the scene, the new CIO's response was to begin an aggressive, top management-endorsed campaign to get at the heart of the business problems and corresponding opportunities that the end-user departments were attempting to solve themselves. He did this by adopting the reengineering concepts and techniques described earlier. As you will see, his case is not unique.

Rightsizing Snapshot: A National Credit Corporation

A national credit corporation provides a good example of a company that has blended all the concepts introduced so far—rightsizing information systems, business process reengineering, and applying information for competitive advantage—into a successful formula.

Background

This corporation was a subsidiary of a very large insurance company. In 1990, the company began rethinking its five-year strategic plan within the context of the increasingly competitive premium finance industry. The cornerstone of the new strategic plan was a "Vision Statement" that clearly defined the company's business, products, markets, and approach. The only problem with the Vision Statement was the limitations posed by inadequate management information systems and antiquated processes that would prevent the company from achieving the stated goals. Drastic change was required.

After targeting PCs and LANs for their development environment because of the low price/high potential, the company sought out a systems integrator. With the help of the integrator, the company began rewriting eleven mission-critical applications in a client/server environment. Application and technical architecture teams worked concurrently to expedite the deployment of the target environment. This environment would allow users to access information in all 10 branch offices and to leverage the technology for more effective customer service and loan packaging.

Problem

To achieve the broad scope outlined in the Vision Statement and systems integration strategy, the team leveraged the flexibility of an object-development environment (ODE) and methodology and customized it in specific development life cycle activities to meet the company's requirements.

Because of limited resources, the project was divided into three phases. The first phase focused on rolling out the Technical Architecture platform to enable immediate learning and use of Windows, Lotus Notes, and several other personal productivity tools. The second phase focused on delivering four custom front-end applications with the highest added value for branch-office personnel. The third phase focused on corporate and back-end applications, including disbursements execution, accounts receivable, income recognition, insurance company management, credit, incentive, and regulation issues.

The Technical Architecture component of the project included integrating new and proven technologies to create an "open" architecture. To prepare for the first phase roll-out of the technical architecture, however, the company faced challenges in communications, development tools, and desktop products.

Solution

For communications, the company looked at commodity X.25 and private line services from third-party vendors. Although these offerings were mature, they were aging poorly and the jump to the next generation of technology was very risky. One of the methods used to limit the risk was by outsourcing the wide-area network services. Outsourcing limited capital exposure and training needs in a rapidly evolving area, and removed the need for an in-house 24-hour management facility. In addition, a condition for implementing any solution was the ability to "test drive" it prior to production. In the end, frame relay services were used.

Development tools were also changing rapidly. Powersoft's PowerBuilder was the specified development tool, utilizing BSG Corporation's BluePrint as the architecture. Based on design notes, developers prototyped in PowerBuilder 1.0 and designed for coding and implementation using release 2.0 of both products.

A primary success factor was the BluePrint ODE, a collection of base classes and other tools that contain value-added features that eliminate much of the redundant coding. By subclassing and over-riding and/or extending the services provided, application developers moved beyond the mundane tasks and focused on the business-enabling features and functionality.

Results

With the successful development and deployment of the first phase applications in December 1992 (including lead management, pricing and quoting, and booked contracts), the project team completed prototyping and began developing the Phase Two applications. The project team also optimized specific conversations from Phase 1. With Phase 2 applications scheduled to be coded and with integration and user acceptance testing completed in a late 1993 time frame, this company will aggressively pursue its Vision Statement, going into its highest volume months ever in early 1994.

Other Reengineering Success Stories

In virtually every company that has reengineered its business processes, the managers involved needed MIS support. This marks a turning point. In the past, new technology led to automating existing processes. Now, I/T enables totally new processes. From thinking about I/T, one logically moves to reengineering discussions.

Despite the importance of I/T to reengineering—and vice versa—MIS executives rarely lead reengineering efforts. Business reengineering advocates sometimes even downplay I/T's transformative powers altogether. Although reengineering does require a change in how information is collected and distributed, just changing information systems doesn't change the way you do business.

MIS played an active role in the reengineering efforts of Westinghouse Electric Corporation. The company's electronic systems group, which manufactures radar and missile systems under government contracts, tested a computer and communications system with which employees can create, store, and distribute information anywhere the group has offices. Although the system—called Westinghouse Integrated System for the Enterprise (WISE)—was developed by a team from the design engineering group, the MIS group is acting as a central coordinator for the integration of various systems that feed into WISE.

Through a reengineering project strongly led by MIS, Tupperware built a computer system to process customer orders and shipping requests. This system has reportedly saved eight times its cost in its first year of operation. The company also is building a global manufacturing and distribution system to track demand, inventory, manufacturing capability, and local costs. The system will run electronic document interchange (EDI) transactions over a public data network. The company also wants to develop an automated decision-making system, based on expert systems software linked to the EDI network. Tupperware sales managers would use the smart system to help forecast sales for new products or new markets.

MIS groups must be sensitive to internal politics preventing them from taking the lead on many reengineering projects. For example, New York Life hopes to move the company from a predominantly IBM mainframe environment to one made up of distributed UNIX workstations; local area networks; radio-linked, hand-held computers; image-processing systems; and client/server software. MIS management believes only 20 to 25 percent of the gains from the project will come from automation; the rest will be the effect of eliminated processes and other direct results of reengineering.

At the far end of the spectrum, some very I/T-intensive reengineering projects have had very little input from MIS departments. The Dallas-based diagnostics division of Abbott Laboratories, for example, engaged in two reengineering projects, both with plenty of I/T.

One project planned to create nine self-directed work teams in a group that makes analyzers and monitors for hospitals, laboratories, and physicians' offices. It was designed to use databases on computers linked by local area networks, a move to eliminate certain data-gathering chores and enable the 15-person teams to shrink to 11. The other project planned to link manufacturing employees of the diagnostics division with the staff doing engineering research and development.

The involvement of Abbott's MIS group was limited to representation on a cross-functional council overseeing the two projects. One reason for less MIS involvement was that the reengineering projects made use of UNIX-based systems, with which the MIS group had no experience. In addition, Abbott's corporate MIS group focuses on accounting, payroll, and other back-office jobs; the reengineering efforts involve engineering and other specialized functions and systems.

MIS professionals possess a problem-solving, multidimensional way of thinking that makes them the strongest candidates for the role of corporate reengineer. In fact, at some future time, CIO may more appropriately come to stand for "Chief Innovation Officer." However, consultant Mike Hammer admits MIS executives often underestimate the complexity of human relations in organizations. In his opinion, MIS tends to follow a "Mr. Spock" logical model that fails to account for the feelings, politics, and resistance that can torpedo the finest process design. Overcoming these resistance points is the subject of the next chapter—"Change Management."

Change
Management

7

Change Management

It is sufficiently agreed that all things change and that nothing really disappears but that the sum of matter remains exactly the same.

—Francis Bacon (17th c.)

Objectives:

1. To understand how people create perceptions of personal and organizational change.
2. To understand the life cycle of change acceptance by people.
3. To understand how to plan for change.
4. To learn key guidelines to follow for successfully implementing change.

In the previous chapter, you learned about the need to start the rightsizing planning process with reengineering: breaking tradition and examining how to radically and positively affect the business. Implementing rightsized information systems then becomes a major part of the radical change. An essential part of a successful information systems rightsizing project is successful change management. This chapter briefly deals with this important subject.

Perceptions and Future Shock

Change management is the process of adjusting people's perceptions of change so that they welcome—or at least tolerate—change, as opposed to resisting it. Affecting perceptions is key, because people react to change based on their perceptions. We perceive change to be *positive* when our capabilities exceed the challenges we face. This allows us to exercise control or at least have some influence over the event. We perceive change to be *negative* when the challenges we face surpass our capabilities and we are not able to achieve what we want.

Today's challenges chiefly are represented by the tremendous competition in the marketplace. This competition has caused acceleration in the volume, speed, and complexity of change in the workplace. The result has thus been more turbulent workplaces and perceived negative change. Characteristics of this turbulence include:

- More required interaction among people, tasks, issues, problems, and opportunities
- More unanticipated consequences

■ Less time to react to events and less predictability and control

■ Less durability of solutions

The result, manifested on an individual basis, can best be termed *future shock*, first popularized by Alvin Toffler in his book of the same name. Future shock is that point in time when people no longer can assimilate change without displaying dysfunctional behavior. Future shock often occurs because of the aggregate impact of several changes. Figure 7.1 illustrates some different kinds of change and how they can force people over the threshold. Notice that there are micro, organizational, and macro changes. The micro, or personal, changes have more impact; macro changes, albeit important, have the least impact.

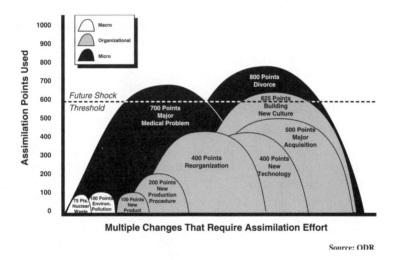

Figure 7.1. The aggregate impact of several changes on a person.

The High Costs of Failure

Among the chief causes of organizational change are events such as incorporating new computer systems as an integral part of business and production strategies, and adapting to fluctuations in the economy by rightsizing. These types of changes usually are considered strategic or major tactical changes. Because they are so critical (and visible), there can be some especially high costs and risks if the changes are not accepted and assimilated properly. They must be planned for.

Money, time, and people resources; the job security of those involved in or affected by the information systems rightsizing project; and the confidence the organization has in its senior leader, its mission, and its strategic directives all are risk factors. Hence, when planning a new system, it is absolutely critical that the impact of failing to implement changes recommended from reengineering be well quantified and that contingencies be determined before moving ahead with this radical change. Only when the objectives and potential impact of changes are well understood and documented should the process of implementing the changes—and the new system—begin.

Guidelines for Change

Because change is a process and not an event, there are certain markers you can use to guide the process as it relates to a rightsizing project, some of which are discussed in the following paragraphs.

Positive Response to Change Takes Time

Figure 7.2 shows stages in the progression of individual "buy in" to change. Early in a project, there is a certain level of uninformed optimism. Depending on the circumstances, however, not much time needs to pass before an informed pessimism sets in. It is during this phase that pessimism reaches its highest levels with individuals, and it is when they are most likely to "check out."

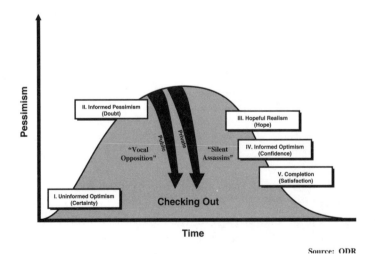

Source: ODR

Figure 7.2. *Life cycle of positive response to change.*

Checking out of the change process is essentially the public or private decision by a person to completely resist the change. Checking out publicly—doing so in a way that people become aware of it—is better than doing so privately because, if you can change the person's mind, you can turn the defection into an advantage. Private checking out is much more dangerous because it means that people are outwardly going along with the change, but are silently resisting—and perhaps even working against—the change.

When you get beyond this point, however, you arrive at hopeful realism, soon followed by informed optimism—in other words, confidence that the new system will work. The final stage, hopefully, is satisfaction with the results of a new production system in place, successfully meeting its objectives. Recognizing that it takes time for people to move through all of these stages of change is important to survival through them.

Anticipate and Tolerate the Transition State

During the transition between old and new systems, some temporary instability emerges. High emotional stress, high—often undirected—energy, battles for control (which can become a major issue during any transition), and increased conflict typically becomes apparent.

Remember that problems will occur during this period of transition. Expect them, plan for them, and seek allies when you have to. External consultants who are experienced in reengineering can be extremely valuable in helping you anticipate mistakes and respond to the expected reactions, while at the same time fulfilling the role of an objective "honest broker" of change.

Think Globally, Act Locally

Don't underestimate the power of positive change that comes from providing individuals with the means to rise up and face the new challenges they are called to meet. For example, treat geographically dispersed resources as though they were centralized. Information should enter the system once—at the source. Have those who use the output of the process perform the process and put the decision point where the work is performed. Build individual control into the new processes.

Recognize that economy of scale and service response need not be constrained by information systems design or existing information systems. On the contrary, information processing should be integrated into the real work that produces the information.

Recognize Roles and Involve Those Affected

Make sure you recognize the roles in the change process. These roles include the sponsor, agent, and target. The sponsor is the individual or group who legitimizes the change. The agent is the individual or group responsible for implementing the change. The target is the individual or group who must actually change. A more thorough discussion of group dynamics among those in these different roles is beyond the scope of this section. Suffice it to say that changes in information systems have their best chance of succeeding if they are championed down through each key level of personnel via an expanding tree of sponsorship (see Figure 7.3).

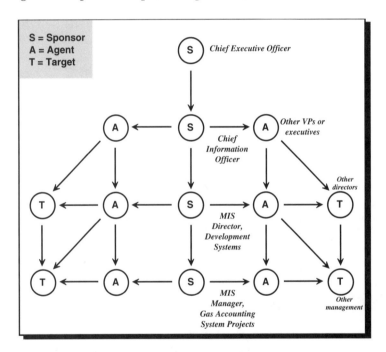

Figure 7.3. Positive change through sponsorship.

When it comes to system development, MIS traditionally has been a change agent, whereas line management and staff have been the change target. It is often the case with rightsizing information systems, however, that these roles are reversed. The line management is the advocate and agent of change, whereas the MIS organization is the target—typically resisting the perceived radical changes brought on by rightsizing.

Understand and Respect the Frame of Reference of Targets

It is important to treat target users as if they're experiencing the death of a close associate. They are! Usually, for better or for worse, the only system they have identified with, relied on, or mastered is being taken away from them. To get them to better accept the new systems, you must show users your sensitivity to their information systems needs, wants, and habits.

The energies of users on a rightsizing project can be harnessed, like that of parents and friends anticipating the birth of a new family member—they'll prepare tirelessly for the new arrival. If people have a personal stake in the process, they are much more likely to support it and advocate that others get involved as well.

Finally, don't underestimate corporate culture. Corporate culture plays a strong role in affecting and managing change. You should recognize that changes perceived as being out of character with the corporate culture cause more disruption and stress.

Communicate, Communicate, Communicate

To borrow from the real estate brokers' maxim, the three most important things to remember about managing the process of change through your rightsizing project are to communicate, communicate, and communicate. Successful change is best ensured by establishing and maintaining communications through the series of cascading sponsorship shown in Figure 7.3. Have meetings, write memos, or even start a monthly newsletter about the project. Keep everyone informed in any way you can think of. You want to foster a cascading, direct line of active sponsorship and increasing knowledge through all groups affected by a rightsizing project; otherwise, it is all too likely to fail to achieve its ultimate success.

Build In Resilience

The single most important factor necessary to increase an organization's ability to accept change is the degree to which people are *resilient*. Resilience is the ability to absorb high levels of disruptive change while displaying minimal dysfunctional behavior. Although resilient people face no less of a challenge than others when they engage change, more often than not they

- Regain their equilibrium faster
- Maintain a higher level of productivity

- Are physically and emotionally healthier
- Achieve more of their objectives than people who experience future shock
- Tend to rebound from the demands of change even stronger than before

How do you know whether your people are resilient? Some of the characteristics of resilient people include the following:

- Positive

  Strong self-esteem

  See change as opportunity
- Focused

  Mission-oriented/directed

  Goal-oriented—Have a course
- Flexible

  Tenacious

  Creative
- Organized

  Can define order in chaos

  See structure in ambiguity
- Proactive

  Engage, not run away from, change

  Selective

Given these characteristics, there are some steps you can take to improve the resilience of your organization. First, you can hire, train, and reward resilient people. Second, you can teach people patterns of change (for example, informed pessimism). Both of these steps generally assume that there is some level of predisposition to change. The next two steps do not. The first involves making tough choices; implementing business imperatives; prioritizing and even taking some things "off the plate" of your people. Second, implement change with discipline. This means follow and don't waver from practicing the processes you've implemented in your organization to effect change, such as communications mechanisms.

What Is Success?

Put simply, the definition of successful change is achieving stated human and technical objectives of change on time and within budget. The bottom line is that MIS executives often underestimate the complexity of human relations and their reactions to change in organizations. They fail to realize that feelings, politics, and resistance can torpedo the finest process design. By following some of the guidelines presented here, you have a much better chance at success in a major applications rightsizing project.

Rules for
Rightsizing
Success

8

Rules for Rightsizing Success

Success is counted sweetest
By those who ne'er succeed.
To comprehend a nectar
Requires sorest need.

—Emily Dickinson

Objectives:

1. To help you learn four basic rules for managing your rightsizing project.
2. To provide you with some guidelines for success on the technical side of implementing the project.

Most success stories are the result of good *management*. From observation, some fundamental rules of rightsizing project management have emerged. They are these:

1. Secure top management support for the rightsizing project.
2. Reorganize, refocus, distribute, and rightsize the IS department.
3. Staff the rightsizing team carefully—include both PC and mainframe people.
4. Use outside help and education including conferences, consultants, and integrators.

Some common technical rules seen in successful implementations include:

5. Modularize applications to machines.
6. Use extra hardware for help in solving problems.
7. Limit the diversity of the installed base.

This chapter explores these seven rules in depth.

Top Management Support

One of the most important issues involved in rightsizing is the need to secure the cooperation of both your technical and management staff. As Howard Fosdick of Fosdick Consulting stated at the February 1993 Rightsizing Expo in Chicago, "What we're really doing is rightsizing the IS culture. This is a management issue, not a technical issue."

Gaining top-management support, where "top" is defined as company president (outside the realm of IS), should be no problem. After all, what top executive is going to reject a plan that promises budgetary savings in addition to a data-processing movement toward commodity and away from cult status?

Gaining top-management support where "top" is defined as CIO or Vice President, Information Systems may be another matter. Because rightsizing implies possible (and probable) staff reductions and reduced IS department budgets, we shouldn't be surprised to expect resistance from this segment.

The front-page cover story in the February 17, 1992, *Computerworld* was about the issue of IS resistance to rightsizing. The article raised the point that *CIOs are losing their jobs* as companies rightsize and distribute processing. More recently, the March 1, 1993, *Information Week* cover story discussed this same issue:

> *"As companies re-engineer, rightsize, and shift IS decision making to departments and business units, many CIOs and other high-ranking IS executives find they've outlived their usefulness...as client/server networks decentralize processing even further and companies lean toward departmentalized IS structures...the CIO position may soon be obsolete."*

In fact, many of the prime movers and motivators behind rightsizing projects have moved on to new jobs at different firms after the rightsizing was successfully completed. The kind of person who has the talent to successfully implement the changes implied by rightsizing may not be interested in sticking around and running the new environment.

Rightsizing doesn't affect just the CIO. It clearly changes the skill set and procedures of most IS employees. Consider the following impacts:

> *Data Center Staff*—These employees are no longer needed as the care and feeding of mainframe consoles, disk drives, and tapes disappear. Larger shops may still operate a server room with air conditioning and fire protection, but it's likely to be manned by a much smaller staff than a mainframe glass house. One new job required is that of LAN administrator; depending on the skill set of your operations staff, some of these people may be appropriate for the job.

> *Programmer*—In the late 1980s, as leading-edge companies rightsized, there emerged a problem in retaining experienced staff. A typical mainframe programmer's salary was $45,000; someone with comparable skills and more productivity on the PC could be hired for closer to $30,000. Many mainframe programmers faced with this reality decided that their fortunes were better served in another company where they could continue to do mainframe applications. High turnover was commonplace in these situations. In some cases, IS staff turnover reached 100 percent!

Many people with mainframe skills such as COBOL, CICS, and DB2 are finding themselves almost unemployable (see Figure 8.1). As a recruiter commented in the August 24, 1992, issue of *Computerworld*, "These guys with just plain COBOL/CICS skills are dead in the water…the mainframe guys are becoming dinosaurs. We have not placed one of these guys in a year." Programmers who are to be retained need a new skill set that includes GUIs, client/server computing, object orientation, and SQL. For many programmers, the nature of their job will change from one of original development to one of component assembly and debugging. Some programmers will now develop client systems and, therefore, should be located in user departments. Others will work on the network or database and should be located within the central IS unit.

Figure 8.1. *Those with mainframe skills need to leap into the '90s.*

Computer user's lives are seriously affected by a move to rightsizing technologies. For one thing, they must become more closely involved in their department systems development process. Many of the people doing the development work should now be located in end-user departments for closer contact with the consumers of the developed product. In addition, prototyping with GUIs is becoming a more critical and common development technique: this involves users. Finally, user management may now be managing a portion of what was previously controlled by the IS department.

Reorganize, Distribute, Refocus, and Rightsize the IS Department

The nature of an organization is likely to change substantially as distributed, network-based computing takes hold. Changes will occur in the business units using new systems as well as in the IS department that is developing (at least partially) the new environment. The concept of business-process reengineering concerns what happens in the business units as new communications and computer systems take hold. Typically, the end result is an organization that has fewer management layers in the organization hierarchy. Walter Wriston, former chairman of CitiCorp, wrote in his 1992 book *The Twilight of Sovereignty*, "The middle managers who used to convey information and the upper managers who 'owned' it and held power thereby are losing that power and in some cases their jobs. Information systems flatten the management hierarchy. They change the very meaning of management and the skills needed to do it well."

Data processing techniques are now coming full circle and changing the culture, organization, and approaches used by IS professionals. Over time, the size of the typical corporate IS department will shrink as users become more intimately involved with computer-based systems. In addition, the focus of the IS department has to change away from applications and towards networks and databases. In other words, the successful data-processing department of the future will focus on databases, connectivity, and standards. The development of much client-side work will be left to the consumers of these new systems.

In the past, the IS professional was concerned with the mainframe. That concern is now replaced by the management of shared data and networks. Previously, the typical user department was concerned with a dedicated mini-computer that ran the department applications. Now the user department is dealing with a series of applications that run on the client workstations and are, in turn, supported by data accessed locally over a LAN server or remotely through wide area networks, distributed databases, information warehouses, or other appropriate technologies.

Staff Carefully—Include Both PC and Mainframe People on Your Team

A rightsized system often includes important elements from both mainframe and PC technologies. Word processing is not rightsizing. Word processing has always made more sense on a PC, stand-alone or networked. *Rightsizing means the use of networked workstation and PC technology to build enterprise-oriented, transaction-processing applications.* Such applications must be supported by robust systems. Robust means that data integrity and security are built-in features. A robust system has recovery techniques to ensure that no transactions are lost or half completed; transactions are to be either fully completed or all interim changes should be backed out.

The essence of mainframe systems has been robustness. PC systems have focused more on usability and immediate responsiveness. With Windows and Macintosh GUIs now predominating, PC systems provide ease of learning and adaptability as the user interface remains similar across applications.

In many shops, there has been a great wall separating the PC support staff and the mainframe systems people. However, successful rightsizing requires skill sets from both camps. The mainframe group can bring expertise in large scale systems and project management; they understand the requirements for applications that must support large numbers of people or must operate in a 7 X 24 mode. PC people bring experience with GUIs, DOS, Windows, NetWare, and the like.

Those organizations that build development teams out of both groups will do a better job of rightsizing. It is important to make sure that you have communications between your PC and mainframe people. Even something as obvious as staggered, mixed offices between the two groups can help.

Use Outside Help, Including Conferences, Consultants, and Integrators

It should be obvious that a move to any new technology requires some major investments in learning and training. Yet, this is something frequently underestimated, even by the most experienced people.

Much of the technology in this field changes so rapidly that it should all be considered current events. Conferences and industry literature are a good way to keep current, and it's essential to keep current if your rightsizing investment is to return its due.

Probably the most frequent "morning after" comment about rightsizing projects is that consultants or systems integrators should have been used more frequently than they were. We are dealing with new technologies, and bringing in knowledgeable advice is usually cheaper in time and money than trial-and-error discovery approaches. When you identify the technologically tough areas, line up consultants who can help when they are needed.

Modularize Applications to Machines and Throw Extra Hardware at the Problem

One of the best things about rightsizing is that hardware is cheap. You should not hesitate to use or even squander it if it provides any benefit.

There are many ways that extra hardware can help:

- One of the problems with NetWare is that no protection is provided between various NLMs (NetWare Loadable Modules—applications running under the control of the server) in the same machine. One method of obtaining application protection in this environment is to use a different machine for each major NLM application. For example, a database server such as Sybase, Gupta, or Oracle should always run on its own machine (with no other significant live applications running).

- If extra machines and machine parts are kept stocked, trained user personnel can substitute working parts (or machines) for the down hardware. This will lower your requirement for on-site, emergency maintenance support. Slow turnaround maintenance is far less expensive.

- If your database response is slow, buying additional servers to split up the database, obtaining a faster server, or purchasing additional network cards are all easy, relatively inexpensive, and fast solutions.

- Adding more client terminals so there is never a wait for service goes a long way towards improving the image of a system.

Limit the Diversity of Your Installed Base

One of the nice things about the rightsized world is that "open systems" rule. There are plenty of technologically based answers for almost any data-processing problem. For those "answers" to be successful, they have to interoperate with established industry (market) standards. (The Macintosh, Windows, DOS, MVS, NetWare, and UNIX all are examples of market standards.) In other words, these products are so successful that independent developers have added functionality and designed products for these architectures. Having such a wide choice of products is one of the best things about the networked, rightsized world.

An important point here is that it's nice to have this choice at selection time. One shouldn't, however, expect a reliable, robust environment if too many of these alternatives are selected and then, in turn, supported in a live production system.

We are now starting to see some cases in which severe maintenance problems are caused by a lack of attention to implementation standards during the fielding of a system. Variations in operating system release levels, interrupt controls, slot availability, add-in boards, disk drives, video displays, and the like can cause network or compatibility problems.

A wide variety of both software and hardware is good at selection time. At implementation time, however, is best if you have limited the number of different system components and vendors.

Assembling the Team for Client/Server Applications Development

To know all things is not permitted

—Horace

Objectives:

1. To help you understand the skills needed to implement client/server applications systems.
2. To help you understand that client/server applications development is a team process, because different team members contribute different skills.
3. To help you define the benefits of an appropriately designed client/server applications-development training program.
4. To help you assess the skill level of existing staff and determine which skills must be supplemented in order to ensure a successful implementation in the client/server applications environment.
5. To help you begin the training-needs assessment process.

One of the serious barriers to fulfilling the promise of client/server networked computing is the lack of people with the skills needed to design, develop, maintain, and operate applications in this environment. In a 1993 report "Closing the Skills Gap" by Forrester Research, 70 percent of the sample of senior IS executives from Fortune 1000 companies said their applications development plans are limited by the capabilities of their staff. Earlier chapters discussed the technical and organizational risks associated with rightsizing. The biggest risks, however, may arise from

■ Ignorance. Existing mainframe MIS personnel undertake network application projects with undue confidence—they don't recognize what they don't know.

■ Undue optimism. Management underestimates the learning period associated with the new technology and raises expectations that cannot be fulfilled.

You can reduce these risks. To do so, you must understand what skills are needed, who needs to have those skills, how to find out whether you already have those skills on your staff, and what steps to take if you don't.

One of the first steps is to understand that development in this environment is a team process. Only a handful of individuals have all the skills needed to address such diverse issues as data analysis, high-level application program interfaces, SQL, gateways, graphical interfaces, object-oriented programming (OOP), office-productivity products, stored procedures, and more. Developing all these skills in one person is a prohibitively long and expensive process. You therefore apportion skill requirements among team members, ensure good team communications, and use a solid methodology so that team members with the right skills are involved at the right points in the development cycle.

Defining the Team

The team consists of a core group—a client/server-application developer, an application architect, and a project manager—who usually are assigned full-time to the project. Their work is coordinated with that of the database administrator, the distributed database administrator, the connectivity (enterprise-wide network) architect, the LAN engineer, and the MIS director, who provide assistance at different points throughout the project. The workgroup manager typically becomes involved as the project is readied for production status. A possible team organization is shown in the chart in Figure 9.1. The roles and responsibilities of each team member are discussed after the figure.

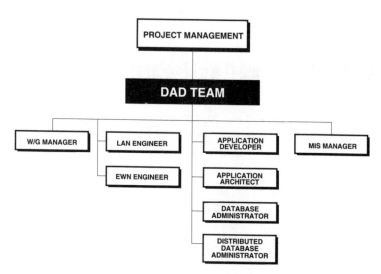

Figure 9.1. *The distributed-application development (DAD) team.*

Distributed-Application Developer

The *distributed-application developer* is responsible for the core effort of the development process. He or she must participate in JAD sessions, conduct follow-up interviews with users, perform data analysis, develop prototypes, write and test programs, and often assume responsibility for systems conversions and user procedures.

Distributed-Application Architect

The *distributed-application architect* is responsible for the "look and feel" of the system. He or she determines the project standards, often establishes means and methods of program-to-program communication, creates the test environment, tunes program performance, and implements security.

LAN Engineer

The *LAN engineer* is responsible for installing the local-area network (LAN) environment, monitoring and troubleshooting LAN operations, and tuning LAN performance.

Enterprise-Wide Networking (EWN) Engineer

The *enterprise-wide networking (EWN) engineer* is responsible for EWN aspects of the application including data communications, interoperability technology, and gateways. (This team member is optional if the development project has only local communications and no interoperability considerations.)

Database Administrator

The *database administrator (DBA)* is responsible for validating the data analysis (and sometimes participates in the data-analysis process), installing the database management system, implementing the physical database on the database management system, tuning database performance, and implementing data validation and integrity procedures. This role may be assumed by an application developer on projects of limited scope.

Distributed Database Administrator (DDBA)

Managing a distributed database is significantly more complicated than running a monolithic single-location database. The *distributed database administrator* has all of the design and implementation issues of a single location, *plus* the added complexity of distribution, network latency, time shifts, and remote administration. The following are examples of work the DDBA must perform:

- Designing and planning the distributed DBMS or replication system, including how and when data is to be shared amongst users. It's only after this work has been done that the local DBA can input the necessary information to set up the replication system.
- Coordinating the installation and system configuration at the various sites where the data will be located.
- Monitoring the operation, performance, and recovery of the system from an enterprise, rather than a local, perspective.

This team member will be needed only when data will be distributed or replicated.

Project Manager

The *project manager* is responsible for supervising the project team, planning and assigning work, and ensuring quality. Depending on the application project, the project manager may perform one or more of the other team functions.

MIS Manager

The *MIS manager* is responsible for controlling and setting the direction of the team and ensuring the validity of the technical and application direction.

Workgroup Manager

Finally, the *workgroup manager* is responsible for front-line help to the user community regarding workstations, network operations, common office applications such as spreadsheets and word processors, and operations of the business application. Although this role is not currently recognized by many companies, experience has shown it to be critical to achieving real user-productivity gains.

Development Team Skills

This chapter has identified the process of client/server migration, the general skill requirements in the process, and the members of the development team and their respective roles. You now will learn about the specific skills each member needs in order to perform his or her role effectively. For example, a partial skill set for an application developer includes

- An excellent working knowledge of relational data design, front-end development tools, procedural languages and report writers, user-interface design, program and system testing, and the development cycle
- A conceptual understanding of networks, mainframe connectivity, and data communications

Figure 9.2 is a skills-assessment matrix for the development team. When you use the matrix for your environment, substitute specific product names that reflect your technical platform. For example, if you have selected Powersoft's PowerBuilder as your front-end development tool and SQL Server as the relational database management system, substitute "PowerBuilder" for "Front End" under *Development Tools* and "SQL/Transact SQL" for "SQL" under *Relational Database Management System*. Other skill areas, such as relational data design and user-interface design, are platform-independent. The network platform is discussed in Chapter 12, "The Network Platform."

The skills assessment matrix is designed to help you identify the skill levels needed by team role, and then compare this with the skill levels of your staff. There are four skill levels:

- *Conceptual level*. Has good understanding of the operational theory involved.
- *Works under supervision*. Can perform effectively if good supervision and additional subject expertise are available.
- *Works independently with the technology*. Can be an effective resource for others and provide technical supervision.
- True expert- or instructor-level mastery of the topic.

The next step after tailoring the assessment matrix to reflect your platform is to develop some objective performance criteria associated with each skill level for the skill of relational data design (for example, see Figure 9.3). Once performance criteria are established, you then ask staff members to assess themselves individually with regard to the skills matrix, and you perform an independent assessment of their skills. Then compare the two assessments. Areas in which your assessments differ need discussion and resolution. (A consultant may be helpful in this area also.)

	MIS Manager	Distributed Applications Developer	Project Manager	Database Administrator	Applications Architect	LAN Engineer	EWN Engineer	Workgroup Manager	Network User	Your Current Skill Level
PC Operating System	2	3	3	2	4	4	4	3	1	
EWN/WAN										
Data Communications	1	1	1	1	2	2	4	1		
Bridges and Routers	1	1	1	1	1	3	4			
TCP/IP	1	1	1	1	2	2	4	1		
LAN Protocols/Access Schemes	1	1	1	1	1	3	4	1		
OSI Model	1	1	1	1	2	3	4	1		
Mainframe Connectivity	1	1	2	2	3	2	4			
DEVELOPMENT PROCESS										
Development Cycle	4	3	4	3	4	2	2	2	1	
CASE Tools	2	3	3	3	4	1	2	1		
User Interface Design	1	3	3	1	4	1	1	1	1	
Relational Data Analysis	2	3	3	4	3	1	1	1		
Object Oriented Design	1	1	2	3	3					
Testing	3	3	4	3	4	1	1	1		
User Procedures Development	2	3	3	2	2	1	1	1		
NETWORKS										
Operations	1	1	1	1	1	4	4	3	1	
Installation	1	1	1	1	1	4	4	2		
Design	1	1	1	1	2	3	4	1		
DEVELOPMENT TOOLS										
Front End	2	3	3	1	4	1	1	1		
Report Writers	1	3	3	2	4	1	1	2	1	
Data Analysis	3	3	3	4	3	1	1	1		
Procedural Languages	2	3	3	2	4	1	1	1		
Object Oriented Languages	2	2	2	1	3	1	1	1		
RELATIONAL DATABASE MANAGEMENT SYSTEM										
SQL	2	3	3	4	4	1	1	1		
Database Administration	1	1	2	4	2	1	1	1		
Tuning	1	1	1	4	1	1	1			
COMMUNICATIONS										
Oral Presentations	4	3	3	2	3	2	2	3	*	
Persuasive Writing	4	3	3	2	3	2	2	2	*	
Business Case Development	4	2	3	2	2	1	1	1	*	
Interviewing	3	3	3	2	2	2	2	3	*	
PERSONAL PRODUCTIVITY TOOLS										
Word Processing	3	3	3	3	3	3	2	4	*	
Spreadsheet	3	3	3	3	3	3	2	4	*	
Personal Information Manager	3	3	3	3	3	3	2	4	*	
DEVELOPMENT MANAGEMENT										
Effective Supervision	4	3	3	3	2	2	3	1		
Project Administration	4	2	3	3	2	3	3	2		
Project Planning	4	2	3	3	3	2	3	1		
Technical Architecture Direction	3	2		3	4	2	3	1		
OPERATIONS MANAGEMENT										
Backup/Security	3	2	2	3	4	3	3	2	1	
Version Control	3	3	3	1	3	2	3	1	1	
User Training	3	3	3	1	2	2	3	3		

Figure 9.2. A skills-assessment matrix.

To demonstrate conceptual mastery of this skill, the participant should:

- Be able to define: *Entity*, *Attribute*, and *Relationship*.

- Define and give examples of 1:1, 1:Many, and Many:Many relationships

- Resolve a Many:Many relationship and create the correct resulting data entities.

- Describe the relationship between an entity and a table.

- Define the terms *primary key* and *foreign key*.

To demonstrate the ability to work under supervision with this skill, the participant should:

- Have participated in three or more user interviews and drawn the resulting entity/relationship diagrams.

- Be able to define the terms: *dependent entity*, *time-sensitive relationship*, *derivative data*, and *recursive relationships*.

- Have diagrammed a moderately complex data model: at least 15 data entities.

- Explain the significance of "No duplicates," "No nulls."

- Define the seven rules associated with primary keys.

- Provide at least two situations where system assignment of the primary key would be appropriate and two situations where user assignment would be appropriate.

- Explain the relationship between relational data design and SQL.

To demonstrate independent working knowledge/technical mastery of this skill, the participant should have:

- Participated in the data analysis phase of three or more projects; with a minimum assigned time of four months.

- Demonstrated mastery of the data analysis process through reviews with the database administration staff.

- Completed a project where he/she had data analysis responsibilities (so as to see the results of the final data model).

- Correctly create a data model requiring effective data entities.

Figure 9.3. A sample performance criteria: relational data design.

In a process independent of the skills assessment, you should estimate the staffing requirements for the project (that is, "need five developers, and one architect, and one project manager," and so on). After you've completed this process, you normally will determine that you have some skills deficits. To assemble your team, your options are to upgrade existing staff, hire new staff, or contract with another firm. Often, the step taken is a combination of all three options. Even if outside integrators and consultants are used, however—and you are fortunate enough to hire new staff that have *both* the downsizing technology skills *and* knowledge of your business applications—ultimately you still must find or develop an approach to training your existing staff in the new environment.

Distributed-Applications Development Training

Any approach to client/server-applications development training must recognize the team approach already discussed in this chapter. The training program must recognize that there will be different roles, for example, developers, architects, and so on.

Second, training must coordinate with work assignments. "Just-in-time training" is more than a cliché. To get the most return from the training investment, team members finishing a course must be able to return to the job site with immediately usable skills in the tool sets (development languages and other design and programming products) available in their organization. Delays in starting the project or acquiring development tools prevent team members from being as effective as they can be.

Third, training must be both measurable and measured. This includes independent, objective testing of the participants and reviews by company personnel to measure effectiveness.

Finally, training must be intensive and accomplished in as short a time as possible. It is simply too expensive to let the training period extend over several months. In a matter of weeks or days, the team members must have intense exposure to the concepts and products with which they will be working. This doesn't mean that all the needed training courses should be taken in immediate succession. Rather than stay in continuous "training mode," participants could move directly from each training class to a project role, and back for additional training as their project progresses.

Figures 9.4 and 9.5 are sample curricula developed for the distributed-applications developer and architect. Note that there are certain core courses, which are assumed to be platform-independent. These courses are mixed with specific product courses that reflect the technologies being used by the organization.

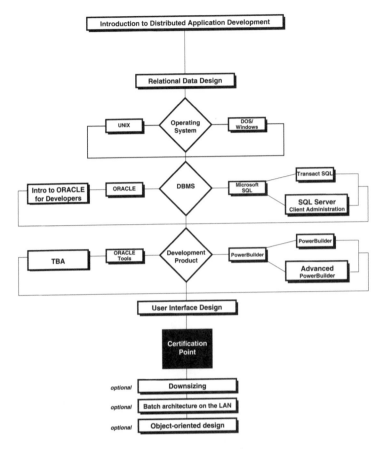

Figure 9.4. A sample distributed-applications developer curriculum.

Sources of Training

Training is normally provided by one (or more) of three sources: internal training departments, software and hardware vendors, and independent training organizations. Internal training organizations often are excellent sources of training in courses that are repetitive in nature, or courses in which the instructor can develop subject mastery in a relatively brief period. For example, courses in supervisory skills or Excel spreadsheets are often available internally.

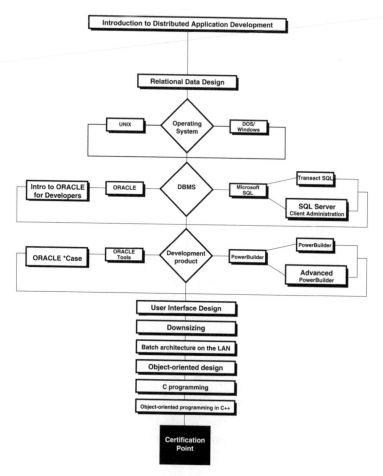

Figure 9.5. A sample distributed-applications architect curriculum.

Hardware and software vendors normally offer training in the specific technologies associated with their products. This training is offered through two different channels:

- Directly from the vendor
- From training organizations authorized by the vendor

For example, Novell training is provided almost exclusively by training organizations authorized and certified by Novell. Microsoft offers training both at its sites throughout the United States and at authorized network training centers. Oracle trains almost exclusively in its own centers. You can get information about vendor-sponsored or authorized training by calling vendors directly and requesting information about their offerings.

If you need training on a specific product, you generally want to be sure that the training vendor is authorized or certified by the product vendor. When the product vendor authorizes the trainer, it normally maintains a quality-control interest in the training provided, ensures the trainer has the latest product change and upgrade information, and makes certain the training vendor is using the correct version of the software and hardware.

Independent training organizations can offer training in specific product technologies (such as in the use of Visual Basic), interoperability issues (such as how to make Windows and NetWare work together), and platform-independent skills (such as relational data analysis). Independent training organizations may offer curriculum-planning and skills-assessment services. They should be willing to work with your organization to help develop the objective performance measures you need in order to assess skills and develop a tailored training plan for your organization.

Costs of Training

Training from product vendors and independent training organizations currently costs between $275 and $400 per participant per day. Most offer training at your site for six or more students, which lowers the per-day cost for each student. Depending on the team role and experience of the team members, the total training requirement for a person varies from just a few days to more than 40 days.

For purposes of estimating your transition to this environment, you can use $4,000 to $7,000 per person for individuals such as workgroup managers and LAN engineers, and $9,000 to $14,000 per person for client/server-applications developers and architects. These costs are incurred either directly (as training dollars) or indirectly (as project lost time, missed deadlines, network downtime, and so on). Usually, costs are much higher when they are incurred indirectly. These costs are real and must be factored in to the calculations used to analyze the economics of downsizing.

Benefits of Training

In a 1990 survey of Fortune 500 companies, the cost of a single hour of network downtime averaged $34,000—and this survey was taken before most of the participants had placed any mission-critical applications on the LAN. Recently, a Houston energy company undertook a rightsizing project as a cost-saving move. Every day that it remained on a mainframe system cost them $9,600 more than operating on a LAN. A delay of only one month in project completion could cost that company $288,000.

Although quantification of benefits is elusive, the risks of inadequate training are clear: excessive downtime, project delays, and applications that fail to work because of platform incompatibility or performance issues.

Priorities for New-Breed Developers

After the team is assembled and trained, the company is at the point at which it is just then ready to begin rightsizing. In the meantime, however, as the team has been assembled, the simple fact is that the technology will continue to change unabated.

Developers can take steps to keep current and survive in this environment. First, they must adopt a modular, reusable, function-specific approach to code implementation. Tools that help to do this are discussed in Chapter 15, "The Rightsizing Development Environment."

Second, developers must evaluate new tools on the job and incorporate them when appropriate. Even though a specific tool-selection step is included in the downsizing methodology, constant review of new tools is necessary to keep abreast of the best options available.

Third, developers should be encouraged to choose tools from reliable vendors that have a likelihood of surviving over the longer term. Simply because a standard was developed more than a few years ago does not mean that it's an option for today. For example, an advantage of COBOL is that it has demonstrated remarkable staying power. Compared to a language such as C++ or SmallTalk, however, COBOL is not well designed to handle the development requirements of most GUI-oriented applications today.

Fourth, developers and their management should make a commitment to self-development: subscriptions to technical journals, time for skills upgrades, attendance at user-group meetings, and technical presentations at department meetings.

Last, management and the development staff must realize that training and retooling are ongoing processes.

PART III

Design

Part II discussed the key steps in the planning phase of rightsizing methodology. Part III describes the key steps in the next phase of the rightsizing methodology—design, as shown in Figure III.1.

In the design phase, the assumption is that the overall objectives of the system to be developed have been identified, the company has verified that it can afford (or can't afford not to have) the system, and the company has identified and assembled the team of professionals that will be involved in the systems development activity.

If these assumptions are correct, the first step in the design phase is determining the application's inputs, outputs, and primary functions. This step is best conducted in a SWAT-team-like manner called *joint application design* (JAD), which is discussed in detail in Chapter 10, "Joint Application Design (JAD)."

In this step, you develop the initial concept for the major components of the system. Later, when implementation begins, a series of iterative, detailed design activities occurs, at the same time that program development is occurring. This parallel activity is represented by the overlap of the design and implementation steps. The overall goal is for the design activity always to stay one step ahead of the programming activity.

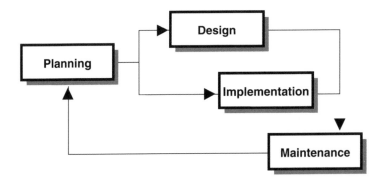

Figure III.1. Rightsizing development methodology.

When the initial SWAT-style design session is completed, several important selection activities must occur. First, a technical architecture for the system must be selected. (An explanation of architecture, the criteria for selection, and choices available are discussed in Chapter 11, "Architecture.") Next, the network platform for the rightsized information system must be determined. (This selection process and related issues are discussed in Chapter 12, "The Network Platform.") The development environment, which primarily means tools, also must be selected. (This selection process is discussed in Chapter 15, "The Rightsizing Development Environment.")

During each of these detailed steps, you should focus on particular elements to make the best selection for the system. As Figure III.2 shows, these elements influence each of the steps as the steps are feeding each other. As you proceed further in selecting the sum of architecture, platform, and tools, feedback occurs that may influence previous choices, either by verifying them or by concluding that a better choice exists.

Because of these selection activities, the design portion of the rightsizing methodology is the first stage in which products are handled, evaluated, and installed. Because personal preferences, both likes and dislikes, come out at this stage, it is more important in this step than at any other time to understand and verify the strengths and weaknesses of the various products and technologies chosen. Even though the design process traditionally has taken about 20 percent of the overall systems development effort (as shown in Figure III.3), it weighs heavily on the end results.

Detailed Downsizing Task   *Focus Elements*

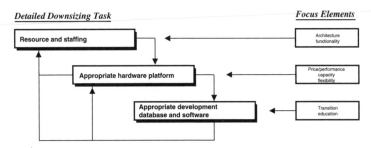

Figure III.2. *The focus elements that drive rightsizing methodology tasks.*

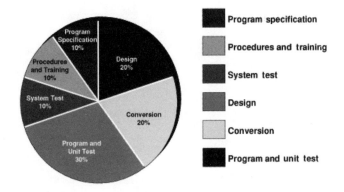

Figure III.3. *Relative development costs by phase.*

Joint Application Design (JAD)

Joint Application Design (JAD)

10

There can be no economy where there is no efficiency.

—Benjamin Disraeli
(1868)

Objectives:

1. To help you understand the advantages of joint application design (JAD) and similar design approaches for rapid development of systems and maximum user participation.
2. To teach you the history of JAD.
3. To help you learn who the main JAD participants are and how to run a JAD session.
4. To help you understand the JAD deliverables, especially the inputs and outputs and design approach.

After the decision to rightsize has been made, JAD will help you design your rightsized system in the quickest and most cost-effective manner. Developed in 1977 by IBM as a method to design software, JAD and modified versions of it have blossomed into the preferred method of development for software, systems, database design, cost estimation, and many other types of projects. Although JAD is certainly not the only method of rightsizing design, it and similar approaches fit the rapid-development philosophy of rightsizing projects like a glove.

JAD enthusiasts say that using this method improves development productivity by as much as 60 percent. That translates into direct cost savings. The traditional design method—interviewing—takes significantly longer; preparing for interviews, conducting them, documenting results, and combining them into a homogeneous set of requirements easily could occupy a number of analysts full-time for several weeks. JAD was designed to shorten the requirements analysis phase by weeks and, consequently, to reduce the cost of analysis personnel. You save not only the cost of design time by using JAD, but also the costs associated with redesigning and modifying a system that does not meet your established requirements.

Although JAD requires a substantial amount of time from a group of your employees at the onset of the development process, this time commitment is minimal compared to what would be required for redesign and modification. In addition, the group development and consensus atmosphere of JAD enables you to fully utilize one of your most important resources, your people.

What Is JAD?

JAD (joint application design) is a design method that uses a high degree of organization coupled with group dynamics to produce a system designed and accepted by a group of designated individuals consisting of users and MIS professionals. The users are the most important members of the JAD team. This group of highly competent people gathers for a two- to five-day workshop to discuss, conceptualize, and analyze. They design the system themselves, based on their everyday needs and their knowledge of how the company's business functions operate.

Using traditional systems development methods, MIS professionals—often outside consultants—interview users individually and then determine the overall system requirements by consolidating the interview results. This process allows for a large margin of error because

- Different users communicate their needs in different ways.
- The MIS professionals may not resolve conflicts to the users' satisfaction.

In some cases, because of miscommunication, the people developing the system do not have a clear idea of what the users require, which results in a final product that creates user dissatisfaction, contains bugs, requires modification or constant maintenance, or is never used.

Anyone who has asked technical people and nontechnical people to describe the same process knows that they may even use the same terms, but that those terms have different meanings. JAD alleviates this fundamental communication problem between users and technical professionals who do not speak the same language in defining system requirements. During a JAD session, users and MIS professionals work together to achieve a common understanding of system requirements and, with the help of visual aids, ensure that the end product is exactly what the users need.

Why JAD Is Successful

Because the JAD environment encourages teamwork and cooperation, users and MIS professionals communicate more effectively, and everyone feels committed to the success of the system they helped design. JAD fosters consensus and acceptance of the project early in the development cycle.

JAD builds on systems-development techniques from the early 1980s—group interviews, prototypes, and user-friendly documentation—and allows users a larger role in the development process. Because of the recent proliferation of computer equipment in the business world, computer-literate users understand the strategic importance of information systems and are aware of the technology available to them. They are more prepared than users of 15 years ago to design a system that meets their requirements.

JAD design procedures are predicated more on the participation of users than are traditional interview methods. JAD methodology emphasizes the role of the user and allows for the inclusion of design aids to ensure a consensus between users and MIS professionals. Visual presentation devices, such as overhead projectors, slide projectors, video projectors, magnetic boards, and flip charts, can display screen elements or other visual aspects of the system so that everyone can see and agree on the design.

In addition, the highly structured guidelines for JAD ensure that the process produces accurate, acceptable results. JAD begins with the determination of the high-level, overall system purpose and requirements. These requirements may be defined in a pre-JAD planning session or determined by the executive sponsor. These overall requirements, business objectives, assumptions, strategic considerations, and budget, time, and hardware constraints should be documented and distributed to all participants before the JAD session. This is very important; otherwise, more than half of the JAD session can be wasted in establishing and rehashing this preliminary information. The participants should keep these elements in mind during the session, and the session leader should make sure that all aspects of the design process reference these overall system requirements.

The JAD Participants

Who are the JAD participants, and what are their roles? They include, at a minimum, an executive sponsor, a JAD session leader, users, MIS professionals, a scribe or analyst, and on-call specialists. In addition, JAD support people and observers may take part in a JAD session, filling out the list of attendees. The roles and responsibilities of each are discussed in this section.

The participants must be people from each area of the organization affected by or involved in the application. They should have the authority to commit to things; otherwise, you have a group developing a "wish list." Management therefore must identify key players, make them available for the JAD, make them accountable for the output, and support their decisions. Without this commitment, business users will not want to participate because they will perceive themselves as scapegoats. MIS designs in a vacuum, makes a best guess at what users want and need, and it turns out wrong. The final result in such a worst-case scenario? The JAD didn't fail. The programmers didn't fail. Management failed to manage.

A more detailed description of each type of participant is in the following subsections.

Executive Sponsor

The executive sponsor is a member of high-level management, often someone who oversees the department or departments that will use the new system. This person may be responsible for defining the overall structure and requirements of the system. The sponsor is responsible also for ensuring high-level management's commitment to the system, including funding and staffing the project, and therefore is involved in the initial JAD planning stage. Both before and at the start of the JAD session, the sponsor should provide high-level, strategic insight into the project. This type of information enables JAD participants to incorporate a future into the system, ensuring that the system allows for future needs and does not quickly become obsolete.

The sponsor may or may not be present during the entire JAD session, but should be available to resolve issues that may require high-level input. In particular, the sponsor is responsible for ensuring that the JAD process produces results consistent with the company's goals and policies. The sponsor reviews and approves the final outcome by signing off on the JAD document (that is, the final report).

JAD Session Leader

The JAD session leader is a neutral individual whose purpose is to ensure the success of the JAD session. The session leader is responsible for organizing and coordinating the JAD session, as well as for educating the participants in JAD methodology. During the session, the leader moderates the activities and keeps the participants on track. Ideally, the leader does not have an interest in the outcome of the design, either as a user or a programmer.

This person should not contribute to the design effort or make judgments on the quality of the design produced. Energetic, outgoing people with excellent interpersonal, presentation, and communication skills make effective JAD session leaders. The leader should be familiar with information technology, have a good working knowledge of the system to be modified or automated, and understand the company's business practices.

Users

The users should be drawn from every level of the employees who will use the system to be designed, from top-level user management to user supervisors to professionals to staff assistants to clerks. All user representatives should be experienced employees with knowledge of the company's organization, functions of other departments, and fundamentals of computer systems. They should be creative, team-oriented individuals with the ability to speak in a group, think analytically, and make decisions.

MIS Professionals

MIS professionals provide technical expertise during the JAD session by informing users about computer systems they may not be aware of and by explaining the benefits and tradeoffs of using particular systems. They should be familiar with the company's overall information systems strategy and therefore should ensure that the solution remains within the boundaries of that strategy, as well as within the cost parameters allocated to the project. Their presence in the JAD session not only ensures that all participants are aware of the information systems technology available to them, but also that the MIS department fully understands the requirements and desires of the users when they begin implementation of the design.

Scribe or Analyst

Not everyone agrees on the name for the scribe position, but this person is responsible for recording the events and conclusions of the JAD session and preparing the JAD document (the final report). Some people suggest that this role is important in all phases of JAD, including planning, organization, and design. Others limit this role to merely recording information during the JAD session. *You* decide. This role should be filled by someone with information systems knowledge and an understanding of the system being modified. The ability to take accurate and understandable notes is an important one and ensures that the JAD document reflects accurately the outcome of the JAD session.

Specialists on Call

A specialist is someone who uses only one aspect of the current system and, therefore, has extensive knowledge of a limited area. Specialists have to attend only the portion of the JAD session that concentrates on their area. A specialist should possess the same qualities required of the other users.

JAD Support Person

A JAD support person is optional. This person assists the JAD session leader in all aspects of organization and may take over such tasks as scheduling, appropriating equipment, and distributing memos. This person should be knowledgeable in JAD methodology and in the system being designed so that he or she can act as session leader during a session leader's absence.

Observers

Observers are optional. Observers may be additional technical experts from MIS or another area, or people training to be JAD leaders.

Try to keep the number of people involved in a JAD session between 8 and 15. A group larger than 15 is less productive because it does not communicate and cooperate as well. Larger groups split among themselves and thus diminish the community feeling of the session.

Setting Up and Running a JAD Session

A JAD session requires preparation, most of it done by the session leader. In addition to scheduling the JAD and obtaining the room, equipment, and refreshments, the leader must choose and educate all participants in JAD methodology and conduct interviews and research to prepare the initial, pre-JAD document on the project. This document should contain information about the overall requirements and scope of the project, including the project's purpose, high-level management's strategic insight, and time constraints. The document should be distributed to all participants well in advance of the JAD session, allowing them sufficient time to read it and then consider their roles and prepare ideas for the session.

During the session, the leader should guide the participants through a structured analysis of the system requirements and specifications, keeping to the schedule and steering participants away from unrelated topics. Some good issues to begin with include an overview (by the executive sponsor), assumptions, and workflow. After workflow analysis, you should cover data elements, screens, screen access, and reports, and then resolve any open issues. In IBM seminars and guidebooks, the company suggests that workflow analysis should cover the following points:

- *Planning*—What are the sources that tell users what work to expect and when to expect it?
- *Receiving*—Where and how is work received? Where and how are resources—people, machines, materials, supplies—to do the work received?
- *Receipt processing/tracking*—How are receipts reported, and how is received work uniquely identified? Are other locations notified of receipts?
- *Monitoring and assigning*—How will planned work be received, received work be processed, and priorities and resources be monitored? What identification documents, instructions, and reports does the system provide?
- *Processing*—How is the work done, by whom, and on which machines? How does the system monitor and guide progress? How does it report?
- *Recording*—How does the system record events about the work and notify clients when required?
- *Sending*—Where is the work sent after completion? What labels, directions, and other documents are required? Who is notified of completion? What billing or accounting data is produced?
- *Evaluating*—What management information is required to show trends, summary data, measurements, or exceptions to plans, objectives, and budgets?

IBM's structured guide is well-adapted to the automation of existing manual workflows and to the redeployment of aging systems. Used correctly, the guide can be helpful in integrating transaction systems with client/server technology—a major source of information systems development incoming years. In this way, JAD is a critical link between the process of business reengineering and the development of new information systems.

Throughout the JAD session, the leader should facilitate interaction and promote consensus by encouraging less-vocal participants to express their ideas or their agreement. The leader is responsible for informing the scribe or analyst of what should be recorded for inclusion in the final document and for determining when the participants require a break.

Documentation

Documentation is important throughout all phases of the JAD process. The entire purpose of JAD is to facilitate communication and understanding among all parties involved; clear, understandable documentation makes this possible. This includes the pre-JAD document that informs participants of the overall system specifications as well as the final JAD document. Some people advocate the what-you-see-is-what-you-get (WYSIWYG) documentation approach, which suggests inclusion of all overhead transparencies and other visual presentations in the final JAD document. To assist in the development of JAD documentation, most books on JAD include sample fill-in forms that can be used for all phases of the JAD process, including some for the initial planning and others for the actual JAD session.

Figures 10.1 and 10.2 show sample forms from the JAD documentation.

In addition to these forms, your JAD document might include these sections:

- Management objectives
- Scope and limits
- Business questions the system will answer
- Information required to answer the questions
- Relationship with other systems
- Issues
- Assumptions
- Data-element definitions
- Screen design or layout
- Report design

- Menus
- Processing rules
- Operating procedures
- Performance and operational requirements

When the first JAD session is conducted, you can estimate the total design time that will be required for the system. Figure 10.2 illustrates a blank Estimating Rules of Thumb worksheet.

EDIT & VALIDATION

Function Name: Add an Order
Screen Name: Order Identification (Screen 1 of 3)
Use Codes: R = Required;   O = Optional
    D = Displayed;   P = Protected

Item No.	Abbreviated Name	Use Code	Edit/Validation
1	Order No	P	System generated Sequential number
2	S/Rep ID	R	Validated for match in system table.
3	Order Date	R	Prior or equal to Entry Date (system date)
4	Cust No	R	Validated for match in customer file.
5	Cust Name	P	
6	Cust Ref	O	
7	Entry Date	P	System Date
8	Ship to Dept	D	
9	Ship to Street	D	
10	Ship to PO	D	
11	Ship to City	D	May not be blank.
12	Ship to State	D	May not be blank. Validated for match in system table.

Figure 10.1. A sample Edit-and-Validation JAD form.

```
SESSION  PHASE
Step    1a.    Sum number of large/complex screens plus major processing routines      _____
        1b.    Sum number of medium screens, medium processing routines,
               large reports plus interfaces                                           _____
        1c.    Sum number of small/simple screens, simple processing routines,
               small to medium reports*                                                _____
Step    2a.    Divide result of step 1a by 5              _____
        2b.    Divide result of step 1b by 6              _____
        2c.    Divide result of step 1c by 7             _____
Step    3.     Sum results of steps 2a, 2b, and 2c.                                    _____
Step    4.     Add to result of step 3 between 1 and 3 days for JAD/Design kickoff, requirements,
               scope, workflow diagram, and workflow description, as follows:
                         If result of step 3 is less than 3, then add 1 day.
                         If result of step 3 is 3 - 4, then add 2 days.
                         If result of step 3 is 5 - 7, then add 3 days.               _____


CUSTOMIZATION  PHASE
Step    1.     Number of calendar workdays equal to number of session phase days (session phase,
               step 4). Note that this is irrespective of whether one or two analysts are assigned to
               the project because the session leader tends to be the critical response.   _____


WRAP-UP  PHASE
Step    1.     Multiply session phase days (Session phase, step 4) by 3                 _____
Step    2a.    Divide result of step 1 by number of people documenting (full-time or percentage
               thereof). This is the amount of time to allocate for producing the document's first draft.
                                                                                        _____
Step    3.     Add 3 to 6 days for document review and update as well as executive sponsor
               presentation.** (partially parallel)                                     _____
Step    4.     Add prototype development time.** (parallel)                             _____


FINAL  WRAP-UP
Step    1.     In the case of a multi-JAD/Design project, add final wrap-up time to the end of the last
               JAD/Design. Multiply the number of JAD/Designs in the project by 2 to determine the
               number of calendar workdays.                                             _____


* The typical simple menu screens are collectively counted as one small simple screen for estimating
purposes.
** Some or all of the executive sponsor presentation preparation time and the prototype development
time may be scheduled in parallel with the first draft documentation tasks and would therefore not
add calendar time to the wrap-up effort.
```

Figure 10.2. A sample Estimating Rules of Thumb worksheet.

Common Pitfalls

Try to get the best people involved in JAD as well as in the overall systems-development effort. Too often the temptation is to assign people other than the best, which inevitably affects the project results in a negative way. Also, recognize that although there may be a core team of designers from the end-user organization, many people's work will be directly and indirectly disrupted by the application development project. The JAD sessions should be an early opportunity to identify the potential disruption points so that plans can be made to minimize them.

Even if you experience success with a JAD session and are eager to try it again on another project, don't get carried away with JAD. Some good JAD textbooks provide an excellent starting point for how to use JAD most efficiently and effectively. (Refer to Appendix G, "Bibliography," for suggested readings.) Allowing your employees to use JAD in inappropriate situations is an inefficient use of resources: JAD is not a substitute for managing people. For example, do not use JAD to handle personality conflicts, complete highly detailed tasks, or resolve situations that could be handled just as well using other means. JAD should be reserved for highly complex projects that require a substantial time commitment and involve users from different departments.

Try not to raise false expectations from the method. After all, JAD produces only what can be expected from a two- to five-day concentrated effort. The team approach is powerful; it cannot, however, solve all business problems by itself, nor can it solve the technical and implementation problems of later phases.

Good Design: The Results of JAD

A good design is one that a user does not even notice. When you use a well-designed object—a hammer or a pen, for example—you have no conscious perception of the tool. An ill-designed tool makes a user more conscious by causing awkwardness or irritation. It is when a tool breaks or does not function properly that its user consciously perceives it. (Picture what happens when a hammer's head flies off its handle.) This view applies directly to the design of user interfaces; in particular, to interactive workstation interfaces. Other elements of good interactive design are clarity, consistency, performance, and respect for the user.

The design concept of unobtrusiveness is applicable also to less-interactive media, such as reports. A well-designed report (on-screen or on paper) is one that presents information so clearly that its readers do not need instructions to interpret it. The report never offends with elements of poor appearance, such as pale ink, misaligned characters, too many colors, and so on.

By far the most important factor in interface design is knowledge of which tasks a user is to accomplish and how they are to be accomplished. To design an easy-to-use system, JAD designers need to know something about the user—his or her prior knowledge of the application and of computers—and about the pattern of use—daily, intermittent, or infrequent. This knowledge enables the designer to create mental models, or *metaphors*, that users already know (for example, the metaphor of a spreadsheet package).

Translating Design to Programs

At this point, a word about translating design to programs is appropriate. Because one of the JAD deliverables is high-level data design, as well as input and output design, it is helpful to have an idea of the approach to be used in the actual programming. There are three possible design approaches you can take in translating JAD results to program design specifications: process-driven, data-driven, and object-oriented.

The traditional way of structuring a program, called *process-driven* design, is to group related processing functions into related modules: A mainline module acts as "traffic cop" and passes control to each subordinate module in turn.

In contrast, the premise of *data-driven* design is that the program structure should match the data structure. Designing a program consists, therefore, of designing a hierarchical data structure. The structure of the program does not depend on which data are on which files. Whether a program uses data from one file or multiple files, the program is written no differently.

For client/server network computing-based systems, however—which generally are some portion (if not all) of the result of the rightsizing process—a new programming and program-design paradigm is becoming increasingly popular: object-oriented design and programming. Object-oriented design and programming attempt to eliminate the controversy between process-driven design and data-driven design by combining the two.

Object-oriented (OO) programming has its commercial origins in a language called SmallTalk. A SmallTalk object is a piece of data to which is attached all the processing that the data can undergo. For instance, a number is stored together with the rules of addition, multiplication, printing, rounding, and so on that apply to it. The programmer never can have access to the data other than through one of these processes, also called *methods*.

In a very simplistic sense, the goal of object orientation is to allow software applications to be built using manufacturing assembly techniques. The idea is to have reusable software components (objects and classes) that can be maintained and enhanced through the technique of inheritance. The building of applications, becomes a process of software component assembly.

Object-oriented development environments are characterized by four principals: encapsulation, inheritance, polymorphism, and late binding. Here's a very short discourse on these principals.

> *Encapsulation* refers to the way in which object-oriented systems package data and processes together. The only way to access data is through the procedures that surround and maintain them. A mechanism known as messages, analogous to function calls, is used to access the procedures and functions of an object. Using an object's functionality only requires knowledge of the object's user interface, not of the object's internals.

> *Inheritance* is the basic mechanism of code reusability. Objects can be organized into "Is a" classes and inherit functions from objects higher in that class. Appropriate maintenance changes are therefore automatically propagated throughout the hierarchy.

> *Polymorphism* simply refers to the behavior of an object-oriented system to messages. The same message can be sent to objects of different classes and elicit different but appropriate behavior in each case.

> *Late binding* is an operational characteristic of object-oriented systems. Objects can be created on the fly by the application. Because of this, the system can't be "compile time bound."

Class Libraries

OO doesn't offer any magic. What it does offer is a different view of programming organization. In an object-oriented system, the programming language and DBMS are constructed to encourage the reuse of code and the building of class libraries. As for the productivity of application developers, that simply isn't going to happen until a development environment has a full, rich set of object classes that can be reused.

The basic assumption of object-oriented development is that small groups (the brightest people) will do the difficult work of developing class libraries. Other groups will then assemble application systems by using the developed class libraries. Developers of libraries and objects will be done both by software vendors and within businesses' IS organizations. At this point, the market split of work between generic objects by vendors and user-specific objects built by IS departments is unknown.

Although object-oriented design for traditional host-based systems has been less well known, it is increasingly becoming the approach of choice for network-based applications (in combination with certain low-level C compilers), whether these are oriented for decision support, query, or transaction processing. JAD members therefore should be familiar with object orientation to help guide the development of JAD deliverables that are easiest for the programming team to use.

Architecture

Architecture

11

Microsoft's MS-DOS and Windows operating environments may be the world's two leading computer brands—eminently more valuable than brand names like Intel or Compaq.

—Rappaport and Halevi,
Harvard Business Review,
(1991)

Objectives:

1. To introduce you to the key client/server computing architecture concepts.

2. To help you understand the importance of designing an appropriate architecture for developing rightsized systems.

3. To introduce you to the major competing client/server computing architectures and some of their key differences.

A client/server computing architecture is a computing architecture in which applications are partitioned between clients and servers. A *client* is a software or software/hardware component that accesses services provided by one or more servers. A *server* is a software or software/hardware component that provides services accessed by one or more clients. Note that it is possible for one computer to have both clients and servers executing on it. However, in most client/server architectures, clients and servers are on separate computers.

At a high level, a client/server computing architecture contains two major architectural components: the technical architecture and the application architecture. The *technical architecture* is a structured collection of computing technologies that supports the execution of applications. The *application architecture* is the organization and location of a set of software components that perform business-related tasks and that together make up an application.

Technical Architecture

Technical architectures for client/server systems vary in complexity from fairly simple architectures, which require only a handful of technologies, to very complex architectures, which require the integration of two dozen or more different technologies. Generally the complexity of the technical architecture increases with the size of the system, where size is measured by the number of users, the transaction volume, and the size of the geographical area over which the system is used. However, there are a few components that are common to every client/server technical architecture: clients, servers, and networks. This section provides an overview of these common components.

Clients

A client, as defined earlier in this chapter, can be a software-only or software/ hardware component. The common usage of the term, however, is to refer to a client workstation. A client workstation is a computing device at which a user interacts with the client portion of a client/server application. Typically it is a small computer packaged in a desktop or deskside configuration.

Client/server computing technologies were first developed in the mid-to-late '80s primarily for the technical computing environment. A technical computing environment is one in which most of the computing is for scientific or engineering purposes. In this environment the client workstations, often called "engineering workstations," were usually small, relatively expensive, high-performance computers with large, high-resolution graphical displays. Usually they ran a variant of the UNIX operating system and had built-in networking capabilities.

As client/server concepts and technologies began to be used for mainstream business computing, the preferred client workstation became the personal computer. This is primarily because the rapid increase in personal computing during the '80s had already led to the placement of PCs on or beside the desks of most office workers. In addition, personal computers were generally less expensive than engineering workstations, and the operating systems that ran on them were usually perceived to be easier to use than UNIX.

Today the most common choice for a client workstation is an IBM-compatible personal computer running a version of Microsoft's MS-DOS or IBM's OS/2 operating system. Microsoft's Windows graphical user environment is often layered on top of MS-DOS.

Servers

A greater variety of hardware and operating systems are found on the server side of the client/server architecture. The three most common types of servers are file servers, print servers, and database servers. A file server provides file sharing capabilities. Users at several different client workstations can store and retrieve data in files on the disk drives connected to and managed by the file server. To the client workstation, the file server's disk drives are "virtual disks." The client workstation accesses them across the network, almost as if they were actually part of the workstation.

Print servers allow users at several different workstations to share printers. Printers connected to and managed by a print server can be accessed across the network by a client workstation almost as if they were directly connected to the workstation.

A database server is a server upon which a database management system (DBMS) is executed for the purpose of managing one or more databases. Although client/server applications don't have to be built using a database management system, most of them are because a DBMS provides a mechanism for managing multiple user access to a set of structured data. The database management systems most often used for client/server applications are based on the relational database model and support a version of the Structured Query Language (SQL) for retrieving and manipulating the data in the database.

Networks

A network is a collection of hardware and software services that enables computers connected to it to communicate with each other. Networked computers have networking software configured into their operating systems so they can send information over the network, using well-defined protocols and message formats. In a client/server technical architecture, the network serves as the "glue" between clients and servers. It provides the communication mechanism by which clients access the services provided by servers.

Putting It Together

The basic components just described are combined to form the foundation of a client/server technical architecture. A typical technical architecture for client/server computing includes one or more file servers running a NOS, one or more print servers for distributed printing, and a database server. The file and print servers are there primarily to support the day-to-day productivity needs of the users: sharing files; running productivity software like spreadsheets, word processors, and presentation graphics programs; and printing. Actual client/server applications are usually distributed between the client workstations and the database server.

Small client/server systems with only a few users can be implemented on a condensed technical architecture. Some of the popular relational database management systems are available in versions that run on a NOS (network operating system). Therefore, for systems with a relatively low number of users, a single high-performance PC server can be used as both the file server and the database server. However, because the processing requirements of most production client/server applications exceed the capacity of a single server to meet the demands of both file sharing and database management, the DBMS is usually located on a dedicated database server. The operating system on the database server is often a version of UNIX, because UNIX-based systems provide a wide range of scalability and excellent price/performance ratios (probably because of the high level of competition in the UNIX server market). Several vendors now sell families of compatible servers with the processing capacity to support a few dozen users on the entry-level server, up to a few hundred users on the most powerful model.

Application Architecture

Most client/server applications being implemented today are based on a two-tier architecture. There are two processing tiers, or locations, where the application code execute: the client workstation and the DBMS. The client portion of the application allows users to enter data, to submit requests to retrieve data from the database, and to summarize and display data in various ways. The client application code interprets the user's inputs, translates them into SQL statements, and then transmits the SQL across the network to the database server. Actual insertions of new data, updates to existing data, or retrievals of data in response to a query from a client workstation are performed by the DBMS. In the case of a query, the DBMS prepares the return set of requested data and transmits it back across the network to the client application code on the appropriate workstation.

Important Architectural Choices

Architectural choices have a significant impact on the success of client/server systems. The capability of the system to meet both the business objectives and performance expectations of users is directly affected. For example, if one of the business requirements for a client/server application is that it must be able to automatically distribute reports to users via e-mail, the technical architecture must have the appropriate technology components to provide this functionality. Other considerations are the processing capacity of the database server and the bandwidth of the network. If neither is large enough to support peak processing demands, periods of degraded performance will occur, during which the users' satisfaction level may drop considerably. The processing capacity of the client workstations has a direct bearing on the performance of the client application code. If the client workstations do not have enough memory and powerful enough processors, the users are likely to be disappointed with the performance of the application.

The most important part of designing the application architecture is *partitioning* the application. Partitioning is the process of deciding which portions of the application should execute on the client workstations and which should execute on the database server. Application routines that must manipulate large sets of data and perform a series of complex calculations may best be executed on the server. This is especially true when the client application is developed using an interpretive 4GL that is executed in a Windows environment.

Network computing offers numerous choices in development architectures. The correct architectural solution depends on many things, including the problem to be solved, the organization that must solve it, the platform to be used, and the tools available. Changes in any of these parameters can change the recommended approach. Although this diversity of correct approaches increases the options available to the designer, it also makes selecting the final architecture more difficult. As always, the first step in determining how to do it is to ask the question, "What do we want to do?"

Industry trends, such as rightsizing, systems integration, and enterprise-wide networking, have created the need for standards that allow for and facilitate the implementation of multiple-vendor systems. In response, many computer manufacturers have worked together to build a set of industry-accepted standards, and they now produce products and systems that conform to those standards. In the process of developing a standardized product line, manufacturers have developed architectures or all-encompassing plans for their product lines.

The Big Issues

Astute MIS directors, faced with the obvious and compelling business benefits of rightsizing information systems, most often ask these questions:

- How do I make the transition without scrapping everything we've done in the past 20 years?

- How can I convince my staff to head in this direction without scaring them all away and causing my systems to fall apart?

- How do I choose tools without paying a king's ransom to evaluate them all?

- What tools really are needed, and how do they fit together?

- How can I be assured that I won't lose any more sleep from operating in the new environment than I'm currently losing today?

- How do I build or buy application solutions that really solve the big problems without costing another fortune to implement?

These are the big issues. The rest—the technical issues typically debated in the press—resemble the arguments of medieval scholars discussing angels dancing on pins: interesting but irrelevant. The beauty of the mainframe environment is that answers to these questions are known, well-defined, and relatively unchanging. The beast is that the answers are too expensive and no longer meet the rapidly increasing expectations of system users.

Key Functions and Products

The network computing world is filled with products that address a wide array of architecture functions. This section discusses the state of the market and makes suggestions about how you can address each functional area in building a technical architecture. A detailed discussion of selection issues for network platform and development environment products is in Chapter 12, "The Network Platform," and Chapter 15, "The Rightsizing Development Environment," respectively.

Operating Systems

Two types of operating systems typically are used in rightsizing situations: network operating systems (NOS) and application operating systems (OS). They could be one and the same, but usually are not. The NOS is important because each type is optimized for some specific purpose. The three main types are Novell's NetWare for file I/O, Banyan's VINES for communications and WAN, and Microsoft's LAN Manager and Windows NT. The application OS provides functions that are directly useful to the application. Characterizing the products in short form, one would describe Microsoft's LAN Manager as the product with a Presentation Manager and IBM SAA flavor; Banyan's VINES as the high-end, full-function product with a UNIX flavor; and Novell's NetWare as the market leader with the fastest product best suited to office environments. Services provided by operating systems include memory management, task management, timer control, interprocess communications, authorization checking, and so on.

The reality and the power of the network computing environment is that there are likely to be as many operating systems as are necessary to optimally solve an array of business problems. A typical environment in a large corporation includes MVS, OS/400, VMS, a UNIX variant or two, perhaps a real-time OS, and one of the three main network operating systems. Today, each is likely either to exist in an isolated environment or to be tied to the rest by way of file transfer facilities. Only the most sophisticated companies have created interactive ties between the different environments.

The network operating systems (NOS) were originally created to function as a collection of utilities capable of sharing files and support services among PCs. As PC networks expanded, however, it became clear that networks, PCs, and servers needed to have the capabilities necessary to replace mainframes. The NOS has been attempting to cover such functions as task management and coordination across the network.

There is still no PC or LAN equivalent to the full functionality of any mainframe software environment, with the exception of application development languages, however. In a mainframe environment, operating systems, transaction monitors, time sharing monitors, database management systems, and development languages are assembled in a coordinated fashion to complete the transaction processing functions. What vendors are now attempting is to use UNIX—combined with a transaction processing monitor, an RDBMS (relational database management system), and (perhaps) the OSF DCE—to become the new transaction processing platform.

Communication

In a mainframe environment, the central computer is constantly responding to terminal messages; it is never disconnected. In terminal-to-terminal communication, all messages are sent through the mainframe. Communications in a rightsized environment are more peer-to-peer, with computers directly interfacing to cooperatively process a message.

Over time, PCs have emerged as single-user devices. This raises the question of how to manage, from a software point of view, a network of single-user devices operating in concert as a multitasking, multiuser system.

The answer has been to connect another server onto the existing network and provide services to other users through the NOS. In effect, the combination of single-user operating systems running on clients over a LAN network allows the network and its constituents to emulate mainframe communication and connectivity functionality. Of course, this is a loose use of the word *emulate* because a network can handle the transaction workload of the mainframe at a fraction of the total hardware/software cost. Ultimately, networks will supply graphical interfaces, run Lotus 1-2-3 and Word for Windows, and do a host (pun intended) of things that mainframes can't handle.

NOSs currently perform the following services:

- Account for network and resource usage
- Assign tasks to idle workstations
- Provide audit trails
- Remotely administer the server
- Do interprocess LAN communication
- Monitor performance
- Provide access to multiple servers
- Support security through passwords and other mechanisms

Transaction Processing (TP) Monitors

A TP monitor may be needed to manage access to distributed databases. A front-end process would send the TP monitor a unit of work, which the monitor then executes. This provides a much more efficient processing model than the process-per-connection (or terminal) model that many RDBMSs require. TP monitors may also provide excellent deterministic scheduling and transaction control features. Transactions can be prioritized by type, so response levels can be guaranteed. Certain TP monitors can run processes when system utilization falls below a specified threshold. Often, the overhead of using a TP monitor is more than made up for by the additional control over transaction load. Novell and Digital's Tuxedo products, NCR's Top End, and Transarc's Encina are examples of TP monitors.

The Development Environment

What is needed is a single, integrated, extensible development environment for designing, coding, testing, and supporting all aspects of production-level, large-scale systems. You should not assume that it can solve all problems, but it should provide the framework within which individual sites can implement their unique solutions. Unfortunately, this area is one of weakness in the architectures for network computing-based systems today. Some vendor-specific architectures provide solutions, but often the solutions lock you into a single supplier.

The Development Language

No single development language is appropriate for solving all problems. You can, however, define a core set of conditions under which certain languages are appropriate. Probable candidates are C, C++, COBOL, Smalltalk, Visual BASIC, SQL, GUI scripting languages like PowerScript, and distributed object-oriented development environments like Forte and Dynasty.

Security Management

The architecture must include standards for integrating security control into business applications. It must strive to be integrated, redundant, centrally maintained, extensible, and include high-performance security maintenance and authorization checking. The Kerberos Authentication Service developed by MIT is the basis of most message exchange systems. Kerberos uses a two-key system that proves the identity of those exchanging messages. CA's ACF2 for networks and for other platforms is a candidate product for security management in the world of rightsized systems.

Storage Management

Such storage management functionality as file migration and archiving control should be considered when determining your architectural choices.

Report Distribution

Report distribution is one of those mundane, but important, components of the technical architecture. Products such as CA-DISPATCH/PC provide a limited start. Existing e-mail systems are another good starting point, especially if an organization is networked at all locations and to all personnel and divisional levels.

Capacity Management

Most NOS vendors provide elements of capacity management, but what's lacking is the comprehensive environment management available in the "glass house," in other words, the central computing systems facility. On-line performance monitoring, performance trend analysis, and capacity planning tools are now available for the UNIX operating system.

The final major component of technical architecture mentioned in this discussion is database access. Chapter 15 provides a detailed description of key success factors and functional requirements of databases.

Vendor Architectures

Some standard features available from most vendor-developed architectures include graphical user interfaces (GUIs), application programming interfaces (APIs), and network protocols. In addition, these architectures support system management and security, client/server computing, object management, computer-aided software engineering (CASE), and database management systems (DBMSs). The development of these standardized architectures has facilitated interoperability across multivendor platforms, but the development of "open systems" is far from complete. As customers continue to demand quicker automation of functions, less redundant data, lower product implementation costs, easier-to-use systems, and the capability to integrate diverse systems, vendors seek to support these demands by developing standardized architectures.

Industry coalitions also have assisted in the development of standards. Some accept submissions from architecture designers and then offer them to others through licenses. These coalitions include Corporation for Open Systems International (COS), Object Management Group (OMG), Open Software Foundation (OSF) (see Figure 11.1), and X/Open Company Ltd.

Vendors view architectures as a twofold plan:

- A method for meeting the current demands and needs of customers.
- Assurance of customer stability and devotion. Standard architecture enables customers to keep old equipment when new equipment is added.

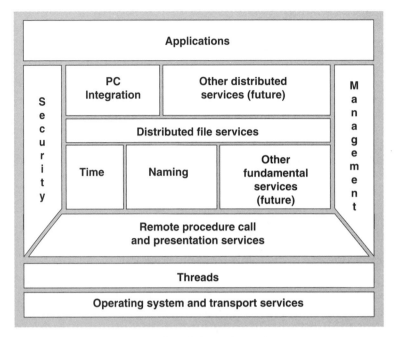

Source: Open Software Foundation

Figure 11.1. *OSF's distributed computing environment (DCE) architecture.*

The rest of this section provides descriptions of the architectures relevant to rightsizing that are available from major computer manufacturers. This discussion shows how a few of the better-known vendors compare in their approach to system architecture.

Hewlett Packard Company

Architecture: NewWave Computing (NWC)

NWC arose from Hewlett Packard's efforts in distributed computing, industry standard networking, and RISC hardware. Unlike other architectures, however, NWC is based on object-management technology and object-oriented networked services. HP NewWave 4.1 includes several NWC features for MS-DOS computers, with future releases planned for OS/2 and UNIX.

NWC uses HP's distributed object-management facility (DOMF) technology. In addition to controlling how objects are defined and cataloged and how they interact with system resources, DOMF tracks where objects are stored and handles communications between objects. Using an RPC mechanism, DOMF supports HP's Network Computing System (NCS) and Sun's Open Network Computing (ONC) network interconnection protocols for transmitting requests in a distributed environment.

IBM Corporation

Architecture: Open Distributed Computing Structure (ODCS)

IBM worked on its architecture for the multivendor, enterprise-wide client/server environment for years. IBM is now working on implementing its architecture through various products. Its implementation strategy will likely be to first adopt open systems technologies like OSF (Open Software Foundation) and OSI (Open Systems Interconnection) in its own systems. Later, it would go on to making its own technologies available for other vendors' systems. At some point in the future, IBM will take the most meaningful step and use such industry standards as those developed by Novell and Sun.

NCR Corporation

Architecture: Open, Cooperative Computing Architecture (OCCA)

OCCA—a client/server architecture based on open systems standards, networked distribution of computing functions, and consistent user interfaces—offers information, network and systems management, and transaction processing. NCR Cooperation for MS-DOS servers is an object-oriented application-integration environment consisting of more than 50 software modules that implement OCCA in multivendor systems.

Rhapsody, a similar product from recent NCR partner AT&T, focuses on workgroup features, combining an enterprise-wide orientation with workgroup features. In addition, NCR Desktop, the interface for NCR Co-operation applications, provides the object-management facility and task-automation technology of HP NWC and NCR's remote method.

Microsoft

Architecture: Open Database Connectivity (ODBC)

ODBC is Microsoft's architecture for data access across a heterogeneous environment. Based on the Call Level Interface (CLI) specification of the SQL Access Group, it is a portable API used by Microsoft and Apple Computer.

Apple Corporation

Architecture: AOCE

This 1994 architecture is a framework for creation of collaborative or workgroup applications and also a platform that uses hardware and software resources to their best advantage. Security and the integration of such technologies as voice mail, fax, and e-mail are integral to it.

Emerging Architectures

A growing "hot" market is architecture for development of rightsized information systems. In order to support changing business needs in an enterprise environment, a three-tiered client/server architecture such as that suggested by Open Environment Corporation (OEC) may be needed. Systems using OEC's three tiers—presentation, function (or logic), and data—may yield a competitive advantage. The trick is to use different experts to design each component, then interface them in a way that totally shields the system from the underlying platforms. In such a scenario, components could be run on one machine or across a network.

The Network
Platform

The Network Platform

12

The LAN is the new hardware platform and the group is the new user.

—Larry Moore
Vice President
Lotus Development
Corporation

Objectives:

1. To remind you of the difference between client/server and other network models.

2. To help you understand what a network operating system is and its key selection criteria.

3. To help you understand the major differences among the three key network OSs.

4. To teach you what the cabling plant and other components of the network OS are.

5. To help you understand the major categories of networks and their advantages.

6. To teach you about the key selection criteria for network servers and clients.

The PC local area network (LAN) and its bigger brother, the wide-area network (WAN), have emerged as the preferred platforms for rightsized applications. The reason for this emergence is that PC LANs are best suited to adapting to the "structure of the moment" in organizations. They can shrink, grow, and relocate as fast as people do. This chapter describes the kinds of networking models and the technological choices to be made in selecting a networking platform for a rightsizing application.

Networking Models

There are two primary models for networking:

- Peer-to-peer
- Client/server

The peer-to-peer networking model enables any node in the network to be a client, a server, or both for any given application. Conceptually, peer-to-peer networking is attractive because it provides for total network flexibility and device independence. Practically, however, peer-to-peer networking becomes difficult and less desirable to implement when network size and application complexity grow beyond the small and simple. The reason for this difficulty is that PCs, which operate as both clients and servers (that is, as "peers" to other computers in the network) can greatly slow down when used as servers. In addition, it can be difficult to manage applications on a peer-to-peer

LAN because data and applications can be run and stored anywhere. Most peer-to-peer LANs don't yet have sufficiently sophisticated network management capabilities.

The other networking model, client/server networking, provides for certain nodes to operate as clients and others to operate as servers in an application. Clients typically provide the user interface and functional processing for an application. Servers typically provide file service and network management functions. The client/server model is more practical than peer-to-peer because it provides for a level of specialization of hardware in the network. Each device can do what it does best: 286/386 PCs work as clients, 386/486 PCs work as servers, and so on. Most mission-critical, rightsized applications are designed for a client/server network.

A client/server computing environment consists of three principal components: client, server, and network (see Figure 12.1).

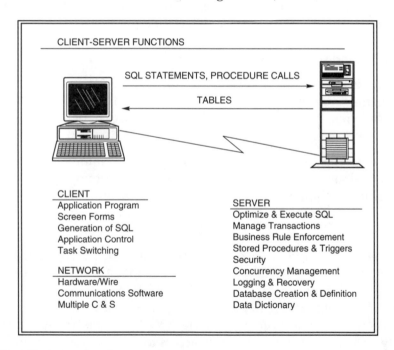

Figure 12.1. Client-server functions.

The client is where the application program runs. Normally, client hardware is a desktop computer, such as an IBM PC, PC clone, or Apple Mac. The application program itself may have been written in a 4GL or 3GL language, such as C or COBOL. There is an entire new class of Windows 4GLs that allows the painting of applications under leading desktop, Windows-based operating systems.

Such Windows 4GLs support both windows-oriented application development and execution. Leading examples now on the market include Powersoft's PowerBuilder, JYACC'S JAM, Uniface, and Gupta's SQL Windows. Using any of these application-building approaches results in a runtime configuration in which the I/O and application controls come from the client, whereas the database and associated semantics run on the server. At the desktop level, most software supports the emerging windows-based standards, that is, Windows 3.x for DOS, Presentation Manager for OS/2, Motif and Open Look for UNIX, and Mac OS for the Macintosh.

The network connects the clients and servers. Normally, networks are based on either EtherNet or token-ring topologies, and have appropriate interface cards in both the client and server boxes. The communications software typically handles different types of transportation protocols, such as SPX/IPX, LU6.2, and TCP/IP. Most network environments provide support for multiple clients and servers.

The server is responsible for executing SQL statements received from a client. Sometimes data requests are not communicated through SQL, but rather through a remote procedure call that triggers a series of pre-compiled, existing SQL statements.

The server is responsible for SQL optimization, determining the best path to the data, and managing transactions. Some server technologies support advanced software capabilities, such as stored procedures, event notifiers, and triggers. The server is also responsible for data security and requester validation.

The server handles additional database functions, such as concurrency management, deadlock protection and resolution, logging and recovering, and database creation and definition. The idea of managing data on a separate machine fits well with the management approach of treating data as a corporate resource. In addition to executing SQL statements, the server handles security and provides for concurrent access to the data by multiple users.

The Benefits of Using SQL

An important benefit that the set-oriented SQL language provides is network efficiency. When using traditional, file-serving, PC LAN approaches, the entire data file had to be transmitted across a network to the client machine. Using SQL as a basis in the database management system on the server solves this problem because only the necessary query response data (a subset of one or more tables) is transmitted to the client machine.

Having SQL on the server also allows the database implementation of advanced facilities, such as triggers and automatic procedures. As relational DBMSs evolve, they will confer the capability to build rules directly into the database engine. Systems that are built with this approach will be more robust than traditional application-based logic approaches.

Although client/server computing is being planned for environments that use minicomputers and mainframes as servers, the largest market likely to develop will have a mix of Windows 3.x, Windows NT, MS-DOS, OS/2, and Macintosh on the client and either UNIX, Windows NT, NetWare, or OS/2 for the server. Server software will provide mainframe levels of security, recovery, and data integrity capability. Functions such as automatic locking and commit rollback logic, along with deadlock detection and a full suite of data administration utilities, are available on the server side. Another way of looking at this, then, is that SQL client-server technology allows cheap PCs to be made into "industrial strength" computing engines.

Network Operating Systems

The network operating system is a client/server network's central nervous system. It consists of software that manages the LAN and provides file service, print service, file-access security, and other management functions. Network operating system selection is crucial to the success of a LAN. You should follow certain technical and design guidelines in selecting a network operating system software package:

- *Application compatibility*—Applications that will be used on the network must be capable of running on the selected operating system.
- *Manageability*—The operating system should have tools available to make managing the network simple. LAN administrators should be able to add or delete users, directories, and applications and upgrade or reconfigure without disrupting the network.
- *Ease of use*—New users should be able to adjust quickly to system functions. An effective menu system, with few new procedures and commands to learn, is beneficial.

- *Reliability*—Downtime should not be a major concern. An operating system prone to failing probably is worse than having no operating system at all. An operating system that works with a redundant hardware setup, for example, providing duplicate disks or disk channels, is beneficial for those who cannot afford any downtime.

- *Security*—The operating system should have security to provide proper channels of access to files, encrypted passwords, and so on.

- *Performance*—The operating system is the crucial component in system performance. Hardware cannot make up for an operating system that cannot perform.

- *Expandability*—As network requirements increase, it's essential to have a system that can add users with little difficulty. The operating system should be capable of adjusting for new software requirements, including expanded memory. It should be able to add processors and processor sizes; that is, it should be scaleable.

In addition to these considerations, other more practical criteria enter into the purchasing decision. As Figure 12.2 shows, the reputation of the vendor and the product, as well as the product price, weigh heavily in the selection decision. Appendix C, "Choosing a NOS from the Leaders," provides a detailed comparison of the marketplace's leading network operating systems.

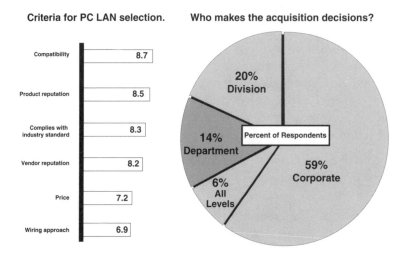

Figure 12.2. LAN purchasing patterns.

The Physical Plant

The phrase used to describe the combination of cable and connecting devices that tie the clients to the servers into a network is the *physical plant*. Often ignored, the physical plant can be the network's greatest source of stability or trouble, depending on the attention it receives in design and implementation.

Here are some questions to ask in designing the physical plant:

- Where will the clients and servers be located?
- How many clients and servers will there be?
- How far apart will the clients and servers be?
- Is there the possibility that the cabling will be in an area exposed to a large amount of electrical "noise"?
- What kind of response times are necessary for the network?

The following sections describe some basic considerations to keep in mind in selecting the cabling and other network connectivity devices for a network.

Cabling

With the network operating system selected, the next network platform choice is the cabling plant design. There are two primary standards for network cabling plant design, or *topology*, in a network computing environment: bus and ring. In turn, each of these cabling plant designs is associated with a major protocol—EtherNet and token-passing ring—discussed in the following sections. The kinds of cable over which these standards can operate have increased in variety and capability during the past few years.

As Figure 12.3 shows, there are three major choices in cable type. The primary difference in these types has to do with price versus performance, with *twisted-pair cable* at the low end of both price and performance and fiber-optic cable at the high end. *Coaxial cable*, in the middle, is likely to be chosen less often as twisted-pair increases in performance and fiber-optic decreases in price. Note that fiber and shielded twisted-pair (IBM type 1) are very close in price, especially when *plastic optical fiber* (POF) is used in the comparison. The primary price difference arises from the cost of "punching down" (that is, connecting the wires to the servers), with an approximate cost of $75 for fiber, $15 for STP (shielded twisted-pair), and $5 for UTP (unshielded twisted-pair).

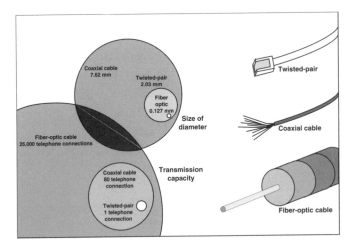

Figure 12.3. *Comparing cable size and capacity.*

EtherNet

EtherNet uses the Collision Detect/Carrier Sense Multiple Access (CD/CSMA) cable-access method (or *protocol*). This method enables nodes to compete for cable access. When a node on the network sends a command to another node or the file server, it first checks the cable to see whether another node is transmitting information. If the line is being used, the node waits and checks the line at random time intervals until the line is free. If the line is clear, the sending node transmits its data. When data is transmitted, it is sent across the entire network, but accepted and acknowledged only by the station to which the data is addressed.

Data being sent from one workstation can collide with data being sent from another workstation. When a collision occurs, the workstations involved wait a random period of time (to reduce the possibility of a recollision) and attempt to transmit again. If there are many collisions, the network can reach a saturation point, which leads to performance degradation.

EtherNet cabling is widely accepted by the networking industry. The original cable was a thick, coaxial cable. A matchbox-sized device, called a *transceiver*, connected nodes to the cable and served as the collision detection device. Today, the newer thin EtherNet cable is widely used because it costs less than the original cable. Even better is unshielded twisted-pair (UTP), or telephone wire, that now can be used in many instances with the introduction of 10BASET adapter cards.

EtherNet cabling is linear in design. This design most often is referred to as *bus topology*, as shown in Figure 12.4. Flexibility is provided, however, by using additional devices, such as repeaters (explained later in this chapter). Interfaces and operating software for EtherNet LANs are readily available, with dozens of EtherNet network interface card (NIC) vendors in the market and support from all three major network operating system vendors—Novell, Banyan, and Microsoft.

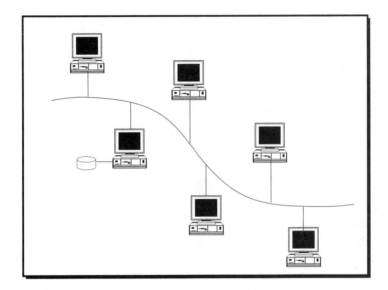

Figure 12.4. Bus topology.

Token-Passing Ring

A token-passing ring network is a closed loop through which communications travel in one direction, passing data from one node to the next. A *token* is a permission-to-transmit signal. The best-known proprietary implementation of this cabling standard is IBM's Token-Ring Network. Each station is connected to the previous node and the next node in the ring, as shown in Figure 12.5. Some token-passing ring networks utilize multistation access units (MAUs) to allow for easier connection and disconnection of nodes. At a centrally located MAU, or hub, all nodes are connected to their next and previous nodes, thereby maintaining the integrity of the ring layout. MAUs also automatically connect or disconnect nodes as they are turned on or off.

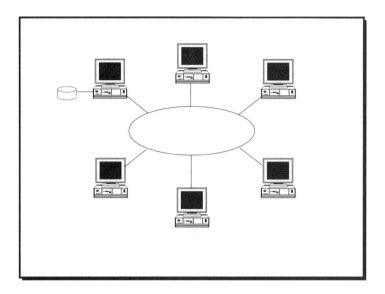

Figure 12.5. Ring topology.

Through this kind of network an electronic signal, or token, is passed from node to node in a predetermined order. A finite amount of information can be transmitted from a node only if it is in possession of the token at the time transmission is requested. A node must wait its turn in order to transmit data through the network. This method eliminates the kinds of contention problems that can occur on EtherNet networks and guarantees orderly network access. EtherNet network access is random and may cause many contention problems, especially during times of heavy traffic.

When IBM built Token Ring, it was built to run at 98 Mbits; IBM is currently internally running Token Ring 98 Mbits over shielded, twisted pair wire. The shielded wire is used not to prevent electrical interference from outside, but because when Token Ring runs at 98 Mbits, the wire radiates like a 50,000 watt FM radio station. Why don't we have 98 Mbits Token Ring running in our corporations? Because of IBM's marketing plan. Every two to three years, IBM plans to speed up the Token Ring available to the public. When Token Ring first came out, companies bought 4 Mbits Token Ring. A few years later, IBM made the 16 Mbits card available. In a year or two, IBM will announce a 32 Mbits Token Ring card, and then a 64 card. With each update, IBM is collecting large revenues. Get the picture? IBM wants to sell a new Token Ring card every three years to large accounts who are building production subsystems that need Token Ring cards in quantities that begin at 10,000.

Connectivity

The basic network cabling, along with the required linking devices, such as connectors, transceivers, and MAUs, typically provides the physical plant for LANs. The trend for most businesses that rightsize their systems, however, is to build applications for more than one location. The four primary devices for connecting LANs to construct a wide-area network are repeaters, bridges, routers, and gateways.

Repeaters

A repeater is the simplest method of connecting long segments of a single LAN or multiple LANs. *Repeaters* are powered hardware devices that amplify and distribute transmissions from one LAN to another LAN. Because repeaters contain multiple cabling ports, they enable the installation of additional nodes on a network. LAN cable distances can be extended because of the amplification of transmissions by repeaters.

Repeaters can connect only identical LANs: LAN connections must be EtherNet-to-EtherNet, token-ring-to-token-ring, and so on. Repeaters are technologically very simple and therefore do not filter or change transmissions other than through amplification. All transmissions through repeaters are propagated to all other workstations, which can lead to decreased LAN performance.

Bridges

Bridges are similar to repeaters because they also connect at the hardware level. Also like repeaters, bridges can be used only to link similar LAN cabling networks, that is, EtherNet-to-EtherNet or token-ring-to-token-ring.

Unlike repeaters, bridges use *routing tables* to determine whether transmissions should be allowed through the bridge. Any transmissions sent to other clients or servers on the same side of the bridge do not pass through the bridge. If a transmission is sent to a client or server on the other side of the bridge, it is routed through the bridge. In this manner, local traffic stays local and does not interfere with performance on the other side of the bridge. Only inter-network traffic crosses the bridge.

Bridges that are well-designed in the physical plant can lead to better performance across a network. For example, a LAN can be divided into local working areas by use of bridges. When a LAN is divided properly, local transmissions remain in one area, without bridging to another area. Only transmissions addressed to devices in another working area have to cross the bridge. This method reduces overall LAN traffic and, therefore, leads to better performance. If bridges are not used effectively, however, they can become transmission bottlenecks, leading to a decrease in network performance.

Routers

Routers perform basically the same function as repeaters and bridges; they differ, however, from repeaters and bridges because they are hardware-independent. This independence enables routers to link together and operate on many types of networks (EtherNet-to-token-ring, for example). Although most existing models of routers are still protocol-specific and cannot communicate across different protocols, more and more multiprotocol routers are being introduced. Wellfleet, Cisco, 3Com, and Proteon all have developed routers that support multiple protocols.

Routers transmit only data addressed to devices on the other side of the router. As with bridges, this helps reduce inter-network traffic by keeping transmissions local whenever possible. Like bridges, a poorly designed router configuration can cause bottlenecks.

Gateways

Gateways work at the protocol level and provide protocol conversion, enabling different protocols to transmit data between each other. Gateways also provide conversion between physically different networks and computer systems. X.25 gateways are used to connect LANs to WANs (wide area networks). The gateway for an X.25 protocol usually consists of a PC desktop computer, a wide area communications board, communications software, and a high-speed, synchronous modem.

X.25 gateways typically encapsulate from a PC LAN protocol in the international standard X.25 protocol format and transmit across the WAN. The contents and structure of these packets are transparent to the protocol. X.25 is not concerned with the data in the packet. Communication is completed if the receiving X.25 switching device understands the data transmitted by the sending device. An X.25 gateway enables multiple users to access a WAN through a single connection simultaneously. Several users can be running different processes through a single, dedicated X.25 gateway.

Note that X.25 merely acts as a shipping mechanism. It packs up the data from the LAN and sends it while the receiving LAN unpacks it. Remember that X.25 is a point-to-point protocol; only if the LAN protocol is *reliable* (meaning that it guarantees delivery, such as SPX) do the sending and receiving LANs enforce reliable transmission.

A LAN-to-host gateway connects multiple workstation PCs on a LAN to a mainframe or minicomputer not locally connected to the LAN. The host gateway usually is a PC on the LAN that is dedicated to gateway communication. In some cases, gateways work also as nondedicated workstations. The host gateway contains a special communications board and special communications software to communicate with network PCs and the host computer. Although the gateway serves as the link to the host computer, individual LAN workstations using the host computer must run communication software and terminal emulation software to be capable of talking directly with the host computer.

Terminal emulation software enables each PC workstation to act as a *dumb terminal*; to the host computer, each workstation seems to be another standard mainframe terminal. LAN-to-host gateways vary widely in performance, screen display, and functionality.

Other Remote Data Communications Issues

Connectivity devices, such as routers and gateways, extend network connectivity beyond local or campus distances. They enable networks that are remote to be logically connected and to form what seems to the user to be one giant, wide-area, or enterprise-wide network.

The term used in linking together devices over long distances is *remote data communications*. Because of the extra distance typical in remote data communications, links must be fast and efficient. Data transmission can be done through asynchronous or synchronous communication alternatives.

In *asynchronous* communication, data is transmitted as a continuous bit stream. Start bits and stop bits also are sent to indicate the beginning and end of each character. When problems occur during transmission, the entire bit stream must be retransmitted. There are two modes of asynchronous transmission: *full duplex* and *half duplex*. With full duplex transmissions, both sides can transmit signals simultaneously. With half duplex, only one side at a time can transmit signals.

Asynchronous communication is beneficial because it is simple to set up and use on standard, dial-up telephone lines. Because of the overhead use of start bits and stop bits and retransmission requirements for error recovery, however, synchronous communication is more efficient. *Synchronous communication* transmits data in blocks, with a leading *synchronization character* to identify the data sent. Because synchronous communication does not have to send start bits and stop bits for each character, error recovery is better and transmissions are faster. In addition, with the advent of high-speed (9600 baud) synchronous modems, the use of normal, voice-grade, dial-up lines has become a feasible solution to remote linking.

Remote data communications can occur through many mediums. The slowest medium is voice-grade dial-up lines (9.6K per second), followed by conditioned data-grade lines (56K per second), with high-speed T-1 lines and satellite links (1.544 Mbits per second) as the fastest medium. Remote access through modems is extremely slow. Faster media, such as T-1 lines, are much preferred and more closely resemble LAN speeds. Monthly costs for a high-speed method, however, can be very expensive.

Clients and Servers

Conventional wisdom, from the days of traditional computing, said that you should always choose your software first, then your hardware. In building the network platform, however, this process is much more parallel than ever before. True, you still want to let the particular business need that the application will meet drive your hardware selection; but, you want to choose the client and server computers at least at the same time—if not before—you choose the network operating system and other physical plant components.

This process is parallel because so many decisions about the rest of the network are contingent on the clients and the servers—which workstation operating system they use, how much memory they can hold, what processor they use (and whether they have multiprocessor capability), what kind of internal bus they use, and so on. Thus, the following sections discuss some key issues regarding the selection of clients and servers for the network.

Clients

Because of the commodity nature that PCs have taken on during the past few years, the question of product brand in selecting the network client is hardly an issue anymore. Instead, the issue is more one of ensuring that the network client has the greatest likelihood of living up to the model of the ideal client, as shown in Figure 12.6.

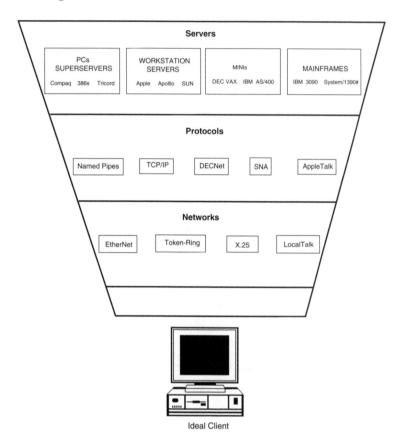

Figure 12.6. The ideal client.

As the figure shows, the ideal client is one that can easily become part of a *seamless* network, in which a user does not have to take extra, system-oriented steps to get work done on the computer. The ideal client allows a user to manipulate any data using any combination of data analysis and presentation. The ideal client is scaleable—it can grow without unduly disrupting the user.

The figure shows also the flexibility requirements of the ideal client as they exist today. The client must be able to work with any number of networks, interpret any number of protocols, and interact with any number of different kinds of servers. Clearly, not all these requirements are the function of the client PC itself. The key, however, is to buy clients that don't inhibit any of these "ideal" attributes because of their technological limitations.

There are many choices in selecting a server platform, and there are just as many decisions to be made at the client/workstation level. Using a 286 workstation is clearly a possibility. However, the 386 is more popular and a better choice. If you're thinking about going to client/server, you should begin thinking about using 386s for all of your clients; 286s will not handle client/server applications well because they lack memory capabilities. Each client should have a minimum of 8M of memory.

You can employ RISC workstations, which are very good workstations, especially if you have a UNIX server. There's a certain symmetry to a RISC client talking to a RISC server. But remember, just as RISC machines are very powerful, they are also relatively expensive. It is hard to cost-justify the use of RISC boxes as X-terminals, because they are so expensive both in terms of hardware and required software. Most cost-benefit studies have found that they rarely are worth the extra cost.

Network Servers

In the late 1980s, vendors introduced high-performance microcomputers for use on LANs. These *superservers*, although technically still considered microcomputers, are more powerful than normal microcomputers and were designed specifically for use as LAN file servers. Part of the impetus for their development came from the fact that the major NOS vendors really do provide "dedicated" platforms. This means that, although you can run an application on the server, its performance suffers when it is not dedicated to the task of providing network services.

Superservers have high-performance disk and input/output (I/O) systems and can support a larger number of users than can a normal PC. Many superservers offer multiple processor configurations, usually based on the 80386 or 80486 Intel processors, with storage capacities that rival mainframes. Superservers are being designed with additional capabilities that improve their survivability as engines for mission-critical applications, such as disk shadowing and uninterruptible power supplies.

In a LAN using a superserver, the network can be set up using any variety of cabling options. Desktop computers are used as workstation PCs. Rather than install another PC as the file server, you connect the superserver to the network as the dedicated file server. The end result is improved performance.

A major disadvantage of multiprocessor superservers is that not all operating systems are designed to utilize multiple processors. This situation is changing quickly as software vendors, such as Novell, are becoming committed to supporting multiprocessor superservers. Microsoft's LAN Manager supports *asymmetric multiprocessing*, in which one processor is dedicated to the file system and network applications and the other processor runs OS/2 applications. Banyan System and Santa Cruz Operation also support synchronous mode multiprocessing, dividing tasks between the processors as available.

Many companies are potentially saving millions of dollars a year in maintenance and software costs by switching from mainframe- or minicomputer-based systems to PC LANs served by a superserver. Superserver costs are comparable to minicomputer costs, ranging from $20,000 to $100,000. Companies are discovering also that reliability and scaleability are improved with superservers.

There are other choices for server hardware platforms. You could buy an inexpensive 386 or 486 machine—they are very popular. Both the 386 and 486 are good machines, but there is always the chance that serious problems will stem from their memory limitations. Inadequate memory can cause both system and I/O performance problems: a database won't work if the I/O channel becomes choked quickly. Memory limitations also dictate the number of concurrent users. If you have an adequate machine and a good DBMS software server, a 386 or 486 could probably support 30 to 50 users. But that's only if you have a good (efficient) DBMS server. If you don't, you could possibly be stuck with an upper limit of *three* or *four* concurrent users. Obviously, it is important to be very careful when choosing both the hardware server platform and the DBMS. A poor choice can translate into limited processing capabilities.

If you have a PC-based server running OS/2 but you need more power, and you've done a good job in picking a DBMS server and product tools, you have the option of moving to a superserver that runs OS/2. Parallan and NetFrame are two examples. These two companies have pushed and pulled OS/2 to produce greater memory and I/O capacities.

A different hardware solution is NCR's new 3600 product line, which is fully scaleable and allows the user to run either OS/2 or UNIX. You can have anywhere from one to 1,000 processors. The problem with such scaleability is that in running the same software across such different machines, you can't be guaranteed to receive the full potential speed and power of that system.

Note that without support for symmetric multiprocessing yet, OS/2 won't be able to take advantage of the high end of the NCR line.

Other choices for server platforms include RISC-based processors, such as SPARC from SUN and Precision Architecture from Hewlett Packard. These products work well as servers. Using RISC or SPARC will afford you more concurrent users and I/O capabilities. When there are so many concurrent users, however, you need more software—such as performance monitors—and more administration support—such as DBAs and LAN administrators—to understand, monitor, and control this environment. For the most part, these essential control aids are still missing from UNIX platforms.

Building the Enterprise View

This chapter has described various hardware and connectivity products required to set up a basic network platform. The next two chapters move from basics to the more advanced subjects of additional key networking technology (Chapter 13, "Developments in Networking Technologies") and network management (Chapter 14, "Network Management"). Both are essential elements of today's mission-critical networks. The application-development environment that is implemented on the network is discussed in Chapter 15.

One thing you shouldn't lose sight of amid the discussion of all these devices, protocols, wires, and so on is that the objective is still to build a single-enterprise view of the information system. Through rightsizing, you can take the network platform and replace dozens of cubic yards of big, mainframe iron in the glass house with a silent, linked-together set of PCs, servers, and specialized connection devices that are on your desk, under the bookcase, and in the supply closet.

Developments
in Networking
Technologies

Developments
in Networking
Technologies

13

All things make room for others and nothing remains still.

—Heracleitus (500 BC)

Objectives:

1. To help you understand changes that are driving the need for new networking technologies.
2. To help you appreciate the limitations in present circuit-switching and X.25 packet-switching environments.
3. To help you understand the advantages of new technologies such as frame relay and cell relay.

The evolution toward many small but powerful computers has had several effects on data networks.

- First, there is an inherent increase in the need to share files and data as systems are rightsized.
- Second, workstations are increasingly graphics-oriented, and transmitting a high-resolution graphics image requires millions of bits. This move from textual to graphic interactions creates the need for much higher throughput.
- Third, the communications requirements for accessing files and databases have been increasing rapidly in recent years as part of the natural growth of an expanding field.

All these effects create the need for networks to support large blocks of data. The data rates of today's wide-area networks, however, are insufficient to transmit large blocks with acceptable delay.

The performance experienced with local networks is driving changes in the wide-area network also. The link capacities available in local area networks have been much larger than those in wide-area networks. Unlike wide-area networks, the cost of a local area network is not dominated by transmission costs. Coaxial cable and even twisted-pair cable can achieve relatively high-speed communication at modest cost in a building or campus environment. As workstation users become accustomed to sending images and large files over local area networks, they expect to do the same over wide-area networks with similar service response. Today, local area networks are forced to operate at wide-area network speeds. Tomorrow, wide-area networks will have to operate at local network speeds.

As data communications requirements have changed, there have been dramatic reductions in the costs associated with networking due to three main events. First, the costs of wide-area networks have, until recently, been dominated by the costs of transmission. Advances in optical-fiber technology, however, are reducing the cost of transmission, particularly at high data rates.

Carriers such as AT&T, Sprint, and MCI are rapidly deploying optical fiber, which soon will be the primary mode of transmission. The result will be the availability of much higher-capacity links at much lower costs.

Because nodes within the network are small computers, the cost of a given amount of processing within the network has been decreasing rapidly. This cost decrease makes it feasible to perform data computational tasks in the network that until now were cost prohibitive.

Finally, the equipment serving as end devices for the network has changed. In the past, networks were primarily hierarchical in design, dumb terminals being connected to mainframe computers. As a result, all network processing had to be performed within the network itself. Now that intelligent terminals and workstations are prevalent, some processing tasks can be offloaded from the network, improving throughput efficiency.

Limitations in Networking Technology

As more network applications have to operate at high speeds across a wide area network with the same connectivity, and because of the response times to which users have become accustomed in their local communications, the limitations of present day switching techniques become an issue. Users often attempt to connect local networks with bridges and routers using dedicated lines. As the complexity of such networks grows, serious drawbacks can result, including higher transmission costs, lower reliability, and limited network-management capability. Today's two major switching technologies, TDM circuit switching and X.25 packet switching, do not measure up to the requirements being placed on networks.

TDM Circuit Switching

Time division multiplexing (TDM) divides transmission bandwidth into multiple, fixed-length time slots. Attached devices are assigned one or more time slots, depending on their requirements. When a device is sending data, the bits are simply placed in the time slots. No address information is required because the receiver understands which bits belong to which device according to where they appear in the time sequence. This approach is efficient from a network-delay point of view.

When a device is not sending data, however, the time slots are empty and go unused. TDM circuit switching therefore is well-suited for applications, such as voice, that are characterized by a relatively constant stream of bits, the need for high speed, and a low tolerance for network delays. The primary drawback is the inefficient handling of *bursty* applications, because bandwidth is allocated to a time slot whether or not traffic exists.

One of the key characteristics in both LAN-to-LAN and graphics-based applications is the need to transmit high volumes of data in bursts. TDM circuit switching is not well-suited for transmitting this type of traffic.

X.25 Packet Switching

Packet switching solves the problem of empty time slots by dividing the user data stream into packets that contain both source and destination addresses. When a device needs to send a large burst of data, the equivalent of several time slots can be used to accommodate the data. This is known as *statistical multiplexing* because it depends on not every device needing to send a burst of data at the same time. Most present-day packet switching is based on the international X.25 standard. Packet switching is widely used for transaction-oriented applications such as reservation systems, banking, and electronic point-of-sale.

The major drawback of X.25 packet switching is its lack of speed. The full-featured X.25 protocol was developed at a time when transmission lines were much lower in quality. This low quality required complete error detection and correction. As a result, a relatively large amount of processing is performed on each packet. The price paid for the efficient handling of bursty data is lower throughput and more network delay than with TDM circuit switching. For these reasons, X.25 packet switching is not suitable for LAN-to-LAN and graphics-based applications networking, which require much higher speeds.

In summary, present switching technologies cannot support the new demands being placed on networks. Circuit switching provides high throughput but does not use bandwidth efficiently. X.25 packet switching improves the utilization of bandwidth but is limited in throughput and can introduce unwanted delay. As a result, a whole new suite of switching technologies, often referred to as *fast packet switching*, has developed. The only commonly available fast-packet-switching technology is called *frame relay*.

Frame Relay

Fundamentally, frame relay is statistical multiplexing over a shared network. It can be thought of as a streamlined version of X.25 packet switching. When X.25 was developed, transmission lines were not of the high quality we have today. As a result, a significant part of X.25 overhead is associated with error detection and correction. At each node, the incoming packet is stored and checked for errors, and is not forwarded until errors are corrected.

Frame relay, on the other hand, does not perform error correction. It assumes the use of an error-correction protocol operating in the end devices. This assumption is practical only in using high-quality transmission lines. Otherwise, performance deteriorates because too much time is spent retransmitting messages. X.25 was developed at a time when most terminals had little or no processing capability. Because frame relay is intended for use between intelligent end points, error correction can be performed outside the network.

This reduction of processing within the network gives frame relay much higher throughput. Frame relay is being implemented at DS1 (1.5 megabits per second) speeds. In contrast, X.25 networks typically use 56 kilobit-per-second transmission facilities. Although frame relay has been standardized at the DS1 rate for now, no technological reason prevents operation at higher speeds.

Frame relay equipment and services are readily available in the marketplace. Virtually all the carriers offer, or have announced plans to offer, public frame relay services. The major manufacturers of bridges and routers support frame relay, as well as most of the T-1 multiplexor and X.25 switch suppliers.

What, then, are the limitations of frame relay? Frame relay is not well-suited to the transmission of both voice and data, because frame relay uses a variable length framing structure. Frames can vary from a few characters to thousands of characters. If a voice frame were transmitted just after several very long frames, an intolerable delay would be experienced. Further, the delay on voice transmissions would be variable, depending on the makeup of other frames being transmitted. The solution to the variable frame problem is called *cell relay*.

Cell Relay

Broadband ISDN (BISDN), Switched Multimegabit Data Service (SMDS), and Asynchronous Transfer Mode (ATM) are all examples of *cell relay* technologies. Cell relay uses a fixed length, 53-byte cell rather than a variable length. The length of the cell was selected partly because of its suitability for voice. The fixed small-packet, or cell, size is suitable for delay-sensitive traffic. Moreover, using a fixed-length format simplifies processing and further improves throughput.

Proponents of cell relay believe that it represents a single, unifying technology that can accommodate a different mix of transmission speeds and delay requirements. Some even argue that cell relay technologies such as ATM will be used in high-speed, local area networks, and replace the Fiber Distributed Data Interface (FDDI) technology. They argue that FDDI, unlike ATM, is a shared media interface and will encounter performance problems at very high speeds. The main attribute of ATM is its support of a wide range of data, video, and voice applications in the same public network. ATM supports transmission speeds of 155 Mbps and 622 Mbps. A generic ATM-based network can support services such as cell relay, frame relay, SMDS, and circuit emulation. Further, the concept of a single technology encompassing local and wide area networks is appealing. Cell relay will be implemented in the future, as it requires a new generation of hardware technology and additional standards development.

Fast Ethernet

Another promising development to support high bandwidth applications, such as multimedia, video, and imaging, is Fast Ethernet. Fast Ethernet (100 Mbps) is run over Category 3, 4, and 5 unshielded twisted-pair (UTP). Thus, companies with UTP cabling already in place may not have to purchase cabling to incorporate Fast Ethernet. Fast Ethernet is still under development as standards committees are trying to formulate IEEE standardization for it.

Network planners face several key issues. They have to consider the implications of emerging technologies, such as ATM and Fast Ethernet. Some believe that frame relay is an interim technology, soon to be replaced by cell relay. The implication is that conversion to frame relay is not worth the effort. The carriers are strong proponents of cell relay because they want to attract all traffic to their public networks. The network planner must decide whether this is acceptable or whether private networks should be maintained for at least mission-critical applications. Some argue that frame relay at high speeds will be more efficient because it supports large frames, while cell relay had to compromise with a small frame size to be capable of supporting voice and video. If this argument is valid, private frame relay networks may exist for a long time.

The private-versus-public network debate is central to the network planner's dilemma. In the mid-1980s, many companies integrated voice and data onto T-1 multiplexor networks. In recent years, several users have resegregated voice and data. Voice is being removed from the T-1 networks because of the attractive pricing of the carrier's virtual private network services. The re-integration of voice and data is not a foregone conclusion.

One thing is clear: The move to broadband networking is highly dependent on the growth of LAN-to-LAN and graphics-based applications. Without the added network requirements created by these applications, the new technologies are not needed—a simple fact that escapes many people!

Network Management

He has put to hazard his ease, his security, his interest, his power, even his darling popularity, for the benefit of people whom he has never seen.

—Edmund Burke
(18th c.)

Objectives:

1. To help you understand the critical role of network management.
2. To introduce you to the components of network management.
3. To teach you the importance of understanding network management from a management point of view.

As networks proliferate and become more critical to the operation of a company, network management is developing into one of the most important areas in the field of communications. A network is of little practical use if it cannot be managed effectively. In fact, many communications managers now list network management as their primary concern.

It is difficult to place too much emphasis on the value of powerful network-management capabilities. Networking experts unanimously agree that one of the biggest problems today in dealing with the explosive growth of LANs is that no one knows what is the real traffic on the LANs or between the LANs. A diagnostic capability also must exist so that downtime can be minimized and problems solved.

As is not really surprising or unusual in the communications industry, most network-management discussions center around technical concepts. In most cases, the people assigned to solve the problem have technical, rather than managerial, backgrounds. This is not to say that technical issues are not meaningful, but without a sound management basis, technology becomes somewhat inapplicable. In reality, many "technical dreams" involving network management capability may not come to fruition for several years. The network manager, however, must devise a solution that meets the needs of the firm based on capabilities presently available.

Network Management: A Working Definition

A sound, working definition of network management must include all activities required to ensure that the network cost-effectively provides a satisfactory level of service. This includes activities traditionally associated with network management, such as being able to identify, diagnose, and repair problems in the network (network maintenance activities are discussed more thoroughly in Chapter 19, "Maintenance"). Also included, however, are network design, cost controls, and effective administrative procedures. Moreover, the overall context should be centered around providing service levels that meet the needs of the end users.

Network Design

The importance of network design often is overlooked. The key to network management is to design the network correctly in the first place—otherwise, you're always trying to catch up no matter how sophisticated your network management capability is.

Network design emphasizes quality through engineering, documentation, and processes. To accomplish this quality, certain elements are needed, including:

- Design and verification procedures
- Mechanisms for managing the network elements
- A thorough understanding and documentation of all procedures
- The use of suppliers' capabilities and technologies

Security must also be addressed on a network, and the number of people allowed to change the system must be kept to a minimum.

Administrative Management

Finally, there are the less glamorous parts of network management, which fall into an administrative category. These parts include the capability to bill users, validate vendor invoices, monitor costs, and manage network-related projects.

The Evolution of Network Management

Successful data networking is dependent on sound network management. Except for backup dialing capability, limited public alternatives are available; they must be designed into the network. You could argue that an occasional delay in placing a call in a voice network is more of a nuisance than a real problem, especially when you consider that truly important phone calls almost always can be placed on the public network. Data networks, on the other hand, usually are far more critical to the day-to-day business of the firm. Not surprisingly, then, network management in the data network arena has concentrated on

- Real-time monitoring of the network
- The capability to diagnose faults

■ The capability to control, to some extent, the correcting of the problem and employing back-up capability

Because there was no market for integrated solutions until the late '80s or even the early '90s, suppliers of network management products tended to concentrate on specific aspects of the problem. Some suppliers marketed call accounting packages; others marketed data test equipment. Still others marketed performance-monitoring systems. Many tools that have been available were developed by suppliers to augment their particular equipment or service. In many cases, the suppliers were driven by a proprietary marketing motivation, which resulted in tools that worked well with only their own equipment. Attempting now to integrate tools from different suppliers is still extremely difficult. Users who have done a good job with respect to overall network management find themselves with a hodgepodge of difficult-to-maintain software, incompatible functional modules, and duplication in areas such as network inventory databases and trouble ticketing systems.

Network Management Today

Network management is changing, however. The demands being placed on network management systems today require a more integrated approach. First, as network expenditures continue to grow, the need for improved cost control and administrative procedures continues to receive more emphasis. Further, more and more data networks are becoming utility networks, responsible for processing several applications and creating a need to address billing and cost allocation. Companies therefore are attempting to place this part of their operation in order.

The primary area of concern, however, is data network performance. Data networks are becoming more vital to the day-to-day operation of companies. Even minor outages cannot be tolerated. For example, if an airline or hotel chain reservation network ceases to function, even for a brief time, the impact is serious.

Almost all predictions agree that this heavy dependence on information systems will continue to grow, which leads to the premise that the successful companies will be the ones that can best manage their information. This statement implies a tremendous reliance on networks. As a result, it can be assumed also that network management will continue to grow in importance in the years to come.

Trends in Network Management Tools

Network management tools have evolved in a very short time from isolated tools solving single network management problems to highly integrated "umbrella" managers that attempt to provide the network manager with a single view or a command center from which to manage the entire internetwork. Some trends that are affecting the architecture and feature sets of network management tools in current and future releases include:

- True integration of network management products from multiple vendors through a common data model instead of pseudointegration consisting merely of providing access to add-in products through additional menu bar choices.

- Automation and simplification of tedious configuration and administration tasks performed manually today. Examples include automatic discovery of new networked devices and the use of device configuration templates that allow managers to find and start managing new devices quickly and easily.

- "Process frameworks" that involve enabling network management tools to take a broader, process-oriented view of network management instead of being narrowly focused on single network management problems.

- Distributed management agents that receive and interpret data from network devices and optionally initiate corrective actions without the need to send all of the status data to a centralized management console and wait for operator input.

- Separate network management domains that distribute responsibility for network management to remote sites. This allows individual managers to be responsible for the service level of a remote site while keeping a centralized network management information repository constantly updated. For domain management to succeed, network management platforms must support peer-to-peer relationships and must allow multiple users to operate the network management software from multiple locations simultaneously.

- Intelligent event processing using rules-based logic and filters to send a minimum amount of network management data to the network management console. This reduces the load that network management information places on network capacity and allows the network operations staff to focus on only those events that require attention instead of wading through masses of nonmeaningful status messages.

Providers of Network Management Tools

In today's highly distributed, heterogeneous networks, it is unlikely that a single vendor will provide all of the components of the network management solution. The trend to incorporate SNMP (Simple Network Management Protocol) agents and RMON (Remote Monitoring) problems directly into networking equipment will further heighten the need for multivendor interoperability.

The component that is most affected by the need for interoperability is the network management console. The network management console usually consists of a UNIX workstation that collects and analyzes information from networked devices such as hubs, routers, file servers, and UNIX application servers. Status information is compared to user-defined thresholds to determine whether problems that will impact network service-level goals have occurred. The status information is also used to update a simple "network map" to provide the network operator with visual indicators of the health of the network.

There are several vendors that provide DOS- and Windows-based network management applications. However, these products are limited by the ability of DOS to quickly process large volumes of data generated by the managed network devices. They are best suited to networks with a relatively small number of managed devices or networks that can afford to collect status information on an infrequent basis. Novell's Network Management System and Hewlett-Packard's OpenView for Windows are examples of network management consoles that do not require a UNIX workstation.

UNIX-based network management consoles include the following:

- **Hewlett-Packard (HP) OpenView Network Node Manager**— Widely recognized as the network management market leader today, OpenView's key strengths include its strong support from third-party add-in products, automatic discovery of network devices, and availability of Application Builder for customizing OpenView without programming. HP's plans to support "process frameworks" and object technology in OpenView Version 4 should help keep OpenView at the top of of the list of many network managers.

- **SunConnect SunNet Manager**—Probably still has the largest install base of any of the major vendors. However, SunNet's technology is somewhat dated and its market share is starting to slip. SunConnect has recently tried to regain market presence by joining in an agreement with NetLabs, Inc., for its DIMONS technology.

- **IBM AIX System View NetView/6000**—Originally based on OpenView code licensed from HP, this IBM product has big improvements in ease of use and multiprotocol support. IBM's licensing agreement with HP, which should result in versions of NetView for other platforms besides the RS/6000, ends in 1994.

- **Digital Equipment Corp. (DEC) POLYCENTER Manager on Netview**—In August, 1993, IBM and Digital announced that they would jointly port IBM NetView/6000 to Digital's Alpha AXP platforms and codevelop all future versions. POLYCENTER adds support for DECnet Phase IV protocol and provides for tight integration with installed POLYCENTERmcc applications. The companies also plan to port POLYCENTER to run on MicroSoft's Windows NT operating system for DEC's Alpha processors.

- **Cabletron Systems SPECTRUM for Open Systems**—SPECTRUM's "network virtual machine" creates a working model of every device in the network and updates this model with real-time data. The information in the network model is used by SPECTRUM's inference engine to process events and to automatically take corrective actions, if desired.

- **Netlabs, Inc. DIMONS**—The key strengths of DIMONS include "Domain Management"—which allows multiple DIMONS managers to be interconnected to create a network management hierarchy— and the "NerveCenter" alarm system—which filters network information, generates alarms, if needed, and automatically initiates corrective actions, such as sending e-mail, beeping a pager, or launching a third-party application.

- **AT&T Global Information Solutions OneVision**—AT&T GIS and HP have announced a partnership that will involve porting HP's OpenView to UNIX SVR4 on AT&T hardware. OneVision should combine AT&T's BaseWorX Applications Platform, targeted primarily to the management of highly complex public telecommunications networks, with OpenView's capability to manage private internetworks. Because AT&T's current Star SENTRY product is based on technology from Netlabs, Inc., HP has agreed to migrate NetLabs NerveCenter technology into future releases of OpenView to give current StarSENTRY customers an easier migration path.

- **Objective Systems Integrators NetExpert**—NetExpert gained a reputation as an integrated manager of multivendor, multiprotocol networks in the cellular telecommunications industry. Its strengths include rules-based event processing, the capability to interface to nonstandard network components, and the capability to store network management information in a variety of SQL databases, such as Oracle, Sybase, Informix, and Ingres.

Network Management Tool Evaluation Criteria

When you evaluate network management tools, you should consider the following features and functions:

- Event processing
- Data sharing
- Multitiered, distributed management
- Adequate capacity
- Availability of add-in tools
- Support for target environment
- Hardware/operating system support
- Support for object-based technology

Some of these evaluation criteria are straight-forward. For example, either the existing hardware, software, and other aspects of the environment are supported or they are not. Other features, for example, event processing and distributed management, may need to be quantified in terms of the degree to which they are supported.

Network-Management Misconceptions

Many difficulties surrounding the network-management arena stem from approaching it as a purely technological problem. There is a concentration on subjects such as expert systems, artificial intelligence, OSI interfaces, graphic displays, multiple-alarm processing, special protocol handling, and other esoteric topics. The issue is not that these concepts are an unimportant part of network management—they are essential—but that you get the impression that these concepts comprise the entire problem. Management issues don't receive the attention they warrant. As a result, certain weaknesses exist.

Neglecting the Nontechnical Aspect of Network Management

Several elements to successful network management don't depend on technical solutions, but rather require sound management practices and discipline. Change management is a case in point. Veteran telecommunications-operations managers appreciate that it is impossible to manage a network successfully without good change control procedures. This area involves such items as design reviews, sign-offs by all affected personnel, and perfect communication of all change information. Part of this process involves updating the network inventory database so that accurate knowledge about what constitutes the network exists at all times.

Although successful change management can use technology to facilitate the process, the challenge is managerial. You must create an adequate process and then instill the management discipline for that process to perform effectively.

Neglecting the Role of People

Many ignore the "people part" of the network-management equation. There seems to be an assumption that the tools for managing networks will be so sophisticated that even inexperienced people will be able to operate them. In reality, the more sophisticated the technology, the more skillful people need to be. Employee knowledge, skills, competency, and attitudes are at least as important as the technology. As networks become more complex, network management becomes more complex. It is hopelessly naive to think that network-management systems being developed are so refined and foolproof that the networks can almost run themselves. It may be an admirable goal, but the probability of achieving fruition in any reasonable timeframe is not good.

Overlooking the Advantages of Integration

Many network managers tend to view network management as a set of discrete problems. Each problem tends to be addressed separately, resulting in a number of corresponding "solutions." There probably are three reasons for this:

- First, technical people tend to specialize. For example, network engineers rarely are expert in all aspects of data networking. They tend to focus, therefore, on a piece of the total problem.
- Second, many network management problems are not technical in nature. In these cases, another group of people, such as MIS specialists, tend to be assigned to the problem.
- Third, many network management tools are supplied by equipment and service vendors who specialize in their own product and service.

Those who view the problem with a managerial focus quickly become concerned with the fragmented approach being taken. Such an environment breeds duplication and lack of control. Problems can "fall through the cracks." Duplication of information and conflicting data is likely. Consider the need for good inventory management. That you cannot validate an invoice from a supplier unless you know what is in the network implies a need for some type of network inventory. Similarly, diagnosing a problem is difficult unless you know exactly what is in the network. This too implies the need for a network inventory. Thus, two very different aspects of the total network management problem rely on an accurate network database.

Lack of Customer Orientation

Network management systems commonly use measures that are difficult to relate to the satisfaction of the network end users. The right questions to ask are those such as "What does this customer really need?" rather than "How well can we really do?" For example, a network might provide 99.5 percent availability to its customers. The network manager must go one step further and determine whether the measure is adequate for the needs and expectations of its customers. Perhaps for the needs of its customers, this percentage is more than adequate. In that case, the company probably should not strive to improve availability; or, as is more likely, maybe 99.5 percent is not sufficient.

The point is that the company must look at its measurement standards from a user viewpoint. Establishing service-level contracts with end users probably is a good idea. Customer satisfaction must be the driving principle. To do this, technical measures and goals of network performance must be translated into customer-relevant measures.

Insufficient Attention to Network Design

Lastly, a network must be designed with management objectives in mind. If the network design is inadequate, a sophisticated network-management system does nothing more than tell you in elegant terms what you already know—you have a problem. Sound network management begins with sound design.

The fact that many suppliers of network-management products do not offer network design capability does not mean that it's not part of the network-management problem. It means simply that the suppliers have chosen not to offer a design capability as part of their product.

Conclusion

The key to a successful network-management system is to view the problem from a managerial, rather than a technological, perspective. Network management must be approached as a total problem. Addressing each individual aspect separately does nothing more than create independent solutions that have no common ties to the total problem.

Companies first must reevaluate the type of people they have assigned to solve their network-management problems. People adept at addressing technical issues usually are not the type who excel in installing management systems. A good network-management team must include members who possess these strengths:

- A management focus. These people understand the business activities of the organization, yet possess sufficient technical expertise so that technical objectives can be related to business objectives.
- A service orientation. These people interface with the network users and, therefore, should possess good interpersonal skills.
- Technical expertise. These people not only must be able to solve technical-network problems but also must be adept at creating a working set of network-management tools.

It's not likely that one person will have all these traits. The network management team must be composed of people with a blend of these skills.

Looking at all the elements of network management, you can see that network management no longer can be regarded solely as a technical function. If a company hopes to manage its information efficiently and be successful in applying information technology, it must begin to view network management from a broader perspective.

The Rightsizing
Development
Environment

The Rightsizing Development Environment

15

Time is the only thing I can't get more of.

—Anonymous end user

Objectives:

1. To help you understand the objectives of a network-based transaction processing system.
2. To teach you the key criteria in selecting a network-based development environment for transaction processing applications.
3. To help you understand the issues and key criteria regarding the selection of a database and DBMS tools for the development environment for transaction processing applications.
4. To teach you about other development environment tools associated with creating mission-critical transaction processing applications on a network platform.

Many recognize the benefits that client/server network computing offers in terms of flexibility and personal productivity. For rightsizing to be a real solution to the challenges facing the Fortune 1000 and other large companies, rightsized systems must be able to match the processing capability and system reliability of traditional mainframe systems while performing the same tasks that historically have been the domain of these large systems.

In some extreme cases, companies are intent on removing all hosts and going to 100 percent PC-based information systems. Others are finding that, for now, a heterogeneous (that is, multilevel and multivendor) computing system makes the most sense. Fortunately, the technology exists to enable these firms to enjoy the benefits of rightsized systems while using their existing resources.

An important part of the technology developments that make this heterogeneous system possible is the shifting role of applications over the past decade. As Figure 15.1 shows, the trend has been to isolate many system-level functions of an application—such as displaying information or communicating with the network—and make them the responsibility of other software tools. This trend has enabled developers to focus their application development work on just the key functions to be accomplished.

This chapter describes various software tools for a development environment that supports the rapid development of information systems based on client/server network computing technology.

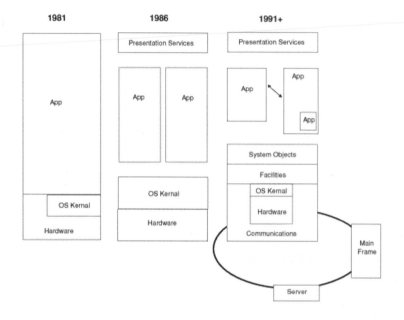

Source: Revelation Technologies

Figure 15.1. The changing role of the application.

Transaction Processing on a Network

A fundamental assumption driving large-scale rightsizing is that LAN-based platforms are capable of providing *online transaction processing* (OLTP) activities, often as well as mainframes. OLTP systems include applications such as order entry and billing, payroll, and purchasing—applications that support a company's day-to-day operations.

One of the distinctive characteristics of transaction processing systems in general is their heavy use of batch processing, or batch. *Batch* refers to the sequential processing of a series of like business transactions until all are complete. For instance, in a typical batch system, all new orders are processed, then all returns, and finally all other adjustments.

There is no shortage of mature development tools for PC systems. Requirements for transactional systems, however, differ fundamentally from those for which typical PC-based development tools were diagnosed. Fortunately, transactional architectures for client/server networks are emerging.

To accelerate rightsizing, these tools must provide a complete environment with functionality every bit as rich and comprehensive as that available on larger computers. The remainder of this chapter covers the key development products that provide this functionality, including:

- Database management systems (that is, the "servers" in client/ server)
- Dictionary and repository tools
- Front-end development tools (that is, the "clients" in client/server)
- Compilers and debuggers
- Editors
- CASE tools
- Source code control tools

The good news is that network computing tools usually "deliver the goods" when it comes to many of the much-touted advantages over their mainframe counterparts: they're efficient, have attractive user interfaces, and are easy to use. The bad news is that, in many cases, the network application development products available are immature or incomplete in comparison to their mainframe counterparts. In some cases, as with operations management utilities, the products are virtually nonexistent. This is the reality of rightsizing. Although rightsizing has many compelling advantages, it has its pitfalls, to be discussed in more detail in Chapter 17, "Avoiding the Downsides of Rightsizing."

Criteria for Development Tools

To choose the right development tools, you first must define selection criteria. The most important criteria for development tools on a rightsizing project are covered in the following sections. Specific tools are discussed in depth later in this chapter.

Maximizing Productivity

One of the most common frustrations of users is the lengthy time it takes to see changes implemented in their information systems to better accommodate their business needs. In MIS terms, this is the applications backlog. The size and growth rate of the applications backlog in rightsized environments can be addressed in three ways:

- Use a modular or object-oriented development methodology that facilitates rapid and reusable application module development.
- Maximize the use of suitable, packaged applications software.
- Put suitable tools in the hands of end users, especially for query and analysis.

Productivity is more than just quickly creating databases, screens, and reports. Productivity is viewed properly as a lifecycle issue, from the initial conceptualization of the need through the maintenance life of the resulting system. Some tools or techniques may actually reduce immediate productivity for the sake of this long-term gain.

Performance Is Important

Users of personal computer systems have become somewhat spoiled. They now expect host-based applications to perform as quickly, and be as easy to use, as their PC-based spreadsheets and word processors. Transaction processing systems are different from single-user systems, however, and performance characteristics differ between the two. Although a comparison between these two types of applications may be unfair, the fact remains that moving applications to a network platform results in even higher performance expectations—expectations that sometimes are difficult to meet.

Tools for network computing face a similar tradeoff to those on the mainframe: performance versus productivity. Tools, such as ADS/O or Focus, trade machine cycles and I/O for developer productivity, as compared to the standard COBOL-based development tools. In the end, it comes down to the difference between using an interpreted language approach versus a compiled language approach.

One proposed solution to meeting the performance demands of rightsized transaction processing systems that use a client/server architecture is to identify the main sources of performance problems (the *bottlenecks*) and apply additional computing resources—such as more powerful processors—in those problem areas. This approach is supported by the notion that people are expensive, and computers—at least the personal kind—are cheap and getting cheaper.

This solution, although useful, does not negate the issue of network tool performance. Tool selection, even in a client/server environment, must be motivated at least in part by the performance characteristics of the tool.

Multiple Platforms Are a Fact of Life

Heterogeneous computing environments are the norm, not the exception. There is no use for a mission-critical, enterprise-wide application that cannot reasonably accommodate the multiple environments of the organization. This is because any large company is likely to have a mix of PCs operating on DOS, Windows, or OS/2; minicomputers that use some form of UNIX; and mainframes with terminals using MVS.

DOS won't go away any time soon, but not all applications can be run on DOS. The jury is out on OS/2, and UNIX is gaining ground, although there seems to be just as many versions as ever. MVS is not likely to disappear either, at least for large-scale, batch-oriented operations and very large databases.

The challenge, considering this state of affairs, is to select tools that

- Allow these platforms to coexist peaceably on a network
- Enable developers to take advantage of the inherent power available in a distributed environment, without having to concern themselves with the intricacies of communications across the network
- Maintain the controls, recoverability, and operability that are so vital to running mission-critical applications

No single vendor provides tools that address all these objectives. To meet these objectives, therefore, developing customized integration components sometimes is necessary. Such components do not deliver perceptible functionality to the end user, but the end user notices their absence when the system goes down and is unrecoverable.

Reusing Existing Skills—Not of Primary Concern

Through their years of host-based information systems development, most companies have built an extensive skill set in programming and database standards, such as batch COBOL, VSAM, IMS, IDMS, and online ADS/O. The bad news is that many of these technologies are not directly transferable to a rightsized network computing platform. The good news is that you can shift maintenance of the mainframe-based applications from the directly attached mainframe terminals to the PCs on the LANs. Details of this approach and products that support it are covered in Chapter 19, "Maintenance."

More important in today's environment is quickly establishing a skill set that addresses the challenges of developing and maintaining client/server applications. Structured query language (SQL), for example, is a critical skill, still new to many information systems shops. It's imperative, however, that SQL relational technology be considered first for any new applications because of its broad acceptance as the industry standard syntax—even if the organization currently has only a limited relational technology skills base.

The development of network-based applications has myriad different language variants: C, C++, Transact-SQL, SmallTalk, MicroFocus COBOL, Visual Basic, and the list continues. Developers can expect to work with many different language platforms.

In short, the development environment that companies implement for their rightsized systems must be

- Highly productive, from both a developer and end user perspective
- High-performance, in terms of capability to perform high-volume transaction processing where required
- Open to multiple operating system components
- Not so complex that developers are unable to quickly absorb and implement new technologies

Database Decisions

The first critical decision is that of a database management system (DBMS). The DBMS has an impact on all the other development tools and on the production environment. Essentially, a DBMS is software that provides two things:

1. A systematic way to organize and manage data
2. A user interface that lets people interact with the data

The DBMS also may have an application development capability for creating user interfaces and managing data.

Thus, Microsoft's SQL Server, Borland International's Paradox, and Progress Software's Progress all are DBMSs—but they're not equivalent. In fact, they're not really in the same category. The existence of different categories of LAN DBMSs is probably one of the most immediate messages to make clear. (Appendix D provides a detailed chart of the DBMSs available at the time this book was published.)

Paradox, for example, can best be described as a traditional multiuser LAN DBMS. These DBMSs use the LAN file server as though it were a disk drive. That is, the data files are kept on the file server's hard drive, but processing occurs at the user's workstation. When a user application running on a workstation has to update a database table, the server generally must send the entire file across the LAN to the workstation, which executes the update and sends the file back for storage. This approach is viable if the tables are relatively small and the same tables are not in constant demand by multiple users.

Such a traditional file server approach can be satisfactory with numerous, simultaneous users, if the users need only read access to the database and are not authorized to make changes. In more typical situations, however, when several users need to modify data on a regular basis, two problems quickly surface:

- When one user retrieves a table to make a change, the table is locked. In many cases, other users can read the table but cannot make changes.
- Traffic on the LAN may be unnecessarily heavy because of many requests for data by multiple personal computers.

Client/server architecture—the next generation of products beyond the traditional file server architecture—was developed to resolve these problems. Client/server architecture products greatly reduce traditional LAN DBMS problems by interposing a program, called a *database server*, between the database files and applications running on the workstations.

The database server can run on either the network file server or a separate computer. Client software running on multiple users' computers talks to the database server in SQL. In the client/server approach, the database server does most of the data processing so that only specific records of a data table, those that match the search criteria—rather than entire data tables—travel across the network.

A major architectural difference between the file server and client/server models is that, in most cases, the client/server model implies two separate programs. The program that makes up the database server portion typically is called a *back-end*; it is represented by products such as Microsoft's SQL Server and Oracle's Oracle Server. The client portion of the software typically is called a *front-end*. Front-ends often are retrofitted versions of traditional LAN DBMSs. Borland's Paradox and dBASE IV are good examples of DBMSs that were rewritten to work with database server software, such as Microsoft's SQL Server.

Proponents of the client/server approach cite a number of advantages, including

- The capability to more fully use all of the CPU power in a LAN
- The capability to mimic mainframe transaction processing systems
- Improved security
- Portability of applications

Data transparency—another client/server model advantage—encourages tasks at client workstations to be configured so that they can access multiple database servers.

Note that each advantage makes the developer's life easier, but barely affects the user. In fact, the user shouldn't be too concerned about these "technical" issues, because most have been handled previously by host-based information systems. For example, because data transparency permits physically separate or distributed database servers to act as a "single" database, users have no need to be concerned about where the records for their applications are physically located. Thus, network managers can fine-tune network configurations to improve system performance for the user without worrying about complete record accessibility.

In addition to enabling simultaneous access to data on different database servers, a client/server environment enables multiple front-end applications to access the same database. For instance, a certain data entry might be in a form-based application written in Gupta Technologies' SQLWindows, and an analyst might use a spreadsheet to access and analyze the data. A manager might use yet another tool to perform queries on the database.

DBMSs based on the client/server model do have drawbacks. With client/ server systems, multiple requests from workstations must be queued up at the database server until the server can process them; this queuing creates a potential bottleneck. In a file server-based system, each personal computer processes its own data before transmitting records back to the database.

Another issue, regardless of whether the DBMS is a file server or client/server model, is whether data has to be shared across geographical boundaries.

Distributed DBMS products are emerging on the market, and although distributed systems are becoming more widespread, they still are difficult to plan for and implement. Distributing information to end users from a central clearinghouse for data is difficult enough to manage. On-demand access to data located in another part of the network, possibly with the intention to update it, requires much computing and communications power, as well as considerable design expertise.

A final question to be addressed concerning DBMSs is that of how well the DBMS is supported by the main application software packages that the organization uses or is planning to implement. Is there a requirement for the application software to access existing subject databases? Will end users be able to get the required data from the application software transparently? Are batch file interfaces needed between the application software and the rest of the organization's system?

PC users historically have had some latitude in the selection of databases, and users working on particular applications have selected databases based on their individual preferences. This situation commonly has led to a proliferation of data management programs existing on LANs within a single organization.

This diversity, although tolerable in the days before network computing, must be eliminated in selecting a database management system for network applications for at least three reasons.

- Each PC database package tends to carry its own syntax, command language, and other intrinsic "baggage" that makes it unique. As a result, PC database packages are notoriously incompatible.

- It is terribly wasteful from a human resources standpoint to have programmers learn multiple products and support multiple "standards." Although there usually is an argument for the technical necessity of keeping a certain product, when it comes down to it, the technical advantages usually are marginal.

- Most PC databases are not capable of supporting the rigorous technical requirements of servicing robust, network-based client/server applications.

Selecting the Server DBMS

The key requirements for a client/server network computing-based DBMS are shown in this list.

- Compatibility with ANSI-standard SQL
- Support for both LAN- and UNIX-based platforms
- Sophisticated, intelligent features, such as stored procedures and triggers
- Widespread support by vendor and third-party development tools
- Power—the DBMS must be capable of supporting high transaction volumes and significant reporting and query volumes
- A reliable, financially stable vendor company with a clear future product direction
- Accessibility from all GUI platforms and character-based front-ends, including dumb ASCII terminals
- Support for a variety of network interface protocols, including TCP/IP and Named Pipes

Only a few database vendors have products that even approach this level of functionality. The major candidates are products from Sybase, Oracle, Ingres, and Informix. Let's explore where each of these vendors stands on the first three requirements listed above: ANSI-SQL support, platform support, and features.

SQL (structure query language) is the standard RDBMS language, but each vendor has its own variations and extensions. The new ANSI SQL-92 standard substantially broadens the definition of the common language. Oracle has historically emphasized ANSI conformance. However, with the latest releases, Sybase and Informix will catch up.

Another hot area of debate in standards is program-level APIs. Three primary candidates today are Microsoft's ODBC, Novell and Borland's IDAPI, and IBM's DRDA, among others. Look for major RDBMS vendors to support all of them. By writing programs that use these APIs, in the not-so-distant future it will finally be possible to write nontrivial applications that are portable between relational databases.

In general, all the major database vendors support all the major hardware platforms, mostly UNIX, but also VMS and Novell. However, on some machines the database can use proprietary features to boast performance or reliability.

Oracle (and soon Informix) offers a parallel server option for multiprocessor machines, such as Sequent, Digitalk, Vax, and Sun. Oracle also supports *clustering*, where multiple machines share disks and act as a single powerful server.

Sybase supports Symmetric MultiProcessing (SMP), a slightly different approach. Sybase and NCR have also developed something called the *Navigation Server*, which lets users split queries across several disparate databases.

Microsoft SQL Server for Windows NT exploits NT's native support for multiprocessing; if you need more power, you can add more CPUs.

Stored procedures are predefined snippets of SQL code that are kept within the database where they can be executed by users or other programs. Because the RDBMS has already processed the code before storing, it can be executed faster than sending the SQL each time from scratch. In a mainframe environment, this is called "static SQL."

Stored procedures are most often used for centralized high volume or common business functions. Rather than duplicating the SQL across many applications, the applications can re-use a single optimized procedure. When to use and not to use stored procedures is all too frequently the subject of vigorous debate. Some feel all database access should be through stored procedures. However, that complicates development with tools like PowerBuilder. The best answer is this: Unless there are unusual transaction or security requirements, stored procedures should be used for common code where their use saves development or processing time, that is, when appropriate.

Triggers, on the other hand, are basically stored procedures that are automatically called when something happens in the database; a row is inserted, updated, or deleted. In the past, triggers have been used to support *referential integrity*, a concept discussed in Chapter 17, that has to do with the relationships between data entities. However, they are also useful for anything you want to happen automatically: updating summary tables, creating an audit trail, or checking for certain events.

Sybase was the first to have triggers, but now all the major vendors support them. There are usually some restrictions on what SQL can be executed in the actual trigger. All the major vendors now support stored procedures, too, although each has its own features and restrictions.

Dictionary and Repository Tools

The *dictionary* is a reusable pool of information about the objects used in application development. For instance, a dictionary might include information about screens, data elements, and program modules. The *repository* is a more modern extension of the dictionary concept made commercially well-known by IBM's infamous repository product line called AD/Cycle. (IBM's AD/Cycle is infamous because of its cost and delivery overruns. The repository concept, however, is still quite valid.) Information about these objects—such as how they function, how they're used in application systems, how they're stored, and what they mean—is stored in the repository as attributes and relationships. This information supports a set of services and functions that enable the different development tools to work together.

Dictionary and repository tools are used to store information about data entities and relationships, as well as business rules, logical triggers, and data flow information. Ideally, information in the repository is accessed by the development software as well as the production application to save development time, eliminate redundant program code, and ensure consistency, thus reducing the potential for program errors.

We are now entering the third generation of PC/LAN applications development, which can quickly produce major, multiuser applications with high performance and slick user interfaces. Graphic (object-oriented) 4GLs and SQL client/server databases now offer major improvements in the area of application development. But while these new applications are *user friendly*, they—so far anyway—can be *developer hostile*. This is because all of the tools needed to complete the rightsizing and client/server revolution are not yet in place. Certainly one critical, missing element has been the LAN-based repository that will allow data definition sharing between different application development toolsets and among multiple developers.

Do not be deceived. A single, common repository will not cause separately developed CASE and AD tools to suddenly work together easily and flawlessly. Various CASE tools, especially front-end CASE tools, are often based on very different assumptions and methodologies. Even common elements such as "entities" and "processes" can have multiple meanings and attributes. These differences, however, do not mean that repositories can't be made to work over time or that there is no real need for them. The need to communicate between large numbers of developers using different tools will continue to exist.

One of the critical problems for most large organizations in the 1990s, then, will be control—especially the control of the computer networks and the control of data between the networked applications. This represents a significant challenge because application development and data administration have proven formidable even in centralized IS shops that support only a limited number of languages, online monitors, and database management systems.

One LAN repository product that holds some promise is Rochade, from R&O of Lexington, Massachusetts. Figure 15.2 depicts the technology offered by Rochade. This product is capable of running on a LAN and providing dictionary and repository services across diverse CASE tools. As shown in the figure, support is provided for Knowledgeware's ADW, Texas Instrument's IEF, and various Bachman Information Systems tools. Each of these CASE products has its own proprietary dictionary repository. Rochade is able to automatically copy and offer integration services for those diverse CASE tools. In addition, with some customization, Rochade can also provide an information model format that will truly integrate the corporate development information being kept in the diverse repositories. Implementing this corporate integration information model is done on a custom basis.

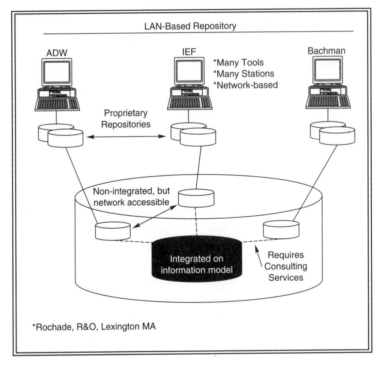

Figure 15.2. *LAN-based repository.*

The Future Payoff

The ultimate use of a dictionary or repository is as a knowledge base for the CASE environment. Figure 15.3 shows the many possible interactions between the dictionary and key parts of the applications-development environment. The idea is that your development group will be able to reuse more and more existing code with only minor modifications to develop more new applications. This reusability speeds development time and provides a consistent "look and feel" to the applications developed by your programming team.

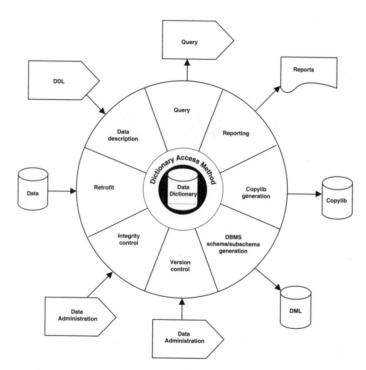

Figure 15.3. Sample data dictionary system flow.

Products such as IBM's AD/Cycle envision users specifying their requirements through an analysis tool that stores this information in the repository. Application and database tools transform these requirements from the repository into a working application. Test cases and data are generated from those requirements to provide a consistent testing environment.

For example, many business rules may be stored in the database in the form of triggers or stored procedures. If SQL Server is the database manager of choice, these business rules are referenced by SQL during operation of the system to ensure system integrity. Other dictionary and repository functions are handled by the front-end development tools, CASE tools, and the DBMS/database server that are used.

The appropriate tools for your dictionary are determined by the choice of database manager, editing tools, CASE tools, and front-end tools. All these tools must interoperate to some degree with the dictionary and repository tools. When a repository tool is adopted, it should become the basis for all future applications development work. Doing so requires that any application development tools provide the capability to tie in to the repository. Tools that do not include this capability should be rejected, regardless of their other characteristics.

Selecting the Client Front-End Tool

A front-end development tool, language, or environment is one that facilitates building the client portion of a client/server system. For the most part, you can think of almost every front-end development tool (or front-end, for short) as falling into one of five categories:

- Desk-top databases
- End-user client/server
- Purebred client/server
- Client/server 4GLs
- CASE tools

Desktop databases are stand-alone database development environments that can access a back-end database. Almost every one of these began as a database product for developing individual applications—such as mailing lists, simple accounting systems, and so on—on a personal computer. Examples include Computer Associates' SuperBase, Blyth's Omnis 7, Borland's Paradox, and Microsoft's Access.

End-user client/server front-ends are GUI-based nonprogramming environments. Many have taken to also calling this category of tools fifth-generation language (or 5GL) tools. Examples of these include Borland's ObjectVision (before Borland ceased selling it), ParcPlace's PARTS, Powersoft's PowerMaker, and Digitalk's VisualWorks.

Purebred client/server front-ends are GUI-based, event-driven database development environments. These include Easel's Enfin, Knowledgeware's ObjectView, Powersoft's PowerBuilder, Gupta's SQLWindows, and Microsoft's Visual Basic.

Client/server 4GLs are based on minicomputer fourth-generation languages (hence, the 4GL) of the past. Some are just "warmed over" versions of essentially the same tool, with a GUI and additional SQL capability thrown in, whereas others are virtually brand new products that have little in common with predecessors except the name or vendor heritage. These products include Informix's 4GL, JYACC's JAM, Oracle's SQL*Forms, and Uniface's Uniface.

Finally, CASE tools are data modeling and code generation tools based on CASE methodologies. These include Knowledgeware's Application Development Workbench (ADW), Andersen Consulting's Foundation for Cooperative Processing, and Texas Instrument's Information Engineering Facility (IEF).

When you are evaluating front-ends to determine their applicability to your situation, there are at least three key criteria to keep in mind. These criteria help you determine how well the front-end addresses the problems in its category. The criteria are

- Database intelligence and sophistication
- Team support
- Power

A sophisticated, "intelligent" front-end has several qualities. First, it assumes a client/server database, like Oracle or Sybase. Second, it provides features to easily build database "forms" or "lists," which are the key constructs in client/server applications development. Third, it abstracts the details of the interface from the developer and the application. For example, it allows you to place buttons on a screen by pointing and clicking, without needing to know a more complicated coordinates system.

A front-end that provides strong team support addresses the following concerns. It includes features that makes it easier to manage multiple developers working on the same client/server system. It also includes features that manage multiple levels, or "views," of the system. Finally, it integrates with (or provides) a version control and source code migration facility.

Front-end power can be measured by the extent that the tool incorporates more advanced technologies. For example, does it have advanced GUI features, such as spin buttons and edit masks? Does it have a strong language and function set, as well as good editing and debugging facilities? Finally, how sophisticated are its object-oriented (OO) features?

Object-Oriented Fundamentals

On this last item, there are three key OO concepts to review when determining the power of the tool. They are inheritance, encapsulation, and polymorphism.

Inheritance is one way that object-oriented systems minimize duplication of code and effort. Inheritance allows you to define a hierarchy of objects, where each object takes on the attributes and behaviors of its ancestors. This hierarchy can be thought of as an inverted tree structure, with the root at the top and the leaves at the bottom. Each lower level of the tree defines more specific attributes about a particular class of object.

Using inheritance, you build a tree of windows, menus, or user objects (called *classes*), with the top-most one implementing the most generic attributes and functions and the bottom-most ones implementing the most specific. With this structure, attributes and functionality can be defined at their highest level of re-use and be inherited by the rest of the objects "below" them. This process is usually called *sub-classing*, as you are creating one class that is subordinate (or descendant) of another.

The benefit of inheritance is that attributes and behaviors do not have to be separately defined for all objects in the system. Therefore, you increase productivity, promote consistency, reduce the chance for errors, and simplify system maintenance. Additionally, when standard functionality must change for a particular class of object, you can change it in one place and all descendant objects will automatically inherit the change with no additional coding.

Encapsulation is a technique of combining data and code into an object class. For example, define a function in a window, menu, or user object, and that function is then a part of that class. This encapsulates the data and processing routines into one package. The main benefit of encapsulation is that it allows you to hide information or shield complexity. When you embed the functions that operate on an object in the object class itself, and only interact with that object through this defined interface, other system components are insulated from the details of these operations.

Polymorphism is the capability of different objects to respond to the same function (or message) differently. Polymorphism enables you to define functions at a high level and let the details of the operation be handled by the object responsible for them. It also allows you to exploit logical similarities between different classes of objects.

For example, to create a drawing application in a traditional language, you need to define functions to draw the different types of objects. Maybe your drawing application needs to draw rectangles, circles, ellipses, and lines. Therefore, you need a function to draw each one: `drawRect`, `drawCircle`, `drawEllipse`, and `drawLine`. The main program has to know which object it is trying to draw so that it can call the proper function.

With polymorphism, you define four object classes: rectangle, circle, ellipse, and line. Each of these objects contains a `draw` function.

The `draw` function is defined at a much higher level of detail (more functional). The main program does not need to know what type of object it is. It only has to tell an object "draw." The details are handled by the object receiving the draw request. Adding new object types has a minimal impact on the main program, because the interface to draw those new objects can be exactly the same. For example, you could add a triangle object with its own `draw` function, and with no other changes, the application would be able to draw triangles.

In what might seem like contrary advice (considering that you just read about selecting a single DBMS in the prior section), the best front-end development tools for most companies are those that are usable in a number of environments; they *should* work with a number of database management systems. Although a certain DBMS may be an appropriate choice now, the choice of the future may be something else. The ability to change to another database platform without affecting the user interface of the application is an important consideration.

Additional Features of Good Front-End Tools

In addition to the features mentioned earlier, desirable features for front-end development tools include

- Support of an iterative approach to programming, enabling the rapid development of prototypes with a minimum of effort. For detailed discussion on this subject, refer to Chapter 16, "Rapid Application Development (RAD)."

- A professional looking, easy-to-use user interface. Today, this is likely to mean delivering the application in a graphical user interface, such as Microsoft's Windows for DOS environments or Presentation Manager for OS/2 environments. You can find more information about this in the section "User Interface Decisions" later in this chapter.

- An intelligent, high-level interface to the back-end database management system. It should not be necessary to specify every detail to access and update database contents.

Luckily, there's a great amount of activity in the front-end development market. Let's take a look at some of the features of one of the purebred client/server products, PowerBuilder by Powersoft. In terms of capabilities, PowerBuilder offers substantial features that many competing products still lack. Some of its advantages include

- Allowing multiple developers simultaneously to edit different portions of the same application

- Allowing the creation of reasonable functions that can be called from anywhere in the application

- Providing a unique, intelligent data window function that interacts with the DBMS at a high level

- Allowing rapid prototyping of applications through screen-building and conversation-building tools

Many features make PowerBuilder well-suited for use by developers who already are familiar with mainframe-based applications development tools. The good news is that vendors appear to be hard at work creating an even more robust and diverse set of tools for network applications development to become available in the coming years.

User Interface Decisions

The decision of which user interface to use for applications is based primarily on three things:

- Video and processor hardware
- System software
- The user

Originally, most network applications were developed with a character-based screen interface. In the past three years, however, graphical user interfaces (GUIs) have become the dominant choice in the network computing industry.

Apple became the first computer company to use a GUI on a large scale when it introduced its Macintosh computer in 1983. Microsoft followed suit by developing Windows as an add-on to MS-DOS. Windows enabled users to interface easily with DOS to open multiple applications, or *windows*, at the same time on the display screen. IBM entered the GUI market with the development of OS/2 and its GUI, Presentation Manager (PM).

Compared side by side, the three products are almost identical. On the PC, many comparisons have been made between Windows and OS/2 PM, with inconclusive results. What is conclusive, however, is that GUIs, in general, are popular and beneficial for some important reasons. First among these reasons are ease of use and productivity, reduced training, and technical capability.

Concerning ease of use and increased productivity, a recent GUI study was commissioned by the Microcomputer Managers' Association (MMA). In the study of more than 400 large corporations, independent researchers determined that applications users were 50-90 percent more productive when they used a GUI rather than a character-based user interface.

In terms of training, GUIs across different software packages have an inherent standard that makes it simple to adjust from one system to another and from one application to another. For instance, after the initial learning curve for the Apple Macintosh computer system, learning how to access and operate additional applications on the Mac is routine. In moving from a Mac to a Windows-based computer, users find that they have little, if any, need to refer to a training manual. Many prompts and screens are similar in operation to Apple Macintosh standards. Only initial training is needed to adjust to these different GUIs.

In terms of technical capability, GUIs are better also for inter-application file handling. GUIs can transfer files to other applications quickly and efficiently. Applications that support GUI inter-application communication links, such as Windows' Dynamic Data Exchange, are setting standards that other software developers are following. This situation creates new opportunities for users. Tools can be linked together, creating new solutions without programming.

Other Development Tools

The next decision concerns development methods and tools, such as programming languages, application generators, compilers/debuggers, editors, fourth-generation languages, and CASE. A large number of tools claim to increase programming productivity and enable end users to develop systems. The contingency approach applied to the choice of style and language weighs project size, degree of integration, and processing volumes against the use of high-level tools.

The general guideline is that the larger the project, the less time is spent, in proportion, on programming and the more on other tasks. The need for communicating specifications and design documents between project members grows exponentially with the size of the project team. It becomes necessary to ensure the coherence of design choices in different parts of the system. Much time also is spent on integration testing; that is, testing to see that all the parts of the application fit together as planned. As a result, extremely large projects (approximately 500,000 lines of code and more) do not benefit nearly as much from advanced tools, such as fourth-generation languages or application generators.

Third-Generation Languages (3GLs)

The tendency today is to choose third-generation languages (3GLs) for very large systems because the toolset that covers activities outside the coding effort tends to be much better established than for the newer languages. Because third-generation languages have been in existence for a long time and are highly standardized, it's easier to leverage the established knowledge base of users as well as the financial investment in code libraries and procedures, using the tools for this environment.

Choosing a third-generation language as the core development language should not preclude the MIS department from using a report writer, query processor, or program generator for low-volume, nonintegrated tasks, such as ad hoc query.

In the network computing world, C is the effective standard for 3GL development languages. Almost all application programming interfaces (APIs) use the C language syntax. Custom programs that must take advantage of such APIs are best written in C. Among the benchmarks for C compilers are products by Borland and Microsoft.

More conventional programs, especially batch programs, can reasonably be written in COBOL. In fact, COBOL often is more syntactically efficient than C for these purposes. Micro Focus's COBOL has many options in addition to the base release compiler. Animator, a source-level COBOL debugger, enables a programmer to step through the execution of the program and view the program as it executes. Other features of the Micro Focus product include

- Mouse support
- Productivity tools for screen development, which vastly improve the speed at which screens can be generated
- Embedded SQL support
- A high degree of portability between operating systems

Other add-on products to Micro Focus COBOL/2 include

- A toolset
- CICS extensions
- Interfaces to Excelerator and other Sage Software development tools

The COBOL tools are available in various releases for DOS, Windows, OS/2, UNIX, and VMS.

Fourth-Generation Languages (4GLs)

Code can be written with great speed in fourth-generation languages (4GLs) and application generators, sometimes creating a mental association between them and prototyping or iterative development. This psychological factor may make it tempting to curtail the design process when such languages and generators are used. This curtailment is acceptable if the prototype developed is truly a prototype—with the objective of experimentation with a specific aspect of the application—and the intention is to throw out the prototype in favor of a designed solution. It's more of a problem if the prototype becomes the operational system, as sometimes happens. In iterative development, you should be sure that the design phase that precedes the first of the iterations is sufficiently solid.

It may prove easy to code an insufficiently designed application the first time. The problem comes with maintaining it and trying to integrate it with other applications. The lack of design and the ease with which code is produced and modified can easily produce such a large number of different successive, or even parallel, versions of the same program that all control is lost.

In some instances, a fourth-generation language has been unsuccessful in handling high transaction volumes. The cause isn't necessarily an inherent inefficiency in fourth-generation languages. Rather, the tradeoff between development productivity and flexibility has been made to favor development productivity. As a result, certain architectural decisions already have been made and are embedded in the product; these predetermined architectural decisions can more readily be incompatible with the nature of the transaction processing required of the application.

An example of this problem occurs in one of the oldest types of productivity tools: report writers. Report writers generally read a sequential file and produce a printout of selected parts of the file, possibly in a different sequence, with totals and summaries where required. A good report writer easily can save 80 percent of the coding effort that would be required to write the corresponding program in COBOL. The problem is that many report writers can produce only a single output report in each pass of the file. If such a report writer is used to produce 10 or more daily reports, the file is read 10 or more times in a day. A custom-written program or a more perfected (but less easy-to-use) report writer could read the file once to extract all the data required as each record is read, do all the required manipulations, and print all the reports, thus eliminating nine passes of the file. In a large file, this consideration is significant.

Other Considerations in Selecting Tools

The range of available tools is wide, from applications generators and fourth-generation languages to third-generation languages with individual tools concentrating on documentation, testing, integration, and design. Most large companies require both fourth- and third-generation products.

An MIS department with multiple tools needs guidelines on which tools to use under which circumstances and on the acquisition of new tools when they are required. The corporate culture should determine how stringently these guidelines are enforced, based on

- The degree of end-user computing
- The balance of centralized, integrated systems as opposed to departmental systems

After the development tools and methodology strategy have been determined, a plan for implementing them must be devised. This plan includes a schedule for

- Acquiring the tools and provisions for training users
- Building up expertise
- Gradually extending the use of the tools

In general, this plan is no different from any other project aiming to change the way people work. As discussed in previous chapters, this change must be managed; it cannot be implemented at breakneck speed, and it requires absolute management commitment and support.

A decisive factor in the selection of the developer's tools, both front ends and compilers, is the choice of the preferred developer's workstation operating environment (DOS, OS/2, and UNIX, for example). For mission-critical applications, developers need truly preemptive multitasking in order to do their job effectively. Only OS/2 and UNIX provide this capability. The chosen platform determines the products to be purchased for developers, although OS/2 is a less effective performer. Production execution is a different question; all of the recommended tools enable programs to be generated for DOS execution in production.

Another key decision in the steps toward choosing development tools is the technical design of the network. Network computing makes sophisticated technical designs possible. Processes can be executed across multiple platforms, sharing data that resides on multiple data serving devices. Implementing such designs, however, requires powerful interprocess communication (IPC) tools to be available. In general, developers have difficulty being productive writing directly to the particular IPCs in a network computing design, for example, the LU6.2/APPC specification or the native IPX/SPX or TCP/IP protocols. Better alternatives for peer-to-peer communications programming must be provided, several of which are described in the following paragraphs.

APPC

One solution for running applications cooperatively on both PC and host platforms, primarily for all-IBM MIS shops, is advanced program-to-program communication (APPC).

With APPC, developers can create true distributed applications that function across a network involving different platforms. APPC is well-supported from a technical standpoint, in that most APPC applications from third-party vendors are IBM-based and offer interoperability with platforms supporting APPC. There are three common cooperative processing architectures for using APPC applications: APPC can be run directly from a desktop machine, through a link over a LAN gateway, or through an intermediary program that queues requests.

The opposition to implementing APPC applications is based on the perception that they are expensive and difficult. The learning curve for programming APPC applications is steep because it is necessary to learn the complex array of network hardware and software from both a microcomputer and mainframe perspective. In addition, development of the APPC cross-platform applications can take a long time.

Remote Procedure Calls

Stepping out of the IBM-only world, the industry standard that has evolved for solving the problem of cross-platform development is available from NetWise. NetWise makes a series of remote procedure call (RPC) compilers that operate between multiple platforms. This product enables programs residing on DOS, Windows, OS/2, UNIX, or MVS (via CICS) platforms to communicate interactively with one another, as shown in Figure 15.4. Although a detailed discussion of RPCs is beyond the scope of this book, this approach is the best one available for implementing an interprocess communications (IPC) mechanism that is fully portable across platforms. (IPC compilers are available for Novell and Banyan network platforms.)

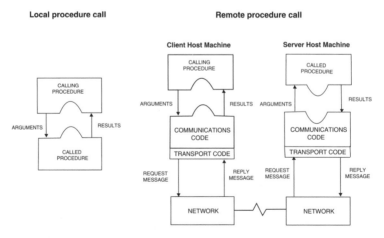

Figure 15.4. Remote procedure call technology.

Editors

Editors for programmers no longer are merely text editors. Powerful functions—windowed interfaces, emulation of other popular text editors, virtual memory management, and configurable macros—all are desirable features. The better editors have advanced error fix integration, such as brace checking in C (in which the editor looks for and validates the left and right brace symbols—important parts of the C syntax).

Editors can be configured to "pop up" on error during compilation, using either of the compilers noted earlier, with the cursor positioned at an error. This capability greatly speeds the programming process.

Perhaps the strongest source code editor in use today is Intersolv's PVCS Professional Editor, which has the features just mentioned and many others. It is language context-sensitive and can be used to automate such routine aspects as the building of Include statements in C.

Source Code Control

Source code control and versioning is a tedious, yet necessary, function in any development effort. Because of the variety of data and programs that more than likely will be distributed throughout hosts and PCs in a network computing environment, source code control software should be among the most flexible of all the rightsizing development products mentioned so far.

Such flexibility and functionality is essential for a version control system to be capable of supporting a programming work group effectively. Some functions that source code control software should offer include

1. Support of heterogeneous computing environments (LAN, UNIX, and MVS)
2. Management of project components across different platforms
3. Support of any development-to-production migration strategy, including
   - LAN development to client/server production
   - LAN development to UNIX host production
   - LAN development to mainframe production

4. An architecture that can adapt to the existing project organization and to changes in network topology

5. Other baseline criteria, including version control, revision control, intelligent difference detection, audit reports, and reusable archives

Of the available products, Intersolv's PVCS is the most popular and among the most functionally rich. Burton Software's TLIB provides good integration with mainframe source code managers, such as Panvalet or Librarian, but does not have a particularly sophisticated interface. PVCS is tightly integrated with the editors and other development tools already mentioned.

CASE Tools

Although we'd like to say that discussing CASE at this point is a case (no pun intended) of "saving the best for last," such a statement would not be true today.

CASE (computer-aided software engineering) tools are intended to automate significant portions of the application system development process. To be effective, CASE tools must work closely with other development tools, such as repositories, code generators, and front-end development tools. Unfortunately, few CASE tools have been able to do this well enough yet. However, for the sake of looking ahead to a time where more CASE products may be available and up to the challenge, the preference is to acquire an integrated upper- and lower-CASE product that can generate applications suitable for execution on a network platform. *Upper-CASE* refers to high-level process and data flow design of applications; *lower-CASE* refers to tools that transform these designs into working applications.

Several products—IEF, from Texas Instruments, and Foundation, from Andersen Consulting, for example—enable all analysis and unit test activities to occur on a network, but these products are heavily mainframe-centric. These are what you might call "Big CASE." It is not clear that any of these mainstream vendors are taking serious, long-term steps toward creating network-based CASE tools.

Then, there are a number of PC-based CASE tools, "little CASE," such as POSE, LBMS System Engineer. For the most part, however, these tools are not fully integrated CASE tools.

Given these observations, CASE remains a good, long-term goal. However, the immediate objective of facilitating developer productivity in a client/ server network computing environment can be achieved through other means. These means include providing developers with good design tools, supporting them with training and architectural standards, and giving them a technical platform that performs effectively. As CASE matures, it may be an appropriate platform for completely specifying and generating the working application. It isn't there yet.

Conclusion

The message is that information systems can be rightsized effectively and reliably with tools and products that exist today. The systems created can have every bit of capability as their mainframe predecessors. Although there is the disadvantage of some immature or missing tools for network applications as compared to mainframe applications, the advantages of GUI, SQL, and the distributed processing power of client/server still provide an extremely effective option to the "traditional" mainframe. You can be assured that more and more of the seemingly separate steps in the development process will disappear as technologies, such as RPCs, become more prevalent.

What's left, then, are the actual implementation and maintenance processes required to get a rightsized system into production, which are subjects covered in the next chapters of this book.

PART IV

Implementation: Putting I/T All Together

Part III discussed key steps in the design phase of the rightsizing methodology. Part IV describes the key steps in the next phase of the rightsizing methodology—implementation, as shown in Figure IV.1.

In the implementation phase, the assumption is that overall design of the system to be developed has been completed, the company has selected a technical architecture, and the network platform and development environment decisions have been made.

When these steps have been completed, the development team has typically already begun programming. A fundamental philosophy of the rightsizing methodology is rapid development of applications. This philosophy is discussed in more detail in Chapter 16, "Rapid Application Development (RAD)." In this chapter, the principles of prototyping and iterative design and programming are discussed as they relate to rightsized applications.

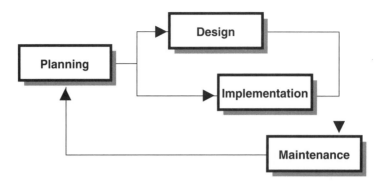

Figure IV.1. *Rightsizing development methodology.*

From development, the discussion moves in Chapter 17, "Avoiding the Downsides of Rightsizing," to tips on avoiding the common pitfalls of the rightsizing process. This chapter discusses the major points of planning, design, and implementation and how to avoid potential problems. Chapter 18, "Putting Design, Architecture, and Platform to Work: An Example," provides an example that integrates the information in several previous chapters, including design, architecture, and platform and tools selection.

Rapid Application Development (RAD)

Power in the marketplace today is directly proportional to the knowledge that the organization can bring to bear, how fast it can bring that knowledge to bear, and the rate of acceleration of knowledge accumulation (i.e., learning).

—Tom Peters (1991)

Objectives:

1. To help you understand what rapid application development (RAD) is and why it's important.

2. To help you learn about the key elements of prototyping and iterative development and how they are important to RAD.

3. To help you understand the potential pitfalls of prototyping and iterative development so you can better avoid them.

4. To explain the differences between prototyping and iterative development.

Rapid applications development (RAD) is a concept first popularized in the 1970s by James Martin, one of the deans of the information technology industry. In his works, Martin created RAD as a trademarked methodology that is still sold today. Since then, the concept has been generalized to represent the development of applications by small teams of highly skilled specialists working very closely with users over a 3 to 12 month time span. This is in contrast to the more traditional approach of a large group of IS professionals coordinating their activities over a longer period of time (24 months or more) and with less contact with the users.

Previous chapters discussed the recommended skill level of specialists on the team, as well as the recommended approach to defining user requirements and design. An objective of rapid application development is to eliminate exhaustive and rigorous project design and review before coding begins. An application's summary description should be no more than a page or two long, not counting JAD deliverables, such as screen, report, and data designs. Anything longer bogs down the project in bureaucracy before it even starts.

There should be fewer formal, ongoing reviews of the project. Rather, progress on the project should be monitored closely and daily by the team members who work side-by-side as the system is developed. This should not be taken to mean that little or no design or review is done. Instead, the effort is compressed into the development phase, with more frequent reviews of less material. Rather than everything being reviewed before the project begins, each piece is reviewed as it is added, modified, or enhanced.

The proliferation of advanced technologies such as Windows and powerful, graphical user interface (GUI) tools has spurred the use and success of the RAD approach. These technologies allow truly rapid development of easily modified components. With older technologies, developing program components took longer, and programs were typically harder to implement in such a way that they were easily modified later. Now that windows, programs, and reports can be easily developed in hours or days, rather than weeks, true "rapid" development is attainable.

Two modern techniques that can now more effectively be accomplished with these new technologies are central to effective RAD: prototyping and iterative development.

Prototyping

Prototyping is the development of a subset of a potential system to demonstrate the feasibility of a proposed approach. It is typically used for four main purposes.

The first purpose is referred to as *proof-of-concept*. This use of prototyping is especially important for projects that are using brand-new tools and technologies or tools and technologies that have never been used together. This can also be an appropriate way to test the performance characteristics of the application. The prototype is a real-world test to prove the technical feasibility of the proposed system. Typically, only enough of the functionality of the system is developed to test the technical hot-spots. There is no need to continue with the development of a system if the technical feasibility is disproved and no other approach can be found.

The second use of prototyping is to ensure that the *user interface* is well-designed: easy to learn and easy to use. This use of prototyping is by far the most prevalent. It can be no more costly than the traditional, paper-based approach for getting users to sign off on the interface design, and it is tremendously more effective. This type of prototyping is part of the user interface design activity of the design phase of rightsizing development.

The third use, *functional prototyping*, is a newer but increasingly popular approach. This kind of prototyping is concerned with iteratively developing the requirements specifications, outside of the user interface. Functional prototyping has increased as the level of ambition of the rightsizing applications in development has increased. In one example, discussed in detail later in this chapter, functional prototyping was used to develop a ship management system for a company's liquid petroleum gas (LPG) products business. Because the time frame for system development was so short—the system had to be available in a few months to coincide with the beginning of peak demand season for LPG—a combination of iterative development and functional prototyping was necessary to confirm the requirements of the users almost immediately.

The least frequent but potentially very beneficial use of prototyping is for performance modeling. *Performance modeling*, which is done at a later stage in the life cycle than is user interface prototyping, is used to evaluate the probable performance of a given design. Performance prototyping is especially popular for applications in which performance may be an issue when the body of experience is insufficient to predict performance without prototyping. Many of the new client/server network computing tools do not provide information about performance. This is especially true for new, Windows-based development products and applications designed to work over wide-area networks. Although functionally rich, their performance can be slower than their mainframe or minicomputer counterparts. It is important to note that, even when performance prototyping is used, peak load performance can only be thoroughly evaluated with volume testing.

It is usually better to do some performance modeling in a proof-of-concept prototype long before the application development effort starts in earnest. There is no reason to embark on a development effort if the application will not perform satisfactorily.

Degrees of Functional Prototyping

There are various degrees of functional prototyping. These have to do with the user's expectations of what the prototype should achieve, the amount of time that can be spent prototyping, and several other factors. An application prototype can be in one of several forms:

Discovery prototyping—In this operation, only a cursory analysis of requirements is performed. The iterative, "discovery" prototype is used to help users focus on determining their true needs. The prototype is revised interactively with users as details emerge and true requirements are uncovered.

Feasibility prototyping—This method is used to resolve problems, assess the performance characteristics of a proposed solution, ascertain levels of risks, or sell abstract concepts. It can also be used to ensure that new technologies actually work as advertised or work together. The objective of this method is fact-finding or presentation, which will cost-justify the effort for these applications. This method is related to proof-of-concept prototypes.

Refinement prototyping—This activity is used to establish user interface requirements and related design criteria that are highly subjective and need to be established according to a consensus of the target user community.

Reusable prototyping—This method reuses high-level software components and enabling technologies to allow rapid application development. For example, the combination of a SQL DBMS engine, component libraries for database access, image viewing, messaging, and standard user interface controls allow prototypes to be quickly built using off-the-shelf tools. Computer-aided software engineering (CASE) tools can assist with reusable prototyping. This method typically takes more up-front training and planning than the other methods.

Prior to beginning any prototyping efforts, it is important to determine which of these methods will be used. Project budget, available technology, available expertise, user expectations, user commitment to the long-term project, and available information are all factors to be considered when making this decision. Any decision made should include the user management's buy-in, as it can significantly affect the course of the project. Whatever option is selected, it is important to identify the cost/benefit factors of each alternative, discuss them with the users involved, and assist the users in making an informed decision.

Prototyping Tools

Prototyping requires computerized tools. A manual prototype is not adequate to demonstrate the functionality of a computer-based application and still get sufficient feedback. Some tools that can be used for prototyping are shown in Table 16.1.

Table 16.1. Prototyping tools.

Tool Category	Sample Tools
CASE tools	LBMS-System Engineer, Popkin-System Architect, Bachman Analyst, JAMM
Advanced GUI development tools	PowerBuilder, SQLWindows, VisualBasic, Visual APPBuilder, ObjectView, Enterprise Developer
PC-based DBMS tools	MS-Access, Paradox for Windows, dBASE for Windows

continues

Table 16.1. continued

Tool Category	Sample Tools
Only Applicable for **User Interface** *Prototyping:*	
Spreadsheets	Excel, 1-2-3
Word processors	Word, WordPerfect
Presentation Tools	PowerPoint, Persuasion, Freelance

There are many tools that can be used for prototyping. Some are appropriate only for prototyping, whereas others are robust enough to support the actual development of the application. The considerations for picking the appropriate tool are impacted by the particular requirements of a potential application, but should address functionality, learning curve, reusability, stability, availability of trained resources, and vendor support. Consider the following:

- The prototyping tool should have a degree of functional richness. For example, a user interface prototype must be capable of showing screens in a default sequence. The prototype must be sensitive to data values, validation requirements, and menu (or function key) choices.

- The tool should be easy to learn and use. The cost of extensive training and surmounting the learning curve cannot usually be absorbed into the budget for a prototype. Availability of trained resources to help "jump start" an effort can often be very cost-effective.

- If a prototype is to be extensive, it can help if the prototype tool will accept design or implementation documentation, such as screen layouts and special key assignments. This capability is typically provided by CASE tools. If CASE tools are not used, object-oriented tools that support the reuse of objects can be another effective approach.

- Tools should work on the same operating systems as the intended application. Depending on the application requirements, availability under other operating systems may also be important.

Advanced GUI Development Tools and Prototyping

The recent, wide availability of robust, graphical user interface (GUI) development tools is the single most important factor for the increased capability to develop successful prototypes. These advanced tools are typically interpreted, rather than compiled, which makes them well-suited to prototyping. They deliver much more functionality than older 4GLs provide. Advanced GUI features can be implemented with the click of a mouse, rather than by writing many lines of code.

With these tools, a developer can sit with a user and develop a running prototype before the user's eyes. As the user provides input, the developer can modify the code on-the-fly, without the need to compile the module, and the results can be viewed immediately. This instant feedback loop allows the user's requirements to be captured more accurately and quickly. Developers can focus on user requirements rather than on more technical issues, such as memory management and compiling.

An additional benefit to using these tools for prototyping can be especially important to a project that has developers who are inexperienced with the new tool. If the same tool used for prototyping will be used as the development tool, developers can practice with and learn the tool while developing the prototype. When real development begins, the developers should be much more comfortable with the tool.

Prototyping Pitfalls

With all of prototyping's merits, there are pitfalls to avoid. The primary pitfall related to prototyping has to do with what happens when the prototype is complete. Although it is often tempting to retain portions of prototype code to include in the actual application, this is rarely feasible.

Prototypes are often done before development and presentation standards are established. The prototype may even be the first attempt to set the standards. It is unlikely that, in this situation, the prototype will implement any standards in a consistent manner. Even when standards are already in place, they are often not enforced for prototypes.

Although new, powerful tools can make it easier to develop a prototype, typically only a portion of the system will receive attention. Other components that will be very important to the operational system are often ignored or only patched together to support the prototype. System controls, such as logical-unit-of-work, referential integrity, and error-handling, are just some of the areas typically neglected. These nonprototyped components often make up the majority of the system. Making the prototype "work" is typically a higher priority than making it "right"—after all, it's a prototype, not a production system.

Attempting to use code that is not of production quality or is lacking system controls is a recipe for failure. The decision to make prototype code the basis of the actual application must be made long before the prototype begins. With sufficient experience and planning, and with the appropriate tools, this can be accomplished, but it will take a not-insignificant, up-front investment.

Another pitfall to avoid in prototyping is throwing large teams of developers at the effort or spending too much time on the prototype. In general, a prototype should not have more than a half dozen or so people working on it—more than that and they will get in each other's way. A prototype should typically take no more than a few weeks or at most a couple months to complete. A year or more is too long for a prototype; the technology that the prototype is based on may very well be out-of-date in that time frame.

Iterative Development

Iterative development refers to an approach in which a RAD team quickly goes through the development cycle—requirements, design, code, review—several times, for small portions of the system. Rather than developing a complete program or area of the system, only a small, functional portion is completed. This is then reviewed immediately by the user to get sign-off or additional input. If sign-off is not received, the process iterates a predetermined number of times until sign-off is received. This approach allows large complex problems to be broken down into smaller, more easily managed components.

With the iterative approach, the development team can avoid long periods of user nonparticipation. Projects typically deliver something of value to the users throughout the development effort; value is delivered before, as well as after, an application is completed. For example, as soon as a report is identified, it can be designed, programmed, tested, and implemented, perhaps in a matter of days or even hours. The development team delivers the report and then goes on to diagnose and implement the next requirement.

The iterative development approach has both positive and negative aspects. The merits of the approach are increased user involvement and rapid return on investment. Users remain involved because very little time goes by between being promised something and seeing it delivered. The development team does not risk spending weeks (or months) developing something only to have the user say, "that's not what I need now." Return on investment is improved because the average time to implement a specific function can be reduced for the same total cost. Therefore, the break-even point of the application—the moment when accumulated benefits or savings overtake the accumulated costs—can come much earlier than with the traditional "waterfall" style of development, mentioned in the introduction to Part II (see Figure II.2).

To people familiar with the waterfall methodology, several questions and potential problems become obvious: How many times do you iterate? How do you manage to complete the required functionality in the predetermined number of iterations? These are difficult questions that you must address before you adopt this development approach. There are different schools of thought that will be impacted by your organization's particular make-up, culture, and experience. Finding resources who are experienced in this approach to assist you in your first effort or in defining your own approach is an effective way to address these questions. If answers to these questions are not developed and implemented, an iterative development approach can easily "spiral" out of control, with no end to the iterations.

Another potential problem with this approach is that it can be difficult to evaluate the economics of an entire system before implementation starts. Often this objection is addressed by requiring that each step must pay for itself, thus ensuring that the entire system achieves at least the sum of the savings of each individual deliverable. In practice, however, this may not be feasible. Some system functions that are a prerequisite for others may not pay for themselves. For example, although invoicing cannot be implemented before a customer database is established, the customer database may not pay for itself, especially if a full-fledged, integrated, total customer database is implemented. It pays only in terms of the applications—order entry, invoicing, marketing, and so on—that it makes possible. So, although this approach has potential cost-benefits, it also has risk factors associated with it.

Prototyping Versus Iterative Development

Although the tools are often the same, prototyping is not the same as iterative development. Iterative development consists of delivering subsets of an application in small increments at frequent intervals—days or weeks. With iterative development, users can start realizing some improvements and return on their investment before the entire application is ready. High-payback functions can be implemented first, improving the period over which benefits can be achieved. In iterative development, each component is developed with ongoing use in mind. The quality of the code, the documentation, the controls, the integration, and the performance are the same as projects developed using the traditional waterfall approach.

Prototypes of applications, on the other hand, are often developed with the idea of throwing away the prototype and "starting from scratch"—perhaps even using a different language or different tools during the implementation phase. This older approach to prototyping is applied less frequently, however, as technology improves. Now, tools that are appropriate for prototyping *and* development are widely available. With proper planning, some of the components of the prototype can be used in the actual application. Additionally, computer-aided software engineering (CASE) tools allow user-interface prototyping, screen, and database designs to be reused. Though these technologies are beginning to blur the distinction between prototyping and iterative development, the two approaches are not yet synonymous.

A Rightsizing Snapshot: A Gas Liquids Transportation Company

One of the largest natural gas products transporters in the United States buys and sells a variety of energy products with customers and suppliers around the world. It has major corporate offices in the United States, France, and the Netherlands.

Business Need

The company needed to integrate its international liquid petroleum gas (LPG) trading business with its ship management business. It required an integrated, automated group of information systems to track its international transactions, including all trading deals, contracts, prices, suppliers, receivers, ports, and vessels. In addition, the company needed a ship management system to store information not only for vessels owned by the company, but also for all vessels that potentially could carry LPG products. Adding to the challenge, the integrated system was needed to be up and running almost immediately to coincide with the start of peak demand periods for LPG (the beginning of winter in the Northern Hemisphere).

A number of systems on a local area network had already been implemented, but these systems were not integrated, and each required enhancement. Integration would help it run efficiently—defined as performing its duties more easily and faster than before—by allowing all employees to access a single, complete database of information in a graphical format. The company needed also to implement the ship management system. When the company began working with a consulting firm toward a solution for this set of problems, they jointly concluded that a LAN-based solution was not only the answer to the company's equipment and application system needs, but also the best solution from a budget perspective and a solution that would allow easy adaptability for change and growth.

System Design

The company worked with the consultants it hired to develop a customized, integrated system that operated using a central database server. This system was to operate on the pre-existing LAN. The consulting team used an iterative prototyping approach to develop the system. The project was divided into four phases:

- System design
- Prototype development
- System implementation
- System support

During the first phase, system design, the consulting team evaluated the existing systems, consulted with the key users to determine functional requirements, designed the database structure, and defined the hardware and software requirements. Two months after the start of the project, the consulting team had developed a prototype system and requested that key users review and test the system. The team also revised the system, based on user feedback and suggestions.

Less than four months after it began work on the project, the consulting team implemented the system, meeting the requirement that the system be in operation for the peak demand period. By this time, the team had completed development and user testing of the system, developed and conducted training programs for all affected users, and converted all information from the existing systems to the new database. During the first month of system operation, the consulting team provided system support including technical support, training, and general user assistance.

Results

This gas transport company has gained many advantages from the changes to an integrated LAN solution. In the short term, this solution is much more cost-effective than a mainframe solution, both initially and for ongoing costs. In addition, quick system development saved costs for consulting, and early training classes saved employee learning time; both allowed for significant productivity improvement in the short term.

But the real gain is long-term. This company now has an integrated trading, ship management, operations, and product accounting system that allows everyone to look at the same data, produces accurate and timely invoices, generates timely management reports, and allows employees to perform their jobs quickly and effectively. In addition, this system easily can be expanded as new needs arise. Because the system is constructed from industry standard tools, leading-edge and developing technologies and extensions to the current system can be implemented in a cost-efficient and timely manner.

Conclusion

The focus of this chapter has been on the principles of prototyping and iterative development. By adopting these principles and combining them with JAD, network hardware, and GUI software tools available for client/server application development, the "rapid" part of RAD becomes a very natural result of the overall rightsizing process.

Avoiding the
Downsides of
Rightsizing

17

Avoiding the Downsides of Rightsizing

A host is a host from coast to coast,
And no one will talk to a host that's close,
Unless the host that isn't close,
Is busy, hung, or dead.

—Anonymous,
(To be sung to the tune of
Mr. Ed's theme song)

Objectives:

1. To help you understand key potential pitfalls associated with such rightsizing activities as planning, design, and implementation.

2. To help you learn guidelines for successfully avoiding or overcoming these pitfalls.

So far, this book has tried to provide a relatively balanced view of the pluses and minuses of rightsizing. Doing so has resembled viewing the beauty and danger of wildlife from a bus tour of Safari World. The sole purpose of this chapter, however, is to get you off the bus and focused on how to walk among the wild animals of rightsizing. This chapter discusses the most likely pitfalls and traps that experience has shown can render null and void many benefits originally expected from rightsizing. If you can negotiate these obstacles, you will have the rightsizing naysayers eating out of your hand.

It All Starts with Planning

Nine times out of ten, a successful rightsizing project, like anything else, can attribute the majority of its success to good planning. Good planning requires answering some common-sense questions well before you ever get to the technical "nitty-gritty." For example, is a rightsizing project being done because it is essential to business survival or just because it is technically feasible? Other than not watching out for these obvious questions, planning pitfalls can occur in several areas, including:

- Hardware and software disparity
- Tools proliferation (or neglect)
- Capacity misjudgments

Let's take a closer look at each of these sensitive areas.

Hardware and Software Disparity

Hardware and software disparity occurs when multiple types of products from multiple vendors coexist in an organization. It's likely that some of the resources are incompatible. The most frequent reason for this disparity is that applications have been developed in isolation. Often, each application development team has chosen the hardware and software that suited the particular application, without regard to other applications. Another reason for disparity is that an MIS department may be the product of a merger between companies, or a consolidation of subsidiaries, and therefore has inherited multiple environments. The bottom line is that having too many products from too many vendors, all with the same purpose, can cause problems.

The two major problems associated with disparity are the *lack of integration* and the *fragmentation of expertise*. A minor problem is *software cost*; having five Windows-based development packages, for example, is bound to be more costly than having two.

The lack of integration caused by disparity usually is found when each application has been developed with its own tools and architecture, without regard to other applications. It then is difficult to make application A deliver data to, or use data from, application B.

Fragmentation of expertise results because each developer can be proficient in only a small number of products and techniques. When developers or maintainers are moved from one application to another with different tools and techniques, their productivity is greatly reduced for substantial periods. The alternative is to assign developers to specific applications and avoid moving them. This alternative frequently is unacceptable because it reduces personnel planning flexibility and limits talented people.

The proper architecture planning for software and hardware environments can force systems planners to choose the environment that best suits the organization over the long term. Properly done, the plan stresses that the technological environment is going to change, and that these changes are independent of the requirements of the applications that are identified today. As a result, it can become somewhat easier to design applications that are less intimately coupled with the technical environment and that therefore will cause fewer maintenance and integration problems later.

As an example, most network applications today are designed with a specific network transport (for example, IPX, NetBIOS) and database management system (DBMS) in mind. If the development team recognizes that the choices made today may not be appropriate three, five, or ten years from now, they may try to design these applications so that the functional part—what the user sees—is less intimately tied to the technical part—the specific DBMS and network transport.

Tools Proliferation

For productivity tools to be effective, their installation must be treated like any other application's installation. The analysts' and programmers' requirements must be analyzed, the tools selected, the users (who, in this case, happen to be MIS professionals) trained, and the process of change managed. In too many cases, tool selection is left to isolated individuals. As a result, tools proliferate as new sets are adopted by only the members of a specific project. Other projects, partly suffering from the "not invented here" syndrome, end up with other tools, often due solely to personal preference rather than technological needs.

The impact of tools on methodology is neglected frequently. The use of some tools practically forces the use of a specific methodology. For example, object-oriented programming tools naturally demand an object-oriented approach, and more traditional, third-generation languages, such as C or Pascal, are by design more processor data-driven. Tool proliferation then also leads to methodology proliferation, which, in turn, causes integration, management, and quality problems. The choice should be made the other way around: Select and implement a department-wide methodology first, and then pick the tools to support it.

Capacity Misjudgments

A key reason for applications planning is to match hardware and software to expected processing volumes and characteristics. Capacity planning is quite different for transaction processing systems than for decision support systems.

Because the recent trend in transaction processing has been toward online processing, batch problems largely have been glossed over. In most transaction processing systems, however, batch processing still plays a large role. With most of the working day devoted to online activity, the so-called batch window—the time frame in which today's batch processing must be done—must be strictly respected.

Historically, most online systems have been designed to be stopped at the end of the day to let the batch system take over. A serious problem occurs if the batch window becomes too small. A recent trend has been to design applications that can operate continuously, processing transactions while the day's processing is being cut off and the databases unloaded. The need for continuous operations must be diagnosed early so that operating systems, communications networks, and the DBMS can be selected to support this requirement.

Capacity—and, more specifically, scope management of rightsizing projects—is critical. If you don't regularly assess how big the IT-based problem is, you cannot determine the solution. This is a risk of techniques such as prototyping. It is possible that, because of multiple iterations of the prototype, the true scope of a problem may not reveal itself until a sizable investment in a particular technical architecture has been made.

Distributed Processing Design Challenges

The next major area of potential pitfalls in rightsizing is in detailed design of the rightsized system: the applications and their network platform. The detailed design of a distributed application, one in which data processes are distributed over multiple processors that run independently of each other, is beyond the scope of this book. Only elementary consideration and illustrations of a few of the difficulties associated with distributed processing design are covered in the next several paragraphs.

Communications Network Design Traps

Communications technology is changing fast, as are the offerings from vendors. Basically, the network design activity is the work of network and telecommunications designers, and consists of anticipating peak and average data transmission volumes and frequencies between different sites. Increasingly, the transmission volumes not only must consider data but also include intracompany telephone conversations, images (as in facsimile, EDI, or other genuine scanned images), and electronic mail. Some specific problem points to be monitored are illustrated in Figure 17.1.

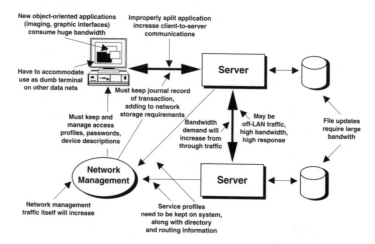

Source: TFS, Inc.

Figure 17.1. How client/server computing affects network traffic.

As the figure shows, no area of the network is immune to poor planning, design, and implementation choices. Thus, transmission volumes, frequencies, and types are key to the design of the network. When these requirements are determined, the designers then decide whether to use the public telephone network, use a dedicated data network offered by a third party, such as Tymnet, Telenet, or IBM, or install leased communications lines. (Unlike switched telephone lines, leased telephone lines always are available and don't require one site to dial up the other in order to connect.)

For example, let's look at a simple distributed data processing design in which the online activity is performed at remote locations (close to the customer or the warehouse) during the day and results are consolidated centrally at night. No communication between sites is required to complete a given online transaction. The problems associated with this type of distributed processing design are fairly simple to solve, requiring only that the design include efficient data uploading and downloading mechanisms and controls that are sufficiently effective to transmit all data that should be transmitted. A typical design consideration is what to download to each site each morning: the entire database required by that location, or only the records that have changed as a result of the night's activity? In either case, the communications network can be a switched/public network.

The communications network problem becomes more complex when a transaction at a specific site requires instantaneous or continuous access to data from another site. A typical design consideration in this case is whether the user or operator must know where to look for the data or whether the system keeps track of it. The latter is the ambition of distributed database management systems, which are not universally available.

Another consideration is how the transaction will be handled if the remote site with the data is unavailable because of hardware or network failures. Can the application work in degraded mode? This question is much more critical than with a single site application because the probability of some link's failing in a distributed network is much higher. (The risk of the entire network's failing is much lower, however.) Based on all these considerations, a leased communications network may be the better choice, with a backup option through a third-party network.

Database Design Traps

One of the most difficult cases to design for is one in which a given transaction requires that several locations in the network update data locally and that these updates be synchronized: Either all the updates are performed or none of them are. This synchronization generally is considered to require a procedure called *two-phased commit* (see Figure 17.2). A "commit" is the action an online user takes to inform the system that the business transaction being processed is complete and correct and that it can be posted to the database. This two-phased commit technique ensures that transactions are not partially posted and, therefore, that they do not endanger the integrity of the database. It locks all data in all locations that are to be affected by a transaction and then doesn't consider the transaction completed or allow any of the updates to be applied until all participating nodes respond with positive indications that the work has been successfully completed at their site.

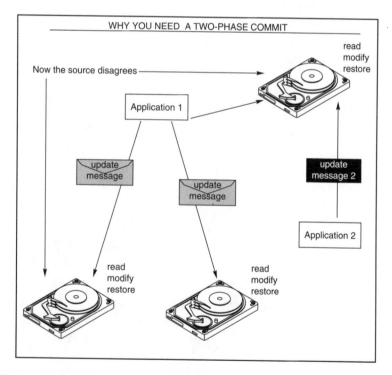

Figure 17.2. An example for the two-phase commit.

In Figure 17.2, Application 1 updates the lower-left database. It does that by reading the before-image of the data to be modified, changing it and then restoring it by writing to this database. That application then goes on to successfully accomplish the same process with the center-lower database. But as Application 1 tries to complete its updates by updating the database at the top right, it finds out that another application (2) has already modified part of the data that is to be updated by Application 1. In other words, the data read now doesn't agree with the values that were read in the first two updates. The end result of such an occurrence for a distributed DBMS is that the first two updates have to be rolled back and the transaction is rejected.

The two-phased commit consists of a transaction at one location asking all other locations involved in the transaction whether they are ready to commit (phase 1). When a positive acknowledgment has been received from each location, the transaction sends the order to perform the commit (phase 2).

A two-phase commit is totally synchronized. When any one node involved in the transaction (or the path to that node) fails, the whole transaction fails. Consider, for example, WAN-based systems operating in developing countries with very unreliable telecommunications. In those circumstances, it is very likely that a distributed database approach using two-phase commit wouldn't work at all.

Because any failure in the network or any of the local participating databases causes the entire transaction to fail, it is a process prone to failure. As distributed client/server applications become more widely used across large enterprises, there is likely to be a requirement for increasing numbers of data copies to support timely local response. As the number of data copies increases, the difficulty of locking them all together in a tightly coupled process for update increases.

Two-phase commit also causes an increase in the network traffic to support the "handshaking" process that consists of messages going back and forth between sites as they coordinate the acceptance of data. This can place a severe burden on corporate networks.

Because of the rigorous requirement for success at all nodes and the overhead of the network traffic, two-phase-commit-based processing is unforgiving and expensive and not likely to be a practical solution for widespread client/server computing.

Two additional problems are associated with the two-phase commit.

- It is time-consuming and resource-consuming. Even a two-second response time is unlikely to be achieved with many wide area communications networks (as opposed to a local area network).

- No standard protocols allow different DBMS software to cooperate in two-phase commit transactions. Therefore, either all sites must use a homogeneous network in which all the DBMS systems come from the same vendor and have a two-phase commit protocol, or a custom protocol must be developed. The latter is costly; the former, hard to find.

There are no standards for implementing a two-phase commit. Various vendors have offered different, partial implementations. It is likely that we will see a future ISO standard dealing with the two-phase commit.

Replication and Two-Phased Commit: A Solution

The asynchronous approach of replication can be combined with a two-phase transaction commit to achieve a distributed environment with many of the advantages of both approaches. The idea here is to consider the transaction to have successfully taken, after it has completed the first part of the two-phase, the writing to the log. The source node looks for a "proof of delivery" message from the target, and when that message is received, the replication message is deleted from the distribution queue. If the target node fails after the log has the transaction but before the local database is updated, the update process is continued when the target reawakens. The first thing that happens then is that the DBMS checks the log to see whether there's a pending transaction. If so, the DBMS completes the appropriate action with the transaction.

Replication can live with periods of inconsistency between different locations, as long as those inconsistencies are reconciled sooner or later. The key point here is that after the first phase, when the update has been written to the local log, the application can proceed, considering the transaction committed.

Transaction-Based Replication and Table Copying

An alternative approach to the transaction-based replication scheme just described is an approach based on table or data copies. A transaction-based approach, such as those provided by Sybase and INGRES, is primarily concerned with preserving database integrity in near real-time processing. The overall integrity of databases is preserved by forwarding transactions that are processed at secondary sites using the same database logic as the primary site.

For example, the Sybase Replication Server uses a distributed transaction model based on asynchronous store and forward of transactions. The transaction log is used to propagate replications. This avoids the use of embedded triggers, which is the INGRES and Oracle approach. The advantage of the Sybase approach is low overhead and minimal impact on the overall system throughput. However, it introduces a single point of failure that could lower the overall system availability when compared with a more distributed peer-to-peer approach.

Table-copying approaches, on the other hand, do what their name suggests; they don't worry about specific transactions. Most users of transaction-based replication want the target databases updated as soon as possible, while table-copying approaches usually operate at scheduled intervals, typically daily or monthly. Table-copying is very efficient and fast if properly implemented and scheduled. On the other hand, this approach doesn't preserve the serial time-based nature of transactions.

Table-copying can become very sophisticated as it is defined in IBM's Information Warehouse architecture, which is illustrated in Figure 17.3.

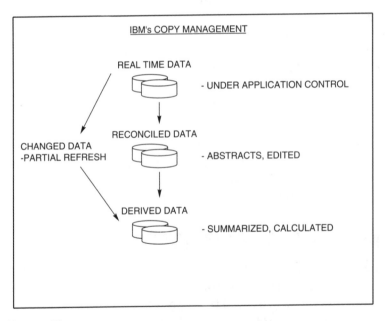

Figure 17.3. IBM's approach to copying data in its Information Warehouse.

What IBM has implemented is copying facilities that offer a sort of three-schema architecture for decision-support purposes. Recognizing that operations-based systems frequently aren't correctly structured for supporting queries, IBM offers reconciled copies and derived data that summarize and add calculation value to the copies of data offered for decision support. The copies can be updated at any time, according to criteria established by the DBA. IBM's and others' data warehouses aren't designed for transaction processing.

So then, transaction-based approaches deliver the highest data integrity and, if replication is based on ASAP timing, the current data availability is maximized at most sites. The downside of ASAP transaction-based replication is its processing overhead and complex replication engine software. On the other hand, table-copying approaches have lower availability of current data or less data integrity (depending on the implementation). They are simpler to implement, however, and can be very dependable if properly implemented.

If you're running a transaction-based production environment, it's a simple decision. Transaction-based integrity is the most important characteristic of any replication system. On the other hand, for decision support or accounting information, having real-time information may not be important. A consistent or stable database for a specific period of time may argue merely for copies of a stable end-of-period database. That may mean table-copying is the best approach. In a decision-support environment, the table-copying may be scheduled for off peak hours, further lowering the cost of creating the copies.

Transaction-based distribution of data done with a two-phase commit of transactions guarantees database integrity. This allows for the discovery of replication conflict problems (that arise from updates during asynchronous intervals), which of course is the first step in their resolution.

In effect, the two-phase-commit transactions approach uses more network and CPU resources and possibly increases the latency time between replicated node updates. The major benefit received for this, however, is that database integrity is guaranteed.

If an interruption occurs during a two-phase-commit protected update at a replication site, and if a "willing to commit" transaction is left on the transaction log file of the destination database, when that node recovers, the database update will be completed. If the target node went down before the transaction was written to the target log, that distribution transaction will stay on the source outbound log and will have to be retried on a schedule determined by the DDBA (Distributed Database Administrator).

Table Snapshots

Snapshots are probably the best known approach to table-based replication. Table-snapshot technology was introduced some years ago by IBM, Oracle, and other suppliers. A snapshot is a copy of a table (or group of tables). The copy is made one table at a time, serially. Transactions can span tables, however, so the general approach to creating a snapshot is to keep the originating tables in a quiescent phase during the copy process.

Oracle supports table snapshots with a goal of backup for primary databases or local decision support. A table snapshot can be refreshed at any DBA-determined interval.

Here are some points to remember about snapshots.

1. The originating DBMS must be inactive (no updates) during the time that the copy is being created. The process is normally one of table copying through a batch program.

2. The snapshot itself is available for read only/decision support processing even though it may be updated by the source database.

3. If a snapshot is defined to be just a timed copy that won't be updated, the DBA is offered flexibility in allowing aggregation or denormalization in that database copy. Aggregation of data or denormalization is definitely something that should not be done when the replicate is updatable.

4. If the snapshot is to be updated by transactions against the original database, the overhead of a two-phase commit process has to be figured in as part of the overall system process.

   An important advantage of snapshots is that the process of table copying can be fast (if it's done relatively infrequently) compared to full processing of transactions at multiple sites (the approach that peer-to-peer replications does). There are exceptions to this rule, however. For example, when transaction volume is relatively low compared to the database size, the total cost of copying a large database may make a two-phase commit with dual updating of transactions a better economic approach.

Peer-to-Peer Replication Versus Master/Slave Approaches

Although replication, which is likely to be offered soon by most DBMS vendors, is becoming a much desired database feature, one shouldn't conclude that replication will be a commodity. Different architectural approaches to the implementation of replication provide fundamentally different capabilities. Table-copying approaches are appropriate for solving certain classes of application problems. Replication approaches that use a two-phase commit around transactions (to preserve transaction integrity) are appropriate in different kinds of applications.

In like fashion, transaction-based replication approaches have been implemented with two fundamentally different architectures by ASK/INGRES and Sybase. ASK/INGRES has built its replicator based on a peer-to-peer architecture approach. Sybase uses a master/slave approach.

All data replication, regardless of vendor, copies data from sources to targets. Master/slave approaches always replicate data from master to slave, requiring updates to successfully complete at the master before the transaction is considered successful from the application's (as opposed to the database's) point of view. Updates in peer-to-peer approaches, on the other hand, can be made at any data location and then copied into other locations. A transaction is successfully completed as soon as any one or a combination of locations is able to update one complete copy of the affected data. Peer-to-peer allows all locations to own and manipulate their own data, broadcasting changes as required.

Although the Sybase architecture is master/slave, the vendor states that its Replication Server can be set up to support a peer-to-peer approach. Replication-conflict detection and resolution software should be provided by any system that supports peer-to-peer transaction replication. The fact that Sybase doesn't have replication-conflict resolution means that the application developer/user would have to develop such code (or decide that the nature of the application didn't need it).

The peer-to-peer INGRES architecture comes with replication-conflict detection and resolution. INGRES states that a master/slave approach could be set up as a default under their system, if desired.

In the master/slave architecture, every table or table fragment is assigned to a primary site. If the primary table's database server fails or access to that server from the network (where a transaction updating that table has occurred) is denied, replication doesn't occur and the transaction is queued. This can present a problem for remotely generated transactions, because those processes cannot update their local or other sites until they are first routed through their primary tables. The advantage of the master/slave approach is that its implementation is simpler, more straightforward than peer-to-peer, and it may be that applications based on master/slave approaches run faster because of lower DBMS overhead.

Fault Tolerance of Replication

One of the principal benefits of replication is that it can provide fault tolerance to a distributed computing environment. Fault tolerance provides the overall system with a capability of continuing to function when a piece of the overall environment is down.

When something breaks, the system—working in combination with the DBA—should provide as much assistance as possible in the recovery process. Necessary steps in such a recovery process should include:

1. Understanding what is broken
2. Understanding what or how the break occurred
3. Determining how to fix the damage and reinstate the broken pieces
4. Bringing the broken pieces back on line
5. Making sure that the recovery of the databases results in consistent data in those databases

The highest level of fault tolerance would come from a system supporting peer-to-peer replication. That's because the system considers an update to be successfully completed when it has completed a database update at any peer site. The site that is updated is like a floating master in this case. The replication server queues the updates to all other data locations.

Recovery of a system based on the master record/slave concept of replication is impossible when access to the primary location is denied. When the master location becomes available, it is then updated. (Until then, however, the application has to consider the transaction as not committed.) After the master has been updated and when there is a failure elsewhere, the replication server queues the updates to the slaves until they are available. This system works as well as a peer-to-peer approach unless the master node fails. In that case, of course, a transaction can't be processed at all.

A related issue to be aware of is that a replication server may require further updates and system processing to be suspended until a recovery process from failure is completed. That kind of approach might work in a small environment but is obviously unacceptable for serious enterprise-level capacity.

In any case, it's important that a system using replication provides the necessary utilities to allow the rebuilding of remote databases from information on the local log and database information on other remote databases. One key utility should be able to "difference" replicates—in other words, to look at a master and slave and determine if inconsistencies exist.

There is a significant difference in the amount of function provided by DBMS vendors and in the ease of implementing replication and its various features. Some products require significant programming with database triggers or database calls to implement replication. Most of the replication functionality in Oracle 7 and much of the service available through Sybase System 10 Replication requires programming with RPCs or DBLib calls by the Distributed Data Base Administrator (DDBA). Setting up database replication with INGRES is easier in that a configuration manager is provided that offers a three-step forms-based approach to defining the replicated environment.

Replication Timing

The replication server, not the user, controls the asynchronous distribution of data to remote data servers after the database local to the transaction has been updated (see Figure 17.4). That distribution can be as follows:

- Immediately, as soon as possible (ASAP). In this case, the data is moved through the queues and replication server as fast as possible.
- Scheduled, as determined by the system implementor. In this case, data remains in the replication server until it is scheduled for distribution.
- Triggered, by user-defined criteria, such as an event happening, the number of records exceeding a limit, or time of day. When a trigger is fired, the server moves the data to the distribution queue for remote processing.
- Under manual control.

The nature of the system usage dictates the type of timing used in replication. For operational systems that expect to be updated with near real-time transactions, the only acceptable approach is ASAP. There is no additional processing overhead attached to ASAP replication in this case because the user is likely to be in a situation in which the replication is under two-phase control at each updated site. In this case, then, there is no processing savings attached to batching the transactions (although off-peak-hours transmission might offer savings).

For decision support or accounting system types, a stable database that is consistent throughout may be preferable to having the most current status. In this case, scheduled replication may be preferable.

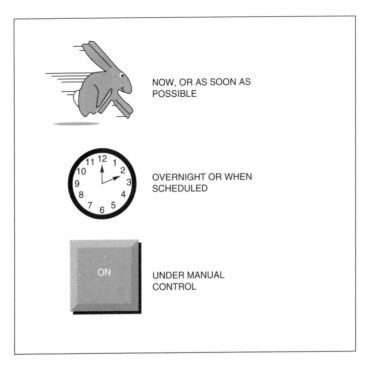

Figure 17.4. Replication offers various timing options.

As mentioned earlier, when an update is not replicated on any target server because of a failure, the update should remain in the replication server's distribution queue. At DBA-set intervals, the replication server reinitiates the remote changes automatically. As the length of time extends, however, some of the target data for the failed replication function may have been updated by some other process.

Replication Conflicts

An important side result of peer-to-peer replication approaches is the possibility of replications conflicts. These occur when the same record, which is physically replicated at two or multiple sites, is updated during the asynchronous latency period. In other words, after a first update occurs, a second update is processed at one site before the propagation of the first update to that site has been completed.

Replications conflicts don't happen with a master/slave architecture such as that of Sybase. This is because the transaction is simply not accepted unless it can be committed at the master site, or what Sybase calls a "clearing house."

For reasons mentioned earlier, a peer-to-peer approach provides a more general solution for transaction distribution. But, peer-to-peer approaches require software for replication conflict resolution. While Sybase indicates that its Replication Server can be set up to manage and implement a peer-to-peer approach, the fact that there's no replication-conflict resolution included makes peer-to-peer implementation using Sybase a risky approach.

To summarize, what replication does is trade away the security of guaranteed no data conflicts for the production fault tolerant advantages of not having to complete a two-phase commit for a transaction to be accepted at the application level. If Figure 17.2 had been set up for replication services, the transaction, as far as the application is concerned, would have been accepted and considered successful at the completion of its first database update. As in the case of Figure 17.2, further processing on the network later resulted in a data conflict, which requires further processing or manual involvement to recover the multiple database copies in a consistent way.

Recovery from a Replication Conflict

From the moment any transaction is committed, the replication server has to keep track of all of the processes that happen in its processing and distribution. The replication server should support multiple DBA-determined options for resolving the conflict. Examples of resolution possibilities include:

- The initial update has priority. Roll back the conflicting (and later) transaction with necessary messages to designated parties.
- The last update has priority. Overwrite the conflict and send the necessary notices.
- Resolve the conflict by firing a user-specified trigger.
- Halt the replication process and send a message to the DBA.

DBMS replication facility must be able to handle conflicts. However, if the replication timing chosen is ASAP and if your databases have been properly designed for replication, the volume of collisions is likely to be very low. Those conflicts that do occur can be handled either by rules in replication conflict resolution software with log entries for manual review or by manual review. Future capabilities for replication servers in this area may include expert systems to help resolve collisions.

It's a Complex Environment but Worth It

The benefits of a properly implemented replication scheme can be substantial. The complexity however, in both a managerial and technical sense, of a distributed environment is much greater than that of a local monolithic environment. This is especially true for an environment that is transaction-based. Data conflicts will occur, and proper recovery requires the cooperation of excellent software and competent administration. It's wise to invest the necessary resources to make sure that the combination of local and global DBA resources is adequate for your environment. Your DBA will have to create a data base design that is correct for replication and tested in the distributed environment. In an operational sense, it's important to not short-change the time it takes for the DBA to become an expert in diagnosing and resolving problems. You should seriously consider consultant assistance as part of the first replication project. It is important to ensure that you understand the architectural, data integrity, and performance implications of a table-based copy management scheme or transaction-based replication. The different approaches to replication have very different cost, performance, and integrity results. You should have a DBMS that supports the requirements of your application environment.

Managing distributed data through replication and copy approaches is non-trivial and requires competent technical management. Review the benefits to understand how you can take advantage of them. Measure them against the costs of the software and extra management that is necessary. It's wise to begin implementing a distributed database with a single vendor. However, if you have a heterogeneous DBMS environment, be sure to understand how your vendor can support a multiple-DBMS approach.

The Referential Integrity Problem

The most important type of integrity constraint on a database is called *referential integrity*. This term refers to making sure that relationships between data entities follow the rules documented during the JAD process.

Referential integrity is ensured when all references between database terms (or entities, in the data analysis vocabulary) are correct. Referential integrity is easy to enforce in transaction-processing systems developed according to a life cycle, by a project team with appropriate standards, training, and management structures. Enforcement is much more difficult in an end user-driven environment, in which users may not be aware of the total model of the database.

This problem has two solutions:

■ *Use the DBMS facilities to refuse update authorization to end users.* They can read the database only; they may be able to modify a local copy that no one else shares, but they cannot modify shared files or relations.

■ *Use a relational DBMS that implements referential integrity.* Such a DBMS would require descriptions of how each relationship is implemented. The DBMS then could perform all the integrity checking required whenever a program attempted to create or delete a row.

Distributed DBMS is where the most interesting action is happening in the large systems DBMS market (minicomputer to supercomputer). As SQL emerges as the standard DBMS language, the principal method by which DBMS vendors are differentiating their products is to add various functions, including

■ Distributed or client/server computing

■ Support for object approaches

■ Addition of database semantics

■ Addition of more relational functionality (typically semantics)

Distributed DBMS software needs to provide all of the functionality of multiuser mainframe database software, while allowing the database itself to reside on a number of different, physically connected computers. The types of functionality distributed DBMS must supply include data integrity, maintenance through automatically locking records, and the ability to roll-back transactions that have been only partially completed. The DBMS must attack deadlocks to automatically recover completed transactions in the event of system failure. There should be the capability to optimize data access for a wide variety of different application demands. Distributed DBMS should have specialized I/O handling and space management techniques to ensure fast and stable transaction throughput. Naturally, these products must also have full database security and administration utilities.

It is important to understand that there is a great disparity between performing distributed DBMS functions at a minimum level and accomplishing them at an advanced level.

Basic Requirements for a Distributed DBMS

The following are fundamental aspects and functions of a distributed DBMS (see Figure 17.5):

■ *Location transparency.* Programs and queries access a single logical view of the database; this logical view may be physically distributed over a number of different sites and nodes. Queries can access distributed objects for reading and writing without knowing the location of those objects. A change in the physical location of objects without a change in the logical view requires no change of the application programs. There is support for a distributed JOIN. In order to meet this requirement, it is necessary for a full local DBMS and data dictionary to reside on each node.

■ *Performance transparency.* It is essential to have a software optimizer create the navigation for the satisfaction of queries. This software optimizer should determine the best path to the data. Performance of the software optimizer should not depend upon the original source of the query. In other words, because the query originates from point A, it should not cost more to run than the same query originating from point B. This type of technology is rather primitive at this time.

■ *Copy transparency.* The DBMS should optionally support the capability of having multiple physical copies of the same logical data. Advantages of this functionality include superior performance from local, rather than remote, access to data, and nonstop operation in the event of a crash at one site. If a site is down, the software must be smart enough to re-route a query to another data source. The system should support full automatic recovery: when down site becomes live again, the software must automatically reconstruct and update the data at that site.

■ *Transaction transparency.* The system needs to support transactions that update data at multiple sites. Those transactions behave exactly the same as others that are local. This means that transactions will all either commit or abort. In order to have distributed commit capabilities, the two-phase commit is required.

■ *Fragmentation transparency.* The distributed DBMS allows a user to cut relational tables into pieces horizontally or vertically, and place those pieces at multiple physical sites. The software has a capability to recombine those tables into units, when necessary, to answer queries.

■ *Schema change transparency.* Changes to database object design need only be entered once in the distributed data dictionary (DD). The dictionary and DBMS must automatically populate other physical catalogs.

■ *Local DBMS transparency.* Distributed DBMS services should be provided regardless of brand of the local DBMS. This means that support for remote data access and gateways into heterogeneous DBMS products is necessary. (This is very much a future capability, as no vendor offers this feature today.)

DISTRIBUTED DBMS - REQUIREMENTS

1) LOCATION TRANSPARENCY

Queries can access distributed objects (distributed join) for both read & write
— without knowing the location of those objects. There is full local DBMS & DD.

2) PERFORMANCE TRANSPARENCY

A query optimizer must determine the best (heuristic) path to the data.
Performance must be the same regardless of the source node location.

3) COPY TRANSPARENCY

Multiple copies of data may optionally exist. If a site is down, the query is
automatically routed to another source. Automatic recovery is supported.

4) TRANSACTION TRANSPARENCY

Transactions that update data at multiple sites behave exactly as others that
are local. They commit or abort. This requires two-phase commit.

5) FRAGMENT TRANSPARENCY

The DDBMS allows a user to cut a relational table into pieces, horizontally or
vertically, and place them at multiple sites.

6) SCHEMA CHANGE TRANSPARENCY

Changes to database object design need only to be entered once in the
distributed data dictionary. The DBMS populates other catalogs automatically.

7) LOCAL DBMS TRANSPARENCY

The DDBMS services are provided regardless of the local DBMS brand. This
means that RDA and gateways into heterogeneous DBMS products are
necessary.

Figure 17.5. *Functions of a distributed DBMS.*

IBM's Four Ways to Distribute Data

Most vendors have been taking many years to develop software that offers distributed DBMS capability. As a way of bringing its distributed SQL products to the market, IBM has proposed a phased implementation with four discrete steps to achieve distribution of data (see Figure 17.6). These four principal steps are defined as follows:

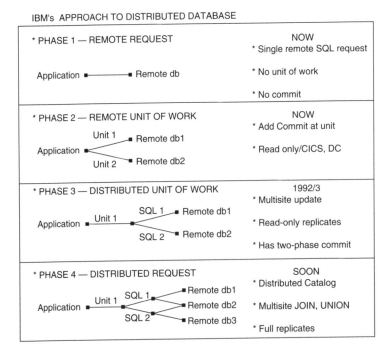

Figure 17.6. *The road to distributed database independence.*

- *Extracts* provide the ability to extract data. This simply means that a batch process unloads and reformats the operational data into a relational view. For example, IBM's DXT allows for batch unloading of IMS and reformatting into DB2. This extraction is manually managed.

- *Snapshots* are becoming a popular technique among many vendors. A snapshot is an extract (as defined above), with a date and time stamp. The advantage of a snapshot is that after it's defined to the system, it is automatically created and managed. Snapshots are read-only and provide an alternative method for decision support access to production data.

- *Distributed tables* can be thought of as the first level of realtime, read/write, distributed DBMS functionality that meets the fragmentation requirement previously mentioned. Such a system, that can support distributed tables, normally manages a single physical copy of data to support the system's logical views.

- *Replicates* are a more sophisticated version of the distributed DBMS capabilities mentioned under copy transparency. This can be thought of as support for a single logical view by up to *n* physical copies (of the same data). Data replicates must be updatable (not snapshots). At a minimum, updatability of physical data replicates requires a software optimizer and a two-phase update commit.

Software Optimizers

When a DBMS is spread over many different physical sites, the cost difference between the best and worst ways of accomplishing a function such as a JOIN can be huge. Consequently, a distributed DBMS must have a cost-based software optimizer. Without a cost-based optimizer, navigation to data is under programmer control, violating a basic precept of relational theory (this is what must be done with several earlier RDBMSs such as Oracle prior to 7.0). Without such an optimizer, only known queries should be handled; the performance of an unanticipated query could be extremely poor.

A software optimizer has to be intelligent enough to ask tough questions and develop a correct search strategy based on the answers to those questions. Examples of the types of issues that should be dealt with are

- How busy are the various machines on the network?
- What are relative speeds of these machines?
- What are the sizes of the tables that have to be accessed?
- How are the tables organized?
- What is the line speed between various nodes on the network?
- How busy are the lines between the various nodes?
- What are the access patterns in the indexes?
- Where should the software optimizer itself run?

For the DBMS software vendor, developing a two-phase protocol is one of the most challenging tasks. The additional complexity in this type of software comes from the fact that there are different types of failure nodes, and the software needs to recover from any combination of failures over all of the supported environments. For the user, operation in an environment requiring a two-phase commit may be very costly. The extra cost is incurred since a two-phase commit requires an extra round-trip message above the normal amount of messages that occur in single computer systems.

There are no standards for implementing a two-phase commit. Various vendors have offered different, partial implementations. It is likely that we will see a future ISO standard dealing with two-phase commit protocol.

More Advanced Capabilities for Distributed (or Client/Server) DBMSs

Other DDBMS capabilities include or should include:

- *Gateways.* Many of the distributed DBMS and client/server DBMS products have optional gateways that allow access to data stored in other DBMSs. Lower levels of functionality provide read-only access, whereas higher levels of functionality allow write access also. This higher level should be accompanied by a two-phase commit capability across the different systems (general availability of this capability is still in the future).

  Distributed access is a technology that is closely related to distributed DBMS. Distributed access is about the building of gateways that allow one DBMS to access data stored in another. This can properly be thought of as a subset of the technologies being delivered by vendors selling distributed DBMS or client/server DBMS technologies. The demand for distributed access, of course, is greatest in popular mainframe file and database environments such as IBM's IMS, DB2, and VSAM, and DEC's Rdb. This is because local DBMS capability is not a requirement for distributed access. Instead, most vendors provide a piece of software known as a requester to be run on the client side of the RDA environment. Some of the products in this market are not finished gateways but tool kits so that users can build custom gateways.

- *Relational integrity.* An important server function that supports increased productivity in application development is relational integrity. This can include features such as referential integrity or the ability to state business rules directly into the database, using stored procedures or program triggers.

- *Triggers.* Triggers are small SQL programs, written in SQL extended language, that are stored in a DBMS catalog. Each trigger is associated with a particular table and an SQL update function (for example, update, delete, insert). They are automatically executed whenever a transaction updates the table. You can write triggers to enforce any database validation rule, including referential integrity.

  Because triggers are stored in a DBMS catalog and automatically executed, they promote consistent integrity constraints across all transactions. Triggers are easy to maintain because they are stored in only one place. They result in rules that are enforced for any application that accesses the database.

■ *Multi-threaded architecture.* For the best performance, a distributed (or client/server) DBMS should implement a multithreaded, single-server architecture. Multi-threaded servers perform most of their work and scheduling without interacting with the operating system. Instead of creating user processes, multi-threaded servers create a thread for each new user. Threads are more efficient than processes—they use less memory and CPU resources. A multi-threaded server DBMS can service 10 to 40 users simultaneously on a machine as small as a 33 MHz 80386 PC with 10 MB of RAM.

■ *Symmetric multiprocessing.* Another advantage of DBMS servers is direct support of multiprocessor hardware architectures in a symmetric multiprocessing (SMP) mode. Most operating systems either currently (UNIX, Windows NT, VMS) or soon will (OS/2) offer support for this functionality. Therefore, there needs to be effective integration between the DBMS and operating system to take advantage of the potentially improved throughput.

Direct support for SMP means the DBMS can take advantage of several parallel processors under the same skin (with an appropriate operating system). The processors can be either tightly or loosely coupled.

■ *Cursors.* A cursor stores the results of a SQL query and allows a program to move forward through the data one record at a time. Sometimes, programmers are also able to move backward within a cursor. Without a cursor, it's harder to program transactions to browse through data.

■ *Text, image, date, and other extended data types.* Support for different types of data can make any DBMS useful in a wide variety of applications. To store a picture, it would be useful to have something like IMAGE data types of binary data. Another useful item is TEXT data types, which are printable character strings.

■ *Remote procedure calls (RPC).* RPCs allow an application on one server (or client) to execute a stored procedure on another server. Stored procedures enhance computing performance because all of the commands can be executed with one call from the application program.

■ *Multiplatform implementations.* Another primary advantage of a robust DBMS is multiplatform portability and networking. If your software runs on the hardware of many different vendors, you have that much more flexibility. For example, Informix has been implemented on approximately 400 different hardware systems.

■ *Disk mirroring.* For companies that want the reliability of mainframe environments on the PC LAN, a disk, or server, mirroring capability is necessary. Mirroring requires that dual operations are executed for each computing step with the generation of error reports whenever there is a difference between the results of the dual steps. Mirroring also allows the system to continue to operate at essentially full speed, even after one of the processors or disks has failed. Disk mirroring is supported through the process called "shadowing." This is a very useful facility for applications that require extremely low amounts of downtime—if one disk fails, the system automatically diverts and uses the other (mirrored) disk without interrupting operations.

■ *BLOB data types.* A BLOB data type (binary large object bin) has no size limit and can include unstructured, nonrelational types of data such as text, images, graphics, and digitized voice. One way to handle BLOBs is as a single field in a record, like a name, date, or floating point number. It can then be governed by concurrency and transaction control.

The ability to create "database macros," which can be executed by the database macros that can be executed by the database engine, should be supported by the DBMS. Such macros would be implemented as centrally stored, user-written procedures that tell the database system how to translate BLOB data to another format. Because they are stored in one place and managed by the database, BLOB macros are simpler to create and maintain than similar code in an application.

■ *Application-specific functions.* This capability allows a user to easily extend the range of database commands by adding new functions, coded in C, to the DBMS kernel. This facility is helpful in the manipulation of BLOB data.

More on Client/Servers

The primary difference between a server DBMS and a distributed DBMS is whether or not each node on the network has a full copy of the DBMS. Almost all of the advanced functions listed in the previous section on distributed DBMS (such as BLOB data types and RPCs) are also available from leading DBMS server vendors.

Many companies are delivering client/server DBMS and associated tools at this time. The very large and active market of the 1970s and 1980s for mainframe DBMS and 4GLs that featured companies like Cullinet, IBM, Software

AG, Cincom, and Applied Data Research has been replaced by a new market. This new environment is built around the client/server or distributed DBMS model with open availability (connectivity) between GUI-oriented tools running principally on the client and a server DBMS principally executing SQL. The reasons behind the current and impending growth of this market are many:

- Developers can use PCs instead of time-sharing terminals as primary development platforms.

- Even though the PC is used as the principle platform, security, integrity, and recovery capabilities comparable to minicomputers result.

- The efficiency of SQL queries and transmissions greatly reduces the network communication load (from that of a PC LAN/file-server-based approach).

- Gateway technologies, which are an important component of client-server computing, allow PC users to gain access to data located in mainframe and minicomputer DBMS products such as DB2, IMS, and Rdb.

- The client/server model isolates the data from the applications program in the design stage. This affords greater flexibility in managing and expanding the database and in adding new programs at the application level.

- The client/server model is scalable because as requirements for more processing come up, more servers can be added to the network, or servers can be traded up for the latest generation of microprocessors.

- A lot of flexibility comes from a computing environment based on SQL because the language is a standard. Commitment to an SQL server engine means that most front-end, 4GL, spreadsheet, word-processing, and graphics tools will be able to interface to an SQL engine.

- Client/server computing provides the industrial strength security, integrity, and database capabilities of minicomputer or mainframe architectures, still allowing companies to build and run their applications on relatively inexpensive PC and minicomputer networks. This hardware and software combination can cut 90 percent of hardware and software costs when building mission critical applications.

The concept of using a large mainframe such as a VAX 9000 or ES/9000 as a database server to networks is discussed by the mainframe vendors. For these machines to play a role in future networks, however, it is clear that they will have to adopt server functionality by acquiring and supporting emerging rightsizing standards such as UNIX, NetWare, LAN Manager for Windows NT, and LAN Server for OS/2.

Performance from a Client/Server Environment

The reader might be skeptical of the claim that PCs running server software can perform as well as mainframes, but there is documented evidence to this effect. Currently available commodity hardware can provide the kind of performance indicated in Figure 17.7. The most efficient PC server operating system at this time is probably NetWare. Tests run in conformance with the Transaction Processing Council's standards have shown that products like Informix and Gupta's SQLBase are capable of running about 50 transactions per second (TPS) on 486-based PCs.

```
DATABASE SERVER PERFORMANCE

LOW END

    * 486 PCs, LOW END RISC, 12 ms ACCESS/4MB TRANSFER RATE
    * 10 - 20 MIPS @ $6,000 TO $18,000
    * 8 - 15 TPC-B/SEC
    * 90 WORKSTATIONS SIMULTANEOUSLY ON A SINGLE SERVER
    * 250 ATM's ON A SINGLE SERVER
    * ETHERNET - 100 TPS ACROSS NETWORK

HIGH END

    * PARALLEL CISC OR RISC GIVES 100's OF MIPS
    * SCSI AND IPI CHANNELS — COMPARABLE TO 3090 CHANNELS




RESULT

OLTP AT $1K - $4K/TPS
```

Figure 17.7. What can an open server do?

Mid-sized banks with over 100,000 transactions per day run complete online teller systems against an SQL DBMS server running on a single processor 486 server (for example, a mixed DOS and NetWare environment with a DOS server running the database and a NetWare server handling file management and transport services).

Hyatt Hotels implemented a UNIX based client/server approach using AT&T minicomputers and Informix SQL-based software to completely replace its mainframe reservations system for 600 hotels, worldwide. This is the kind and size of application that has historically been relegated strictly to mainframe, transaction-style processing. Hyatt has reported an overall 25 percent savings in running the client/server system, but the most important benefit for Hyatt is the improved maintainability and functionality of the new application.

These kinds of systems and performance numbers definitely prove that SQL style client/server systems can be implemented on generic hardware platforms and deliver performance that is the equivalent of an expensive mainframe running IBM's DB2. In fact, many banks running on PC servers have used those machines to replace mid-sized mainframes.

> The transaction capabilities of client/server software working with low-end PC servers or super-servers (minicomputer style cabinets built with merchant microprocessors such as the 80486 or R4000) are quite astounding. PC hardware can support disks with 4-millisecond access time and 8 MB transfer rates. Such a machine can be configured with 600 MB of disk for under $5,000!

If you have had a chance to build PC-based database applications in the last few years, you may be suspicious of any claim that a PC hardware environment could be capable of performing on a level comparable with minicomputer technology. However, it is important to remember that the processing capability of a typical PC increased by a factor of forty between 1984 and 1992. A PC built around the Intel 80486 microprocessor chip running at 33/66 MHz has at least 60 times the computing power of a PC/XT. This high level of service can provide online transaction processing capabilities at a cost under $2,000 per TPS.

This cost is much less per TPS than existing minicomputer and mainframe systems can provide. Using proprietary minicomputers, you can expect to spend between $25,000 and $40,000 per TPS. IMS-based MVS mainframe environments typically cost $50,000–$75,000 per TPS. Alternatively, using the combination of MVS and DB2 as a transaction processing engine typically costs over $100,000 per TPS. What all of this means is that, based on full development, maintenance, hardware, software, and staff costs, SQL client-server computing is likely to result in finished systems that cost only a small fraction of what building transaction systems has cost in the past. Actual case studies confirm this type of important savings in finished, delivered systems.

Of course, there are many applications that are simply too large to contemplate running on even a fast PC. Client/server architectures allow you to design an application, and then, without changes, port it to whichever server has the database processing power you need to manage your database. This allows application development on PC-style servers, with the porting to the new generation of super-servers—minicomputers built to run open operating systems powered by multiprocessing versions of merchant CPU chips. The approach is to take microprocessor-based technologies and combine them with high speed buses, channels, and parallel computing architectures to create platforms that can run with the fastest minicomputers. Vendors such as Compaq, Pyramid, and Sequent are building parallel processing machines using CISC or RISC microprocessor units capable of reaching a sustained processing capability of hundreds of MIPS. Do not be surprised, then, to see a combination of these new hardware systems with software from companies like Informix, Sybase, Gupta, Microsoft, and Oracle delivering computing technologies comparable to IBM's largest machines, but at a tiny fraction of the price.

In the future you can expect multiprocessor-based client/server architectures to regularly take on what are now considered strictly mainframe types of applications. It is reasonable to envision products like Informix, Oracle, and Sybase in combination with high-end super-servers from such companies as Sequent, Pyramid, Concurrent, Compaq, IBM, or DEC. High-end super-server hardware is typically built with parallel Intel 486, 586, and/or RISC chips from MIPS, DEC, or Sun. By configuring a server with a multiprocessor design and an open operating system that supports it (for example, UNIX, VINES, WindowsNT, OS/2, or LAN Manager), a vendor can build a machine with hundreds of MIPS processing power and 250 GB of disk data storage for well under $500,000.

The various advantages of distributed processing and distributed DBMS are both well documented and considerable, especially for companies that want to take advantage of new computing styles featuring graphical interfaces and distributed implementation. Migrating to these new technologies, however, requires serious investments in the training and building of expertise for the new systems. There do exist potential problems associated with taking advantage of the advanced capabilities of Distributed DBMS.

Some of the problems associated with this technology are these:

- Communication costs can be quite high, and using a two-phase commit protocol tends to generate a considerable amount of communications traffic.

- There is the need for gateway technology to handle the SQL differences among different DBMS vendors.

- The predictability of total costs for distributed queries is variable. In other words, it is difficult to predict how much it will cost to get a job done.

- Supporting concurrency, in addition to deadlock protection, is very difficult.

- Supporting automatic full recovery is very expensive.

- Performing a JOIN across different physical nodes is expensive using today's technology and networks.

- Some advanced relational functions, reasonable for single computers, are difficult and expensive across distributed networks (for example, the enforcing of semantic integrity restraints).

- A distributed database administrator must understand the integrity, optimizer, communication, and data owner issues of the distributed world.

- Data security issues are neither well understood nor proven. It would appear that a distributed environment is somewhat susceptible to security breaks.

These potential pitfalls await the advanced user of this new technology. As in the case of most new technologies, the well-advised user would take small steps while the approach is being mastered before moving on to more complex conversions/implementations. Many companies will find the client/server approach to be simpler to implement initially. Investments made in such an approach will likely migrate towards a distributed database if later desired (in most cases).

Development Challenges

When you have overcome the hurdles in planning and design, the next area of potential problems is development. The various RAD approaches are geared naturally toward avoiding the traditional development problem of scope increases. Testing, however, can hold some special problems for rightsized applications. These problems are caused primarily by an increased number of interacting system elements to keep track of in a multivendor system. These elements include multiple data elements, processing modules, interfaces, data and program structures, network transports, adapter drivers, APIs, and so on. No single human brain can manage the ensuing complexity; as a result, not all errors can be eliminated by simply thinking about or reviewing the implementation.

How do you overcome this complexity problem with testing? The recommended way is to mock up the complete system—communications networks, servers, and all—as early as possible to understand the potential limitations of the platform. This method provides you with a benchmark for knowing how the platform should react so that you can pinpoint variances when you test the new system. Close ties to product vendors should help this process go smoothly. Ideally, such a production mock-up should be created at the time tools are selected, before programming is in full swing. Although creating a production mock-up can be expensive—primarily in terms of people's time—vendors usually will provide the products for a no-charge evaluation period. This mock-up, then, is a recommended part of the design phase of rightsizing, as was discussed in Chapter 15, "The Rightsizing Development Environment."

Rightsizing Hype

Companies that rightsize their information systems are often ill-equipped to make an informed choice among the various technologies confronting them. As a result, they attempt to use checklists of features ("buzzwords") to narrow down the field of options. Vendors often encourage this feature-mania by adding lists of features to their products while pointing out limits in their competitors'. Consequently, companies are choosing databases, for example, on the basis of supporting features like BLOBs (binary large objects) without having a clear picture of what BLOBs are or how BLOBs will solve their business problems.

You can get to the bottom of choosing which product is better than another for your business need. But the choice should be made on the basis of fundamentals like technical support, ease of installation and administration, licensing and distribution rights and costs, real product power and robustness, and standards support.

Rightsizing Snapshot: Vendor Benchmarks

How often have you seen a news item or press release like the following?

> BEAVERTON, ORE. (JUNE 23, 1993)—In response to market demand for high availability and high performance in an open systems environment, Sequent Computer Systems, Inc. and Oracle Corporation today announced general availability of the Oracle7 Parallel Server on Sequent's clustering technology. To demonstrate the real-world application of this combination, Sequent has released a benchmark that represents the first time an open system has supported more than 10,000 users and delivered 1,002.37 transactions per second (tpsA) at a cost per transaction of under $10,000.

As part of an audited TPC benchmark, vendors must release a Full Disclosure Report that describes the exact configuration, parameters, and measurements used for the test. Reviewing a copy of the tpsA benchmark Full Disclosure Report, one sees some key items that are quite revealing about the benchmarking process. (The following discussion is *not* meant to be critical of Oracle or Sequent; rather, the process could apply to most any vendor's benchmarks, and shows just how the "game" is played.) Let's take a closer look at what they did:

$9,335,113 worth of equipment was used.

With a calculator and a little knowledge of Sequent's product line, we figured out that they used two Sequent 750s with 24 Intel 80486 processors each ($10,000/tps * 1000 tps). Now, the TPC-A benchmark test requires just three tables (plus a history table):

Table	Number of Records
Branch	1,004
Teller	10,040
Account	100,400,000

The format and number of records are determined by the TPC. You might question whether this resembles a real-world database. (We consider it to be extremely elementary.) For instance, here is the definition of the history table (again, from the Full Disclosure Report):

```
CREATE TABLE history (
                        teller_id        NUMBER,
                        branch_id        NUMBER,
                        account_id       NUMBER,
                        amount           NUMBER,
```

```
timestamp        DATE,
filler           CHAR(36));
```

The database was spread across 124 2GB disks.

The clustered Sequents shared 124 high-speed SCSI disks, for over two terabytes of storage. Now, part of that is the history requirement—you have to specify enough space even though it isn't used during the test. The real reason, however, is performance; the large account table and its rollback segments were spread out over 100 disks. Each machine had five disk controllers. In the real world, maintaining such a configuration would be insanely difficult (the equivalent of the `create database` statement is some four pages long).

There was 672 MB of memory on each machine.

Again, this is a very high-end configuration. The amount of available memory far exceeded the size of the database during the benchmark, so it should have all resided *in cache* (hitting the disks only for delayed writes).

There was only a single 1/4" tape drive for backup (shared by both machines).

Even though there is the potential for 2 TB of data, the TPC doesn't require you to back it up. To achieve less than $10,000 per transaction, those running the benchmark had to use minimal extras (that is, a single 500 MB tape).

Transactions were generated through a teleprocessing (TP) monitor, i.e., simulated users.

Although the benchmark says 10,000 users, there obviously weren't 10,000 people involved. Rather, a series of eight smaller Sequents simulated the transactions. However, the system price used to calculate price performance includes 10,000 clone dumb terminals (again, this is required by the TPC).

The client transactions looked like this:

```
while (true)
    tpcall(service, data);
```

In other words, the clients requested services from a transaction processing monitor. The "services" actually consisted of 110 copies of the same Oracle call, sending a single PL/SQL statement to do an insert and three updates. In fact, here it is:

```
TPCA1(TPSVCINFO *msg)
{
 // five lines of copying variables
```

```
      ociexe(plsqlstatement);
      tpreturn(TPSUCCESS);
}
```

Again, in the real world, few back-end processes are ever this easy.

The test duration was 30 minutes

This $9 million system was actually "used" for 30 minutes, with a five minute ramp-up time. Again, that's okay, given the rules.

A special feature, "Discrete" Transactions, was used.

The TPC requires that the database support ACID properties—atomicity, consistency, isolation, and durability. The atomicity, consistency, and isolation are the important ones. Basically, the database must support a logical unit of work, with a begin-transaction, end-transaction.

Oracle 7 supports a special transaction mode called the "discrete transaction." In a discrete transaction, all changes made to any data are deferred until the transaction commits. This is faster than the normal transaction mode. However, because of this, you can only use discrete transactions on a small subset of normal processing. Specifically, the process must not view the data after modification or change a data value more than once. It just so happens that the TPC-A benchmark meets those criteria.

However, some critics claim that features such as the discrete transactions feature are nothing more than a "benchmark special"—designed to enhance test results with no real-world impact. It's unlikely that a real application could use discrete transactions or that the developer would even know to use them. (The vendor's documentation would seem to further validate this thought, given that it's covered not in the main body but in an appendix of the manuals.)

Conclusion

All of these observations, it should be noted, are made while fully acknowledging that the test was conducted exactly within the boundaries of the TPC-A benchmark. In fact, in many areas, Sequent and Oracle went beyond the letter of the rules for disclosure and configuration. Yet clearly, this is not a real-world test. It's more a game, and it has much to do with marketing and little to do with true performance. That goes for Oracle, Sequent, Sybase, HP, Informix, DEC, Microsoft, Sun, and any other vendor.

Here's what you should know about benchmarks.

■ Don't size your system based on vendor benchmarks.

■ Don't ever put vendor benchmarks in a proposal to your management (if you are part of an in-house IS organization) or clients (if you are a third-party systems integrator).

■ Don't believe vendor benchmarks.

■ Don't let your management or clients believe vendor benchmarks.

Putting Design, Architecture, and Platform to Work: An Example

Putting Design, Architecture, and Platform to Work: An Example

18

It will go all in your day's work.

—Jonathan Swift (1738)

Objectives:

1. To understand the major questions that must be asked in analyzing the requirements for a network-based architecture.

2. To understand the process of evaluating required system components and packaged software options for the sample network architecture.

Most companies contemplating the rightsizing of their computing environment through the deployment of systems on a network platform must face the reality that they must thoroughly revamp their entire approach to systems management, production, and end-user computing. In almost every case, something more sophisticated than the current architecture is required. This chapter builds from the descriptions of architecture and tools in previous chapters to demonstrate the steps in developing a custom architecture to address a specific need.

In this case, a hypothetical Fortune 500 company needs a new reporting system. Through management mandate, the company has decided to rightsize all reporting systems from a high-volume, batch architecture that is run on mainframes. Although many report-writing tools are meant to operate on a PC LAN platform, most of these tools are limited to the tasks of creating and executing ad hoc reports quickly—they are not complete solutions. Thus, the application architecture in this example lays the basic framework for a more robust approach to reporting.

A Strategy for Implementing an Architecture

Implementation of the reporting architecture discussed in the following paragraphs is no simple task. The benefits, however, are worth the effort. For a baseline, the architecture described mimics the functionality of that on many mainframes, allowing reporting processes to be rightsized from hosts on much less expensive networks. Simply replicating the services already offered in mainframe environments is not of sufficient value to warrant such an undertaking. The real value of a system of this type is not producing reports; it is giving to the user community the tools they need to access data and, through the application of an ever-evolving business context, turn it into useful information in a timely manner.

More importantly, however, this architecture also provides functionality not available in many mainframe environments. Functionally sophisticated report grouping, selection, control, and distribution makes it much easier for users to request reports and review the results. This yields improved perception of responsiveness and accessibility to data, with no decrease in controls or security. However, the ability of end-users to manipulate data and generate reports using tools places a great deal of responsibility on the end-users. They must know how to use the tools. This also places a burden on IS to examine and simplify the underlying data structures so the end-user can productively work with unambiguous data. The best architecture in the world will not resolve issues of insufficient training or bad data design.

Some Key Design Questions

As described in Chapter 10, "Joint Application Design (JAD)," there are some basic application needs that must be explored for this sample application. The key requirements fall into three general categories: report specification; report execution; and report distribution. The following list shows some questions you must address in each of these areas:

Report Specification

- Does a report already exist that has the required information?
- If such a report exists, do we still want it as it is currently presented?
- If such a report does not exist, where does the data exist that will enable us to construct the report?
- After the appropriate report has been identified or created, how do you pass parameters to it that will control the amount of data included in the report?

Report Execution

- How does a user control the timing with which the report is executed? In particular, what mechanism allows users to choose between immediate execution, which ties up a workstation while the report is produced, and deferred execution, which does not?
- What techniques ensure that reports use the available data efficiently so that excessive I/O is avoided?
- What mechanisms ensure that all reports are processed and any execution errors are handled properly?
- A variety of tools may be used to create reports. How does the system ensure that more than one tool can be supported using the architecture? For example, can reports be generated using a spreadsheet program as well as a report generator?

Report Distribution

■ Output destinations of reports should never be hard-coded into the process that generates them. How does the system ensure that output destinations are altered and controlled easily?

■ What mechanisms are provided for users to specify output destination, orientation, font, copies, media, and so on?

■ How will users review a report interactively before releasing it for print? Can report output be archived for subsequent reprinting?

■ Should it be possible to scan the output reports automatically, comparing their contents to the information contained in a controlling database structure, and then follow distribution instructions stored there also?

These questions are among the ones you must consider in the design of a network-based reporting architecture. No architecture can fully address every one of these questions. The intent, however, is to ensure that every question is given its due consideration.

Many mainframe platforms include tools not presently available for the network environment. For example, this list shows some of these mainframe tools:

■ OPC/A, by IBM, handles automated production scheduling.

■ JES/2, by IBM, handles batch job processing and output routing.

■ CA-Dispatch, by Computer Associates, handles sophisticated report distribution requirements.

Tool availability in the current mainframe environment, however, is no guarantee of a successful reporting architecture. Likewise, lack of such tools does not guarantee failure for a network-based architecture. However, the last several years have seen the development of products from mainframe vendors that begin to create "traditional" production facilities in the distributed systems environment. These vendors include Hewlett Packard, Computer Associates, and Legent, with newcomers like Patrol, EcoSystems, and Tivoli Systems making inroads in all aspects of the systems management role.

Central to a network-based approach is the principle that functionality can be distributed to multiple locations around the network. This distribution commonly is accomplished by distributing files and CPU cycles to machines that can perform these tasks independently. In the architecture proposed in this chapter, this principle is recognized by providing for function-specific processes that can run either on a single computer or across multiple computers. These processes require two things: an execution platform and an invocation mechanism. In today's world, there are numerous answers to these needs.

A major requirement for the execution platform for this architecture is multitasking. A number of multitasking platform options exist in today's marketplace. These include the UNIX variants, Microsoft's NT, and IBM's OS/2. The variations on these are well beyond the scope of this discussion, but the major criteria applied to the selection should be scalability, maturity, physical distribution of the application, the robustness of the underlying network, and the maturity of network and systems management facilities. Frequently, distributed system efforts fail because they succeed, overwhelming a nonscalable platform or poorly designed/managed network infrastructure. When choosing a platform for this environment, make sure that the software is designed to be portable and the platform selected can grow to meet larger needs. In today's environment, this generally means support for Symmetric Multi-Processing (SMP), which allows the addition of processors within the server chassis. However, it can mean the use of loosely coupled architectures similar to those employed by IBM in its AIX environment.

Processes on a system are invoked by "calls" made from some other process. When the called process is remote from the calling process (on two different systems with a network in between), this gets complicated because machines can order data differently and the network transports can be difficult to code. To manage these complexities as well as provide the flexibility to move processes between systems and networks in the future, there are a number of products on the market that meet the need. These include the following:

- DBMS Vendor Interface: Sybase, Oracle, Informix, IBM
- Netwise RPCTool
- NobleNet NetRPC
- Open Environment Corporation's Encompass
- Momentum Software's messageEXPRESS

A key proposition underlying the development of distributed architecture is the decoupling of the presentation component from the underlying processes. Using "tightly coupled" architectures like PowerBuilder or SQL Windows provides great programmer productivity, but these architectures are very limited in the distribution strategies they support because of their "tight" coupling of the presentation to data access layers. This is a very limiting approach in the long term, because it forces a front-end decision in conjunction with a back-end process definition, which may preclude reuse of the process by alternative interfaces. The products mentioned earlier facilitate this separation, but add extensive complexity to the overall environment.

Report Specification

Report specification is the first of three components in the reporting architecture. Figure 18.1 shows the basic conversation flow that a user sees when accessing the report control data structure. The list of report groups shows all report groups for which the user is authorized. After a report group is selected, all reports within that report group are listed. When a report is selected, all outstanding report requests from the requesting user are displayed. (A user who is authorized can display and manipulate all requests for that report, regardless of who initiated them.)

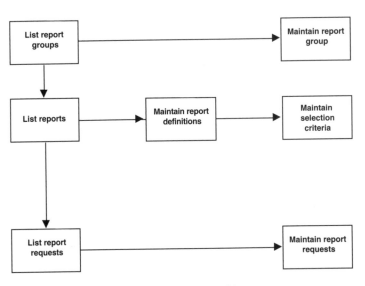

Figure 18.1. List and maintenance specifications for report architecture.

From this list, a user should be able to view the processing status of a specific report, retrieve the report's output online, delete requests, and so on. A user should be able to use the Maintain Report Requests screen to modify or delete a request that has not yet been processed. The user would use that screen also to create new requests.

Figure 18.2 illustrates the logical data diagram that supports Figure 18.1. In Figure 18.2, report groups are a way of categorizing reports. The report groups are used as a security enforcement mechanism and to narrow the user's search for an appropriate report. Descriptions of report groups might include MRP System Reports or Revenue Reports. A report group optionally can contain other report groups and can itself be part of many report groups.

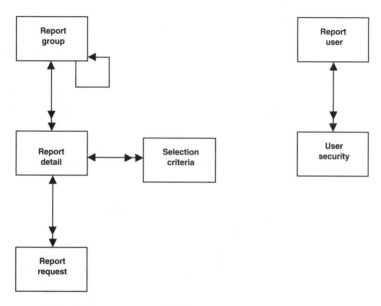

Figure 18.2. A logical data diagram for network-based report architecture.

The Report Detail entity can be directly subordinate to one, and only one, report group. This entity contains default information about the reporting language, batch job name, supported platforms, schedule, destination, copies, and so on. This information is used to provide default values to the report request entry process.

Each Report Detail occurrence can be associated with one or more Selection Criteria occurrences. This generalized data structure describes the data that a particular report will accept when it attempts to retrieve information from the database. Typically, these selection criteria are of two types:

1. Primary selection criteria—These fields govern selection of the main database entities. For example, in a contracts-related report, primary selection criteria might be a range of contract numbers.

2. Secondary selection criteria—These fields govern the subselection of database entities. In the preceding example, secondary database entities could include such information as amendment ranges, effective dates, and so on.

Not all reports include selection criteria. When they do, the data structure provides a general method for specifying which data, in what order, is to be passed to the report. The data structure is used to dynamically format a screen in which a user enters selection criteria when he or she requests the report. Data items in this entity would include internal and external field name, format, length, decimal positions, validation criteria, required/optional indicator, and so on.

When a user requests a report, a Report Request entity is created. Report Requests can also be prepopulated—automatically created at a predetermined time—to control the execution of scheduled reports. Report Requests are the basic unit of communication between the user requesting the report and the report execution architecture. The Report Request entity contains all selection criteria, execution timing, and distribution control information required by the execution architecture to control the report's execution. The format of the Report Request is the same for all report-generation approaches (Focus, Easytrieve, COBOL, and so on).

Note that the dialogue just described must be operable across multiple platforms. The objective is to be able to run the same application on dumb ASCII terminals connected to a UNIX processor, on DOS workstations connected to a network, and on X Windows workstations connected to a network by way of TCP/IP. There are some issues associated with achieving this goal. Because not all interfaces support the same interface primitives, it is generally the case that products filling this role either have to choose the lowest common denominator of functionality, or have to provide emulation for missing functionality on the various platforms. Generally, the decision to run a specific application across multiple platforms is a serious one, requiring the use of lower-level toolsets.

If no report exists that retrieves the data the user wants, this report-execution architecture provides no support other than determining this quickly. An enhancement to the architecture can provide a comprehensive dictionary of all data sources that potentially can be used for reporting. Such a dictionary would define the logical structure of the data, its physical location, any security requirements, and any timing issues to be aware of in using the data. A discussion of the design of this type of dictionary is beyond the scope of this book. Populating this dictionary would certainly be a large effort, but one that is potentially worthwhile in reduced research effort.

Report Execution Components

When a user has determined the report he or she wants to execute and has entered any selection criteria for the report, the report then must be submitted for processing. Processing can occur either online or in the background, depending on the user's preferences. The architecture envisions a number of specialized processes, operating on a single network platform or across the network in a distributed architecture, that collectively perform the functions related to report execution.

Figure 18.3 illustrates the network platform design of the example report-processing architecture. The overall flow of processing through report execution is discussed later in the "Report Execution Flow" section. A few definitions that correspond to the components of the reporting architecture in the figure follow.

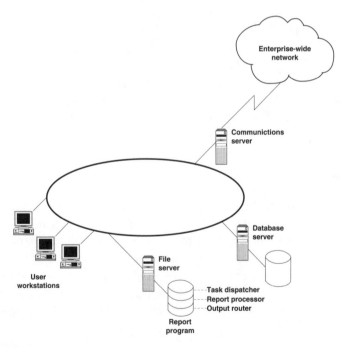

Figure 18.3. Platform design for network-based reporting architecture.

User Workstation

A user workstation can be a DOS, Windows, Macintosh, or OS/2 workstation; a dumb ASCII terminal; or a UNIX workstation running X Windows.

The workstation is used to communicate with the reporting architecture for the purpose of specifying and submitting reports. It also can be used to execute ad hoc reports directly on the workstation.

Task Dispatcher

A task dispatcher monitors activity across the network. When a new task is submitted for processing, the dispatcher determines where that task will be physically executed. It includes a rudimentary schedule-processing function similar to OPC/A on the mainframe. A task dispatcher maintains a database of all tasks dispatched and the results of their processing.

Report Processor

Reports are executed physically on one or more report processors, depending on the amount of reporting load. Both DOS and UNIX workstations can be used as report-processor nodes, depending on the reporting language used. Some products, such as Easytrieve, can execute only on DOS workstations, and others, such as Focus, can run also on the UNIX platform. One of the attributes of the Report Detail entity is the required technical environment and execution process needed for running the report. When report processing is complete, the report processor notifies the task dispatcher of its completion and awaits the next task.

Output Router

When the report output has been generated to a file, the file must be printed (with online review before printing) or distributed electronically (by way of e-mail, for example). The output router is responsible for handling the distribution instructions on the report request and responding to user requests to view or reroute report output. The output router typically makes use of printer queues and ASCII printers to produce its output results. An enhancement to the architecture would support distribution control based on scanning the report itself.

Communications Services

Communications services can be through an SNA gateway, a TCP/IP network, a remote LAN connection, or a general purpose LU6.2 connection. Communications services are the logical processes that provide data communications between the reporting network and other devices.

Database Server

A database server contains all the information used for both reporting control and the production of the reports. In a full production environment, the information is probably in two separate databases. The database server could be a UNIX or OS/2 processor connected to the network using TCP/IP, NetBIOS, or SPX. It all depends on which database engine the company chooses.

File Server

A file server performs standard file-server functions such as program and file access. It includes a network file system for shared storage of UNIX files, and it stores report output files before printing. A file server may also provide interactive access to archived reports on optical disk or tape backup using Hierarchical Storage Management (HSM) facilities, depending on the sophistication of report-archiving features.

Report Execution Flow

Users should generally have the option of running reports on an ad hoc basis without using the architecture. This option is appropriate for one-time reports that will not be executed by others, but this option is not appropriate for reusable reports that will become part of the normal business practice of the company.

A danger exists, however, from a processing time perspective, in allowing completely unstructured, ad hoc queries in a network-based, client/server environment. Many database engines now provide a facility where the duration of a query can be set to prevent runaway processes. EDA/SQL, DB2, and Oracle all provide such a facility.

The processing times to respond to such queries submitted simultaneously could possibly take minutes and, worst case, gridlock the entire system by hoarding computer resources or locking a massive number of rows, thus preventing the processing of updates. One of the most frequent failures of decision support and reporting systems is that they are often built against OLTP (online transaction processing) structures, resulting in poor performance because of record locking and suboptimal database design.

A few important steps should be taken to avoid such scenarios. First, the applications development team must take care to tune and optimize the database server and reporting environment, just as in the mainframe world.

Second, ad hoc queries should be limited by developing preset reporting options that accommodate the majority of users' needs. Lastly, the database designer needs to understand what the common access paths to data are going to be, and design accordingly.

Ideally, many reports can be replaced by optimized, interactive query tools. Inevitably, however, some production paper reports are necessary on the network platform. The architecture is designed to address these reports. Creating and using an architecture for these types of reports ensures that the uncontrolled reporting environment that exists on many mainframes is not replicated on a network.

In summary, in using the architecture, the basic flow of processing is as follows:

1. The user selects the report he or she wants to execute, using the Report Group and Report Detail listing functions.

2. After selecting a particular report for execution, a user can fill in new selection criteria for the current request or copy previously used selection criteria as specified in other report requests.

3. After filling in selection criteria, the user is presented with a distribution control screen that governs how the request is processed. This screen controls information such as media, copies, distribution, and so on. It also determines whether the report will be executed online or in the background. If the processing is to be in the background, the desired processing schedule (hourly, overnight, weekly, monthly, and so on) is specified. Online processing can occur either on the user's workstation or on a back-end report processor, but in either case, it ties up the user's DOS workstation or UNIX task for the duration of the report's execution.

4. When selection criteria and distribution information have been specified, the workstation component of the architecture stores the report request on the database and notifies the task dispatcher of the existence of a new request. If the request is to be processed online, the workstation component waits for the dispatcher to notify it of the report's completion before returning control to the user. Otherwise, the workstation component returns control to the user after notification has occurred.

5. The task dispatcher receives notice of the request, determines whether the request should be processed immediately or on a deferred basis, and handles the request appropriately. Immediate requests are routed to the next available report processor (unless they

are to be executed directly on the user's workstation). Deferred requests are batched and processed as a group on a scheduled basis. The task dispatcher constantly maintains control tables of the current state of all resources the network is responsible for controlling.

6. After receiving notification from the task dispatcher, the designated report processor determines which report requests are to be processed. All report requests of a particular type, based on processing schedule and assigned processor, are handled in a single report process execution.

   The concept behind this approach is that all outstanding requests related to a particular path through the database should be processed simultaneously to optimize I/O performance. Unfortunately, reporting tools such as Focus or Easytrieve do not support this level of control over data extraction. If the tools are ever changed to support this type of processing, however, the architecture is in place to enable the new features to be used to good advantage.

   A report processor is really an instance of a standardized piece of control language that executes the desired report processing. The control language can be a DOS batch file, a UNIX shell script, or a program written in the REXX mainframe scripting language. The process contains certain standard components, however, that enable it to support the architecture features described here.

7. When the report has been completed, the task dispatcher is notified and the next step, report routing, takes control. Reports can be designated as "review before print" or "print immediately" at request time. The output router is notified of the availability of an output report by the task dispatcher, which also notifies the router of the name and location of the file containing the report. The output router then has several options related to archiving, printing, or displaying the report output.

   All of these options are controlled by tables that describe the print output and archiving options available on the network. These tables map the logical output device ID specified by the user to the physical device that should be addressed to output the report. If the device is temporarily unavailable, the report is queued for later printing.

Communication between processes can occur either directly, through remote procedure calls, or indirectly, through database table entries. The method used depends on the degree of recoverability required. This issue should be addressed during the detailed design and implementation of the architecture.

Specific Products

Several commercial products address aspects of the requirements of this kind of architecture. No single product provides all the required functionality. This section discusses specific products and how they can be used within such an architectural approach.

Event Control Server

From Vinzant, Inc., the Event Control Server provides network-aware scheduling-management functions on DOS networks. It can be used to implement a DOS-only version of a reporting architecture that uses DOS machines as back-end report servers.

Qbatch

From Software Clearing House, Inc., Qbatch provides automated batch scheduling functionality for UNIX platforms. This product enables processing to be scheduled across all available UNIX processors on a network. It does not enable DOS applications to be controlled through the Qbatch schedule. Qbatch products can be used to implement the UNIX side of the report-scheduling requirements noted in the previous section on "Report Execution Flow."

RPC Compiler

RPC Compiler, from Netwise, Inc., provides a standardized mechanism for communicating between programs running on different nodes on a network. RPC Compiler automatically handles issues of data format and protocol conversion when moving between IBM and non-IBM environments. This capability insulates the developer from details of particular protocol implementations.

RPC Compiler is used to implement communications between the task manager and the workstation application requesting that a report be run. In another alternative, which avoids the need for RPC, the requesting application writes the request record to the database, and a report-scheduler process on UNIX or DOS constantly monitors the contents of the database to determine whether an action should be taken. If an action is required, the appropriate dispatcher then takes over.

Report Distribution

CA-Dispatch and CA-Dispatch/PC from Computer Associates, Inc. provide an integrated capability to distribute and view both mainframe- and network-generated reports within a single system, using Windows on the LAN, if you want. Custom development of the functionality available through CA-Dispatch/PC would be a time-consuming proposition. Without this functionality, the report-distribution capabilities of the network platform are very limited. The growing popularity of SMTP mail and the use of X.400/X.500 mail backbones have also made the use of off-the-shelf e-mail systems viable for a distribution architecture. Vendors in this category include Lotus and Microsoft, as well as HP. In addition, vendors like Softswitch produce heterogeneous e-mail connectivity solutions that can also be used to route output.

Conclusion

The reporting architecture described in this chapter represents a significant rightsizing project. By moving from a mainframe to a client/server, network-based platform, it is possible for our hypothetical Fortune 500 company, mentioned at the beginning of this chapter, to benefit in cost savings, increased flexibility, faster response times, and other ways.

However, one thing this chapter should have illustrated to you, in addition to the opportunities, is the complexities that remain in rightsizing. For example, this reporting architecture was developed to make optimal use of all available commercial tools. Unfortunately, however, no single tool or collection of tools is available to implement the entire approach. Thus, some custom development is unavoidable. The development required in this case would be with tools and techniques that are not well known. Therefore, although rightsizing benefits may be very sizable, one-time development costs may be just as expensive as development costs on a similar mainframe project.

Maintenance: Keeping I/T All Together

Part IV discussed key steps in the implementation phase of the rightsizing methodology. Part V describes key steps in the next phase of the rightsizing methodology—maintenance, as shown in Figure V.1.

We hesitate to call maintenance the final phase in the methodology because the entire process is so iterative. As the figure illustrates, initial network management and maintenance activities overlap with the implementation phase, showing that before the system is completed, maintenance must begin to keep the programs that have been developed up and running.

In the maintenance phase, the assumption is that components of the system have been developed and potential pitfalls have been recognized, with steps taken to overcome them. Chapter 19, "Maintenance," discusses network maintenance and management, and provides guidelines for how to keep the development and production networks and applications up and running on an ongoing basis.

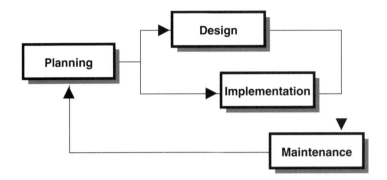

Figure V.1. Rightsizing development methodology.

Chapter 20, "Network Assessment," on the other hand, covers the periodic process of auditing the network platform—an important step in ensuring the short- and long-term success of a rightsized system.

At the end of Chapter 21, "Conclusion: A Call to Arms," you will have been introduced to all the major "pressure points" in the rightsizing methodology. The remainder of the book provides a glossary; reference sections, including one giving a number of approaches to rightsizing an existing DB2 application; a bibliography; and an index for your further use.

Maintenance

Maintenance

19

Whatever you do, do cautiously, and look to the end.

—Anonymous

Objectives:

1. To understand the objectives of maintenance.
2. To observe a structure that provides for ongoing maintenance.
3. To understand alternative approaches to maintenance: departmental, central help and information center, third-party, and so on.

As previous chapters pointed out, rightsized systems based on client/server network computing technology offer tremendous flexibility and power. This is true, however, only if the network is working properly, and if management has a good idea of how the network can and should be used. A good network management and maintenance program is proactive. It builds in such factors as future requirements, leaves open possibilities for using the network in new ways, and continually keeps the components in working order.

Avoiding Maintenance Rigor Mortis

The reputation of MIS departments for being profoundly incapable of taking on new projects in a timely manner has caused cynical end users to compare them to the dead—locked by a backlog "rigor mortis." This reputation for untimeliness is due partly to the nature of systems projects, which are more difficult and take longer to implement than most users realize. But the bad reputation is also due partly to poor personnel planning. Maintenance tends to consume more than 50 percent—and often as much as 80 percent—of the MIS department's personnel, leaving few resources available to cope with new requirements. In addition, planning for maintenance has been inadequate.

Good planning does not reduce the requirement for maintenance, but it can point out to top management the need for more staff in order for new development to take place (with consequently higher budgets), or, alternatively, the need for lower user expectations. In other words, user and management expectations for the speed with which new projects can be developed could be managed better with effective planning.

Planning for realistic levels of maintenance can help management realize also the need for higher quality in the initial development of projects. Many MIS departments tend to skimp on design, documentation, and reviews under the pressure of both top management and users to produce operational applications quickly and within the initial budget.

This problem is not easy to solve because of today's imperfect techniques for reducing maintenance by increasing the quality of the systems design and implementation techniques and tools. Moreover, MIS professionals do not yet have reliable mechanisms for predicting maintenance efforts as a percentage of development effort or as a function of system size.

In the earliest days of end-user computing, the maintenance cost of user-developed systems was even less well-recognized than that of applications developed by the MIS department. In many organizations, this is still the case.

There are two common results of this lack of recognition. First, many end users who develop their own applications (because the MIS department does not have sufficient resources) find the development project to be challenging and rewarding, but they run out of steam when it comes to maintenance. In other words, they commit the same mistakes as early MIS departments did in failing to plan for high maintenance levels. Some of these user departments ask the MIS department to take over the responsibility for the application, thus adding to the maintenance burden of the MIS department.

Second, a more frequent cause of added maintenance is that end-user computing usually places demands for data-delivery systems on the central MIS facility. Analysts and programmers have to be assigned to writing programs to cut off, extract, format, and deliver data to information centers, departmental computers, or PCs.

Even though proper planning does not by itself reduce the levels of maintenance in an organization, designing self-managed, self-maintaining systems should be the first step toward recognizing the maintenance issue and bringing it under control. The remainder of this chapter talks about these systems, focusing primarily on maintenance at the applications and network levels.

Operations Management Utilities

Operations management is the area of greatest weakness for the network computing environment. Software vendors have not yet provided the extensive support for automated data center operations that is available on a mainframe platform. To some extent, such support is less necessary in a network environment; however, some of the fundamentals must be addressed in order for production applications to be executed on a network platform. Among these fundamentals are job scheduling, database backup and recovery, performance monitoring and tuning, and hierarchical storage management.

Job Scheduling

Users should be able to submit jobs for immediate or deferred execution, and system administrators should be able to schedule jobs for timed execution. Controls regarding conditional execution and restart and recovery parameters should be available on a network. LAN-Batch, Event Control Server, and QBatch are products that partially implement these objectives on a network platform. The first two products are competitors on the network platform, and QBatch is a UNIX scheduler.

Performance Monitoring and Tuning

Performance monitoring and tuning tools such as Omegamon, DASDmon, FDR, and others are commonplace in the mainframe MVS environment. Without them, effectively managing the mainframe's resources would be virtually impossible. In a network environment, equivalent tools do not yet exist.

Specialized tools for monitoring network traffic and network performance are widely available, yet tools that monitor operating-system and application-process performance are not. In fact, there are virtually no tools that present a single system image of operating-system and application performance and resource consumption across the network.

Hierarchical Storage Management

On the mainframe platform, hierarchical storage management (HSM) and system-managed storage provide the capability to automatically archive and restore infrequently used files without making them totally unavailable to system users. Such facilities are not yet available on the network platform. For years, Palindrome has provided the most extensive support for network storage-management needs. Other vendors now have similar offerings.

Minimizing Network Downtime

As more and more companies implement critical business applications on client/server network computing platforms, keeping networks up and running becomes increasingly important. Network downtime is very costly in terms of loss of productivity. Major corporations are reporting substantial losses when they have problems with their networks. With studies reporting an average loss of productivity resulting from network problems to be in excess of $3 million per year, it's apparent that minimizing network downtime through maintenance is a serious issue.

The following is a checklist for minimizing network downtime. Many of the items are discussed in the following section.

- Keep detailed documentation on hardware, software, users, and network configuration.
- Document the physical schema of the network, including servers, routers, and gateways.
- Implement change-control procedures to manage network changes as well as to provide detailed documentation.
- Consider signing a maintenance agreement, especially for critical hardware.
- Develop "normal" statistics for reference.
- Develop a troubleshooting methodology to diagnose and treat network problems.
- Consider purchasing network troubleshooting tools such as TDRs, network monitors, and network analyzers.

Documenting the Network

The single most valuable weapon in the war against downtime is documentation. In assembling a network, a network administrator should create a manual file for each component of the network (hardware and software). Establishing a standard form of documentation makes it easy for the network administrator to locate vital information when troubleshooting network problems or contacting technical support departments. Network documentation should include hardware, software, and user information; the physical configuration of the LAN cabling should be documented, along with network addresses and devices (routers, bridges, gateways, and servers).

Hardware Files

For each piece of hardware, you or your accounting department should possess copies of the purchase order, packing slip, invoice, and warranty (including serial number information). When repairs are performed, add related documentation to the file. Organize the filing system by the hardware serial number or by a unique internal asset number.

You may also want to keep electronic records of hardware devices. Several tools are available for tracking hardware; these include PC Tracker, by RG Software Systems, Inc.; NetManager, by Brightwork Development, Inc.; and Micro Resource Manager, by Computer Associates International, Inc. Remember, though, that even when records are available online, you should maintain hard copies of the documentation.

Server and Workstation Configuration Files

Document each server and workstation configuration. File server configuration sheets should include an operating system maintenance record that includes the date and version of the initial NOS installation, as well as all upgrades, patches, additional drivers, and other useful information. File server information should also include general diagnostic information. The leading network operating systems include software utilities that report this type of information. For instance, these statistics can be found using Monitor for NetWare networks. General information includes the number of file server processes; statistics on file server and network utilization, availability, and memory; the number of files open; and the number of users.

Workstation configuration information should also be gathered, including the workstation model, memory, network address, drives, fixed disks, LAN adapter configuration, CONFIG.SYS, SHELL.CFG, AUTOEXEC.BAT, and workstation location. Third party products are available to automatically collect this type of information, including Tally's PC Census or Net Census and Horizons Technology's LANauditor.

Software Installation and Configuration Files

Similar to the files maintained for the network hardware, files should be established for each software package installed on the network. Include in the software files copies of the purchase order, packing slip, invoice, completed registration form, and warranty information, if applicable. It may be helpful also to keep track of who is responsible for the manuals. Maintaining current software information can be very valuable because manufacturers often require detailed purchase information for upgrade offers. Lotus Development Corporation, for example, offered upgrades of Lotus 1-2-3 Version 3.0 free for anyone who had purchased Version 2.01 after September 1988.

Develop a software configuration sheet for each software package on the network. Each software configuration sheet should include the following information: directories in which software was installed, trustee rights for those directories, file flags, and the default configuration. Also include information on how to modify the defaults and how to access the software. Document users' configuration files and search mappings, along with any special hardware or software required to use the package (a plotter, for example).

Finally, create a general information sheet that contains specific information about the software and its required files. Include the application name, executable filenames, overlay files, hidden files, and temporary files used by the software. The protocols required along with the logical drive definition, print queues, and job definition can also assist the network manager.

User Configuration Files

Adding, deleting, and changing user privileges is a routine task for the network administrator. Maintaining files documenting users, groups, and privileges along with log-in scripts can simplify the process. It can also provide insights into how to create logical groups of users.

Physical Connectivity of the LAN

Documenting the physical design of the LAN can prevent crawling around in the ceiling space looking for the end connection of an unmarked cable. The first step in documenting the physical layout of your LAN is to establish a naming and numbering convention. Develop numbering schemes that include the wiring closet number and sequence. Meaningful names should be assigned to identify the router, bridges, servers, and gateways. It's helpful if you can assign your own locally administered addresses (LAA). By using your own addresses, the address location can be isolated quickly to a building and segment if a problem occurs.

A Picture Is Worth a Thousand Words

A graphical representation of the physical connectivity of your network can be extremely beneficial, especially when the network covers more than a single office. The easiest way to create a picture of your network is to use a physical network management system. Physical network management systems, such as Isicad's COMMAND cable management system, provide network information in both graphic pictures and reports.

Physical network-management systems combine a graphical front end with a standard, commercially-available relational database. The database supplements the graphics with detailed information on the network components, and changes in the database are reflected in the graphics. Some reports that can be generated by a network management system are work orders for moves, adds, changes, and repairs; reports on equipment schedules, cable schedules, and cable tray accommodations; and bills of materials. For example, with Novell's NetWare Management Enhanced Map System, users can load bitmap images of their building layouts using a scanner or many standard graphics tools. Automatically discovered network devices represented by icons may be overlaid onto these images by selecting an icon and dragging it onto the appropriate location on the map. This links objects with their exact location, allowing network managers to find a malfunctioning networked device quickly. The key reason for maintaining a physical diagram of the network, however, is to know the exact configuration of the network for troubleshooting.

Change Control Procedures

A LAN is an ever-changing creature. To keep changes under control, a change control system and standard procedures should be developed to ensure authorization. Change control encompasses all network changes including new hardware, hardware upgrades, new releases or patches to operating systems, new operating systems or applications, and modifications to existing applications. Change control system also helps a LAN administrator organize daily requests for adding upgraded software, user and workgroup changes, and more workstations. Effective change control includes the following components:

■ Secured libraries or areas to separate testing, intermediate, and production environments. A test environment should be set up to allow programmers to test their changes. For example, test libraries may be created to allow programmers to test application changes and a separate test server may be set up to allow the testing of NLMs, system patches, and other operating system changes/enhancements. Changes should never be directly applied to the production environment without first authorizing, testing, and approving the changes. Security should be configured so that programmers cannot access intermediate and production libraries. Intermediate libraries should be established to allow testing of changes by quality assurance (QA) and user personnel. Production libraries should be restricted to personnel who need the access to perform their job duties. Changes to objects should be controlled by a version control product such as Intersolv's PVCS.

- Version control for source code. For further discussion of this, see the section on "Source Code Control and Versioning."

- Documentation and authorization of all changes. This serves not only as written authorization to support the requested change, but also as an audit trail of all changes made. The audit trail may provide an effective tool in troubleshooting production problems. For example, an integrated database could contain a detailed inventory of hardware and software, including a listing of all changes. Additionally, the documentation regarding the changes can be used to update disaster recovery plans when appropriate.

- Independent testing, review, and approval of changes prior to implementation into the production environment. This is necessary to ensure that the actual changes were made in accordance with the authorized request for change, the implemented change works successfully and as anticipated, the implemented change has no adverse affect on surrounding areas (for example, no negative impact on dependent programs), and the change was made in accordance with established standards (for example, programs were written in accordance with the organization's information systems methodology). Some changes have a widespread effect (that is, necessitate changes in other areas) and must be communicated to the proper parties for implementation of the "dependency" changes prior to the implementation of the original changes.

- Migration of changes to the production environment by individuals independent of those people who actually made the changes. If migration is not performed by an independent person, change control is a moot point. Why have authorization, testing, and approval of changes when this can all be circumvented by a person with access to the production environment?

- Where possible, backups made prior to implementing the change. Thus, if the newly implemented change adversely affects production, it can be removed and replaced with the backup of the previous production version. The backed-up production versions should be kept for a sufficient period of time in the event that all subsequent changes had negatively impacted production and required restoration of a particular production backup.

■ Timely notification of users of the implementation date of pending changes.

Maintenance Agreements

Maintenance contracts or arranged service contracts are beneficial for LAN environments when it is impractical to maintain a team of skilled technicians and spare inventory. There are three common types of service contracts: *time and material contracts*, *term maintenance contracts*, and *hot spares contracts*. Time and material (T&M) contracts are the least comprehensive of the three types. Parts and labor are provided on an as-needed basis. T&M contracts usually specify service costs, such as set rate per hour, technician qualifications, trip costs, minimum billed hours per call, equipment covered, response time, and warranty repairs. Pay close attention to the areas of the equipment covered under the contract, the response time promised, and how warranty repairs are handled. Some contracts add a fee for repairs performed under warranty.

Term maintenance contracts cover a specific piece of equipment—for example, the file server—over a specified period of time. A term maintenance contract establishes specific contractual performance requirements such as scheduled preventive maintenance, spare parts on reserve, and turnaround time guarantees. Term maintenance contracts differ from T&M because they are particular to a certain item of equipment and provide preventive maintenance as well as a guaranteed maximum length of downtime during repairs.

A hot spares contract, typically the most expensive maintenance agreement, guarantees that duplicate equipment will be available immediately if a device fails. This type of contract usually is used on only critical devices such as file servers, but should include also the device's peripherals, such as the disk drives. Duplicate equipment should be tested regularly to ensure that it will work properly if the primary devices fail.

Problem Management

To ensure sound customer orientation, the problem management system must be working effectively and be carefully monitored. Problem management can include the following components:

■ Network surveillance processes and procedures to correlate causes of alarms with affected applications.

- Centralization of critical alarms in a single console, including the arrangement of alarms into hierarchical levels based on the seriousness of the problem: normal, minor, major, and critical.

- Documented escalation procedures to handle problems. For example, notification procedures should be escalated all the way to top management, depending on the seriousness of the problem.

- A documented trouble-ticketing system to facilitate handling network problems, including a trouble call history database that provides the capability to review previous problems while working on a new problem.

- A Help Desk function staffed with personnel who can answer basic and frequently asked questions, as well as provide the first level of troubleshooting.

- Procedures to address trouble-call coverage during business hours and after hours as needed. Procedures should be set up to manage time, priorities, and resources. Document who is responsible for resolving the problem.

- Response guarantees from those vendors providing services under a maintenance agreement.

- Development and availability of problem-solving tools such as the "Expert Sniffer," a customer-portable PC that reads data online, analyzes it, and provides problem-solving interpretations for use in corrective actions.

Troubleshooting

By following these suggestions, the task of troubleshooting a network problem will be greatly reduced. Preparing for trouble by documenting the network and establishing maintenance procedures and contracts proves its value when the network fails. When the network is down, the administrator's job is to identify the source of the problem and fix it—fast.

Documentation is important; however, it shouldn't be a crutch. It is still the LAN administrator's job to know every detail of the network, cold. He or she should develop a level of familiarity so that things "feel" right or wrong. Developing this feeling helps to avoid relying on documentation, which in some cases can slow troubleshooting.

Troubleshooting Methodology

Like documenting the network, the key to troubleshooting the network effectively is to establish a baseline reference in advance of actual problems. The baseline helps indicate normal network utilization during the day, dominant applications, protocols, and other network performance characteristics. Network interfaces, including the gateways, repeaters, bridges, and routers, should be examined and their normal performance documented before problems occur.

Troubleshooting requires knowledge of network operation and also of the relationship between the symptoms experienced by users and possible causes. First, observe the problem symptoms. Ask yourself these questions:

- Are a few users affected, or are all network users having the same problem?
- Are there particular times when this problem manifests itself (for example, during peak hours)?
- Has anything changed lately?
- Are all the release variables and versions experiencing the same problem?

These questions should provide clues to the range and scope of the problem, the percentage of time the problem occurs, and whether a change in the network may have triggered the problem. The change control log can be invaluable in determining what may have changed recently on the network.

Next, consider how the network differs from the baseline discussed earlier. Could an increase in users have affected the performance of the network, for example? The next step is to develop a theory and then a method to test the theory. Here, a good understanding of network protocols and the applications running on the network comes into play. Finally, when the iterative process of theorizing and testing is completed, you can draw a conclusion about what caused the network problem.

The most common problems encountered in networks have to do with connectivity and configuration. Connectivity can be disrupted by breaks or shorts in cables and by malfunctions in the hardware. Configuration errors usually occur across routers, bridges, and gateways.

Certain network configurations are more conducive to troubleshooting. The token-ring network allows active and passive status monitors to provide feedback information in the form of MAC frames. This network also has the capability to recover from some failures by "wrapping around" the faulty node. Token-ring adapters are also self-checking. If they fail, they do not bring down the network (an exception is IBM's Type 3 wiring scheme); rather, they remove themselves from the network.

The network operating system being used can do part of the troubleshooting for you. Some network operating systems provide tools that log errors as network events and confirm that critical network resources are present. Most network operating systems have built-in utilities for interaction directly with the disk-drive subsystem. NetWare, for instance, provides utilities such as COMPSURF, ZTEST, VREPAIR, DCONFIG, and DISKED.

Troubleshooting Tools

Three common types of tools assist in network troubleshooting: *physical layer tools*, *network monitors*, and *network analyzers*. Physical layer tools include time domain reflectometers (TDRs), oscilloscopes, breakout boxes, and power meters. Physical layer tools help to identify cable opens (for example, cables which are not properly connected), cable shorts, unterminated cables, and poorly functioning connection hardware. The TDR, perhaps the most useful of these items, sends signals along the physical medium at regular intervals. The returning signals' reflections provide a representative waveform that shows the placement of network devices and the location of any cable problems. TDRs cost from $1,500 to $10,000.

Network monitors can monitor all or selected portions of the network traffic. They help in compiling statistics on network utilization, including packet type, number of packets sent, and packet errors. Statistics such as these are useful in establishing baseline performance as well as in helping to identify problem areas. One of the best features of network monitors is that they can watch the network 24 hours a day. Network monitors provide relatively low-cost error-detection facilities and integrate easily into the network management design. Network monitors cost from $500 to $10,000.

Network analyzers assist in locating network problems and testing solutions. Recently, a number of network analyzers have incorporated online troubleshooting guides that provide probable causes for network problems. The analyzers provide extensive, detailed information through real-time, network traffic analysis including packet capture decoding and transmission statistics. In selecting a network analyzer, consider the number of protocols supported, collection capabilities, transit capabilities, maximum capture data rate and sustained data rate, ease of use, and format of display. Prices start at $10,000, but can be well over $30,000 for network analyzers that support multiple physical media and protocol decoding.

Network Security

Network users depend on network administrators to maintain the confidentiality, integrity, and availability of data on the network. This job includes those tasks required to help ensure the security of the network, including controls over unauthorized user access to the network data and maintenance of data integrity, virus prevention and detection, and the use of system fault tolerance. Another facet of maintaining data includes keeping data safe from human disaster and from natural disasters such as floods, fires, and earthquakes—thus, necessitating the backup and recovery of critical records and the development of a disaster-recovery plan. Backup and recovery and disaster-recovery planning are discussed in subsequent sections.

The first steps in determining the security needs of a LAN are to determine the sensitivity of the data and develop a suitable network security policy. Your business needs direct which security approach best suits your network environment. The commonsense approach to security means that network users follow some common security precautions, including locking office doors and desks, changing passwords often, avoiding easy-to-guess passwords (such as a spouse's name), and prohibiting two users from using the same user ID. Changing factory-default passwords and settings in the network software is important when the network is first installed. Make sure that documentation is kept on these changes.

System Security

Steps such as banning automatic logon, ensuring proper logoff, and logging the user off the network after a set period of inactivity help to keep unauthorized people from gaining access by using unattended computers.

A number of products are available for securing the workstation. Programs such as Fastlock and The Gatekeeper encrypt the disk partition table and require a password when the computer is switched on. Certus, a TSR program, compares programs the user is trying to run against an authorization list. Other programs, such as Net/Assure, establish users and privileges at the workstation level and create audit trails for each workstation. Terminal-lock products can be installed to prevent or block physical startup or mask the disk drives from the startup poll that occurs when a network is first activated. Diskless workstations can prohibit copying network files to floppy disks, as well as help prevent the introduction of viruses to the network.

Finally, authentication of users can be used to replace or enhance the logon password. Several devices are available for authenticating users. One low-cost device uses small plastic cards that contain personal user-identification codes; users insert them into readers at each workstation. More expensive devices are available that read fingerprints, retinas, voiceprints, or other unique biological characteristics.

Physical Security

The threat of unauthorized personnel accidentally or deliberately causing network failure is greatly reduced by limiting access to network servers. Restricting access to the server includes removing input/output devices such as the monitor, keyboard, and disk drives. If a disk drive is required to reboot the server, the drive should be disabled when the server is up and running.

Physically restricting access to network media is another important key to keeping a network secure. The cabling plant and devices such as wiring hubs, concentrators, servers, bridges, and gateways should have access limited to authorized personnel because they are the major points of network communication.

Restricting physical access involves keeping the cabling plant out of the way of harm by keeping it in the ceiling and walls and preferably in some type of shielded conduit. The connectivity devices themselves (like the hubs and concentrators) should be kept in locked, environmentally controlled wiring closets or server rooms.

These security steps are low-cost ways of securing network media and can be implemented without much work on the part of the network designers and administrators. If the network requires more protection, however, or contains especially sensitive data, encryption of data is a further measure of security that can be employed.

Virus Prevention and Detection

A policy should exist to educate users on the existence of computer viruses, preventative measures to take, procedures to notify appropriate personnel, and measures to mitigate the damage resulting from a virus infection. Users should be required to scan files from diskettes and bulletin boards prior to using them; service personnel should be required to use write-protected or scanned diagnostic diskettes; and servers and workstations should be scanned on a regular basis. It is prudent to invest in a virus product that will automatically scan network and local drives at specified intervals and provide virus eradication when necessary.

Data Encryption

Data encryption protects against breaches in security such as wiretapping and unauthorized file access at the system level. The encryption process encodes and decodes messages using an algorithm and a key. Two types of encryption systems are commonly used: *symmetric* and *asymmetric*. The symmetric system requires the sender and receiver of the message to use the same algorithm and key. In the asymmetric system, the algorithm and key for encoding the message to a specific person are distributed, but the decoding key is known only to the message recipient. Using encrypted data as a means of security adds a heightened degree of responsibility to the system administrator to track and assign keys and algorithms.

Fault Tolerance

Physical and system restrictions are important. However, mission-critical applications also require fault tolerance to ensure data integrity and thus, ongoing operations. Two popular methods of ensuring data integrity are *disk mirroring* and *disk duplexing*. Disk mirroring (also called *disk shadowing*) uses two disk drives simultaneously. The second (backup) drive duplicates the information on the first drive. The two disks are not identical because each disk can be expected to have unreadable portions in different physical locations—the two disks contain exactly the same data. When a disk fails, the surviving disk takes over.

Disk duplexing is an extension of disk mirroring. The difference is that when data is retrieved from the server, the disk that has the information most readily available is the one the server reads. This enhances server performance as well as provides data protection. Duplexing can be extended to include not only the use of a redundant drive, but also a redundant disk coprocessor board and disk controller. This approach is known as *channel duplexing*. The appearance of newer Redundant Arrays of Inexpensive Drives (RAID) systems is hastening the adoption of fully duplexed systems. RAID is implemented from level RAID 0 to RAID 5, and the new RAID 7 and RAID 10. The most popular implementations are RAID 0, 1, and 5. RAID 0 provides data striping so that data is written across all drives, with each block written to each drive in the array in sequence. RAID 1 involves writing a second copy of data to a second drive (disk mirroring). With RAID 5, data and parity information is written to all drives without an assigned parity drive.

Fault tolerance can be extended from the disk level to an entire file server. Novell's SFT III lets you mirror not only the disk drives but also the CPU, memory, network interface cards, hard drives, operating system, and applications. By doing this, you can protect your network from most server-based hardware (and even some software) failures. However, SFT III v3.11 cannot use many of NetWare's own management and internetworking services to link it with other systems such as NetWare for Macintosh, NetWare for SAA, TCP/IP, and NMS. Additionally, some third-party NLMs are incompatible with SFT III v3.11.

Backup and Recovery

Online systems are typically more vulnerable to hardware and software failures than batch systems because the failures interrupt an activity that is in process; therefore, it is very difficult to know where to restart. In batch systems, recovering from failures is easier because the process normally can be restarted from the beginning, because file updates are usually saved for the last step.

The difficulties caused by recovery and restart procedures long were a major deterrent to online updates. For many years, prudent designers advocated updating in batch, with the only online update advocated being the so-called memo update. Memo update consists of having in each record a scratchpad area that can be updated to provide a running value; this value is erased at the end of the day and recalculated by the batch update program running overnight.

Many decisions on restart and recovery still have to be made by the designer. The main problem to guard against by using restart and recovery procedures is the failure of the system at an arbitrary point during the online session. Without proper design safeguards when the system fails, you may have no way to tell how much work has been completed and recorded on the database or on other external files. Because the contents of memory may be lost, any work that has been done only in memory might as well not have been done at all. For example, Novell incorporated Transaction Tracking System (TTS) into NetWare to protect databases from corruption caused by incomplete updates to related files. TTS automatically rolls back to the previous point of consistency in case of failure. Only the failed transaction is aborted.

The simplest preventative measure to avoid these complications is to make a backup copy of the database every night; if the system goes down, the system can be restored from the copy. Of course, the worst-case scenario of this approach is that users may have to reenter an entire day's transactions. As you can imagine, this way of ensuring recovery is not popular with users.

Rather than back up once every day, the database might be backed up several times during the same day to minimize the work lost in the event of a failure. This solution usually fails because of the volume of data to be backed up. Some databases are so large that it takes all night to back them up.

A more common practice is to make a daily copy of the database and then accumulate on a separate log all the modifications posted to the database. The log contains each modified record as it looks after the update. This technique is called *after-image logging*. Whenever the database is updated, the log must be written to first, and the transaction must wait for the physical I/O to be completed.

The same effect as forward recovery using after-images can be achieved differently and sometimes more economically. Rather than store the modified images of the database records, the log stores the images of the records before they were updated, in a process called *before-image logging*. These images can be used to roll back the database. The log is read in reverse sequence and the before-images are substituted, gradually working backward to the point where each transaction in process at the time of the failure has been undone.

On-the-fly recovery is made possible by logging transactions as well as either after- or before-images. When the database has been restored to a known state, an automatic transaction restart facility can bring the system up-to-date by simulating the work done by the operators at the time of failure, to the point where there is no more data on the log. Then, each user takes over, very close to the point where the work was interrupted.

In the mainframe world, database backup and recovery is largely a location-independent activity. In the network computing world, however, the story can be different.

This process requires that the server platform be physically close to the support staff, a proposition counter to some of the more motivating aspects of distributed, decentralized processing. Until either vendors either correct or prevent limitations, such as this one with SQL Server, or until a third-party utility is introduced to provide "work around" functionality, database restart and recovery remains an issue.

Nonetheless, backing up the network files is vital. These three steps ensure a solid backup strategy:

- Determine the frequency of data backups.
- Choose a backup procedure and backup media.
- Test the backups to ensure the integrity of the data and that the data is retrievable.

The frequency at which data backups should be performed depends on a number of factors, including how critical the data is to the business, the volume of data that must be backed up, and the resources available to perform backups. Because mission-critical data may change several times during a business day, even daily backups may not provide enough protection. Servers that contain mission-critical data should have adequate system fault tolerance in place. For example, NetWare servers with applications that must be continuously online should incorporate SFT III. SFT III provides a redundant server that can take over in an instant if the original server suffers a server-based hardware failure. Also, an uninterruptible power supply (UPS) should be installed to guard against a power outage.

The most practical and popular backup solution for most LANs is a tape backup system. Whenever the LAN is least used (usually at night), network data files should be copied automatically to magnetic tape and the tapes then archived and stored offsite. When a backup schedule has been established, using multiple tapes in rotation can help protect against tape failure. Digital audiotape (DAT) backup drives and tapes are becoming increasingly popular because they can store 8 (or more) gigabytes of compressed data on a single tape, depending on the drive type and tape length. Other backup systems include write once, read many (WORM) drives and optical drives.

A number of automated data-management systems are available that assist a network administrator in maintaining backups. ARCserve, by Cheyenne Software, and an erasable optical drive, LaserStor, by Storage Dimensions, are a possible software/hardware combination for backups. ARCserve performs full and incremental backups interactively using NetWare queuing services to schedule and dispatch to the backup device. LaserStor provides random access to archived data. In a drive failure, LaserStor can be used as a direct-access device and as an emergency replacement for the server's hard disk.

Palindrome's The Network Archivist is a rule-based expert system that combines the activities of backup, archiving, restoration, and file system maintenance. Restoration can be accomplished on selected files, a key feature during any recovery aside from complete disaster recovery. File maintenance features maintain the automatic migration of unused files to tape using rules specified by the LAN administrator.

Legato's NetWorker provides centralized backup and recovery for a heterogenous network environment, including DOS PCs, NetWare servers, and UNIX workstations.

In addition to backing up data files, network operating system files containing the system configuration should be backed up also. The advantage to backing up network files, such as the bindery files in Novell NetWare, is that the files can be used not only in case of failure, but also in case a server must be taken down to load a new process. The network system files can be used to endow new file servers with the same configuration of selected users, groups, and print services.

Planning for Disaster

Although most LAN administrators back up their networks faithfully and have used their backups to recover files accidentally lost by users, many administrators do not take precautions for unthinkable disasters. A University of Texas study estimates that 43 percent of all companies that do not prepare for a disaster and then suffer one never reopen; 90 percent of those that reopen are out of business within two years.

The first step in minimizing network downtime following a disaster is preplanning: determining your risk and the systems necessary to cover critical business functions and supporting system operations. A company is at extreme risk if it copies damaged files, does not store backups offsite, or has not scheduled backup operations correctly.

Estimate the cost of a disaster such as an office fire, flood, or earthquake. The cost of disaster can be calculated as the loss of revenue for the estimated downtime, whether it's a day, a week, or longer. This price should far exceed the cost of implementing a disaster recovery plan.

Software Licensing

The Software Publishers Association (SPA) was formed to police software licensing compliance. This association has performed investigations of major companies accused of copyright infringement of software licenses. In recent years, companies using pirated software have paid millions of dollars in additional licensing fees, fines, damages, and court costs. However, products are available to help ensure that your company is in compliance with your software licensing agreements by automatically metering the number of users of each network application. Auditing and inventory products are also available to determine the number of copies of software on each workstation.

Managing an Expanding Network

Minimizing network downtime—through comprehensive documentation, performance monitoring and tuning, effective troubleshooting, solid backup and recovery procedures, and adequate change control procedures and security to limit unauthorized access and changes to the network—is most of the battle in keeping your network running smoothly. The other component of a well-managed network is being able to efficiently accommodate expansion. These tasks include handling increases in users, creating a productive network environment, updating network software, managing enterprise-wide networks, and maintaining a heterogeneous applications development platform.

A checklist for managing an expanding network is as follows:

- Establish logical groupings of users.
- Learn how to use network-naming services.
- Consider software tools to assist you in managing users.
- Install a menu system or GUI to make the environment user-friendly.
- Selectively upgrade software, balancing user need with network restrictions.
- Carefully test applications for problems before placing them on the network for public use.
- Implement and utilize tools to unify management of all aspects of an enterprise-wide network.
- Maintain a heterogeneous applications development platform by addressing several issues—including source code control and versioning, compatibility testing, test data management, and dictionary maintenance.

Managing User and Group Information

User administration can be simplified significantly if users are grouped functionally according to similar duties and responsibilities. Groups are sets of users that require similar access to network resources. A network administrator can more easily add the privileges for a group once and then add users to the group than add privileges for each user individually.

The leading network operating software include *naming services*, which assist an administrator in adding both users and groups to servers on the network. Before naming services were available, a LAN administrator had to add a user individually to each of the servers connected to a network and then each server would keep duplicate information. Banyan's StreetTalk global naming service, used with its VINES NOS, is a leader in naming services. With StreetTalk, users must be added only once, and they are recognized by all servers on the network. This feature is now available in Novell's NetWare 4.x.

Network naming services are developed on the principle of *domain-based naming*. A server is placed within a *domain*, or group of servers. Because a user logs on to the domain rather than to a single server, the user can share the resources of a number of different file and database servers, without a number of different login IDs. Each leading network software package (NOS) handles naming services differently, so you should know how your network responds when applications and other network resources are moved. For instance, moving an application to a different server may require that you change all the users' drive mappings.

Several third-party packages are available to assist you in tracking user information such as access privileges, rights, group membership, account restrictions, login scripts, and user requirements. Examples of these third-party packages include Frye's Utilities for NetWare Management and XTree's XTree Tools.

Creating a Productive Environment

One often overlooked way of keeping a network running smoothly is to create an atmosphere in which users feel comfortable and confident. An easy way to do this is to develop a menu system to provide users with a list of available services on the network and make it easy to access programs and files. Leading network operating systems provide menu-building systems, and a number of third-party products are available for DOS. Graphical user interfaces, such as Microsoft Windows 3.x, also can make users feel comfortable using the network.

Updating Smoothly

Network users are becoming more aware of the software packages available for the LAN environment and when new versions or upgrades are available. However, LAN administrators should be part of the decision-making process with users in determining whether an upgrade is warranted. An upgrade costs more than just the purchase price—there are costs associated with the technical staff having to learn new features to provide support to users, ensuring compatibility with the files of previous versions, training users, providing in-house documentation, and the time it takes to install upgrades on the servers and workstations. The timing of the upgrade should be considered also, based on the requirements of the departments affected. The key point in determining whether an upgrade is warranted is to balance users' needs and wants with compatibility and value to the network. If users are satisfied with the functionality of the current version and can get their jobs done, consider waiting. If they are demanding more, proceed carefully. Additionally, software distribution products have become available to automatically install software at the client. For example, Frye's Software Update and Distribution System provides automated file updating/replacement and automated PC configuration management.

Testing New Applications

Before a new application is installed on a network, the application *must* be tested and documented thoroughly. Most applications can be used in the network environment, even though some of them may be unaware of the existence of the network or may not specifically use the network in any way. Other applications are for use only on networks. Unfortunately, no real standards exist for design, installation, or configuration of network-based applications. Applications sometimes require multiple configuration files. Generally speaking, configuration files should be distributed to users' personal directories so that users can customize the application according to their own preferences.

Managing Enterprise-Wide Networks

Simple Network Management Protocol (SNMP) has become a critical interoperability element that helps managers to keep track of multivendor networks. There is an increasing need for departmental-computing environments to integrate and share information with enterprise managers. It provides a tool to manage everything—a unified management approach to networks based on TCP/IP. For example, SNMP can allow centralized management of all servers, hubs, and routers.

A Rightsizing Snapshot: Maintaining a Heterogeneous Applications Development Platform

Mainframes are not going away tomorrow. They probably will survive for many years in companies that require centralized processing of certain kinds of activities. Most rightsized systems therefore should be developed in such a way that the network can be used for two very different applications purposes:

- Developing and testing applications that ultimately will be executed on a mainframe platform
- Developing and testing applications that ultimately will be executed on the network platform, in either a DOS, UNIX, or OS/2 operating environment

In most cases, applications-programming work for the mainframe platform takes the shape of maintaining existing applications. Conversely, applications-programming work for the network platform usually is directed toward development of new applications. Contrary to what you may believe or have heard from "mainframe-centric" people, maintaining existing mainframe applications from a rightsized network is straightforward, and performing mainframe-applications maintenance from a PC-based network has distinct advantages.

You can expect some implementation and learning curve issues, especially if your firm has no experience with rightsized systems; this approach to mainframe-applications maintenance, however, is one that many companies are using productively today. In fact, maintaining existing mainframe applications from a network and running them on a mainframe is a suitable intermediate migration step from a completely host-based environment to a purely network-based system. Thus, before you fully implement a network-based maintenance platform, you typically must address several issues—including source code control and versioning, compatibility testing, test data management, and dictionary maintenance.

Source-Code Control and Versioning

Source-code control tools keep track of versions of software under development and track changes between versions. The product PVCS by Intersolv provides version control in an object-oriented programming environment. Through Intersolv's Production Gateway utility, links can be provided between PVCS on the LAN to traditional mainframe source-code control facilities, such as Panvalet and Librarian. These links should be bidirectional and should provide lockout capability on the side that does not "own" the current version of the source.

Many companies' current approach to source-code management—manual downloading of individual files—usually proves to be too time-consuming and error-prone to be useful in a large-scale maintenance or development environment. Panvalet's PAN Life Cycle product provides bidirectional functionality to Panvalet on the mainframe. Life Cycle has a robust user interface, but suffers from some performance problems. Both PVCS and PAN Life Cycle are good products to consider in evaluating products for this function.

Compatibility Testing

In addition to management issues such as source-code control, there are even more fundamental issues in considering moving mainframe-applications maintenance to a network. For example, mainframes use the EBCDIC coding set; PCs and UNIX processors use ASCII. The collating sequences of these systems are different. This rather fundamental operating difference is important when you consider that programs rely on a particular collating sequence for their own internal "decision making." Depending on the codeset translations made and the data used, errors can be introduced when you move information between mainframe and network applications. The only way to prevent this from happening is to establish procedures for performing compatibility testing as part of the migration procedures for an application.

Test Data Management

The current approach to testing at many companies is to make heavy use of copies of production data. This approach is fine for stress testing and final integration testing of the system. It is not a good approach, however, for unit testing of individual programs or planned systems testing of an entire application.

A better mechanism is to provide individual developers with maintainable, individual copies of test data files, stored in a centralized test data repository. This repository then can be used to save and refresh copies of test files across multiple test cycle executions. Ideally, you should be able to save the test data and the results from tests for future regression test cycles during application maintenance.

Dictionary Maintenance

The data dictionary is the central repository for all data elements for your information systems. As applications are maintained or developed, on either the mainframe or the network, so must the dictionary be revised and maintained. Although an automated approach for performing dictionary maintenance is possible, a better approach in a transition environment, in which mainframe applications are being maintained from the network, is to control the process with manual procedures.

The rationale for this approach is twofold. First, no good tools are available today that handle data synchronization across mainframe and network platforms. Second, because few new systems are likely to be built using older mainframe databases, continuing to use the mainframe data dictionary doesn't make sense; and, data maintenance should occur on one platform or the other, but not on both. To illustrate, let's look at an example of a non-DB2 mainframe dictionary.

The Cullinet IDD is the central repository of all information concerning an IDMS application. Keeping the dictionary synchronized between mainframe and network platforms is an important requirement. IDMS-PC, a Cullinet add-on product, provides limited facilities for importing and exporting dictionary contents. It does not provide, however, an integrated, easy-to-use workbench for automatically maintaining control over dictionary updates. The best bet to ensure data synchronization is to maintain the data dictionary with manual procedures during the migration process. After all application development is on the network, dictionary maintenance can be automated.

Conclusion

Maintaining mainframe applications from a network can be addressed immediately with technology available from a mix of mainframe and network vendors. You usually have no reason to wait to begin maintaining production systems on a network platform.

Network Assessment

Now, what I want is, facts…. Facts alone are wanted in life.

—Charles Dickens
Great Expectations

Objectives:

1. To understand the benefits of a network assessment and why it is critical to the ongoing success of network-based applications.
2. To learn the steps in a network assessment and expectations for each step.
3. To understand what network assessment deliverables are and how they should be used.

As you have seen in the past several chapters, rightsizing information systems is likely to introduce entire new sets of hardware and software into a company's systems infrastructure. Even with well-developed maintenance and management policies and procedures, a periodic review of the technical and functional health of the rightsized systems becomes important. A *network assessment* is the recommended method of review.

The primary reason for performing a network assessment is to give your network a checkup. A Network Assessment Analyst (NAA) investigates and analyzes all aspects of your network, including its setup, administration, and security. Companies request network assessments for several reasons:

- To determine the stability of their network to support mission-critical applications
- To establish a baseline for performance indicators, security, and other network components
- To provide supporting documentation to serve as the basis for additional services, such as the development of a disaster recovery plan
- To ascertain opportunities for improvement and efficiencies in network configuration, design, and management

For example, when a new MIS manager for a soft-drink manufacturer began his work, he suspected that something was wrong with the network and requested a network assessment. This assessment in fact revealed serious flaws in the network—flaws that may have cost the company large sums of money and would have impaired its capability to operate in the event of hardware failure, virus infiltration, or a security breach.

Other Network Assessment Benefits

Having your network assessed delivers some benefits with legal implications. Most important, the Foreign Corrupt Practices Act of 1977 requires internal controls to ensure the integrity of financial transactions. In instances in which a corporation's internal controls were not sufficient to restore operation after a disruption, shareholders of publicly held corporations have brought negligence litigation against the officers, directors, and MIS management. Following the recommendations from a network assessment and developing a disaster recovery plan not only ensures the continued operation of the company, but also protects management from personal liability in a worst-case scenario.

Your company may also be liable for the unauthorized release of personal information, such as medical-history or employee-background records, in the event of a security breach in its LAN. An assessment identifies any security issues to prevent a breach from occurring. A secure LAN also protects your company's mission-critical information from being leaked.

In addition, an assessment may identify hardware problems that need immediate attention, such as equipment that is about to fail or that is running inefficiently. Many companies do not perform regular inspections of their hardware—they should.

The Network Assessment Approach

A network assessment is designed to be an extensive, all-encompassing review of a network. As Figure 20.1 illustrates, the assessment consists of more than just an extensive review of operational procedures. It includes also a review of the working conditions of environmental components (such as building HVAC systems), system fault tolerance components, the operating system, and applications.

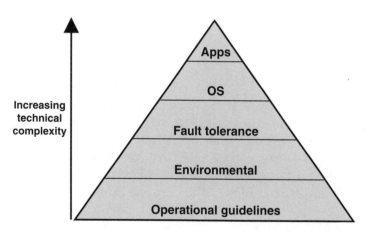

Figure 20.1. A comprehensive network assessment.

Network assessments, like accounting audits, should be performed by an independent team. During its investigation, the team may use resources such as documentation provided by the MIS department to obtain information about the network environment as well as determine whether the documentation contains inaccurate information or is missing key information. Also, an NAA interviews the MIS staff and many of the users to determine everyday practices relating to network security and to determine which systems are mission-critical to the company's operation.

The length of a network assessment and the amount of financial investment required for the assessment depend on the size of the network, particularly on the number of servers and nodes. The NAA can generate thousands of pages of reports per server. The minimum amount of time required to do a network assessment of a small LAN is one week.

A Network Assessment methodology should extensively cover at least the following:

- Administration
- Network design and performance
- Security
- Disaster recovery planning
- Operating-system implementation and maintenance
- Hardware configuration and maintenance
- Fire protection and environmental hazards
- Inter- and intra-office communications
- Help desk (problem resolution)
- Vital records
- Strategic planning
- Documentation

In the administration section, the NAA determines whether procedures have been established to ensure that the network is administered in a cost-effective and efficient manner, in accordance with management's mission. During the review, the NAA examines the network setup for efficient and consistent directory structure on the file servers, consistent software installation on the file servers and workstations, and standard procedures for administering the network. Deliverables can include recommendations for specific automation tools to reduce the amount of manual intervention and provide proactive management.

The network design and performance section includes an examination of the network implementation, including cable plant, bridges, routers, hubs, and gateways. If required, arrangements can be made to use a protocol analyzer to determine performance bottlenecks. The NAA can examine the network design for its ability to support additional traffic and accommodate future expansion.

During the review of security, the NAA reviews how access is restricted to the file server and hard drives of workstations containing critical or sensitive information. This includes login access, access to files and directories, and restricted usage of powerful utilities. If network information is deemed highly confidential or sensitive, the NAA will determine whether sufficient security measures have been taken (for example, encryption of transmissions, authentication devices to prove a user's identity, and so on). As part of the security review, the NAA reviews virus prevention/detection and software-licensing compliance processes and policies.

The disaster-recovery planning portion of a network assessment addresses an organization's current disaster-recovery plan and identifies the major risks specific to the enterprise for which a plan is required. The NAA reviews backup and restore procedures to determine whether a company's information assets are protected in the event of a disaster or disruption. This review includes the rotation schedule for offsite tapes, the location of tapes before they are stored offsite, backup procedures for workstations, the adequacy of the backup software for the size and needs of the company, and a current listing of prioritized applications. The NAA will also ask, "Does a disaster recovery plan exist? Is it tested regularly? Is it current?" The NAA reviews and makes recommendations for the plan.

Figure 20.2 is an example of a network assessment methodology for the platform concentrating on backup.

In the operating-system implementation and maintenance portion, the NAA examines the network operating-system installation to determine whether drivers or other software should be upgraded. The NAA also checks for the existence of backup copies of all system components and determines whether the copies have been stored offsite.

The hardware configuration and maintenance section addresses file server, node, and peripheral device configurations. This is accomplished using one or more network utilities that provide not only documentation but also utilization statistics for load balancing and configuration adjustments. Preventive maintenance logs, the inventory of spare parts, and hardware utilization are also reviewed.

Backup Assessment

A.   Review the current backup procedures in effect for each LAN.

B.   Obtain a copy of the log that shows the tapes located offsite.

C.   Determine the last time a restoration to the system was performed to ensure it is operating correctly. Note if the client has restored security (for example, Bindery information) to the system for testing purposes.

D.   Determine if tapes are secure when not in offsite storage.

E.   Review service agreements to determine the minimum turnaround time, or provision for a loaner tape drive in the event of hardware failure or destruction.

F.   Review procedures in effect to account for tapes that are retired, destroyed, or lost.

G.   Review procedures in effect for the backup of data on users' workstations. Note provisions for handling sensitive data.

H.   Are network servers backed up daily?

I.   Determine how often backups are performed for critical applications/data on individual workstations.

J.   Is the type of backup, and backup hardware/software adequate for operation?

K.   Determine how long the user is willing to wait to restore one file and/or the entire server.

Figure 20.2. An assessment methodology example.

In the fire protection and environmental hazards section, the NAA reviews the physical protection over key components of the network, including the file server, wiring closets, and other critical devices. The NAA performs a fire-protection site survey of the computer room, user facilities, and remote storage areas. The NAA looks for and inspects fire prevention, detection, and suppression equipment. The NAA also investigates the location of water sprinklers that may damage equipment, particularly in a computer room fire.

The inter- and intra-office communications focuses on workgroup communications such as electronic mail, fax, and workgroup software. This is particularly important if the network is part of a WAN. The efficiency of data transmissions to remote locations is also examined.

The help desk (problem resolution) review determines whether the function is properly staffed, trained, possesses documentation of the network, and has adequate resources to provide assistance to its clients. It also determines whether user problems are resolved on a timely basis.

During the vital records review, the NAA determines whether or not the storage (and the location of the storage facility) of vital company records—including magnetic media, manuals, and procedures—is sufficient to ensure that company operations can continue without interruption or legal consequences. Information gained supports an analysis of policies and procedures on custody of information assets and results in recommendations on the enterprise information classification system and methods of archiving data.

The strategic planning review addresses the process to determine future hardware/software platforms on an enterprise-wide basis. It includes a review of issues associated with interoperability, open systems, capacity planning, and expected availability of APIs among the suite of products in use. A review of representative workgroups determines whether the network will support the overall mission of the workgroups and enhance the overall work effort.

The documentation section includes a thorough review of all essential documentation, such as hardware configurations, cabling diagrams, purchasing guidelines, and operational policies and procedures. The NAA examines the policies and procedures for the purchase, administration, and support of network, including hardware and cabling configuration diagrams, hardware and software service contracts, inventory documents, and the MIS strategic plan.

After a review of each area, as well as other areas specific to your LAN, the NAA typically writes a brief report of his or her findings and includes recommendations to correct problems and enhance performance. In most cases, the NAA reviews his or her findings with the appropriate personnel.

Network Assessment Final Report

Rarely does a NAA not discover a number of deficiencies that require immediate attention. The final report from a network assessment is usually a straightforward document listing these deficiencies and recommended changes, as well as any reports generated from network utilities. These recommendations may range from measures that reduce the threat of losing mission-critical systems during a disruption, to measures that reduce administrative effort and increase proactive management of the LAN.

Figure 20.3 provides an example of a finding that might be included in a network assessment report. Notice that the document contains in the Finding section a thorough description of the problem; in the Recommendation section, the action required; and in a third section, a form that enables management to assign the required action and follow up on its completion.

LAN Audit

Client: <u>Company XYZ</u>   Project:_____

Storage of Backup Tapes

Finding:

During our review of the data center we noted that all backup tapes are retained in the computer room. In the event of an incident that destroyed or damaged the equipment, it is likely that the backup tapes would also be subject to destruction. Since these tapes are the only method of recovery, substantial financial loss would result. All copies of telex transmissions would be lost; application data would be lost; all spreadsheets, documents and databases stored on the LAN would be lost; the database server could not be restored; and most mainframe connections would be lost for an indefinite period of time. An extended period of recovery would be necessary, if it were even possible.

Recommendation:

All tapes should be stored offsite in a secured environment. Only those tapes that are necessary to perform the current day's backup activities should remain onsite. A rotation schedule should be developed to ensure that three generations of each file are available.

Assigned To: _____

_____

_____

Estimated Completion Date:_____ Date Completed:_____

Figure 20.3. Company XYZ's network assessment.

Conclusion:
A Call to Arms

Conclusion:
A Call to Arms

21

The past, present, and the future are really one—they are today.

—Harriet Beecher Stowe
(19th century)

Harriet Beecher Stowe was right on the mark. What we do today is based on what we know from the past and future, as well as what we know today. The problem most of us often encounter, however, is that we spend our time reacting to today's problems with yesterday's solutions.

This reaction is the problem with information technology today. Fortunately, the opportunity that rightsizing information systems presents is not really all that dramatic. It just means using more of the technology available today to replace yesterday's technology.

Of course, the question most often asked by skeptics when this kind of change is proposed is "Why bother? Why fix something if it ain't broke?" The answer to this question lies at both the micro level and the macro level.

At the micro level, the answer to the question "Why rightsize?" comes from studies such as the one conducted by Temple, Barket & Sloan, and sponsored by Microsoft. The study found that using PCs led to the following improvements:

- 23 percent more tasks attempted
- At least 35 percent more tasks completed
- At least 16 percent fewer errors committed
- 51 percent less frustration experienced

In other words, increased productivity, employee satisfaction, and quality were (and can be) achieved by doing work on a PC rather than on a mainframe terminal.

At the macro level, the answer to "Why rightsize?" comes from gaining a better understanding of the global marketplace and the socioeconomic world order. The themes that nations and the companies conducting business in them have adopted include competitiveness, management responsibility, and human resources.

These themes force companies to be faster, better, and smarter, and to continually improve by combining all they know about the past and future into their present actions. The client/server network computing revolution provides a new set of technologies that can and should play an important role in these actions.

So, What Do You Do Next?

What do you look for when you are wondering whether rightsizing information systems is a strategy that will work for you? Here are a few telltale signs, or entry points, that indicate a need for rightsizing:

- Business problems related to information or procedures
- High internal MIS cost estimates or MIS cost savings important to the organization
- Insufficient internal resources and a strong user need (mission-critical, tight deadlines to meet, for example)
- External customer complaints about your company (ask customers "If we were to improve our information systems, what should we change?")

Recognizing these entry points is the first step toward getting the rightsizing ball rolling. After the ball is rolling, you can do a number of things to keep it on the right track:

1. Stay focused on your vision. Midway through a multiple-month (or year) plan, it is easy to forget where you are trying to go.
2. Go with your best people. They likely will come from all areas of the company, not just from MIS or the initial group of end users affected by the rightsizing project.
3. Pick the right software partners. Find vendors who will support your vision.
4. Simplify your business processes before you begin rightsizing information systems. Change the process for the better. Challenge the way your business units do their business.
5. Obtain management support and funding before you start rightsizing—for the entire system, if possible, or for as much as you can.
6. Seek and follow industry standards, whether they are "de jure" or "de facto." To successfully accomplish rightsizing, you need standards and an architecture that provide for the following items:
   - Centralized control
   - Standard platforms
   - A clear enterprise-wide networking strategy

- A user support plan
- An applications development and maintenance plan

7. Don't underestimate what it will take. Prepare for the unexpected. For example, areas where the best approaches and technologies are still evolving in rightsizing information systems include these:

   - System integrity and security
   - System reliability
   - Identifying lasting development tools
   - Long-term impacts on the MIS organization

8. Don't accept that doing it right will cost more. Through rightsizing, you can make information systems faster, better, and cheaper.

9. Realize that you are never done. Be prepared to improve continually. The world is constantly changing.

Keep these pointers in mind, and you will be prepared to rightsize your information systems, significantly benefiting your organization for many years.

Vendor List

Vendor List

3COM Corp.
5400 Bayfront Plaza
Santa Clara, CA 95052
(800) NET-3COM
(408) 764-5000

Adobe Systems, Inc.
P.O. Box 7900
1585 Charleston Rd.
Mountain View, CA
94039-7900
(800) 922-3623
(415) 961-4400

Advanced Logic Research
9401 Jeronimo
Irvine, CA 92718
(800) 444-4ALR
(714) 581-6770

Aldus Corp.
411 First Ave. S., Ste. 200
Seattle, WA 98014
(800) 333-2538
(206) 628-2320

Apple Computer, Inc.
20525 Mariani Blvd.
Cupertino, CA 95014
(800) 776-2333
(408) 996-1010

Artisoft, Inc.
Artisoft Plaza
2202 N. Forbes Ave.
Tucson, AZ 85745
(800) 846-9726
(602) 670-7000

AST Research, Inc.
16215 Alton Pkwy.
P.O. Box 19658
Irvine, CA 92713-9658
(800) 876-4AST

AT&T
1700 S. Patterson Blvd.
Dayton, Ohio 45479
(513) 445-5000
(800) 225-5627

Attachmate Corp.
3617 131st Ave. SE
Bellevue, WA 98006
(800) 426-6283

AutoDesk, Inc.
2320 Marinship Way
Sausalito, CA 94965
(800) 445-5415
(415) 332-2344

Banyan Systems, Inc.
120 Flanders Rd.
Westboro, MA 01581
(800) 828-2404
(508) 898-1000

Borland International
P.O. Box 660001
1800 Green Hills Rd.
Scotts Valley, CA 95066-0001
(408) 439-9344

Brightwork Development, Inc.
Jerral Center West
766 Shrewsbury Avenue
Tinton Falls, NJ 07724
(800) 552-9876

BSG Consulting, Inc.
11 Greenway Plaza, Ste. 900
Houston, TX 77046
(800) 937-2001
(713) 965-9000

Bytex
4 Technology Dr.
Westborough, MA 01581-1760
(800) 227-1145
(508) 480-0840

Cabletron Sytems, Inc.
36 Industrial Way
P.O. Box 5005
Rochester, NH 03867
(603) 332-9400

Canon, Inc.
One Canon Plaza
Lake Success, NY 11042-1113
(516) 488-6700

Cheyenne Software, Inc.
3 Expressway Plaza
Roslyn Heights, NY 11577
(516) 484-5110

Cisco Systems, Inc.
3535 Garrett Dr.
Santa Clara, CA 95054
(415) 326-1941

Codenoll Technology Corp.
1086 N. Broadway
Yonkers, NY 10701
(914) 965-6300

COMPAQ Computer Corp.
77070 SH 249
P.O. Box 692000
Houston, TX 77269-2000
(800) 231-0900
(713) 370-0670

CompuServe, Inc.
1000 Massachusetts
Cambridge, MA 02138
(800) 873-1032
(617) 661-9440

Computer Associates Intl.
1 Computer Associates Plaza
Islandia, NY 11788
(516) 342-5224

Cooperative Solutions
2125 Hamilton Ave., Ste. 100
San Jose, CA 95125
(408) 377-0300

Data General Corp.
4400 Computer Dr.
Westboro, MA 01580
(800) DATAGEN
(508) 366-8911

DataEase International, Inc.
7 Cambridge Dr.
Trumbull, CT 06611
(800) 243-5123
(203) 374-8000

Dell Computer Corp.
9505 Arboretum Blvd.
Austin, TX 78759
(800) 289-3355
(512) 338-4400

Digital Communications
Associates, Inc. (DCA)
1000 Alderman Dr.
Alpharetta, GA 30202-4199
(800) 348-3221

Digital Equipment Corp.
(DEC)
146 Main St.
Maynard, MA 01754-2571
(800) DIGITAL

Eicon Technology Corp.
2196 32nd Ave. (Lachine)
Montreal, Quebec
Canada   H8T 3H7
(800) 803-4266
(514) 631-2592

Epson America, Inc.
20770 Madrona Ave.
Torrance, CA 90509-2842
(800) 289-3776
(310) 782-0770

GRiD Systems Corp.
P.O. Box 5003
47211 Lakeview Blvd.
Fremont, CA 94537-5003
(800) 222-4743
(510) 656-4700

Gupta Technologies, Inc.
1060 Marsh Rd.
Menlo Park, CA 94025
(800) 876-DBMS

Hayes Microcomputer
Products, Inc.
P.O. Box 105203
Atlanta, GA 30348-5203
(800) 96-HAYES (U.S.)
(800) 665-1259 (CD)
(404) 840-9200

Hewlett-Packard Co.
Worldwide Customer
Support Operations
3000 Hanover St.
Palo Alto, CA 94304
(800) 752-0900

IBM Corp.
Old Orchard Rd.
Armonk, NY 10504
(800) 426-3333
(914) 765-1900

Informix Corp.
4100 Bohannon Dr.
Menlo Park, CA 94025
(800) 331-1763
(415) 926-6300

Ingres
P.O. Box 4026
1080 Marina Village Pkwy.
Alameda, CA 94501
(800) 446-4737
(510) 769-1400

Intel Corp.
2200 Mission College Blvd.
Santa Clara, CA 95052-8119
(800) 548-4725
(408) 765-8080

LaserData Corp.
300 Vesper Park
Tyngsboro, MA 01879
(508) 649-4600

Lotus Development Corp.
55 Cambridge Pkwy.
Cambridge, MA 02142
(800) 343-5414
(617) 577-8500

Madge Networks, Inc.
2310 N. First St.
San Jose, CA 95131-1611
(800) 876-2343
(404) 955-0700

MCI Communications Corp.
1650 Tysons Blvd.
McLean, VA 22102
(800) 333-1000
(703) 506-6000

MDBS, Inc.
P.O. Box 6089
Lafayette, IN 47903-6089
(800) 445-6327

Memorex Telex Corp.
545 E. John Carpenter Freeway
LB 6
Irving, TX 75062
(800) 944-4455
(214) 449-3500

Micro Focus
2465 E. Bayshore Rd; Ste. 400
Palo Alto, CA 94303
(800) 468-9080
(415) 856-4161

Microsoft Corp.
One Microsoft Way
Redmond, WA 98052-6399
(800) 426-9400
(206) 882-8080

Motorola, Inc.
1201 E. Wiley Rd.
Schaumburg, IL 60173
(800) 233-0877
(708) 576-1600

NCR
1700 S. Patterson Blvd.
Dayton, OH 45479
(800) 225-5627
(513) 445-5000

NEC Corp.
Data & Video Communications
Systems Division
1525 Walnut Hill Lane
Irving, TX 75038
(800) 222-4NEC
(214) 518-5000

Network General Corp.
4200 Bohannon Dr.
Menlo Park, CA 9402
(800) 695-8521
(415) 453-2000

Novell, Inc.
122 E. 1700 South
Provo, UT 84606
(800) 453-1267

Okidata
532 Fellowship Rd.
Mount Laurel, NJ 08054
(800) 654-3282
(609) 235-2600

Oracle Corp.
500 Oracle Pkwy.
Redwood Shores, CA 94065
(800) ORACLE-1
(415) 506-7000

Palindrome Corp.
600 E. Diehl Rd.
Naperville, IL 60563
(800) 288-4912
(708) 505-3300

PowerSoft, Inc.
70 Blanchard Rd.
Burlington, MA 01803
(800) 273-2841
(617) 229-2200

Proteon, Inc.
Nine Technology Dr.
Westborough, MA 01581
(800) 545-RING
(508) 898-2800

Quarterdeck Office Systems,
Inc.
150 Pico St.
Santa Monica, CA 90405
(800) 354-3222
(310) 392-9851

Revelation Technologies
181 Harbor Dr.
Stamford, CT 06902
(800) 262-4747
(203) 973-1000

Saros Corp.
10900 NE 8th St; Ste. 700
Bellevue, WA 98004
(800) 827-2767
(206) 646-1066

Sequent Computer Systems,
Inc.
15450 SW Koll Pkwy.
Beaverton, OR 97006-6063
(800) 854-0428
(503) 626-5700

Silicon Graphics, Inc.
2011 N. Shoreline Blvd.
Mountain View, CA
94043-1389
(800) 800-7441
(415) 960-1980

Software Publishing Corp.
3165 Kifer Rd.
Santa Clara, CA 95056-0983
(800) 336-8360
(408) 986-8000

Standard Microsystems Corp.
(SMC)
350 Kennedy Dr.
Hauppauge, NY 11788
(800) SMC-4-YOU
(516) 435-6000

Stratus Computer, Inc.
55 Fairbanks Blvd.
Marlboro, MA 01752
(508) 460-2000

Sun Microsystems, Inc.
2550 Garcia Ave.
Mountain View, CA 94043
(800) 821-4643
(415) 960-1300

Sybase, Inc.
6475 Christie Ave.
Emeryville, CA 94608
(800) 8 SYBASE
(510) 596-3500

Symantec Corp.
10201 Torre Ave.
Cupertino, CA 95014-2132
(800) 441-7234
(408) 253-9600

SynOptics Communications, Inc.
4401 Great American Pkwy.
Santa Clara, CA 95052
(800) 776-6895
(408) 988-2400

Tandem Computers, Inc.
19191 Vallco Pkwy., Location 4-40
Cupertino, CA 95014-2599
(800) 538-3107
(408) 285-6000

Tandy Corp.
1800 One Tandy Center
Ft. Worth, TX 76102
(817) 390-2774

Texas Instruments, Inc.
13500 N. Central Expressway
Dallas, TX 75265
(800) 527-3500
(214) 995-2551

Thomas-Conrad Corp.
1908-R Kramer Lane
Austin, TX 78758
(800) 332-8683 (U.S.)
(800) 654-3822 (CD)
(512) 836-1935

Tricord Systems, Inc.
3750 Annapolis Lane
Plymouth, MN 55447
(800) TRI-CORD
(612) 557-9005

U.S. Robotics, Inc.
8100 N. McCormick Blvd.
Skokie, IL 60076
(800) 342-5877
(708) 982-5010

Verbatim Corp.
1200 W. T. Harris Blvd.
Charlotte, NC 28262
(800) 538-8589

Viewstar Corp.
5820 Shellmound St.
Emeryville, CA 94608
(510) 652-7827

Vinzant, Inc.
600 E. 3rd St
Hobart, IN 46342
(800) 355-3443
(219) 942-9544

Wang Laboratories, Inc.
One Industrial Ave.
Lowell, MA 01851
(800) NEW-WANG
(508) 459-5000

Wellfleet Communications, Inc.
8 Federal St.
Billerica, MA 01821
(800) 989-1214
(508) 670-8888

WordPerfect Corp.
1555 N. Technology Way
Orem, UT 84057
(800) 451-5151
(801) 225-5000

Xcellenet, Inc.
5 Concourse Pkwy. Ste. 200
Atlanta, GA 30328
(800) 322-3366
(404) 804-8100

Xerox Corp.
P.O. Box 24
Rochester, NY 14601
(800) ASK-XEROX
(716) 423-5078

Xircom
26025 Mureau Rd.
Calabasas, CA 91302
(800) 438-9472
(818) 878-7600

VARS/Distributors

Gates/FA Distributing
39 Pulham Ridge Dr.
Greenville, SC 29615
(803) 234-0736

Ingram Micro, Inc.
1600 E. St. Andrew Pl.
Santa Ana, CA 92799-5125
(800) 456-8000

Kenfil Distribution, Inc.
16745 Saticoy St.
Van Nuys, CA 91406
(800) 36KENFIL

Merisel, Inc.
200 Continental Blvd.
El Segundo, CA 90245
(800) MERISEL

Tech Data Corp.
5350 Tech Data Dr.
Clearwater, FL 34620
(813) 539-7429

Vitek Systems
2052 Corte Del Nogal
Carlsbad, CA 92009
(800) 366-6655

Market Research Services

Aberdeen Group
92 State St.t
Boston, MA 02109
(617) 723-7890

Bell Atlantic B.S.S.
P.O. Box 3528
Princeton, NJ 08453-3528
(800) 688-4469
(609) 936-2900

BIS Cap International, Inc.
One Longwater Circle
Norwell, MA 02061
(617) 982-9500

The Burton Group
P.O. Box 3448
Salt Lake City, UT 84110-3448
(800) 657-6340

Business Research Group
275 Washington St.
Newton, MA 02158
(617) 964-6204

The Chandler Group
4400 N. Federal Highway,
Ste. 210
Boca Raton, FL 33431
(407) 392-9220

Datapro Information
600 Delran Pkwy.
Delran, NJ 08075
(609) 764-0100

Forrester Research, Inc.
One Brattle Square
Cambridge, MA 02138
(617) 497-7090

Freeman Associates, Inc.
311 E. Carrillo St.
Santa Barbara, CA 93101
(805) 963-3853

G2 Research, Inc.
PRTM Building
1503 Grant Rd; Ste. 130
Mountain View, CA 94040
(415) 964-2400

Gartner Group, Inc.
56 Top Gallant Rd.
P.O. Box 10212
Stamford, CT 06904-2212
(203) 964-0096

InfoCorp
2880 Lakeside Dr; Ste. 300
Santa Clara, CA 95056
(408) 970-0304

Input, Inc.
1953 Gallows Rd; Ste. 560
Vienna, VA 22182
(703) 847-6870

International Data Corp.
5 Speen St.
Framingham, MA 01701
(508) 872-8200

LANQuest
1251 Parkmoor Ave.
San Jose, CA 95126
(408) 283-8900

Ledgeway/Dataquest
550 Cochituate Rd.
P.O. Box 9324
Framingham, MA 01701-9324
(508) 370-5555

LINK Resources Corp.
79 5th Ave; 12th Floor
New York, NY 10003
(212) 627-1500

Merrin Information Services
2275 E. Bayshore Rd.
Palo Alto, CA 94303
(415) 493-5050

New Science Associates
167 Old Post Rd.
Southport, CT 06490
(203) 259-1661

Sentry Market Research
1900 W. Park Dr.
Westborough, MA 01581
(508) 366-2031

Summit Strategies
360 Newbury St.
Boston, MA 02115
(617) 266-9050

Workgroup Technologies
140 Second Ave.
Waltham, MA 02154-1129
(617) 895-1500

Yankee Group, Inc.
200 Portland St.
Boston, MA 02114
(617) 367-1000

Evaluation Labs

LANQuest
1251 Parkmoor Ave.
San Jose, CA 95126
(408) 283-8900

Lone Star Evaluation Labs
(LSEL)
Route 2, Box 115
Georgetown, TX 78626
(512) 746-2251

NSTL
P.O. Box 1000
Plymouth Meeting, PA 19462
(215) 941-9600

Ziff-Davis Labs
320 B Lakeside Dr.
Foster City, CA 94404
(415) 378-5560

A Brief History of Computing

B

The early years of computing were marked by the development of crude computers by several universities, federal agencies, and private companies. The first successful electronic computer was the Electric Numeric Integrator and Calculator (ENIAC), completed in 1946. It weighed 30 tons, stood two stories high, and covered 15,000 square feet. It contained more than 18,000 vacuum tubes, implemented from radio technology. An offspring of the ENIAC, the Universal Automated Computer (UNIVAC) was installed at the U.S. Census Bureau in 1960, marking the first practical use of a computer.

The next major leap in computer technology occurred in the 1950s. This "second generation" of computers used transistors and other solid-state devices to replace the bulky vacuum tubes. These innovations made computers much smaller and much more reliable. First developed in 1947, transistors were 1/200th the size of tubes and were much faster. They also were less likely to overheat than vacuum tubes and therefore were much more dependable. Early transistorized computers, however, were plagued by incompatibility. Programs had to be rewritten when they were moved between computers— even between similar models of computers made by the same company. Much of the other computer equipment, such as printers and data-storage devices, worked only on the computer for which they were designed.

The "third generation" of computer technology began in the late 1950s, with the introduction of integrated-circuit (IC) technology, which replaced transistors. Integrated circuits went into production in 1959, with the development of a planar process for producing integrated circuits efficiently. This process used photo-engraving on a wafer of silicon to produce the IC. Integrated circuits not only were faster, more reliable, and more compact than resistors, but also they introduced the term *MIPS*, or million instructions per second, used to rate how quickly a computer can perform calculations. MIPS quickly became a standard measure of computing performance.

IBM released the 360 System, the first to use integrated circuits, in 1965. The 360 System resolved the earlier compatibility problems by using a revolutionary concept of building compatible components using integrated-circuit technology. This concept soon was adopted by other computer manufacturers. Many faster, cheaper computer models have been developed by various manufacturers since the 360 System, but the concept has not changed much. Many of today's modern IBM computer centers still run programs that were written on the 360 System. With the System 360 (and later minicomputers), the overall size of computers was reduced, and the time needed to perform calculations (the *processing speed*) decreased. The stage was set for the development of the microcomputer.

Although the race to develop more powerful and less expensive large computers went on, another branch of companies—led by Micro-Instruments Telemetry Systems (MITS), Apple Computer, and the Tandy Corporation—pursued the possibility of developing a smaller "fourth-generation" computer based on Very Large Scale (VLS) ICs, aimed at smaller companies and individuals who did not need the power of a large computer. The release of the IBM Personal Computer (PC) in 1981 provided needed recognition that microcomputer technology had established itself. When IBM entered the world of microcomputing, it opened up the design used in its computers; this design became the Industry Standard Architecture (ISA). IBM's gift of a standard bus was meant to encourage other companies to help establish a microcomputer market.

IBM also bundled a workstation operating system, PC DOS, developed by the fledgling start-up company Microsoft Corporation, as well as a BASIC programming language interpreter. At the time, IBM did not believe that microcomputing would expand into small business and compete with mainframe technology. *Cloning*, or copying, IBM computers developed rapidly. The cost of purchasing an IBM PC clone usually was less than buying an IBM PC. Today, more than 200 companies in the United States manufacture some 600 types of microcomputer equipment. Table B.1 illustrates some of the key events in the history of computing.

Table B.1. A brief history of computers.

Year	Event
1923	Computer-Tabulating-Recording (CTR) introduces the electric keypunch, a forerunner of the calculator.
1924	CTR officially changes its name to International Business Machines (IBM).
1934	IBM introduces the 405 Alphabetical accounting machine.
1944	IBM presents the Automatic Sequence Controller (known as the Mark I) to Harvard. The machine is 51 feet long by 8 feet high.
1945	Captain Grace M. Hopper finds a moth in the Mark I. The term "debug" comes into use.

continues

Table B.1. continued

Year	Event
1946	The University of Pennsylvania develops the Electric Numeric Integrator and Calculator (ENIAC), the first successful large-scale electronic computer.
1950	Remington Rand acquires an offspring of the ENIAC called the Universal Automated Computer (UNIVAC). The UNIVAC is installed at the U.S. Census Bureau.
1954	General Electric, the first private firm to use a computer, takes delivery of a UNIVAC at its plant in Appliance Park, Kentucky.
1959	Second generation of computers begins with the introduction of transistor technology.
1964	Third generation of computers begins when the integrated circuit replaces the transistor.
1965	IBM releases its 360 System, which introduces the concept of standardized, interchangeable computer components.
1969	First silicon-chip microprocessor, the Intel 4004, is developed by Marcian E. "Ted" Hoff.
1974	Micro-Instruments Telemetry Systems (MITS) releases the ALTAIR 8800 microcomputer.
1976	The Apple microcomputer is released. It becomes widely available in early 1977.
1979	Tandy Corporation begins selling the TRS-80 microcomputer through its Radio Shack stores.
1981	IBM announces its Personal Computer.
1982	Lotus Development Corporation introduces the new generation spreadsheet, 1-2-3.
1983	Novell, Inc. emerges from a reorganization of Novell Data Systems, introducing Sharenet on a 68000-based file server.
1984	Apple introduces the Macintosh.
1987	Steve Jobs, one of Apple's founders, leaves Apple to form a new computer company called NeXT.
1989	Lotus Development Corp. popularizes a new category of software called "groupware" with its Notes product.

Year	Event
1990	Microsoft introduces Windows 3.0, its new generation of operating systems.
1992	Apple announces its Newton Personal Digital Assistant (PDA) ushering in a new future of mobile wireless computing.
1993	Novell and AT&T complete Novell's acquisition of Unix Systems Labs, a move targeted to set an industry-standard UNIX.

As the microcomputer market expanded, the costs of owning one decreased. The proliferation of personal computers on campuses around the United States was led by IBM and Apple. Special student-discount buying programs and computer-supply stores were established on campuses. Libraries were set up with microcomputers for student use. Exposure to PCs while students led individuals to continue using PCs in the work world. The proliferation of microcomputers among middle management was already under way.

The current "fifth generation" of computing history is the age of network computing. With the microcomputer firmly established as a player in the computing world, companies searching for more market share are turning to the possibility of networking their microcomputers (making microcomputers talk to each other) instead of having to upgrade to a minicomputer or even to a mainframe. New computer companies have begun emerging with new ways of networking microcomputers. These companies have provided business organizations with numerous choices in their networking decisions, as more and more software is introduced to meet the unique needs of today's organizations. To follow one of these companies, Novell Inc., through its growth is to follow the emergence of network computing.

In 1983, Novell began creating the technologies that have been at the forefront of network computing in business. When Novell got its start, there was not a clear-cut, dominant workstation operating system, and each brand of microcomputer was a little different. Making an Apple Macintosh transfer readable data to a Tandy TRS-80 was similar to trying to get toast out of a refrigerator. To avoid the problem of committing to one operating system over another, Novell introduced the concept of a remote file system, a cornerstone of the versatility of Novell's network operating system (NetWare) as well as other network operating systems. By not being tied to any one PC operating system, NetWare can be linked to many operating system platforms; these platforms include mainframes, minicomputers, and microcomputers running on many different operating systems, including DOS, UNIX, OS/2, Windows, and others. Innovations by Novell and other network computing companies, such as 3Com and Banyan, have helped to accelerate this current wave of computing. Figure B.1 shows a comparison of the different waves of computing growth.

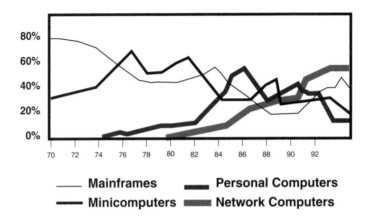

Source: Infocorp, Corporate Reports, and Bernstein estimates.

Figure B.1. *Waves of computing growth.*

Today, computers come in many sizes and with different levels of capability. Rather than possess computers from a single category, most corporations are likely to have computers in all three groups—mainframes, minicomputers, and microcomputers. The differences between these groups can be roughly differentiated by observing a comparison of IBM computers in each category, as summarized in Table B.2.

Table B.2. A comparison of IBM computer sizes.

Feature	ES900 (Series 3090)	AS400	PS/2
Cost	$575,000	$16,990	
Memory (characters)	64–512 MB	8 MB	4MB

Feature	ES900 (Series 3090)	AS400	PS/2
Number of available programs	many	many	many
Complexity	high	medium	low
Simultaneous jobs	many	many	a few
Telecommunications	sophisticated	sophisticated	simple
Size	large cabinets	small cabinets	notebook
Location	climate-controlled computer rooms	end-user proximity	desktop

Choosing a NOS
from the Leaders

C

Because the network operating system (NOS) is the platform on which your information systems will be built, choosing the NOS for your organization is one of the most important decisions you may make. NOS selection has a direct and widespread impact on the usefulness and potential of your information processing capabilities in both the present and the future. In the process of choosing an NOS, you should follow a careful evaluation of your

Company	Product	Platforms Supported D=DOS M=Macintosh O=OS/2 U=Unix W=Windows		Max. no. of licensed clients per server	LAN Support E=Ethernet F-FDDI L=Local Talk T=Token Ring	Communications protocols A=AppleTalk I=IPX N=NETBEUI NB=NETBIOS T=TCP/IP (o) = optional	NIC Standards N = NDIS O = ODI
		Server	Client				
Actrix Systems, Inc. (408) 281-4321	PC/NOS Plus	D	D, W	64	E	NB	
Artisoft, Inc. (602) 293-4000	LANtastic 5.0	D, W	D, W	500	E, F(2), L(2), T(2)	A(o), I(o), NB, T(o)	N(2)
CBIS, Inc. (404) 446-1332	Network-OS Plus 7,27c	D	D, W	254	E, F, T	NB	O
D-Link Systems (800) 326-1688	LANsmart NOS 3.2	D, W	D, W	1,024	E, T	I, NB	N, O
Grapevine LAN Products, Inc. (206) 865-9773	GV LAN/OS 2.0	D, W	D, W	50	E, T	NB	
Hayes Microcomputer Products, Inc. (404) 441-1617	LANstep 2.0	D	D, W	255	E, T	NB	N
Invisible Software (800) 982-2962	InvisibleLAN 3.4	D	D, W	255	E, T	NB	N
Microsoft Corp. (206) 882-8080	Windows for Workgroups 3.1	W	D, W	Unlimited	E, F, T	I, N, NB, T(o)	N
Moses Computers, Inc. (408) 358-1550	ChosenLAN 3.0	D, W	D, W	255	(5)	N(o), NB	N(2)
	MosesALL 3.0	D, W	D, W	8	(5)	N(o), NB	N(2)
Net-Source, Inc. (408) 246-7040	SilverNet 2.10	D	D	254	E, T	N, NB	N(2)
Novell, Inc. (801) 429-7000	Personal NetWare	D, W	D, W	50	E, T	I, NB, T(o)	O
Performance Technology, Inc. (210) 349-2000	PowerLan 2.30	D	D, W	255	E, T	NB	N, O
SunSelect	MacTOPS 3.1	M	M	Unlimited	E, L	A	
(508) 442-2300	DosTOPS 3.0	D	D	Unlimited	E, L	A	
	SunTOPS 3.0	U	D, M	Unlimited	E, L	A	
Tiara Computer Systems, Inc. (415) 965-1700	10NET 5.1	D, W	D, W	255	E	N, NB	N
Webcorp (415) 331-1449	Web for Windows and DOS 4.0	D, W, O	D, W	250	E, T	I	

FOOTNOTES
(1) Price requires, but does not include, vendor's adapters
(2) An additional product is required
(3) Price includes vendor's adapters
(4) Price assumes Windows is already installed
(5) Runs over proprietary LAN only

NDIS = Network Driver Interface Specification
NETBEUI = NETBIOS Extended User Interface
NIC = Network interface card
ODI = Open Data Link Interface

Figure C.1. Peer-to-peers network operating systems.

organization's specific needs and investigate how the available network operating systems can meet those needs.

This appendix is intended to provide information about many of the NOSs on the market, divided into peer-to-peer NOSs (see Figure C.1) and server-based NOSs (see Figure C.2). After the following two figures is more in-depth information about the leading products.

Additional Features E=E-mail G=Group scheduling R=Remote Access T=Tape backup (o) = optional	Encryption D=Data P=Password	Security A=Audit trail D=Directory-level privileges F=File-level privileges	Mgt. User Groups	Price S=Server U=User	Price per user/ No. of Users
E	D				$195/64(1)
E, R(o)	P	A, D, F	Yes	U:$99(1)	
	P	D	Yes	U:$190	$1,988-2,587/ 80-255
E(o)		A, D, F	Yes		$395/ Unlimited
E		D			$275-865/ 3-unlimited
E	P	D	Yes		$595/ 5
E	P	D	Yes	U:$189 (3)	$495/ 2(3)
E, G, R(o), T(o)	P	D		U:$100 (4)	
E(o)		D, F			$499/ 3(3)
E(o)		D, F		U:$99(3)	
E(o)		D, F		U:$99	$1,999/ 254
R(2), T(2)	P		Yes	U:$99	
E, R, T(o)	P	D	Yes	U:$99	$795/ 255
	P	D		U:$299	$399-995/3- 10
	P	D		U:$249	$995/10
	P	D		S:$1,249	
	P	A, D, F	Yes	U:$89	$198-1,999/ 2 - 100
E	P	D, F		U:$99	$259-3,195/ 3 - 100

Source: David Rhodes

Company	Product	Platforms Supported D=DOS M=Macintosh O=OS/2 U=Unix W=Windows		Multi-processing A=asymmetrical S=symmetrical	Max. no. of licensed clients per server	Server Ram M-bytes	LAN Support E=Ethernet F=FDDI L=Local Talk T=Token Ring	Communications protocols A=AppleTalk I=IPX N=NETBEUI NB=NETBIOS NS=NFS T=TCP/IP (o) = optional	NIC Standards N = NDIS O = ODI
		Server	Client						
Apple Computer (408) 996-1010	AppleSharePro	U(1)	M, D(3) W(3)		200	R:16; S: 32	E, L	A	
	AppleShare 4.0	M	M, D(3) W(3)		150	R: 8; S: 8	E, L, T	A	
	AppleShare 3.0	M	M, D(3) W(3)		120	R: 4; S: 4	E, L, T	A	
Banyan Syatems, Inc. (800) 222-6926	VINES 5.525	U(1)	D, M, O, W	S(2)	Unlimited	R:8; S: 12	E, L, T	A, I, NB, T(o)	N
IBM Personal Software Products LAN Systems (800) 342-6672	LAN Server 3.0 Advanced	O	D, M(3), O, W	A(3)	1,016	R: 10; S: 12	E, T	A(o), I(o), N NB, NS(o), T(o)	N
Microsoft Corp. (206) 882-8080	LAN Manager 2.2	O	D, M(3), O, W		256	R: 10; S: 16	E, F, T	A(o), N, NB, T	
Novell, Inc. (800) 638-9273	NetWare 4.0	D(4)	D, M(3), O, W	A(3, 5)	1,000	R: 8; S: 16	E, T	A(o), NB, NS(o), T	N,O
	NetWare 3.11	D(4)	D, M(3), O, W	A(3, 5)	250	R: 2; S: 4	E, T	A(o), NB, NS(o), T	N,O

FOOTNOTES
(1) Runs on proprietary version of Unix
(2) Supported only on VINES SMP
(3) Additional product required
(4) Boots on DOS but runs on NetWare
(5) Supports asymmetrical multiprocessing only when managing a replicated server

ESD = Electronic Software Distribution
UPS = Uninterruptable power supply
NDIS = Network Driver Interface Specification
NETBEUI = NETBIOS Extended User Interface
NFS = Network File System
NIC = Network interface card
ODI = Open Data Link Interface

Figure C.2. Server-based network operating systems.

Peer-to-Peer NOSs

Peer-to-peer NOSs may reside on any system in the network. That system can then function as both a client and a server. They are used when the organization has less stringent requirements for high performance and a smaller number of users. There is peripheral file and data sharing as opposed to true networking. Products in this category were selected based on their ability to fit easily into a complex network environment, security, additional utilities, and price.

Artisoft, Inc. LANtastic 5.0. LANtastic is the most widely installed peer-to-peer LAN and offers fundamental peer NOS services at a low price. LANtastic provides optional drivers supporting AppleTalk, Internetwork Packet Exchange (IPX), Network Basic I/O System, and Transmission Control Protocol/Internet Protocol, thus allowing LANtastic clients to integrate into complex network environments. The product has an electronic mail utility and offers remote access as an option. File- and directory-level privileges are supported, as is password encryption.

Internet-working B= Bridging R= Routing	Directory Services D=Domain naming G=Global naming	Security A=Audit trail D=Directory-level privileges F=File-level privileges	Encryption D=Data P=Password	Fault Tolerance D=Disk Duplexing M=Disk mirroring T=Transaction tracking U=UPS monitoring	Mgt. N=NetView reporting S=SNMP server agent	Utilities E=ESD L=License control R=Remote access T=Tape backup	Price S=Server U=User	Price per user/ No. of Users
		D	P			L	S:$2,399	
		D	P		S	L	S:$1,899	
		D	P			L	S:$1,199	
B, R	G	D, F	D, P	M, U	N, S	R(3), T		$1,495-8,495/ 5-Unlimited
B(3), R(3)	D	A, D, F	D(3), P	D, M, U	N, S(3)	E, L	S:$2,295 U:$75	
	D	A, D	P	D, M, U	N, S	E(3), R(3), T	S:$1,995 U:$65	
B, R	G	A, D, F	P	D, M, T, U	N, S	E(3), R(3), T		$1,395-47,995 / 5-1,000
B, R	D(3)	A, D, F	P	D, M, T, U	N, S	E(3), R(3), T		$1,095-12,495 / 5-250

Source: David Rhodes

Microsoft Corp. Windows for Workgroups. Windows for Workgroups provides client support for LAN Manager and Windows NT NOSs. The product supports IPX and, optionally, TCP/IP. E-mail and a group scheduling utility are standard, with remote access and tape backup optional. Password encryption and directory-level privileges are supported, though data encryption and file-level privileges are not. Price is $100 per user.

Novell Personal NetWare. Personal NetWare is the only peer-to-peer NOS supporting DOS and Windows on both client and server platforms. Systems running Personal NetWare can become full NetWare clients with the addition of a simple shell program that comes free with NetWare 3.11 and 4.0. Novell also supports NETBIOS and, as an option, TCP/IP. Although the product does not have an e-mail or a group scheduling utility, remote access and tape backup are available through third parties. Password encryption and directory-level privileges are supported, whereas data encryption and file-level privileges are not. Price is $99 per user.

Server-Based NOSs

Server-based NOSs reside on a dedicated system. They are typically used when there are a large number of users, high performance is critical, and the organization is network-based. Products in this category were chosen based on directory services and administration of multiple servers, security, support for a range of platforms and environments, fault tolerance, and also additional utilities.

Banyan Systems, Inc. VINES 5.525. As far as enterprise-level directory services and management are concerned, Banyan's StreetTalk global naming, directory and administration facility has long made VINES the strongest contender for nets comprising a large number of NOS servers. StreetTalk has a three-tiered directory structure that combines ease of use with a powerful global naming facility. VINES 5.525 supports DOS, Macintosh, OS/2, and Windows clients as standard features. VINES provides drivers for Ethernet, token-ring, and Apple LocalTalk local-area nets. For security, VINES supports directory- and file-level privileges, and data and password encryption, but lacks an audit trail facility. Fault tolerance features are not a strong suit of VINES, although the company does support disk mirroring and uninterruptible power-supply monitoring, but not disk duplexing or transaction tracking. VINES supports remote access and tape backup but not electronic software distribution (ESD).

Novell, Inc. NetWare 4.0. With the development of NetWare Directory Services (NDS), Novell now offers enterprise-level functionality, which enables users to administer multiple NetWare servers as a single logical domain and locate resources across a network of servers. NDS provides a 15-tier global naming and directory structure that enables net managers to set up directories to parallel the complex structures of many organizations. NetWare 4.0 supports every major client platform and all but one transport protocol, although some support is optional. NetWare 4.0 has strong security features, with support for directory- and file-level privileges, an audit trail facility and password—but not data—encryption. The NOS supports such fault tolerance features as uninterruptible power-supply monitoring, disk mirroring and disk duplexing. Novell is the only vendor that supports a completely redundant server and transaction tracking. ESD, remote access, and tape backup utilities are supported.

Microsoft, Inc. Windows NT Advanced Server. Windows NT Advanced Server provides domain-control capabilities and administration tools, trust capabilities, and centralized security administration, including centralized user profiles. It can be used as a large workgroup, department, or enterprise server in environments with multiprocessor machines or high performance processors. It runs client-server applications using all major protocols, clients, and NOSs. Fault tolerance capabilities include RAIDS, striping with parity, disk mirroring, and disk duplexing. Performance monitoring and server management can be done from any machine.

Multiuser LAN Database Management Systems

D

Company Address Phone	Borland Int'l, Inc. Alto Hills, CA (408) 431-1641	Borland Int'l, Inc. Alto Hills, CA (408) 431-1641	Data Access Corp Miami, FL (305) 238--0012
Product	dBase IV Version 2.0	Paradox Version 3.5	DataFlex Version 3.0
Client/Server? SQL?	dBase Server Edition for Microsoft SQL Server / Yes	With SQL Link/ With SQL Link	Yes / Yes
Database Operating Systems	DOS, UNIX, VMS	DOS	OS, Unix
Provides Referential Integrity?	Yes, Declarative	Yes	No
Lowest lock level/time stamps for shared locks	Field / Yes	Row / No	Row / No
Transaction logs?	Yes	Yes	Yes
Deadlock Resolution	No	Yes	No
Maximum Fields per Record	256	255	255
Application end-user features	4GL Control Center; freeform entry forms; pulldown dropdown lists; query by example	Interactive, menu-driven w/ programmable menus; freeform entry forms; programmable pulldown/ dropdown lists; query by example	Freeform entry forms; pulldown/ dropdown lists
Comments	None	Also supports IBM OS/2 EE, Microsoft SQL server, Oracle Tools 6.0, Sybase, Inc. and DEC Rdb backends	None

Company Address Phone	Information Builders, Inc. New York, New York (212) 736-4433	INFORMIX Menlo Park, CA (415) 541-0873	INFORMIX Menlo Park, CA (415) 541-0873
Product	PC/Focus LANpak Version 5.5	INFORMIX Online for NetWare 4.1	INFORMIX SE DOS / Windows
Client/Server? SQL?	Yes /Yes	Yes / Yes	No / Yes
Database Operating Systems	DOS, OS/2	NetWare 3.11, NT, Unix	NetWare 2.2
Provides Referential Integrity?	Yes	Yes	Yes
Lowest lock level/time stamps for shared locks	Row / Yes	Row-level locking	Row-level
Transaction logs?	Yes	Yes	Yes
Deadlock Resolution	Yes	Yes	Yes
Maximum Fields per Record	3000	Unlimited	Unlimited
Application end-user features	Menu-driven; freeform entry firms; pulldown/dropdown lists	4GL, C and 3rd party tools	4 GL, C and 3rd party tools
Comments	Also supports Microsoft SQL Server, IBM Database Manager, Teradata Corp. Back ends	Can store BLOBS (Binary Large Objects or images and binary data)	None

Company Address Phone	MicroData Base Systems Lafayette, IN (317) 447-1122	MicroData Base Systems Lafayette, IN (317) 447-1122	Microrim, Inc. Bellevue, WA (208) 649-9500	Nantucket Corp. Los Angeles, CA (213) 390-7923
Product	MDBS IV Version 4.2	KnowledgeMan version 3.0	RBase Version 4.0	Clipper Version 5.0
Client/Server? SQL?	Yes / Yes	Interface to SQL Server / Yes	Yes / Yes	Yes / Yes
Database Operating Systems	DOS, OS/2	DOS, OS/2	DOS / OS/2	DOS
Provides Referential Integrity?	Yes	Programmable	Yes	Yes
Lowest lock level/time stamps for shared locks	Row / N/A	Row / No	See comments / No	Column / No
Transaction logs?	Yes	No	Yes	Yes
Deadlock Resolution	Yes	No	Yes	Yes
Maximum Fields per Record	Varies	255	3000	2048
Application end-user features	None	Forms, menus; freeform entry forms; pulldown/dropdown lists; query by example	Menu-driven; freeform entry forms; pulldown/dropdown lists; query by example	Freeform entry forms; pulldown/dropdown lists; query by example
Comments		OLT for large amounts of data; also available for Unix, VMS, and other operating systems	Also supports Microsoft SQL Server Back end; also available for VMS, Sun, Microsystems Inc. Sun OS operating systems	Uses own currency control method

Company Address Phone	Oracle Corp. Redwood Shores, CA (415) 506-7000	Oracle Corp. Redwood Shores, CA (415) 506-7000	Oracle Corp. Redwood Shores, CA (415) 506-7000	Progress Software Corp. Bedford, MA (617) 275-4500
Product	Oracle Tools Version 5.1c	Oracle for Windows DDE/Toolbook Interface Version 1.0	Oracle for Macintosh Version 6.0	Progress 4GL and RDBMS Version 6.0
Client/Server? SQL?	Yes / Yes	Yes / Yes	Yes / Yes	Yes / Yes
Database Operating Systems	DOS, OS/2, Unix	Windows 3.x	Macintosh	DOS, OS/2, VMS, and Unix
Provides Referential Integrity?	No	No	No	Yes
Lowest lock level/time stamps for shared locks	Row / No	Row / No	Row / No	Row / Yes
Transaction logs?	Yes	Yes	Yes	Yes
Deadlock Resolution	Yes	Yes	Yes	Yes
Maximum Fields per Record	254	254	254	32000
Application end-user features	4GL; pulldown/ dropdown lists	Graphical user interface; point-and-click access; embedded SQL; pulldown/ dropdown lists	Point-and-click access, embedded SQL; pulldown/dropdown lists; query by example	Menu-driven- query / report tools; freeform entry forms; pulldown/dropdown lists; query by example
Comments	None	None	None	Progress RDBMS is a client/server database engine that supports distributed processing and distributed database across 400 hardware platforms, as well as numerous operating systems and network protocols

Company Address Phone	Revelation Technologies, Inc. New York, NY (212) 689-1000	Software Products International San Diego, CA (619) 450-1526	Software Publishing Mountain View, CA (415) 962-8910	Wordtech Systems, Inc. Orinda, CA (510) 254-0900
Product	Advanced Revelation Version 2.11	Open Access III Version 3.02	Superbase 4 windows Version 1.3	Quicksilver Version 1.3R
Client/Server? SQL?	Yes / Yes	No / Yes	Yes, w/ Superbase SQL Library / Yes, w/ Superbase SQL Library	No / Yes
Database Operating Systems	DOS, OS/2, Unix	DOS	DOS	DOS, Unix
Provides Referential Integrity?	Yes Unix	Yes	No	N/A
Lowest lock level/time stamps for shared locks	Row / No	Row / No	Row / No with records, yes with sequential files	Row / No
Transaction logs?	Yes	No	No	Yes
Deadlock Resolution	Yes	Yes	Yes	N/A
Maximum Fields per Record	As many fields as will fit within 32K bytes	255	Hardware-dependent	512
Application end-user features	Menus, Windows, pick lists, character-based; freeform entry forms; pulldown/ dropdown lists; query by example	Menu-driven; freeform entry forms; query by example	Windows, graphical user interface, freeform entry forms; pulldown/ dropdown lists	Command line; programmable freeform entry forms
Comments	Also supports Oracle Server, DB2, dBase, SQL Server back ends	Also includes word processing, spreadsheet, graphics e-mail dialer, and so on	Also supports Oracle, SDB and Gupta SQLBase and Microsoft SQL Server back ends	An .exe compiler for Wordtech Systems; dBXL and Borland's dBase that creates independently executable programs; also supports Gupta's SQLBase, Oracle back ends

Company Address Phone	Gupta Technologies Menlo Park, CA (415) 321-9500	IBM Armonk, NY (914) 765-1900	Infopoint Systems, Inc. Richardson, TX (214) 669-4700	Microsoft Corp. Redmond, WA (206) 882-8080	Novell, Inc. Provo, UT (801) 429-8080
Product	SQL Base Server, version 5.0	DB2/2	PCBUS Databus	Microsoft SQL Server, Version 4.2	NetWare SQL, Version 2.11a
Client/Server? SQL?	Yes / Yes	Yes / Yes	Compiler Version 1.5.0	Yes / Yes	Yes / Yes
Database Operating Systems	DOS, OS/2, Unix, Novell NetWare 3.x	OS/2	No / No	OS/2 Version 1.21 and higher, NT	NetWare 3.x
Provides Referential Integrity?	limited	limited	Yes	Yes, procedural	Yes, declarative
Lowest lock level/time stamps for shared locks	Row / Yes	Row / No	Row / No	Page; Yes	Row / No
Transaction logs?	Yes	Yes	Optional	Yes	Yes
Deadlock Resolution	Yes	Yes	Yes	Yes	Yes
Maximum Fields per Record	254	255	Unlimited	250	255
Comments	Supports Microsoft's Windows Dynamic Data Exchange, Dynamic Linked Libraries, and so on	Supports stored procedures in C, COBOL, REXX; C, COBOL, FORTRAN, Pascal, REXX programming interfaces all included	Information not provided	None	Users can call (800) RED-WORD for list of supported third-party products
			An extension of the Databus language		

Company Address Phone	Oracle Corp. Redwood Shores, CA (415) 506-7000	Oracle Corp. Redwood Shores, CA (415) 506-7000	Oracle Corp. Redwood Shores, CA (415) 506-7000	Sybase, Inc. Emeryville, CA (510) 596-3500	XDB Systems College Park, MD (301) 317-6800
Product	Oracle Server 7 for NetWare 386	Oracle Server for OS/2 with PL/SQL, Version 1.0	Oracle Server for Macintosh Version 6.0	Sybase SQL Server	XDB Server, Version 2.4
Client/Server? SQL?	Yes / Yes	Yes / Yes	Yes / Yes	Yes / Yes	Yes / Yes
Database Operating Systems	NetWare 3.x	DOS, WIndows, OS/2, Macintosh, Unix	Macintosh	Unix, VMS, VOS, NetWare	DOS, DOS-Windows, OS/2
Provides Referential Integrity?	Yes, declarative	No	No	Yes	Yes
Lowest lock level/time stamps for shared locks	Row / No	Row / No	Row / No	Page-level locking / time-stamp-based optimistic currency control	Row / programmable
Transaction logs?	Yes	Yes	Yes	Yes	Yes
Deadlock Resolution	Yes	Yes	Yes	Yes	Yes
Maximum Fields per Record	254	254	254	255	750
Comments	Oracle Server also available for Unix, VMS, MVS, OS/2	None	None	None	Supported front ends include Powersoft's PowerBuilder and Precision's SuperBase; 100% IBM, DB2-compatible SQL, Syntax, Error codes, Referential Integrity

Rightsizing DB2
Applications:
Five Approaches

Rightsizing DB2
Applications:
Five Approaches

As stated previously, one of the driving forces behind rightsizing is less expensive hardware. However, for IS shops running legacy systems, there are better reasons for rightsizing. One such reason is new and improved user interfaces. Another advantage is data accessibility; even with relational technology such as DB2, which makes data more available than with IMS, data is still relatively inaccessible. This is particularly true if you're comparing DB2 with the PC model of computing. The bottom line is that, although hardware may be the reason why rightsizing is now both possible and popular, the real motivation for most IS shops should be the desire for better business systems.

Different Rightsizing Approaches

There are several diverse approaches to rightsizing. Unfortunately, often no analysis is available to explain why one approach may be better than another. It is essential to understand the different methodologies and for which environment each will work best. Here are explanations and evaluations for some of the major rightsizing approaches.

The basic five approaches most frequently followed are these:

- Take an existing mainframe application and migrate it to a PC.
- Take an existing mainframe application and migrate it to a PC LAN.
- Take an existing mainframe application, keep it on the mainframe, and add PC front-ends.
- Develop applications on cross-platforms. For the past five years, people have been developing applications on PCs to be shipped to the mainframe for use. This style of development can work the opposite way also: applications can be developed on the mainframe and then shipped to PCs for use.
- Keep your existing mainframe system and add PC LANs and software to increasingly evolve the systems. Eventually, most or all of the applications will reside on the PC, and this move will have been accomplished with an evolutionary approach. This rightsizing method may have the most potential for traditional IS shops.

Following are details on each of these approaches and suggestions as to where each architecture works the best.

Approach One: Mainframe to PC Portability Questions

Porting an existing mainframe application to a PC does provide benefits in the form of lower hardware costs. The issue here is that with a PC, you are limited to single user applications. Therefore, scalability is not simply a hardware function, but is also a software concern. In addition, remember that the PC and mainframe environments must be compatible unless rewriting applications is your idea of fun. You will quickly discover, if you choose this form of rightsizing, that the world of mainframe software is divided into several classes, some of which are portable but many of which are not.

Another major factor to be considered when porting mainframe applications to PCs is the different architectures. First, each machine has a unique character set. Although most software translates rather easily, occasionally you will run into problems such as collating sequences. In addition, between these two different types of computing, files systems are different, transaction monitors are different, and so on. There is an endless slew of small (or large) variations.

Approach Two: PC LANs

Given the single-user limitation of PCs, when people talk about porting mainframe applications to a PC environment, they usually intend to use a local area network of PCs. The normal assumption here is that on the PC LAN, there would be either a client/server architecture or a DBMS client/server architecture. This isn't true all of the time, but it is usually the structure that you will see.

The important issue then becomes this: How compatible is that rightsized PC LAN environment with your mainframe? In most cases, these environments are not very compatible. If you are planning to move from a mainframe to a multiuser LAN environment, you will essentially have to re-design your software. If you have a mainframe DB2 application that uses CICS as a monitor, how are you going to re-architect that to fit into a Microsoft SQL Server environment? If you use the same design as you did for CICS, it will not work. Take this as a warning about what you have seen in the press. There has been an abundance of wonderful articles about companies who have unplugged their mainframe and replaced it with a PC LAN environment, but how common (or practical) is this for the average IS shop?

Approach Three: A Face-Lift

The third popular approach to rightsizing is to keep your applications on the mainframe and add PC front-ends. This means adding a PC product similar to EASEL or Mozart in front of your mainframe DB2 application. Then, effectively, when a 3270 block comes down to the PC, users see a GUI rather than the traditional, less interesting, character-based display. How does this type of architecture classify as rightsizing? Users are taking advantage of the PC by using cheaper MIPS and employing a graphical interface.

The largest benefit of this method is that you're upgrading the interface, which makes users happier, but you haven't had to change the underlying application. For such reasons, this method of rightsizing is nondisruptive to corporate computing.

There are downsides to this technique that require attention, however. With this scenario, the PCs are not event driven. The user may have a mouse and click on icons, but behind the scenes, the result is the same as if the user had pressed the Enter button on a 3270: the screen freezes as information is sent to the mainframe for processing, and it remains frozen until information is returned. If all you change is the interface, there will always be that menu-driven, 3270 computing philosophy.

Approach Four: Cross-Platform Development

Another of the rightsizing trends that has been both popular and successful over the past five years is cross-platform development. When this is done, software is developed on a PC and shipped to the mainframe for production, *or* the application is developed on the mainframe for production use on a PC. This first scenario of PC development is more common and has been well proven in the last half-decade. The benefit it provides is that software developers can take advantage of the interactivity of the PC. At the same time, by shipping the application to the mainframe for production, users can still take advantage of mainframe software and administrative functionality and organization.

The other cross-platform development option, developing applications on the mainframe for PC production, is not very common, but it is done. This setup allows the user to take advantage of the standards and procedures that have been in mainframe environments for years. Then, at the PC level, users are able to benefit from the lower cost of hardware.

Approach Five: Distributed Access

The last and the most reasonable rightsizing avenue to follow consists of taking a central mainframe shop and evolving it into a distributed access system. This process entails doing nothing with legacy applications residing on the mainframe, but instead entails progressively using a connected PC LAN or single PCs to develop and run new applications. Using this technique over time, more and more applications and data will be moved onto the PCs until, perhaps, it's all there.

There are two popular ways that such a system could be configured: the two-tiered system and the three-tiered system (see Figure E.1).

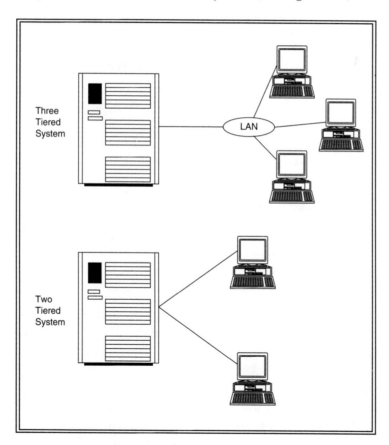

Figure E.1. Two-tiered and three-tiered approaches.

The two-tiered system basically provides a direct link between the PCs and mainframe. The three-tiered configuration adds another layer interposed between the PCs and the mainframe. Currently, the three-tiered approach is most popular among vendors. However, the two-tiered approach has been proven to work well in certain situations.

As far as products for these environments are concerned, for the three-tiered approach, you need an operating system on the server, perhaps NetWare, OS/2, or UNIX, and depending on which operating system you choose, you need a compatible DBMS server such as SQL Server or OS/2 Database Manager.

After you obtain a DBMS server, you need front-end software on the PCs that allows you to develop applications—either character-based or GUI—such as Windows, DOS, or OS/2. Finally, not to leave anything out, communication software is another piece in this puzzle. A lot of shops have trouble with these user-related, interdependent decisions. It is difficult to determine which system to pick first.

If you decide to pursue the development of such an environment, it is easiest to place read-only applications on the PCs as a first step. Applications with update needs can be more difficult to establish on PCs and, therefore, should be implemented at a later date when your IS shop has had more experience the new environment.

One of the advantages of slowly and gradually pushing applications down from the mainframe to PCs is that you can proceed at your own rate. Such migration can be nondisruptive if you carefully choose which application to port first. This type of environment is great for query applications and starts to capitalize on PC hardware and software for more user-friendly environments at lower costs.

For this setup, compatibility is nice, but NOT required. Because the applications are migrated at your own pace, you're not going to necessarily unplug your mainframe DB2 application. Instead, you will increasingly upgrade the application and put both the upgrades and the data on the network.

There are disadvantages with this form of rightsizing. You need to examine how IS is going to partition the data—by location, department, or whatever. In addition, it will be very hard either to estimate or to predict the system's performance. There are not many tools available to help do this. Because this is not a dramatic, instantaneous restructuring of your entire computing system, you can feel confident that you won't run into any serious trouble. Trouble-shooting and monitoring can be a concern in such a distributed-access environment. On a mainframe, you can chose between three or four monitoring tools. But who has the equivalent of those tools that work for a mainframe with a PC LAN plugged into it?

Software Compatibility Issues

Both software and SQL compatibility play a large role in several rightsizing scenarios. In a total replacement situation in which the IS department is moving all applications to either a PC or a PC LAN, if the software is not extremely compatible, you end up rewriting all of the applications. The bottom line is this: the older your IS shop and the more legacy systems you have, the more important are compatibility issues between applications. When rightsizing applications from a mainframe to PCs, there are several items that need to be examined: program logic, screen-handling techniques, and the database. These turn out to be three different forms of software that you have to deal with when rightsizing.

SQL Compatibility

When rightsizing within IBM environments, there are several areas in which software compatibility must be examined: SQL compatibility, operational differences, application development, and support environments.

How has IBM attempted to create compatibility between their various environments? See Figure E.2. For starters, IBM has 15 SAA manuals in which it lists every SQL statement for all of its operating environments. However, although compatibility between systems appears from these manuals to be excellent, when you actually starting working within these environments, you quickly discover the truth. If you were to actually obtain manuals for each DBMS and compare SQL statements, you would find that there are many omissions and inconsistencies between systems. One reason for these discrepancies is environmental differences: some statements that make sense in DB2 aren't applicable to OS/2 Database Manager. Similarly, there are keywords or phrases that make sense on a mainframe but not in a PC architecture. This subject is far more complex than just asking a vendor, "Do you support this or that SQL statement?" Insuring an acceptable level of compatibility can be a very complicated exercise for the user with whom the burden lies.

SAA to the rescue?

To aid the development of portable applications, SAA was introduced in 1987. SAA was IBM's grandiose plan to make all software portable and compatible between different platforms. Now that SAA has been around for five years, it has had a large impact. This may be an odd thing to say because SAA is no longer in the limelight, but its usefulness has grown tremendously. IBM has not been able to provide perfect portability between all platforms, but substantial progress in this direction has been made. You will find applications written on your mainframe using SAA guidelines are significantly more portable than pre-SAA applications.

Figure E.2. SAA to the rescue.

So, what is the bottom line concerning SQL compatibility? Comparing the different versions for DB2 and OS/2 Database Manager, the data manipulation language (DML) is primarily the same. You can get a lot of mileage out of this similarity. When you look at a DDL, you'll find that the logical object is the same but that physical objects are treated very differently. On a mainframe and a PC, the method in which data maps onto the disk drive is very different.

Vendors tend to key on SQL because there is an ANSI standard. Therefore, products can be conformed to meet these standards. This is a fairly easy thing to do. However, in this process, operational and environmental differences between the products tend to be ignored. Just a few of the "details" that tend to be overlooked include catalogs, limits, security, locking, isolation levels, concurrency, logging, utilities, and referential integrity (see Figure E.3).

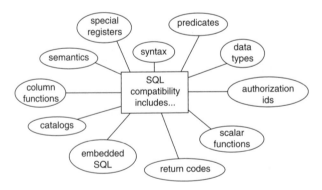

Figure E.3. SQL compatibility.

These are DBMS internals that become very important when rightsizing applications. This is why most companies decide to rightsize decision support, read-only applications first, and then progressively rightsize more ambitious applications.

Physical Objects

Let's take one quick example of the discrepancies between physical objects: DB2 employs objects such as table spaces and index spaces; OS/2 Database Manager basically doesn't have physical objects. OS/2 Database Manager has something called a database that uses rules about mapping logical objects. To the extent that your application cares about these physical dependencies, you've got a major concern. If applications are transparent in terms of physical objects, you will have better luck rightsizing. SQL/400 looks at physical objects in an entirely different way than does SQL DS. So, even within the IBM family of products, you can find some major compatibility problems.

Utilities

Most people are familiar with DB2 utilities. The question here is: What are their equivalents in a rightsized environment? For example, how are backup and recovery handled in the LAN DBMS environment? One answer is that very different types of utilities are available in PC architectures. You could, for example, rightsize a COBOL CICS application with certain products and be very successful in terms of code. But what about backup and recovery? To our knowledge, not one vendor currently offers a package that also rightsizes and ports DB2 utilities onto the PC. This is a big concern.

SAA Benefits for the IS World to Date

How far has the IS world moved in terms of the benefits provided by SAA? The world has improved greatly. SQL DML and logical DDL have high degrees of compatibility. In terms of programming languages, procedure languages, and application generators, there is a high software compatibility. The things to look out for are physical DDL (or DCL) that have differences still between platforms. As previously mentioned, when you get into operating system dependencies, issues such as security and teleprocessing interfaces make rightsizing difficult. When you look at an application in terms of portability or downsizability, in this narrow sense, you can achieve significant results with the appropriate rightsizing tools. As you broaden the scope to include issues such as development, maintenance, and support environments, rightsizing becomes much more of a burden (see Figure E.4).

	High Compatibility between DB2 and downsized software	Low Compatibility between DB2 and downsized software
SQL	DML logical DDL	physical DDL DCL
Environment	SAA programming languages procedural languages application generators	TP monitors O/S control languages security
O/S		backup, recovery concurrency issues maintenanace issues

Figure E.4. *Summary of compatibility issues.*

SAA has given greater benefits to high-level users. If you have a similar SQL on your LAN and mainframe for queries that programmers use (such as DB2), you will receive a great deal of benefit. But, as you progress into the lower levels of software that include operational issues, database management, or technical support, you will receive less advantage. This is where the cost of rightsizing is currently increasing.

The Complete Costs of Rightsizing—Knowing to Look Beyond Hardware

If you don't rightsize all of your DB2 applications concurrently, you will have to maintain new PC platforms in addition to the mainframe. Typically, shops end up maintaining both systems with several applications running in parallel for some period of time. Most commonly, there is part of an application on the PC LAN with other parts still running on the mainframe. Operating in such a manner accounts for part of the cost of rightsizing. This is a good example of why looking solely at hardware costs isn't an accurate measure of the total rightsizing costs. Whereas the cost of the hardware for rightsized systems may be inexpensive, supporting both the old and new environments is not. The administrative and training costs alone can absorb a large portion of your savings.

Conclusions: Rightsizing Is an IS Management Challenge, Not a Technical Issue

The overall key to successful rightsizing is to rightsize IS culture. There is much more involved than just hardware. IS culture has evolved over time to the point where we are currently in an evolutionary phase. To some degree, IS is unsettled due to the pace of change now in contrast to that of ten years ago. These are some of the issues we have to face. The most critical issues involved in rightsizing are going to be faced by management. It is these managerial issues, rather than product selections or hardware costs, that will basically determine how successful corporations are in the rightsizing process.

The Importance
of Cost-Reflective
Pricing

F

Classical microeconomic theory can be used to establish that a cost-reflective accounting systems does, in fact, maximize the benefit produced by the computer dollar. In other words, if a computer or network center attempts to make a profit or sell services below cost, forces have been created that encourage suboptimum conditions. In *The Economics of Computers*, W. F. Sharpe argues that the computer center should be established as a cost center rather than as a profit center. His analysis can be used to show as well that the price set for computer services must be a reflection of cost to maximize the company's profit.

In Figure F.1, the Total Cost (TC) curve represents the cost to the computer center, and thus to the firm, of providing capacity for a specific quantity of computer work. Q represents units of computer work. In other words, a cost of TC_1 dollars is required to install computer systems capable of producing Q_1 work units.

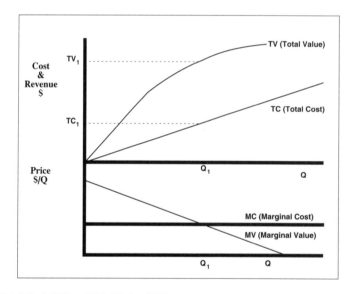

Figure F.1. Total Cost (TC) and Total Value (TV) curves.

The Total Value (TV) curve represents to the user, and therefore to the firm, the value of that work. Its shape (increasing at a decreasing rate) reflects the law of diminishing returns. The more you have of something, the less valuable an additional unit of that something is to you.

Figure F.2 represents the Marginal Cost and Marginal Value curves that correspond to the Total Curves in Figure F.1. These curves represent the cost and value of an additional unit of capacity. The optimum operating point for the firm is the point at which the Marginal Value of an additional unit of work is equal to the Marginal Cost, shown at Q_1 units in Figure F.1. Producing any more is akin to spending \$10 to receive \$8 in value. In Figure F.2, you can see that the total profit to the company is equal to $TV_1 - TC_1$ dollars. This point is the profit maximization point; producing any other quantity of work results in decreased profit.

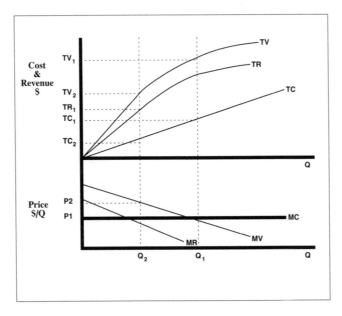

Figure F.2. Marginal Cost (MC) and Marginal Value (MV) curves.

Consider, however, a case in which the computer center is attempting to maximize its own internal profit. Previously, the revenue to the computer center corresponded to the TC curve. To examine the computer center as a profit center, a revenue curve must be added above the cost curve. This is represented by the TR curve in Figure F.2.

The TV curve in Figure F.1 represented the total value to the buying division and, therefore, to the firm. Because the objectives now are to maximize computer center profit, however, the value curve to the computer center is the TR curve. The TR curve is also the cost curve for the buying division. This curve is, by necessity, below the TV curve because revenue is price times quantity, and a buying division will not pay a price higher than the value received. The profit-maximization point for the computer center is the point at which the Marginal Revenue (MR) equals the Marginal Cost (MC). You can see in Figure F.2 that this point is at a capacity of Q_2 work units. The price the buying division will pay for Q_2 work units is not more than the value received, or P_2.

In this case, the total profit to the firm is equal to TV_2-TC_2. This profit is divided between computer center and buying division, with the computer center receiving a total profit equal to TR_1-TC_2 and the buying division a total profit equal to TV_2-TR_1. The total profit, however, TV_2-TC_2, is less than the original TV_1-TC_1 profit when the computer center operated as a cost recovery center. Therefore, establishing the computer center as a profit center works to the detriment of the firm.

The profit center concept, in this case, encourages exploitation of one division by another. This problem could be lessened by allowing the buyer to purchase outside services, which theoretically could force the computer center to sell at a price lower than P2. When the computer center operates as a cost recovery center, however, the theoretical maximum profit to the firm cannot be greater than the profit realized.

A similar analysis can be used to demonstrate that setting computer prices below cost also produces a suboptimum condition. The analysis demonstrates that if a computer center sets its prices at cost, and if buying divisions respond to these prices in a prudent fashion, value to the firm is maximized. The computer center's obligation is to establish prices that properly reflect costs, and this seems to be a reasonable limit to its responsibility. It does not seem proper to expect the computer center to police the buying division's actions, nor to bestow on it the power to manipulate those actions.

You should note that a sensible reaction to the prices established is implicit in this entire discussion. If users do not respond in a cost-sensitive manner— in other words, if the prices set on computing and network services are not a factor in their decision-making process—the internal transfer accounting process has not provided any benefit. In fact, the firm will incur a loss because of the costs associated with establishing and maintaining an internal transfer payment system. The point is that distributing costs among users is not intrinsically a good idea, and the user must react as expected for benefit to be derived.

For example, imagine a computer or network center that sets prices of $150 on services that actually cost the firm $100. If the potential buyer perceives the value of the services as $125, a decision will be made not to use the service, and the firm will suffer an "opportunity loss" of $25. Similarly, if the computer center establishes a price of $100 on services that actually cost $150, the buyer who values the services at $125 would decide to use the service, resulting in a $25 reduction in the firm's profit.

An argument often presented against this type of analysis is that users don't respond to internal prices for services and that the accounting allocation process is merely a game played to satisfy the firm's financial community. Rather than being a refutation of cost-reflective pricing, this argument is in opposition to the entire process of charging internal customers.

Perhaps these questions should be asked first:

- Does the charging process really have an effect on computer and network usage?
- Do users receive "rubber stamp" approval for the information-processing parts of their budgets?
- Do the people developing systems really care what are the costs to run their application?
- If those costs were available, would system developers make efforts to reduce costs through more efficient techniques?

If honest answers to those questions are negative—and this may be the case in no small number of installations—then an internal charging system constitutes an unnecessary expense, and efforts probably should be directed toward reevaluating the organization's financial control philosophy.

On the other hand, if the user community is responsive to the prices set for services, it's difficult to support an accounting system that does not attempt to reflect actual costs. A successful, cost-reflective accounting system provides the user with the information required to maximize the benefit that the installation receives from its computing and network resources.

Bibliography

Suggested Reading

Chapter 2, "Rightsizing Origins"

> Jennings, Karla. *The Devouring Fungus: Tales of the Computer Age.*
> New York: Norton, 1990.
>
> Barry, John A. *Technobabble.* Cambridge, MA: MIT Press, 1991.
>
> Naisbitt, John. *Megatrends.* New York: Warner Books, Inc., 1982.
>
> Peters, Tom. *In Search of Excellence.* New York: Harper & Row, 1982.
>
> Peters, Tom. *Liberation Management: Necessary Disorganization for the
> Nanosecond Nineties.* New York: Knopf, 1992.
>
> Toffler, Alvin. *Future Shock.* New York: Random House, 1984.
>
> Tomasko, Robert M. *Downsizing: Reshaping the Corporation for the
> Future.* New York: AMACOM, American Management
> Association, 1990.

Chapter 3, "Where We Are Today and Opportunities for Tomorrow"

> "IBM in the Nineties." *Byte.* v15n11.
>
> "PC LANs Taking Center Stage" and "MIS Staff Fear Downsizing."
> *PC Week.* September 10, 1990, v7n36.
>
> "When Bulletin Boards Save the Day" and "PC, Phone Home."
> *Network Computing.* June 1991, v2n6.
>
> Clark, David James. *The Complete NetWare Construction Kit:
> A Professional Blueprint for Designing, Installing, and Managing
> LANs.* New York: Wiley, 1993.
>
> Isaacson, Portia. *PC Trends and Forecasts: What's Hot and What's Not.*
> New Desktop Strategies Advisory Service.
>
> McCann, John T. *The NetWare Supervisor's Guide.* San Mateo, CA:
> M&T Books, 1989.
>
> Tomasko, Robert M. *Rethinking the Corporation: The Architecture of
> Change.* New York: AMACOM, American Management
> Association, 1993.

Chapter 4, "Finding and Measuring Rightsizing Benefits"

> Clemons, Eric K. "Evaluation of Strategic Investments in Information
> Technology." *Communications of the ACM.* January 1991, v34n1.
>
> DeBoever, Larry. Talk given at the DCI Database and Client/Server
> World show, "Report from the Downsizing Front: A Manager's
> Guide to Combat," 1993.
>
> Porter, Michael E., and Victor E. Millar. "How Information Gives
> You a Competitive Advantage." *Harvard Business Review.* July-
> August 1985.

Scheier, Robert L. "Effectiveness, Not Dollars, Drives Downsizing." *PC Week*. September 10, 1990, v7n36.

Chapter 5, "Cost Justifying and Financing Rightsizing"

Chivvis, Andrei. "Downsizing: The Business Decision." *LAN Times*. May 20, 1991.

Freedman, David. "The ROI Polloi." *CIO*. April 1990.

Klinkow, Peter D. *Financing Alternatives*. Chicago, IL: Strategic Systems Funding Corporation.

Chapter 6, "Reengineering"

"The Human Factor." *InformationWeek*. June 10, 1991.

Ardnouse, Donald M. "Needs of the 1990s: Call for a New Breed of IS Professional." *PC Week*. August 27, 1990, v7n34.

Carlisle, Patti. *Reengineering Handbook*. 2nd rev. ed., edited by Brian Leary. AT&T, 1992.

Hammer, Michael. "Reengineering Work: Don't Automate, Obliterate." *Harvard Business Review*. July-August 1990.

Hammer, Michael and James Champy. *Reengineering the Corporation: A Manifesto for Business Revolution*. New York: Harper Business, 1993.

Kavanaugh, Paul. *Downsizing: Re-Engineering Business for Open Client-Server Systems*. New York: Bantam, 1993.

Morris, Daniel C. and Joel S. Brandon. *Reengineering Your Business*. New York: McGraw Hill, 1992.

Chapter 7, "Change Management"

Nagel, John. *Change Management*. Organization for Developmental Resources, Atlanta.

Chapter 8, "Rules for Rightsizing Success"

Schussel, George, Dr. "Rules for Downsizing Success." Andover, MA: Digital Consulting, Inc., May 1993.

Chapter 10, "Joint Application Design (JAD)"

August, Judy H. *Joint Application Design: The Group Session Approach to System Design*. Englewood Cliffs, NJ: Yourdon Press, 1990.

Wood, Jane, and Denise Silver. *Joint Application Design: How to Design Quality Systems in 40% Less Time*. New York: John Wiley and Sons.

Chapter 11, "Architecture"

Inmon, W.H. *Developing Client-Server Applications,* rev. ed. QED Technical Publishing Group. Wellesley, MA: QED Information Services, Inc., 1993.

Nunemacher, Greg. *LAN Primer: The Definitive Guide to Networking Fundamentals,* 2nd ed. San Mateo, CA: M&T Books, 1992.

Schatt, Stanley. *Understanding Local Area Networks.* 3rd ed. Carmel, IN: Sams, 1992.

Schussel, George, Dr. "LAN Operating Systems." Andover, MA: Digital Consulting, Inc., 1993

Chapter 12, "The Network Platform"

"Superservers Are the Network Wave of the Future." *PC Week.* June 24, 1991, v8n25.

Corrigan, Pat, and Aisling Guy. *Building Local Area Networks with Novell's NetWare, Versions 2.2 and 3.x.* San Mateo, CA: M&T Books, 1992.

Corrigan, Patrick and Aisling Guy. *Building Local Area Networks with Novell's NetWare: Version "X".* San Mateo, CA: M & T Books, 1993.

Day, Michael. *Downsizing to NetWare.* Carmel, IN: New Riders Publishing, 1992.

Finkelstein, Richard. Talk given at the DCI Database and Client/Server World show, "How to Evaluate and Choose Client/Server Systems," 1993.

Glines, Steven. *Downsizing to UNIX.* Carmel, IN: New Riders Publishing, 1992.

Lawrence, Bill. "The State of ARCnet: Low Bother, Low Cost." *Network Computing.* June 1991, v2n6.

Lawrence, Bill and M. Hansen. *Using Novell NetWare 4: Special Edition.* Carmel, IN: Que, 1993.

McCann, John. *NetWare Performance & Tuning.* Carmel, IN: Sams, 1993.

McCann, John and Rick Segal. *NetWare LAN Management Toolkit.* Carmel, IN: Sams, 1992

Schussel, George, Dr. "Distributed and Client/Server DBMS: Underpinning for Downsizing." Andover, MA: Digital Consulting, Inc., 1992

Chapter 15, "The Rightsizing Development Environment"

"APPC and HLLAPI" and "Building Enterprise Applications: Bridging PCs and Mainframes." *Network Computing*. June 1991, v2n6.

"Microsoft to Boost Windows and Undercut OS/2." *Wall Street Journal*. July 29, 1991.

"Oracle lagging in database replication," *Computer Reseller News*. March 14, 1994.

"PC GUIs Go Head to Head" and "Looking at the Graphical User Interface." *Byte*. Fall 1990, v15n11.

Andriole, Stephen J. *Rapid Application Prototyping: A New Approach to User Requirements Analysis*. Wellesley, MA: QED Information Sciences, 1991.

Inmon, W. H. *Building the Data Warehouse*. Wellesley, MA: QED Information Sciences, 1992.

Inmon, W. H. *Data Architecture: The Information Paradigm*. 2nd ed. Wellesley, MA: QED Information Sciences, 1991.

Martin, James. *Rapid Application Development*. New York: MacMillan, 1991.

Schussel, George, Dr. "Replication, the Next Generation of Distributed Database Technology." Andover, MA: Digital Consulting, Inc., 1994.

Chapter 16, "Rapid Application Development (RAD)"

Andriole, Stephen J. *Rapid Application Prototyping: A New Approach to User Requirements Analysis.* Wellesley, MA: QED Information Sciences, 1991.

Martin, James. *Rapid Application Development*. New York: MacMillan, 1991.

Mullin, Mark. *Rapid Prototyping for Object-Oriented Systems*. Reading, MA: Addison-Wesley Publishing Company, Inc., 1990.

Chapter 18, "Putting Design, Architecture, and Platform To Work: An Example"

Schussel, George, Dr. "Distributed and Client/Server DBMS: A Note on Repositories." Andover, MA: Digital Consulting, Inc., 1992.

Chapter 19, "Maintenance"

"Sybase Server to Add Complexity." *Communications Week*. December 6, 1993.

Schussel, George, Dr. "Replication, the Next Generation of Distributed Database Technology." Andover, MA: Digital Consulting, Inc., 1994.

Chapter 21, "Conclusion: A Call to Arms"

Bochenski, Barbara. "How to Work Mainframe Code into a Client-Server Style." *Software Magazine*. June 1991, v11n7.
Bochenski, Barbara. *Introduction to Client Server*. New York: Wiley, 1993.
McDowell, Robert. "Information at Your Fingertips." *Computer Conference Analysis Newsletter*. January 28, 1991, n269.

Appendix E, "Rightsizing DB2 Applications: Five Approaches"

Fosdick, Howard. Talk given at the DCI Downsizing Expo, "Downsizing DB2 Applications: Five Approaches," 1993.

Appendix F, "The Importance of Cost-Reflective Pricing"

Sharpe, William F. *The Economics of Computers*. New York, NY: Columbia University Press, 1972.

Additional Reading

Baker, Richard H. *Downsizing: How to Get Big Gains from Smaller Computer Systems*. New York: McGraw Hill, 1992.
Computer Technology Research Corp. Staff. *Downsizing for Cost-Effective Enterprise Computing*: 1993.
Davis, Stan, and Bill Davidson. *2020 Vision: Transform Your Business Today to Succeed in Tomorrow's Economy*. New York: Simon & Schuster.
Schussel, George, Dr. "Converting Existing Applications to Client/Server Approaches." Andover, MA: Digital Consulting, Inc., 1993.
Flatten, Per O., Donald J. McCubbrey, P. Declan O'Riordan, and Keith Burgess. *Foundations of Business Systems*. Hinsdale, IL: The Dryden Press, Holt, Rinehart, and Winston, 1989.
Peters, Tom. *Thriving on Chaos*. Alfred A. Knopf, New York: 1987.
Pournelle, Jerry and Michael A Banks. *Pournelle's PC Communications Bible: The Ultimate Guide to Productivity with a Modem*. Redmond, WA: Microsoft Press, 1992.
Maynard, Herman B., Jr., and Susan E. Mehrtens. *The Fourth Wave: Business in the Twenty-First Century*. San Francisco: Berrett-Koehler, 1993.
Toffler, Alvin. *Power Shift*. New York: Bantam, 1990.

Glossary

Glossary

API (application programming interface) A format or language used for communication by programs.

application A software program (or group of programs) that carries out some useful task. Database managers, spreadsheets, communications packages, graphics programs, and word processors all are applications. A specific use of a computer. Payroll, inventory, and accounts receivable are business applications.

application system A suite of programs, sometimes very similar in appearance and behavior, designed to meet a relatively broad purpose. Sales order entry and warehouse inventory tracking systems are application systems.

architecture The manner in which hardware, software, or applications are structured. Architecture typically describes how a system or program is constructed and how its components fit together, and the protocols and interfaces used for communications and cooperation among modules or components of the system. **Network architecture** defines the functions, data formats, and procedures used for communication between nodes or workstations.

back-end The portion of a program that does not interact with the user and that accomplishes the processing job that the program is designed to perform. In a local area network, the back-end typically runs on a specialized server. For example, a database back-end such as Sybase SQL Server is run on a database server.

batch Typically, sequential, off-line processes. For example, instead of executing a time-consuming, file-intensive process like audit trail reports of master files in an online, interactive manner, the process could be submitted in a batch manner for execution at a time when the computer is less busy.

CAD(computer-aided design) Using specialized or high-performance computers for product design.

CAE(computer-aided engineering) Using software that performs engineering analyses on product designs.

central processing unit (CPU) The part of a computer in which the fundamental operations—such as memory management, allocation of computing cycles to requesting processes, and so on—are performed. The heart of the computer.

centralized processing Processing performed in one or more computers in a single, centralized location. Implies that all terminals throughout an organization are connected to computers in the data center. Contrast with **distributed processing** and **decentralized processing**.

CIM (computer integrated manufacturing) 1. Integrating office and accounting functions with automated factory systems. Point of sale, billing, machine-tool scheduling, and supply ordering all are part of CIM. 2. (CompuServe Information Manager) See **CompuServe**.

client In a communications or a local area network, the machine requesting services (usually a workstation or personal computer).

client/server computing A form of distributed processing in which computing processes are split between servers (typically providing services such as file input/output or database management) and clients (typically processing data and presenting it to the computer user).

clipboard A reserved area in memory that temporarily holds data being copied.

communications Electronic transfer of information from one location to another. Data communications refers to digital transmission, and telecommunications refers to all forms of transmission, including analog voice and video.

CompuServe A public information service providing a variety of information. Available by subscription, CompuServe includes online versions of trade publications, bulletin boards, and such general information as weather, news, and sports.

computing resource A source of information systems processing. A computing resource can range from a specific piece of hardware (for example, a PC) to a subroutine of a program that accomplishes a very specific task that other programs need.

cooperative processing Sharing a job among two or more computers such as a mainframe and a personal computer. Implies splitting the work load for the most efficiency.

CPU Abbreviation for central processing unit, the part of a computer in which logical and mathematical operations are performed. The heart of the computer.

data Factual information, stored on magnetic media, that can be used to generate calculations or make decisions.

database A collection of related information about a subject organized in a useful manner. It provides a base or foundation for procedures such as retrieving information, drawing conclusions, and making decisions. Any collection of information that serves these purposes qualifies as a database, even if the information is not stored on a computer.

data communications See **communications**.

data model A representation of all or part of the data used by a particular application system or its logical subset. A data model is used to facilitate the understanding of relationships between various subsets of data.

decentralized processing   Computer systems in different locations of an organization with limited or no daily communications with each other.

directory services   A set of mechanisms for associating information with and accessing network resources, for example, specific users or databases. An information system uses directory services for electronic mail distribution, network management, and other applications requiring directory lookup.

distributed processing   The processing of information in separate locations equipped with independent computers. The computers are connected by a network, even though the processing is dispersed geographically. Often a more efficient use of computer processing power because each CPU can be devoted to a certain task. A LAN-based CIM system is a good example of a distributed application.

DOS   Disk operating system, as in MS-DOS, which stands for Microsoft disk operating system, or PC DOS, which stands for (IBM's) personal computer disk operating system. DOS is the software that organizes the way a computer reads, writes, and reacts with its disks (floppy or hard) and talks to its various input/output devices, including keyboards, screens, serial and parallel ports, printers, modems, and so on. The most popular operating system for PCs is MS-DOS.

drop-down list   In a graphical user interface, a list of command options that doesn't appear until you select a command. After you "drop down" the list, you can choose one of the options. A drop-down list box enables a programmer to provide many options without using a lot of space on screen.

dynamic   An operation done while another process is running, often only on an as-needed basis.

environment   A computer configuration that refers to the sum of the technical architecture, hardware, and systems software. Environment component standards apply to the applications and application systems that run in it. For example, the statement "this program is running in an Oracle for NetWare environment" gives environment information and implies relevant standards.

execution time   1. The amount of time taken to complete a task. 2. The event of running a program; for example, as in the statement "the results of the formula are determined at execution time."

file server   See **server**.

front-end   The portion of a program that processes on a local computing resource and that, typically, users directly interact with. In a local area network, the portion of the program that is distributed to each workstation and that interacts with the back-end application on the file server.

graphical user interface (GUI) An interface that replaces the familiar command-line prompt with a metaphor for real-world work areas such as a desktop. Instead of typing a command, users carry out actions on this imaginary desktop by pointing, clicking, and dragging representations of information called *icons*.

host In an information system, the computer that performs centralized processes such as running programs or making data files available to workstations in the network.

icon A small graphic picture of a file, disk drive, process, or application used in a graphical user interface.

implementation The sum of the programming, testing, and installing of application systems; the selecting, procuring, testing and installing of hardware and systems software; and the writing, testing, and installing of documentation and procedures to run an information system.

integration Making diverse components work together.

interface 1. A mechanical or electrical link connecting two or more pieces of equipment. 2. A shared boundary. A physical point of demarcation between two devices at which the electrical signals, connectors, timing, and handshaking are defined. The procedures, codes, and protocols that enable two entities to interact for a meaningful exchange of information.

InterNet An international network oriented toward computer- and computing-related research.

interoperability The state of operating compatibility of many different types of network devices and software for transmitting and receiving data communications.

interprocess communications (IPC) The exchange of data between programs either within the same computer or over a network. Implies a protocol that guarantees a response to a request. Examples are OS/2 Named Pipes, Windows DDE, and Novell's SPX. Although IPCs are performed automatically by the programs, an analogous function is performed interactively when users cut and paste data from one file into another by using the clipboard.

interrupt A signal that "gets the attention" of the CPU and usually is generated when input or output is required. For example, hardware interrupts are generated when a user presses a key or moves a mouse. Software interrupts are generated by a program requiring disk input or output. An internal timer may continually interrupt a computer several times per second to keep the time of day current or for timesharing purposes. When an interrupt occurs, control is transferred to the operating system, which determines what action should be taken. Interrupts are prioritized; the higher the priority, the faster the interrupt is serviced.

layer　In the OSI model, refers to a collection of network processing functions that together compose one layer of a hierarchy of computing functions. Each layer performs a number of functions, essential for successful data communications. See **OSI model**.

library　A collection of programs, data files, or subroutine functions that are linked into a main program. It may be linked in when the program is compiled, or it may be *dynamic*, meaning it is linked in when the program is running. The term often refers to a collection of subroutines written in a given programming language such as C or Pascal.

load balancing　The practice of splitting communication into two or more routes. By balancing the traffic on each route, communication is made faster and more reliable. In data internetworking, bridges and routers perform load balancing by splitting LAN-to-LAN traffic among two or more WAN links. This process enables the combination of several lower-speed lines to transmit higher-speed LAN data simultaneously. In local area networking, load balancing is a function performed by token-ring routers.

local area network (LAN)　The linkage of personal and other computers within a limited area by high-performance cables so that users can exchange information, share expensive peripherals, and draw on the resources of a massive secondary storage unit (called a file server). The basic components of a LAN are cables, a network interface card, a file server (which includes the central mass storage), a network operating system (NOS), and personal computers or workstations linked by the system. Alternative network topologies (methods for interconnecting the network's workstations) exist, including bus networks, ring networks, and star networks. In addition, there are two methods for communicating via the cables: baseband and broadband.

Macintosh　A family of Apple microcomputers that represents the first wide-scale PC (personal computer) deployment of icons, windows, "mice," and a consistent user interface, now called a graphical user interface (GUI). Apple introduced the Macintosh in January 1984.

mainframe　1. A multiuser computer designed to meet the computing needs of a large organization. 2. The metal cabinet that housed the central processing unit (CPU) of early computers. 3. The large, central computers developed in the late 1950s and 1960s to meet the accounting and information-management needs of large organizations.

message   A unit of communication between stations or processes, with a beginning, content, and ending. A message can be composed of a single packet or a series of packets.

microcomputer   Any computer with its arithmetic logic unit (ALU) and control unit contained on one integrated circuit, that is, any computer with a microprocessor. When personal computers first appeared in the mid-to-late 1970s, people often referred to them as microcomputers, because their CPUs were microprocessors. Microcomputers were designed to be single-user machines. For the first time, microcomputers placed the processing circuitry entirely under the end user's control.

migration   To move from one information system platform and development environment to adopting another.

minicomputer   A multiuser computer designed to meet the needs of a small company or a department; developed in the 1970s and early 1980s. Compare **microcomputer**.

modeling   Simulating a condition or activity by performing a set of equations on a set of data.

multiselect lists   In a Microsoft Windows environment, this term describes a graphical object that contains a list of choices. More than one of these choices can be highlighted and selected by the user for further processing.

multitasking   The execution on a computer system of more than one program at a time. Multitasking should not be confused with multiple program loading, in which two or more programs are present in RAM but only one program executes at a time. Among the operating systems that provide multi-tasking are OS/2 and SCO's UNIX.

native mode   A state in which programs are written and optimized specifically for a particular component of hardware or systems software, as opposed to being written for portability. See **portability**.

network architecture   The design and method of control of a communications system, including hardware, software, access methods, and protocols.

network computing   A form of computing in which a mix of intelligent computing resources, with various levels of capability, are all attached together through a common communications link.

nodes   Points in a network at which service is provided, service is used, or communications channels are interconnected. The term "nodes" is sometimes used interchangeably with the term "workstations."

object A data structure or data. Object code is machine-executable code produced by a compiler or an assembler. In object-oriented programming, an object contains both data structures and commands or methods for manipulating them.

open systems An approach to building information-processing systems using hardware, software, and networking components that comply with industry-accepted standards such as OSI (Open Systems Interconnect) or POSIX. This approach provides users with the ability to move applications between systems provided by many vendors and to incorporate the latest advances in information processing into their organization's information architecture.

optimization The act of making a computing resource or code as perfect, efficient, effective, or functional as possible.

OS/2 Single-user, multitasking PC operating system for 286s and up, developed jointly by Microsoft and IBM. OS/2 is more advanced than DOS and is designed to run multiple programs concurrently; however, it requires a fast CPU and, like Windows, 3–4 megabytes of RAM for maximum efficiency. It can address all available memory (16 megabytes of RAM and 1 gigabyte of virtual memory) and isn't restricted to DOS's 1 megabyte limit. Although new commands have been added, many are the same as in DOS.

OSI (Open Systems Interconnection) model A functional guideline for communication tasks created in 1977 by a subcommittee of the International Standards Organization (ISO). It is made up of seven layers: application, presentation, session, transport, network, data link, and physical. Each layer executes specific functions and communicates with its peers in other computers, but must do so by sending messages through the layers in its own computer. It is not tangible; the model itself does not cause network communication to occur.

packet A fixed-length string of data bits transmitted in a network.

peer-to-peer computing A file-sharing technique for local area networks in which each user has access to the public files of all other users in the network, located on their respective workstations. (Each user determines which files, if any, he or she wants to make public for network access.)

personal computer (PC) A standalone computer equipped with all the system, utility, and application software, and the input/output devices and other peripherals that an individual needs to perform one or more tasks.

platform Hardware architecture and systems software of a particular model or family of computers. The standard to which software developers write programs. Sometimes refers to the hardware and its operating system.

pop-up menu A menu that appears on-screen anywhere other than in the standard menu bar location (at the top of the screen).

portability Refers to an attribute of software that provides the capability to move it easily from one type of machine to another. Implies a product that has a version for several hardware platforms or that has built-in capabilities for switching between platforms. However, a program that can be converted easily from one architecture type to another also is considered portable.

process 1. The act of manipulating data within the computer; for example, processing a request. 2. The program, application, or system that manipulates the data. For example, in the statement "the online process will run for five minutes."

protocol 1. A specific set of rules, procedures, or conventions relating to format and timing of data transmission between two devices. 2. A standard procedure that two data devices must accept and use to be capable of understanding each other. Protocols cover such areas as framing, error handling, transparency, and line control. The three basic types of protocol are character-oriented, byte-oriented, and bit-oriented.

pushbutton In the industry standard and graphical user interfaces, a large button in a dialog box that initiates actions after you choose an option. Most dialog boxes contain an OK pushbutton (which confirms your choices and carries out the command) and a cancel pushbutton (which cancels your choices and closes the dialog box).

radio buttons A series of small buttons that allow only one selection at a time. When a particular button is selected, the previously selected button is deselected. One use of radio buttons is for on/off switches for specific application functions.

remote communications A technique that enables one computer to control or duplicate the operation of another in a remote location. Software resides in both machines and enables you to be an interactive participant in the remote computer. Support personnel can oversee users running their applications.

replication A database technique used in open, distributed applications that uses a mail or store-and-forward approach to update data, maintain data integrity, and provide data management capability.

repository A product used on the network to store (and update) data definitions so they are accessible to all members of the project team and systems staff.

scalable The ability of a computing resource to be increased or decreased in size.

server A computer providing a service—such as shared access to a file system, a printer, or an electronic mail system—to LAN users. Usually a combination of hardware and software. A computer in a network system shared by multiple users.

Structured Query Language (SQL) A language used to interrogate and process data in a relational database. Developed by IBM for its mainframes, many implementations have been used to work interactively with a database, or they can be embedded in a programming language to interface to a database. When SQL becomes a standard, computer systems running different DBMSs will be capable of communicating and easily exchanging data with each other by simply trading SQL commands.

Systems Application Architecture (SAA) A set of standards developed in 1987 for communication among various types of IBM computers, from personal computers to mainframes. Although SAA is merely a set of standards, it calls for a consistent user interface, APIs, consistent protocols, and consistent system terminology across all environments.

Systems Network Architecture (SNA) IBM's layered communications protocol.

systems software The sum of the operating systems, data communications, and database software.

telecommunications See **communications**.

thread One transaction or message in a multithread system.

Transmission Control Protocol/ Internet Protocol (TCP/IP) An important and established internetworking protocol that works at the third and fourth layers of the OSI model. Developed by the Department of Defense, TCP/IP is designed to be rugged and robust, and to guarantee delivery of data in the most demanding circumstances. TCP/IP is increasingly popular with networking and computer vendors who want to connect their equipment to a variety of other systems and protocols.

transparent The attribute describing a hidden computing resource or network operation or process that is made invisible so that the user does not have to deal with it.

transport In the OSI model, the layer that assures that messages sent between a source and destination are successfully transmitted. It is responsible for breaking larger messages into smaller packets at the source and reassembling them back into the larger message at the destination.

tuning To adjust an information system (or a component of it) for precise or efficient functioning.

two-phase commit A database management technique that locks data in all locations to be affected by a transaction until all participating nodes indicate that the work has been successfully completed.

UNIX An immensely powerful and complex multitasking operating system for computers that was developed in 1969 by Ken Thompson of AT&T Bell Laboratories. Many varieties of UNIX are marketed today.

windowing A technique of displaying information on a screen, in which the viewer sees what appears to be several sheets of paper much as they would appear on a desktop. The viewer can shift and shuffle the sheets on the screen. Windowing can show two files simultaneously. For example, in one window you might have a boilerplate letter from which you can take a paragraph and drop it into the letter you are composing in the other window. Being able to see the two letters on the screen makes writing the new letter easier.

windows 1. (Capital W) A graphics-based operating environment from Microsoft that coexists with DOS. Different applications, or multiples of the same application, are kept active in windows that can be resized and relocated on screen. Users can switch back and forth among them. The windows can be converted into icons and placed on the desktop when not required. 2. Separate viewing areas on a display screen as provided by the software. 3. Periods of time during which an event can or must occur.

workstation 1. Input/output computing equipment at which someone works. A station to which a user can send data or receive data from a computer for the purpose of performing a job. 2. A high-performance, single-user microcomputer or minicomputer that has been specialized for graphics, CAD, CAE, or scientific applications. 3. In a LAN, a personal computer that serves a single user, in contrast to a file server that serves all users in the network. 4. Any terminal or personal computer.

Index

Index

Add to Your Sams Library Today with the Best Books for Programming, Operating Systems, and New Technologies

The easiest way to order is to pick up the phone and call

1-800-428-5331

between 9:00 a.m. and 5:00 p.m. EST.
For faster service please have your credit card available.

ISBN	Quantity	Description of Item	Unit Cost	Total Cost
0-672-30173-3		Enterprise-Wide Networking	$39.95	
0-672-30473-2		Client/Server Computing, Second Edition	$40.00	
0-672-30512-7		DB2 Developer's Guide, Second Edition	$59.99	
0-672-22804-1		Reorganizing MIS: The Evolution of Business Computing in the '90s	$34.95	
0-672-30380-9		Windows NT Unleashed	$34.95	
0-672-30298-5		Windows NT: The Next Generation	$22.95	
0-672-30295-0		Moving into Windows NT Programming	$39.95	
0-672-30382-5		Understanding Local Area Networks	$26.95	
0-672-30209-8		NetWare Unleashed	$45.00	
0-672-30501-1		Understanding Data Communications, 4th Edition	$29.99	
0-672-30119-9		International Telecommunications	$39.95	
0-672-30326-4		Absolute Beginner's Guide to Networking	$19.95	
0-672-30465-1		Developing PowerBuilder 3 Applications	$45.00	
❏ 3 ½" Disk		Shipping and Handling: See information below.		
❏ 5 ¼" Disk		TOTAL		

Shipping and Handling: $4.00 for the first book, and $1.75 for each additional book. Floppy disk: add $1.75 for shipping and handling. If you need to have it NOW, we can ship product to you in 24 hours for an additional charge of approximately $18.00, and you will receive your item overnight or in two days. Overseas shipping and handling adds $2.00 per book and $8.00 for up to three disks. Prices subject to change. Call for availability and pricing information on latest editions.

201 W. 103rd Street, Indianapolis, Indiana 46290

1-800-428-5331 — Orders   1-800-835-3202 — FAX   1-800-858-7674 — Customer Service